W9-AFC-480

WITHDRAWN

FRENCH LITERARY FASCISM

FRENCH LITERARY FASCISM

NATIONALISM, ANTI-SEMITISM,
AND THE IDEOLOGY OF CULTURE

David Carroll

PRINCETON UNIVERSITY PRESS   PRINCETON, NEW JERSEY

Copyright © 1995 by Princeton University Press
Published by Princeton University Press, 41 William Street,
Princeton, New Jersey 08540
In the United Kingdom: Princeton University Press,
Chichester, West Sussex
All Rights Reserved

Library of Congress Cataloging-in-Publication Data

Carroll, David, 1944–
French literary fascism : nationalism, anti-Semitism, and the
ideology of culture / David Carroll.
p. cm.
Includes bibliographical references and index.
ISBN 0-691-03723-X
1. French literature—20th century—History and
criticism. 2. Fascism and literature—France—History—
20th century. 3. Nationalism and literature—France—
History—20th century. 4. France—Politics and
government—20th century. 5. Antisemitism—
France—History—20th century. 6. Antisemitism in
literature. I. Title.
PQ307.F3C37 1994
840.9'00912—dc20 94-20035

This book has been composed in Sabon

Princeton University Press books are printed
on acid-free paper and meet the guidelines
for permanence and durability of the Committee
on Production Guidelines for Book Longevity
of the Council on Library Resources

Printed in the United States of America

10 9 8 7 6 5 4 3 2 1

For my parents,
Lillian and Roger Carroll

And my sons,
Thomas and Matthew

Contents

Acknowledgments

I WOULD like to thank once again the first readers of my work, Richard Regosin and Suzanne Gearhart, for their careful readings, their encouragement, and most of all for their criticisms and suggestions for cutting a very long manuscript down to manageable size.

I am also very grateful for the invaluable assistance Anne Tomiche and Elizabeth Constable gave me in the early stages of my research for this book.

In 1992, I received a John Simon Guggenheim Memorial Fellowship and an American Council of Learned Societies Fellowship, which freed me from teaching for a year and allowed me to complete research on the book and finish writing a draft of the manuscript.

Sections of this book have previously appeared in print. A part of Chapter 1 with a different introduction was published in *Paragraph* 17.2 (July 1994) as "The Use and Abuse of Culture: Maurice Barrès and the Ideology of the Collective Subject." Chapter 4 is a revised and expanded version of an article published in *New Literary History*, v. 23, no. 3 (Summer 1992), and entitled "Literary Fascism or the Aestheticizing of Politics: The Case of Robert Brasillach." A section of the Afterword is a revision of a small portion of an article entitled "The Temptation of Fascism and the Question of Literature: Justice, Sorrow, and Political Error (An Open Letter to Jacques Derrida)" and originally published in *Cultural Critique*, no. 15 (Spring 1990).

FRENCH LITERARY FASCISM

Introduction _____

Literature, Culture, Fascism

IN SPITE OF A GROWING NUMBER of important studies arguing the contrary, fascism in its various forms is still often depicted as an aberration within or a radical departure from the dominant Western political tradition and is treated by many as a violent rejection of basic rational principles, enlightenment values, and Western cultural ideals in general. Elements of this picture are not entirely false, of course, but the picture as a whole is one-sided and often self-serving. For the all-too-frequent denial or de-emphasis of the roots of fascism *within* the history of European philosophy, culture, and politics has made it easier to consider all fascist leaders and intellectuals as deranged or evil, and all those who actively participated in fascist movements or supported the goals of fascism to be less than rational and human themselves—in other words, not like "us."

What is especially difficult to understand from such a perspective is how fascism could have appeared as an attractive alternative to democracy to political theorists, writers, and intellectuals who were not irrational nihilists but in fact were deeply committed to traditional values, art, and culture, and even to a form of classical humanism. Such writers and intellectuals saw fascism as a way of restoring the political and cultural values they claimed were an expression of a more profound and truer sense of "Man" than that allowed by democracy, liberalism, and modernity in general. In fact, many saw fascism as the way to revitalize a rational, classical, humanist tradition that had, in their mind, been practically destroyed in modernity. It was not the way to destroy the humanity of "Man" but rather to restore it to him.

In terms of the general denial of common roots between mainstream European values and thought and fascism, France is an especially interesting case. For the desire to emphasize the distance between rational thought and traditional humanist culture, on the one hand, and fascism, on the other, has meant in France, until fairly recently, that fascism was considered to be doubly foreign to France and French history. First of all, if fascism is considered essentially a collectivist irrationalism and antihumanism, then it is profoundly alien to a dominant French tradition that has generally been defined in terms of rational thought and humanist principles. By definition, then, fascism would be diametrically opposed to the France of the Revolution, to France the defender of the "Rights of Man" and the integrity, creative force, and inalienable rights of the individual.

And second, from the moment France was liberated, republican, Gaullist France began promoting the picture of the French people as having been first and foremost victims or even martyrs of fascism—except, of course, for an allegedly limited number of traitorous collaborators. The French in general were in this way encouraged to see themselves as having little if any responsibility for the active collaboration of Vichy France with Nazi Germany. Because France itself never had a fascist government or a state fascist party, the French could claim that they had always been fundamentally opposed to fascism and therefore essentially exempt from any responsibility for the rise of fascism in Europe or for attempts to create a new fascist order. Not just Gaullist France but socialist France and communist France as well have all depicted the "real France" as the France of the resistance to fascism, not the France of collaboration, anti-Semitism, antidemocratic institutions, and severe political and cultural repression.

Much of the serious and important historical work done in the last twenty years on Vichy France and the collaboration of the French with the Germans during the Occupation has of course been aimed at debunking the myth of a predominantly unified antifascist France. The picture has been challenged of a France that took no initiatives on its own but was forced by the Germans to pass anti-Semitic statutes and assist in imprisoning and deporting Jews, and of a France that was generally blameless for the crimes and injustices committed by a small minority of unpatriotic, that is, "un-French," traitors in its midst. In fact, recent studies have shown the opposite to be the case, and as Michael R. Marrus and Robert O. Paxton, for example, have demonstrated in *Vichy France and the Jews* (New York: Schocken Books, 1983), Vichy France consistently went much further and took more initiatives against the Jews than Nazi Germany demanded. Its programs had a rigorous internal logic to them and were developed first of all to serve French nationalist rather than German goals, the primary one being the political and cultural homogenization of France.[1]

Concentrating on the elements of the European intellectual tradition that led a number of writers and intellectuals to see fascism as its culmination, Zeev Sternhell has argued in *Neither Right nor Left: Fascist Ideology in France*, translated by David Maisel (Berkeley: University of California Press, 1986), that fascism must be considered "a phenomenon that is inseparable from the mainstream of European history" (ix–x), that a "fascist type of thought was at that time [the 1920s and 1930s] very prevalent, that its roots went deep, and that its influence was considerable" (xi). But also in the specific case of France, Sternhell argues that France should be seen as "the country in which the fascist ideology in its main aspects came into being a good twenty years before similar ideologies appeared elsewhere in Europe. . . . French fascism was thus in every respect an indigenous school of thought: in no way can it be regarded as a foreign importation" (27). Rather than being considered a totally alien ideology imposed on a victimized country, French anti-Semitism and fascism in this and other studies, then, are treated as phenomena with specifically French characteristics and roots.

In this book, I am interested in the literary dimensions of those roots and the particular *literary* forms that fascism and anti-Semitism took in France. A critical analysis of the literary aspects of fascism and the indigenous traditions and concepts called on to support French literary fascism is essential if we are to gain a better understanding of the rise of fascism in Europe and its attraction not just to political leaders and masses of people but to so many writers and intellectuals as well.

In the hands of some, however, both the rigorously documented analysis of the responsibility of the Vichy government and many French sympathizers for criminal actions taken against Jews and the argument that insists on the indigenous roots of the fascism of various French intellectuals have been transformed into a general indictment of almost everything French. An important though not dominant or exclusive part of French history, culture, and thought has thus been made into "*the* French ideology," transforming the image of victimized, martyred, and resistant France into that of the country in which all of the evils it claimed to have suffered from were actually born and nurtured. Resistant France, the France of the "Rights of Man," has become, for those bent on sensationalizing the issue of fascism in France, not just collaborationist France but, even worse, fascist and anti-Semitic France, France as the original source of fascism and anti-Semitism in general. One myth has thus been created to replace another; the image of unequivocal goodness has been replaced by that of unmitigated evil.[2]

What interests me is neither the innate goodness nor the evil of French society or French culture. Like all societies, France has just and unjust, benevolent and criminal, and democratic and antidemocratic moments in its long social and political history. Like all cultures, both homogenizing, hegemonic, xenophobic, and racist traits and heterogeneous, decentralizing, and antiracist elements can be found in its cultural and political history. These are also present in its dominant aesthetic ideals and in the different versions of its collective sense of self. The problem of understanding the nature of what I am calling French literary fascism and the tradition it calls on and (re)creates to found and justify itself has nothing to do with an all-too-prevalent general condemnation of French (or European) culture in general, for the various forms of French culture and thought and the multiple political traditions in France are much too diversified, contradictory, and conflictual to constitute anything like a single, totalized ideology, especially if this ideology is deemed to be essentially protofascist and racist. This means that neither the simple denial nor the grotesque sensationalizing of the problem of the indigenous roots of fascism in French thought, culture, and politics can be considered a defensible or responsible position.

In this book I focus on the literary side of French fascism in order to understand better what constituted fascism for a diversified group of French writers and intellectuals and how fascism was for them both a nationalist (or Europeanist) political ideology and a nationalist aesthetics—an aesthetics-as-ideology. Because literature and art constituted for these writers the basis of their concept of fascism, I argue that their commitment to art and literature formed and justified to an important extent their politics. For them—and they are certainly not representative of all of France or all of French culture—the cause of literature and art and the cause of fascism were basically one and the same.

The task of understanding the attraction to fascism is not a simple matter of separating the good from the bad, the pure from the corrupt, the rational from the irrational, the historically progressive from the decadent, the humanist from the antihumanist, the modern from the antimodern, the healthy from the sick. For this is the language of the extreme right and the kind of opposition on which it constantly relied. That it has also been the language of a certain left should concern us and is part of the problem of dealing with the issue of fascism in a critical way, and of confronting fascism in its most nuanced intellectual and aesthetic forms as well as in its specific political practices. What could be called the "high" and "low" forms of fascism (some would call these the "utopian" and "practical" or even the "intellectual" and "vulgar" forms), no matter their differences, are in fact inextricably intertwined. In order to understand and criticize the effects of the latter, it is necessary also to analyze the intellectual and aesthetic attraction and emotive power of the former.

For many intellectuals on the extreme right in France, fascism implied among other things a particular relationship between literature and politics. To focus on this relationship means to study the various kinds of exchanges between the two fields: how one field or area opens onto, supports, and at times determines the other. It is a question of understanding the implications of what Walter Benjamin called the fascist "aestheticizing of politics."[3] In a broader sense, I am concerned with the specific role played by art and literature in fascism, an ideology whose goal was the fabrication or fashioning ("fictioning") of a people or state—a politics that was presented as an *art of the political*.[4] Understanding the commitment to fascism of various intellectuals and writers, therefore, is as much an "aesthetic" as a "political" problem, one in which aesthetics and politics are both at the same time fundamental issues, inseparable from each other, no matter the singularity or autonomy attributed to each.

"Literary fascism," in the strong sense I want to give to this term is not the *application* of fascist ideology to literature, a form of determination from the political "outside"; rather, it concerns the "internal" relations of fascism and literature. In a sense, literary fascism exploits the totalizing tendencies implicit in literature itself and constitutes a technique or mode of fabrication, a form of fictionalizing or aestheticizing not just of literature but of politics as well, and the transformation of the disparate elements of each into organic, totalized *works of art*. I focus on the logic of such aestheticizing and on the assumptions about art and literature at the basis of both the aesthetics and politics of literary fascists. By doing so I show why fascism should be treated as an extreme but logical development of a number of fundamental aesthetic concepts or cultural ideals: namely, the notion of the integrity of "Man" as a founding cultural principle and political goal; of the totalized, organic unity of the artwork as both an aesthetic and political ideal; and finally, of culture considered as the model for the positive form of political totalization, the ultimate foundation for and the full realization and unification of both the individual and the collectivity.

One thing that is made vividly clear by a study of the work of nationalist extremist writers of the turn of the century and French fascist writers and intellectuals of the 1930s and 1940s is that their literary and aesthetic sensibilities and critical skills did not save them from, or act as alternatives to, political dogmatism. A sensitivity to art and literature did not prevent them from being insensitive and indifferent in the face of the worst forms of injustice, or in most cases from being biased, xenophobic, or racist and actively promoting hatred and violence against others. On the contrary, it was precisely their particular literary and aesthetic convictions and ideals that led them to and supported the anti-Semitic prejudices and extremist political positions they formulated and defended in their literary and critical texts as well as in their more directly political writings. The question that interests me is how literature was made to serve such a function—how a certain form of fascism came to be formulated in *literary* terms.

Like everyone else, artists, poets, novelists, critics, and philosophers are capable of both the best and the worst. And literature, art, and culture can be made to serve and support both the highest ideals and the basest crimes, to function both as critical alternatives to political dogmatism and as supports for ideals that, when *applied* to society and used to determine its form by repressing or eliminating all nonconforming elements, are themselves dogmatic, unjust, or even criminal. The notion that an "authentic" artist, writer, or critic, in his or her function as artist, writer, connoisseur, or critical reader, could not be at the same time a political ideologue, racist, or anti-Semite, that art and literature are in themselves opposed to political dogmatism and racial biases and hatred, constitutes nothing less than a mystification of art and literature as well as of the artist and writer. French literary fascists proved that the most extreme political ideologies could be formulated and defended in terms of literary and aesthetic principles that are themselves seemingly far removed from and even at times the antithesis of the politics they support.

In this book I am interested in what could be called the negative potential of literature and, more specifically, in the theories of literature and literary models that were given a dogmatic political function by the French writers and critics I am calling French literary fascists. To claim, as I shall, that their politics were more literary, aesthetic, or cultural than strictly political is in no way to excuse or explain away their political commitments; rather, it is to analyze them critically and begin to understand better the attraction of fascism to a large group of French intellectuals and writers precisely *because they were intellectuals and writers*, a group that was no more limited, demonic, irrational, or inherently "evil" than other groups of intellectuals or writers of the same period who were indifferent to or even opposed to fascism. Their choice of fascism—as mistaken, as unjust in its effects, and thus as condemnable as it certainly was—cannot be understood, therefore, as constituting a rejection of traditional humanistic values or cultural ideals. On the contrary, they conceived of fascism as the means for restoring, protecting, and realizing such values and ideals as completely as possible.

Culture can serve many functions, but one of the functions it has always served is ideological. It should come as no surprise, therefore, that writers, intellectuals, and literary critics, especially at moments of social and political crisis, would propose solutions to social, economic, and political divisions and conflicts that could be called aestheticist or culturalist, and that they would use culture both as an ideological weapon against all national, ethnic, or cultural differences and as a model for political unity. French literary fascists, in the name of an idealized notion of French culture, proposed extreme, authoritarian political strategies and defended harsh and unjust political measures, especially against the Jews. The principal question I pursue in this book is what literature had to do with their political extremism and anti-Semitism—what specific theories and forms of literature were evoked not just to justify their anti-Semitism, which was for the most part "cultural" in form, but also to form their notion of fascism itself. In fact, it was as much their confidence in the formative powers of art and literature, and in the benefits to be gained by fashioning the political in terms of literary-aesthetic strategies and models, as it was their extremist ideological convictions as such that led them to fascism. As my reading of their political and cultural essays will show, the ideological and the literary-cultural are inseparable in their work. Political extremism and the defense of the integrity of literature and culture constitute one and the same position.

The book is divided into two parts: the first part deals with three French "fathers" of literary fascism; the second part analyzes the work of five important French writers, critics, or intellectuals whom I am calling literary fascists. In the original project for the book, I intended to work solely on the fascist writers themselves; but I soon found it impossible to isolate them completely from the nationalist writers of the turn of the century to whom they constantly referred. For all of the literary fascists treated (except Céline), the work of Maurice Barrès, Charles Péguy, and Charles Maurras provided a vigorous defense of, and a direct, modern link to, French tradition and to a radical, antidemocratic form of politics. It was not that fascists servilely imitated the traditional culturalism of Barrès, the neoclassical aesthetics of Maurras, or the antidemocratic, aestheticist spiritualism and populism of Péguy; rather, they used their work as models for how the classical could serve as the foundation for a postclassical modernism that would supposedly have nothing to do with democracy and "modernity" per se, but would constitute nothing less than a new, "purified," more authentic, revolutionary form of modernity. The five writers treated in the second part of this book saw fascism as a radical break with the recent past and at the same time as constituting a profound continuity with the authentic past, as a new beginning, the (re)birth of a "new man" paradoxically modeled after a radical notion of an original, poetic, revolutionary, totalitarian "classical man."

To understand better how literary fascists could enthusiastically support the notion of the "new fascist man" and at the same time defend the superiority of traditional French culture, it was first necessary to analyze the place of the French classical tradition and the formative powers assigned to art, literature, and culture in the work of Barrès, Maurras, and Péguy. In the case of each of these "fathers" of French fascism, I have focused on the relation between literature, aesthetics, culture, and politics in their work in order to introduce the major problems and issues I deal with in the work of the fascist writers themselves.

Certainly, there is nothing surprising or controversial in evoking extremist, antidemocratic nationalists and anti-Semites such as Barrès and Maurras in such a context, for their links with fascism have frequently been treated, even if not from the perspective of how their views of literature, art, and culture shaped their extremist nationalist, anti-Semitic politics.[5] I show how the groundwork for what would become literary fascism is laid in the work of both Barrès and Maurras, and how their formulation of a specifically French aesthetics of politics that is rooted in a reinvigorated classical tradition provided the models in terms of which literary fascists later developed their even more radical literary and political ideals and totalitarian cultural strategies. Barrès and Maurras provided literary fascists with a specifically French origin for their own aestheticizing of politics—an interpretation of both the literary and political traditions that made extremist forms of nationalism and fascism originally and primarily products of French culture.

Péguy, however, is another case altogether. As a militant Dreyfusard, a defender of the Republic (of a particular ideal, mystical concept of the Republic), and allergic to all forms of anti-Semitism, his inclusion in such a grouping might seem to some to be a mistake. It is certainly true that he is a far less likely "father" of fascism than the two extremist nationalists and anti-Semites in whose company I have placed him. But since his name appears as a positive reference in the work of so many literary fascists, especially those with Catholic backgrounds and with ties to the Action Française movement, I felt that there was no way to avoid confronting the political essays of Péguy in this first section. My reading of Péguy focuses on the literary-cultural foundations of his utopian "socialist" political vision, which was constantly evoked by fascists as a support for fascism. My goal is not to indict Péguy as a protofascist but simply to bring to light and analyze what could be called the darker side of his legacy, what within his idealization and aestheticizing of politics took on a fascist form after his death. It is to determine why it was in the work of Péguy, antidemocratic, antimodernist "republican," that so many French fascists felt they found support for their own militantly antirepublican views of literature and politics and for their commitment to a form of fascism that was fundamentally literary or aesthetic.

The second section presents and critically analyzes the political and literary-critical essays, pamphlets, and books of five important French fascist writers and intellectuals whose different views of fascism were rooted in and formed by their views of art, literature, and culture and whose commitment to fascism thus represented as much a commitment to literature and culture as to politics. There is, of course, no shortage of French writers and intellectuals from this period who could be studied in terms of their relation to fascism. My focus on the work of Robert Brasillach, Pierre Drieu la Rochelle, Louis-Ferdinand Céline, Lucien Rebatet, and Thierry Maulnier was motivated by their visibility and importance as both literary and political essayists or pamphleteers from at least the mid-1930s until the end of the German occupation of France. Except for Céline—who until he wrote his anti-Semitic pamphlets had few if any relations with the extremist nationalist or fascist press and was generally considered a leftist or anarchist writer—they all were well-known journalists and essayists, whose essays and reviews on literature, art, music, film, and culture and their status as "men of letters" gave "credibility" to their fascist politics. They wrote prolifically on art and politics for numerous extremist journals that were overtly fascist or closely associated with fascism, and they were among the most important literary voices denouncing democracy and advocating a "national and social (fascist) revolution."

My interest in these particular figures also has to do with the specific nature of their commitment to politics, for it could be said of all of them—as it has often been claimed by those attempting to defend them and mitigate their political responsibilities—that in spite of the energy and conviction with which they defended fascism, they were in fact more profoundly interested in and committed to literature and art than to politics. I would agree with such comments, but not to exonerate any of the literary fascists, for their literary interests are the basis for their political dogmatism. In any case, a form of fascism rooted in and supported by a particular view of art, literature, and culture is still fascism, and often, as is the case with these writers, it represents a more idealized and radical, absolute form of fascism than strictly political forms. In the end, a commitment to *literary* fascism cannot be claimed to mitigate political responsibilities in any way, because a commitment to literature is in fact a commitment to politics in these instances, not just because literature and literary criticism are ideologically driven—influenced from the outside by political concerns—but rather because literature and art are considered to represent nothing less than the truth of politics. They embody the ideals that literary fascists claim all politics should strive for and that fascism for them came the closest to realizing.

Certainly the choice of Brasillach and Drieu la Rochelle needs little if any explanation, given their prominence among the self-declared fascist essayists, critics, and novelists before World War II and the fact that they were among the most visible pro-Nazi collaborators during the Occupation. Brasillach became an especially influential voice in literary and political debates at a very young age. He was given the responsibility for the principal literary column, "La Causerie Littéraire," at the newspaper *L'Action Française* at the age of twenty-two. In 1937, when he was twenty-eight, continuing his weekly column for the anti-Semitic, royalist, extremist nationalist newspaper, he also became editor-in-chief of the nationalist, pro-fascist, anti-Semitic weekly *Je suis partout*. Brasillach stopped writing for *L'Action Française* at the time of the defeat, but he continued to direct and write for *Je suis partout* until he broke with the journal—although never with fascism—at the end of 1943. He wrote seven novels, published books on Virgil and Corneille, and edited an anthology of Greek poetry, as well as coauthored *Histoire du cinéma* (Paris: Denoël, 1935) with his friend and brother-in-law, Maurice Bardèche. In addition, he published several collections of his literary essays from the different journals for which he wrote. Soon after the Liberation, he was tried for collusion with Germany during the Occupation, and with the evidence against him based almost exclusively on his newspaper articles, he was condemned to death and executed at the age of thirty-six, on February 6, 1945.[6]

Brasillach's case is in a sense the model case for literary fascism, for he is the writer and critic who most clearly transformed Charles Maurras's royalist, classical aesthetics of politics into an explicitly modern, fascist politics. In my analysis of Brasillach, I focus on both the classical and modern elements of his extremist nationalist aesthetics. I show how his fascism and anti-Semitism are derived from and modeled after the ideal of the organic work of art as the perfect fusion of force and form, the ultimate goal of politics being the ideal of immediacy allegedly realized in the experience of the totalized aesthetic work and the totalitarian community modeled after it.

Pierre Drieu la Rochelle had already published collections of poetry and numerous novels and essays on the state of literature, culture, and politics in modernity before he announced his conversion to fascism in 1934 and joined Jacques Doriot's fascist Parti Populaire Français in 1936. After the defeat, he became one of the most visible and vocal of the French literary collaborators. Drieu la Rochelle not only contributed to almost all of the right-wing extremist and fascist journals before the war and during the Occupation, but he also replaced Jean Paulhan as editor-in-chief of the prestigious *Nouvelle Revue Française* in the fall of 1940 and was nominally responsible for its publication for almost three years during the Occupation.[7] Rather than be captured and tried by the Resistance forces, he committed suicide on March 15, 1945.

In the two chapters devoted to Drieu la Rochelle, I deal with two very different but nonetheless related issues in his work: first, the literary or aesthetic dimensions of the myth of an imaginary, European community at the foundation of his fascism, and, second, the contradictory ambivalence of the question of gender raised by his and other fascists' notion of the birth of a "new fascist man." By focusing on the literary or aesthetic roots of his decidedly Europeanist and gender-determined politics, I show first how both traditional and modern, avant-garde notions of literature and art were used by Drieu la Rochelle to support an apocalyptic, totalitarian political vision. After analyzing the assumptions of a series of important antifascist theorists—Sartre, Adorno, and Theweleit—who discuss the issue of the gender of fascism and the nature of "fascist desire,"

I demonstrate how an idealized aesthetics of the body determines the contradictory place of gender in Drieu la Rochelle's particular "male fantasies" and in his view of fascism.

The inclusion of Lucien Rebatet, a critic and writer who is less well known than either Drieu la Rochelle or Brasillach, is equally easy to justify in a book on French literary fascism, since, like Brasillach, he was a member of the Action Française until the Occupation and an active contributor to *Je suis partout* and other extremist journals both before the war and during the Occupation. He was best known at the time as the author of *Les Décombres* (Paris: Denoël, 1942), his virulently anti-Semitic, pro-Nazi memoirs, which had the highest sales of any book published in France during the entire Occupation. Rebatet fled France with other collaborators in August 1944 and was arrested in Germany in 1945. Convicted and given the death penalty on November 23, 1946, his sentence was commuted to life imprisonment in 1947. He was freed from prison in the amnesty of July 1952 and continued to write novels and essays on music and art and to contribute to right-wing journals until he died in 1972. A sophisticated connoisseur and critic of art, music, literature, and cinema (under the name François Vinneuil), he was also one of the most militant and vicious anti-Semites among the French literary fascists. My analysis focuses precisely on the relation between his aesthetic sensibilities and literary ideals, on the one hand, and his virulent anti-Semitism, on the other. It reveals the aesthetic basis of his totalitarian political vision and his enthusiastic support for the use of unlimited force in the resolution of the "Jewish question."

Céline and Maulnier, for very different reasons, may seem at first glance more problematical choices. I must admit that when I first began forming the project for this book, I had no intention of including Céline among the literary fascists to be treated, for Céline was never as directly involved in political journalism as the other intellectuals and writers I intended to study. In addition, his infamous anti-Semitic pamphlets represented such an extreme, delirious form of anti-Semitism that it could hardly be considered typical of the self-proclaimed "rationalism" and "restraint" of French literary fascists in general. In the end, his "atypicality," his lack of political sophistication or even realism, and above all his extremism were the very reasons I chose to include a study of his anti-Semitic pamphlets in this work. Beginning with an analysis of the project of Edouard Drumont—the turn-of-the-century extremist nationalist and anti-Semite—in *La France juive* to construct a "total picture of the Jew," I focus then on the *logic* of Céline's anti-Semitic "ravings" and show how his pamphlets constitute a radical extension of a long French anti-Semitic literary tradition. Inseparable from his absolutist theory of the poetic, Céline's anti-Semitism constitutes an extreme, unlimited aes-

14 INTRODUCTION

theticism or poeticism. Céline may be the most exaggerated and least typical of the literary fascists, but at the same time he is the most poetic and
the most literary, and it is precisely the extremity of his vision and the
unbounded nature of his poetics of anti-Semitism that reveal the full, terrifying, destructive potential of the literary or poetic when it is absolutized in or as fascism.

Thierry Maulnier is undoubtedly the most philosophically rigorous
and sophisticated of the writers treated in this book; he is also the most
difficult to place. A friend of Brasillach's from the time they were *lycée*
students and then at the Ecole Normale together, he began writing for
L'Action Française at the same time as Brasillach. He also wrote essays
for almost all of the major extremist nationalist and fascist literary and
political journals in France until the defeat. He himself cofounded and
ran two "revolutionary" nationalist journals, *L'Insurgé* and *Combat*, to
which a wide range of extremist writers such as Brasillach and the young
Maurice Blanchot contributed. He is the only one of the group of writers
studied in this work, however, not to have directly collaborated with the
Germans during the Occupation; he remained loyal to Maurras and continued to write for his royalist journal until the Liberation. He is also the
only one not to have overtly declared himself to be a fascist or not to have
associated himself without important reservations with anti-Semitism.
After the war, Maulnier had a very successful academic and literary career and was elected to the Académie Française, where he was a member
until his death in 1988.

Maulnier's idealist view of fascism was highly critical of all existing
forms of nationalism and fascism; it proposed the ideal of a totally spiritual form of fascism that no actual fascism could ever attain. Considered
by almost all the fascist collaborators during the Occupation as a traitor
to their cause, he was at the same time the most rigorous and "purest" of
fascists, so rigorous that he could not associate himself completely with
what he considered compromised or not sufficiently spiritual forms of
fascism—any fascism that accepted being simply fascist; that is, primarily
political rather than literary. I include Maulnier in the group because of
his close association with many extremist nationalist and fascist publications and because he represents the opposite pole from Céline in terms of
the problem of literary fascism. His is a highly intellectualized, critical,
nuanced, and yet extreme, spiritualized form of fascism; what I call a
literary fascism beyond fascism. In Maulnier's work, culture functions
not as an instinctual endowment one inherits at birth but rather as the
ultimate rational foundation for society—as an ideological construct with
which one identifies intellectually rather than emotionally or instinctually, a construct that determines the essence of the human. The ideal of an

authentic, literary-cultural form of fascism represents for Maulnier the most complete realization of "man," the ultimate, most radical stage of the classical humanist tradition—as opposed to democracy, which represents the antithesis and destruction of that tradition. With Maulnier, French literary fascism achieves its fullest spiritual and even critical potential, its most sophisticated, nuanced philosophical articulation.

As Maulnier's case vividly demonstrates, the term literary fascist should not be applied only to a small group of self-proclaimed fascists, militant anti-Semites, and enthusiastic Nazi sympathizers. On the contrary, the influence of literary fascism extended well beyond such monolithic political extremism. As an example of such influence, in an Afterword I relate my analysis of French literary fascism to the controversial case of the young Paul de Man's wartime journalism in the collaborationist Belgian newspaper Le Soir. This is done not in an attempt to equate de Man with any of the figures discussed in the book but rather to understand better his temptation with fascism and to show how, in his case as well, an interest in defending the autonomy and integrity of literature was the basis for a political position that was nationalist, collaborationist, and profascist. For the literary concepts and critical strategies on which de Man relied in his newspaper articles to defend the autonomy of literature and art (as in the case of all of the French literary fascists treated in this book) served rather than countered the extremist nationalist and fascist politics he also defended in these articles. My point is not to demonize de Man as many have done, or to discredit in any way his later work as a critic and theorist, but rather to analyze the literary roots of his brief and misguided political commitments during three years of the war. My purpose is not to condemn some allegedly "evil" side of de Man (or of any of the literary fascists) but rather to insist on the destructive power of such literary ideals when they are applied to politics, as well as to understand the political responsibility of literary critics and writers for their aestheticization of the political.

As a whole, this work makes no claim to offer a general theory of fascism, because the case of these particular writers and intellectuals is not presented as being typical of fascists or fascisms in general. I do argue, however, that as a whole these French literary fascists represent a significant and still largely overlooked or undervalued perspective on fascism, and by studying their work one can better understand fundamental aspects of fascism as well as its attraction to vast numbers of intellectuals and writers. I would hope that my analysis of French literary fascism reveals with some precision the theoretical basis for the fascist aestheticizing of politics as well as its aesthetic and political implications. My analysis is also intended to demonstrate why a critical approach to the aestheticizing of politics should not take the form of a simple rejection of art and literature and certainly not their subordination to politics. What is needed instead is the dismantling of the culturalist and aestheticist concepts and arguments that make both the aestheticizing of politics and the politicizing of art possible. This study is intended as a contribution to such a critical enterprise.

Part One

THE FATHERS OF FRENCH
LITERARY FASCISM

One

The Use and Abuse of Culture:
Maurice Barrès and the Ideology
of the Collective Subject

> Moralists contradict themselves when they forbid
> egotism to man and approve patriotism, for
> patriotism is nothing other than national egotism,
> and this egotism makes one nation to the next
> commit the same injustices as personal egotism
> among individuals.
>   Saint-Simon, *Mémoires*

> Before the war, well before, there was someone
> who had presented fascism, who had given it its
> first expression. It was Maurice Barrès who was
> the first to see the possibilities and the necessity of
> merging socialism and nationalism. . . . Here are
> our origins. We find our riches at home.
>   Georges Valois, *Le Fascisme*, (1927)[1]

The Cult of the Self

For the great majority of French nationalists at the end of the nineteenth century, no matter how extreme their nationalist beliefs and the racism and anti-Semitism they preached, the determination of who was truly French was never exclusively a political, legal, or racial question; that is, it was not strictly a matter of citizenship, ethnic or racial background, or the national origins of one's parents. Of course, if someone did not meet all the "material" and political requirements of the French nation, the question of his "Frenchness" would not even have been raised at all. But a person could meet all of the legal requirements for citizenship, and be seemingly totally assimilated into French society, and still be considered by nationalists to be a foreigner if he were judged not to belong to the "national family," the symbolic unity or spiritual identity allegedly determined by French tradition and culture. Culture in such nationalist contexts could be considered the ultimate determining factor of national identity, a spiritual force more basic and essential (and restrictive) than race in the formation of the French people.

Culture, defined as the most profound expression of an authentic, unified people, could be and was of course used as an explicit political weapon against all those who did not, or who were not allowed to, identify or be identified with the national collectivity. This included all those who ultimately were considered dangerous "parasites" and whose influence the nation would thus have to limit, control, or even eliminate so that the national culture and the people could exist in and as themselves. The "spiritual principle" of culture, whose chief function was to form and unify the French people, to give them a distinct identity, was therefore at the same time a dogmatic ideological force of division, discrimination, and repression when it came to "foreigners," especially those "foreign French" who were considered not to be an integral part of the authentic French spiritual family.

The notion of a homogeneous national culture provided those who were judged to have met the nationalist cultural requirements with (the fiction of) an enlarged rather than a diminished sense of self. A far from insignificant part of the attraction of fascism to numerous French intellectuals and writers in the 1930s had to do with fascism's culturalist aims, its postulation of a collective subject deeply rooted within French culture and tradition that served as the source and model for the individual subject and its fusion with the national community. In this sense, extremist forms of nationalism and even fascism could be considered to be extreme political philosophies or ideologies *of the subject*, rather than ones that are antithetical to or destructive of its fundamental principles.

One of the most extensive and dramatic elaborations of the links between the philosophy of the subject and extremist nationalist ideology is found in the work of the influential novelist and militant nationalist, Maurice Barrès, whom French literary fascists unanimously acknowledged as an important source and model for French fascism. Barrès, whose early political influences were socialist and populist, emerged during the Dreyfus affair as one of the most powerful extremist, ultranationalist, anti-Semitic, anti-Dreyfusard voices in all of France. His work could be seen to have accomplished a kind of fusion before-the-fact of the different and sometimes contradictory aesthetic-political strategies that French fascists, decades after Barrès, also used, not just to defend an inflated, absolute image of the nation, but explicitly to promote the cultural politics of fascism. Of particular interest are the aesthetic and philosophical concepts and assumptions that support Barrès's notion of culture and that remained unchanged in his work despite the radical shift of emphasis that occurred in it about the time of the Dreyfus affair: a shift from an idealization of the individual ego or self in his early works to the idealization of the nation, seen as a collective, culturally defined subject, in his later, post-Dreyfus-affair works.[2]

Barrès's vision of France as a unified spiritual totality depends on the myth of an original, authentic national culture, which is presented as the alternative to social and political disharmony and the "decadence" of the nation in modernity. Barrésian nationalism has its foundation in a subject whose unity is prefigured, always already given in advance through its immediate relation to what Barrès called "la terre et les morts" (the land and the dead). Culture is conceived as a collective subject whose voice manifests itself in philosophy, art, and literature and is echoed in and supported by the voices of model ancestors, and by monuments and memorials, local customs, and the land itself as it speaks to and is symbolically cultivated by its "native sons." The authentic individual subject is at one with itself only inasmuch as it is immediately at one with its past, an aestheticized, collective past that is postulated as an organic unity and that guards in itself the truth—the form or "typology," as Philippe Lacoue-Labarthe would say—of both the individual and the collective subject.[3]

Barrésian nationalism in fact conforms in its broad outlines to what Philippe Lacoue-Labarthe and Jean-Luc Nancy, in an article entitled "The Nazi Myth," call the "logic of fascism," and in this sense it can legitimately be considered protofascist. Lacoue-Labarthe and Nancy make the following claim about fascism and its relation to the philosophical/political question of the subject: "The *ideology of the subject* (which is a pleonasm), that is what fascism is."[4] The claim at first glance seems provocative and even outrageous, for it appears to assert that all philosophies of the subject—whether humanist, idealist, phenomenological, existentialist, even Marxist; whether nominally located on the left, center, or right—are somehow equivalent to fascism. But the word *ideology* is the key to their claim, for, as they acknowledge, they are using the word in Hannah Arendt's sense as the "totally self-fulfilling (and willfully self-fulfilling) logic of an idea, . . . an explanation of history . . . on the basis of a single concept," one that seeks to be "a *total* explanation or conception" (293).[5] Thus, when the philosophy or metaphysics of the subject is "absolutized," when it is presented as the basis for a total explanation of history and the world, then and only then can it be considered an equivalent of fascism. But even if the metaphysics of the subject does not often realize its absolute, negative potential, it does contain this possibility within it, and for Lacoue-Labarthe and Nancy this means not only that fascism should be analyzed in terms of its roots in the history of metaphysics and not treated as fundamentally "irrational" (294), but also that philosophies and politics centered on the subject cannot be considered *in themselves* to represent radical alternatives to fascism.

If there are important links between the philosophy of the subject and fascism, then Barrès's "religion" of nationalism must be given an important place in the development of fascism precisely because it represents an explicit dramatization of the process of totalization of the subject and the fusion of the individual and collective subjects.[6] In this way it also exposes the philosophical premises supporting the extreme form of nationalism at the foundation of what I am calling French literary fascism. Especially important, the ideology of the subject is in Barrès's work—and in the work of his fascist heirs—inextricably intertwined with the ideology of culture and the notion of a unified self, and inseparable from and supported by the myth of a homogeneous, totalized culture.

In his "Examen des Trois Romans Idéologiques" (originally published in 1892),[7] Barrès left no ambiguity as to what was the first principle of his culturalist ideology, the fundamental reality in which it was rooted: "Our morality, our religion, our feeling of nationality are all crumbled things . . . from which we cannot derive rules for living, and while waiting for our masters to reestablish certitudes for us, it is advisable that we hold on to the only remaining reality, the Self" ("Examen," 14–15). The Self—almost always capitalized—asserts itself as an irrefutable *reality*, then, in a world not of Cartesian doubt but of political and cultural devastation, one in which all institutions and systems of belief had effectively failed and in which the nation itself no longer stirred positive feelings. At a time in which Barrès and many others perceived the culture of the present as being in shambles, the Self was not only the last remaining basis for culture, it was *the ultimate basis*.

Barrès saw the Self as the starting point from which to build a new sense of morality (and politics) and a new feeling of national unity—a new or renewed cultural identity. For such renewal could not occur until the primary reality of the Self had been recognized, nurtured, or "cultivated," as Barrès put it, and allowed to realize itself completely. Empirically, logically, and sociohistorically, as well as emotionally, the Self came and had to come first. Which means that the Self first had to be itself before it could rediscover the harmony that Barrès claimed supported it in tradition and in the underlying reality of culture—culture as a deep structure that made possible the (re)formation of the Self necessary for its own renewal.

To be a Self is not, however, to be oneself, an individual; for the world is a hostile place for the Self, and in the world the Self is, more likely than not, *not* a Self but an Other, formed by alien, exterior forces. To realize itself as a Self, the Self must work on itself, form itself, and actively and even violently defend itself against the world of others. The Self is thus always struggling against all exterior elements, especially all nonselves, whom Barrès called foreigners or "barbarians," as in the title of his novel, *Sous l'oeil des barbares*: "Barbarians, that is the name of the non-self, that is, everything that can harm or resist the Self" ("Examen," 23). Barrès's defense of the Self thus consists of a declaration of total war against everyone and everything, for even if those with whom one lives "are in other respects superbly learned, they are for [the Self] foreigners and adversaries" (20). The reformulation and protection of the Self admit no compromises; they constitute a total project with a single principle as its origin and end. The Barrésian philosophy or metaphysics of the Self must thus be considered logical, coherent, and absolute, for all reality must conform to *it* or be negated. All others must also identify with it or be violently excluded or repressed as "barbarians" or "foreigners." The Self, in itself, is totalitarian.

Barrès held that the Self constitutes *a world*, that is, a culture unto itself, which he compared to the world of the Greeks: "In the same sense, the Greeks saw only barbarians outside of the Greek homeland. With contact with foreigners, and regardless of their level of civilization, this people, jealous of its own culture, experienced a strain analogous to that felt by a young man constrained by life to associate with beings who are not of his psychic homeland" (20). The other, the barbarian, constantly menaces the Self and must be "hated" and constantly combated (21), which reveals that the Self is never complete or fully formed but is always in the process of creating itself and defending itself in its war against all others. "Our Self, in fact, isn't unchangeable," argues Barrès. "We must defend it every day and every day create it. . . . The cult of the Self is not to accept oneself completely. . . . It is a culture that is made up of prunings and growth: we have first to purify our Self of all the foreign particles life continually inserts into it, and then add to it" (22). Self-creation is thus an unending *process*, even if the form or cultural typology of what is created exists prior to its creation as a regulating principle or ideal. A Self is known by the way it cultivates itself and remains faithful to the cult(ure) of itself.

The culmination of the successful cultivation of the Self is presented in *Sous l'oeil des barbares*, the first novel of the trilogy titled *Le Culte du Moi*, as a state of intense feeling of plenitude and even ecstasy, one in which the Self "becomes a god" (238), the "principle and universality of all things," and the source of all ideas (230), totally at one with itself, self-made, "totally fashioned according to its own desire" (241). At such moments of self-fabricated plenitude, the main character is presented as being complete, limitless, absolute, or at least he feels or imagines himself to be so. Barrès describes one of these moments of ecstasy as consisting of

the "delights of understanding, developing, vibrating, creating harmony
between oneself and the world, of being filled with undefined and profound images. . . . The universe penetrates me and develops and harmo-
nizes in me" (243, 245). As lyrical and as solipsistic as such scenes are,
they clearly indicate that the passage from individual to collective Self,
which the later trilogy develops, is already contained within the logic of
even a radically individualistic and emotive presentation of the Self. The
absolute principle of the Self cannot be confined to itself and has nothing
less than the perfect harmony of the world as an *internal* element of the
Self, and it has the harmony of Self in or as the world as its ultimate
project.

In his preface to the 1904 edition of *Un homme libre* (Paris: Plon,
1921), Barrès describes the hero of this novel, the second in the trilogy, as
"a self that is not submitted to anything. . . . Don't submit! That's salvation" (xi). The Self is "saved," that is, "free," only insomuch as it is self-
affirming and rejects everything coming from the outside, admitting into
itself only that which is truly its own. At the same time, this radical individualism is intimately linked to an activist collectivism. Barrès acknowledged also in the 1904 preface that the novel failed perhaps to "provide
the young with a clear knowledge of their authentic tradition," but he
also claimed that it did "pressure them to free themselves and to rediscover their own filiation" (xi). The cult of the Self demands that all individuals subordinate themselves to their own filiation, the filiation *of* the
Self that *is* the Self. In doing so, they will eventually discover their "authentic tradition," the culture of their region and nation, and the collective cultural being underlying and forming their individual being.

In the vocabulary of Barrès, submission is always submission to the
other, the sign of a weakness in the Self. Subordination, on the other
hand, recognizes the cultural identity that precedes the Self, forms the
Self, and is the same as the Self, and that therefore the Self must recognize
in order to be itself: "My merit is to have derived from individualism itself
those great principles of subordination which most foreigners possess instinctively or find in their religion" (xiv). The religion or ideology of the
Self thus supplements in Barrès's thinking the absence of religion and an
instinctual identification with race, which he claims other peoples but *not
the French* possessed. The French needed the religion of the Self, the very
culturalist nationalism he was proposing, precisely because their collective Self lacked a unique and determining biological or religious foundation. Culture was the *French* answer to the question of natural origin,
with a collective, cultural subject serving as the replacement for the spiritual subject of religion or the biological subject postulated by racism.

The cult or culture of the Self in Barrès's work possesses a rigorous,
even dogmatic logic, but the concept that founds the realm in which the

Self originates is not reason but instinct. The Self does not first *think* itself
a Self; it *feels* itself a Self; it has the experience of its own force. Most
critics have considered Barrès's instinctual-based "cult of the Self" (and
later, his extreme nationalism, or what I would call his "cult of the Nation-Self") an "irrationalism."[8] It all depends, I suppose, on what one
means by irrationalism. Emotion, feelings, instinctual drives are fundamental to Barrès's thinking, but a rigorous logic derived from the concept
of the Self unifies and gives meaning and form to them from their inception. Barrès's overall project—both for the individual and the Nation-
Self—was, regardless of the importance of instinct, profoundly "rational"; that is, coherent and even dogmatically logical. For Barrès, there
was even a "science of the mechanism of the Self" (*Sous l'oeil des barbares* 41), which resulted from giving oneself over to and understanding
the instinctual, a science that would leave the Self not just at one with but
also master of the fundamental instinctual forces constituting it, forces
that originate outside of and prior to its existence. As a culture, the Self is
rooted in the prerational or extrarational; and as a culture, it imposes or
discovers a logic and order in its instinctual, emotive roots and in this way
is able to identify with them, make them its own, and simultaneously
remake itself in terms of them. There is thus no realization of the Self
without the spontaneous and boundless ecstasy or feeling of Selfhood;
but there is also no genuine realization of Self without a rational practice
predetermining the proper formation of the Self. And the same *logic* is at
the basis of Barrès's nationalism: "Nationalism is not only a product of
sentiment; it is a rational and mathematical obligation" (*Scènes et doctrines du nationalisme* [Paris: Editions du Trident, 1987; originally published 1902], 75).

Barrès chose the Lorraine region as his "native province," and as the
privileged model for the collective Self and even the model for the Nation-
Self in all his work, but regardless of his personal and psychological reasons for doing this, Lorraine fits perfectly into the logic and culture of the
Self already delineated. Lorraine exemplifies the ideal collective Self in
Barrès's terms, not because it has remained identical to itself and un-
scarred throughout the ages, but rather because it "was born by constituting itself as a homeland through an effort against foreigners" (*Un homme
libre*, 98). The "Lorrainian race" is treated as a product not of blood but
of this struggle, and the chief character in the novel explicitly identifies
with *the process* by which the people of this province transformed themselves into the "race," the Self they were destined to be: "Through armed
struggle, the Lorrainian founded his race; through armed struggle, he he-
roically tries to protect it" (122). The Self is born occupied by foreigners
and is born again when it is able to resist and overcome this "injustice"
and in this way become an authentic Self. The province of Lorraine—

invaded, conquered, occupied but still resistant, more French than those provinces that have escaped such trials—is thus the ideal model for both the collective and individual Selves. "Race" in this context is not a natural, biological concept, therefore, but a cultural ideal that must be *created* and then vigorously protected.

The collectivity thus becomes a race (a Self) not by birth or blood but rather through the struggle to rid itself of what is foreign to it and in this way found itself. The individual Self likewise realizes and manifests itself as a Self by waging its own struggle against the foreign and thus identifying with and becoming one with the collective Self, its race. As an identity and through identification, the (individual) Self thus becomes the (collective) Self it was predetermined to be. Barrès's extremist nationalism must therefore also be considered a theory or cult of the Self, an absolute, uncompromising (at least in theory) politics for an uncompromising, absolute, collective subject.

Some commentators have felt that Barrès's extremist nationalism constitutes an antisubjective collectivism and determinism and is thus opposed to the radical subjectivism or egotism—the cult of the Self—of the first trilogy. It is certainly true that Barrès argues in *Scènes et doctrines* that the Self is never responsible for its own origin, or even the origin of its "own" thoughts or expressions. This argument seems to contradict his earlier statements concerning the necessity for the Self to struggle against everything that is foreign and barbarian, and that does not originate in itself. In his overtly nationalist works, the grandeur of the Self always comes from its ability to be at one with what precedes it, to follow the path indicated by previous generations, and to become an integral part of national culture and tradition:

> We are not the masters of the thoughts that are born in us. They do not come from our intelligence; they are ways of reacting in which very ancient physiological dispositions are translated. . . . Human reason is linked together in such a way that we all pass again in the steps of our predecessors. *There are no personal ideas.* . . . We are the continuity of our parents. This is anatomically true. They think and they speak in us. The entire series of descendants only makes *one and the same being.* (*Scènes et doctrines du nationalisme*, 18, my emphasis)

It would be difficult to imagine a clearer expression of cultural determinism than this, in which the individual subject seems to be nothing in itself and has no thoughts that are its own, with its unity and identity, its very being, determined not by itself but by its ancestors. The "cult of the Self" of the first trilogy has thus apparently been replaced in Barrès's nationalist writings and in his second trilogy (*Le Roman de l'énergie nationale*) by nothing less than the total determination of the Self—what some have claimed is a radical antihumanism and the destruction of the individual subject.[9]

Such, I would argue, is not the case, for Barrès's nationalist-culturalist determinism has an explicit goal, as we have seen; that goal is not the simple negation of the individual subject but rather the full realization of the Self. It is true that in his later work he argues repeatedly that the individual must founder and be transcended in the collectivity, but it is not in order to be destroyed but rather so that an authentic, fully realized Self can be (re)born: "The individual founders in order to rediscover himself in the family, in the race, in the nation" (19). For if it is true that the slogan of the Barrésian nationalist Self was not "I am myself" but "I am themselves" ("Je suis eux-mêmes"), it should not be forgotten that the others which the Self *is*, are not really *other*, the sign of a radical alienation or heterogeneity at the heart of the Self—as in the case of Rimbaud's famous phrase "Je est un autre"—but are the *same* as the Self, constituting its deep roots and cultural identity. All culturalisms have some sort of collective self as their ideal or as their regulating principle, and this collective self is not opposed to but is a radical extension or inflation of the individual self, its profound origin, truth, and destiny. Barrès never in fact abandons his cult of the Self; rather, he pursues it all the more dogmatically when it is expressed as a nationalist-culturalist mythology and politics.[10]

Cultural and Racial Typologies

Les Déracinés is the title of the best known and most influential novel not just of Barrès's second trilogy, *Le Roman de l'énergie nationale*, but of his entire corpus. The novel's chief political and cultural purpose is to draw portraits of both the positive and the negative cultural "types," of those who fit and those who do not fit into the cultural collectivity constituting the nation. The negative type is characterized in the novel as being "deracinated," which is another way of saying undetermined, unformed, unaesthetic. It consists of those selves who suffer from the moral and political disease of being cut off from their regional-national roots and their native culture, and thus from themselves, and who are unable or unwilling to identify with and be associated with the Nation-Self, the ideal collective Self. As Barrès put it, "The fatherland is stronger in the soul of a rooted individual than in that of a deracinated one" (*Scènes et doctrines*, 70), and this is because to be rooted in the land means to possess the identity of the collective Self and to be identified as a son of the fatherland. The deracinated are both the exterior enemy, the foreigners or barbarians, and the interior enemy, those who in France serve the foreign, either knowingly or unknowingly, and interrupt or postpone the perfect identification of the Self with itself and with its native land and culture.

The struggle against deracination has to be as constant and uncompromising as the struggle against "barbarians" in the first trilogy, but it is now overtly both a collective and an individual war, in which the opposing armies are clearly marked and thus easy to identify, attack, and—if it literally is war—eventually destroy. Clearly, one of the explicit ideological purposes of Barrès's overtly nationalist novels was to identify the enemy both outside and within. The Dreyfus affair, to which he energetically devoted himself from just after the publication of *Les Déracinés* in 1897 until 1902, was for Barrès precisely a war against the "deracinated," in which nothing less than "the life or death for the nation" was at stake (*Mes Cahiers*, v. 2 [Paris: Plon, 1930], 116). In this war, the enemy identified himself through his support of Dreyfus, and the ally identified himself through his attacks not just on this "traitor" to France but on what he represented: the foreign type par excellence, the Jewish antitype, the extreme opposite of the national type, who represented the greatest threat to national identity and culture.[11]

Barrès admitted that he was convinced of the guilt of Dreyfus not because of any proof against him but because Dreyfus was Jewish and thus the full embodiment of the deracinated enemy, *the* negative type:

> [Dreyfus is] the deracinated individual who feels ill at ease in one of the plots of your old French garden . . . because he had no roots . . . that associated him strongly enough with the soil and the conscience of France to keep him from looking for his happiness, his peace, his life, in foreign lands. I don't need to be told why Dreyfus betrayed. Psychologically speaking, it is enough for me to know that he is capable of betrayal to know that he betrayed. The gap is filled in. That Dreyfus is capable of betrayal, I conclude from his race. (*Scènes et doctrines*, 111–12)

The last phrase of the quotation brutally reveals the intimate links between Barrès's nationalism and his anti-Semitism, encapsulating the dogmatic, tyrannical logic that demands that the defense of the Nation-Self entail a war against all "foreigners," but first and foremost against the Jews, representing all those who, according to the culturalist anti-Semite, can never be rooted in and formed by French *culture*, those who do not have "French tastes."

Barrès's culturalist nationalism postulates a unity of tastes and aesthetic values as a way of distinguishing between the foreign and the native, the deracinated and the culturally rooted, and thus makes aesthetic taste a determining force in politics. To take an especially vivid example, once Emile Zola had been defined by Barrès as a *déraciné*, his role as a militant Dreyfusard needed no further explanation. "Predestined to be a Dreyfusard" out of "profound interior necessities," Zola was quite simply "not French" (35). Barrès went on to say that Zola, separated from "us" by the Alps, because of his Italian ancestry, remained a "deracinated Venetian" (35). His foreignness was especially evident in his lack of aesthetic sensitivity, with this considered to be as much a political as a literary fault: "Insightful minds have always sensed what was foreign, that is, anti-French in the talent of Zola. Everyone of us, inasmuch as he shares French taste, is disgusted by the clutter of the Rougon-Macquart" (36). And this lack of French aesthetic sensitivity was considered to be precisely the root of Zola's political and cultural insensitivity: "Insensitive to our venerations, which his foreign soul cannot even imagine." Zola thus used Dreyfus as his pretext to take his revenge on France and its sensitivities and aesthetic tastes.

According to Barrès, Zola defended Dreyfus not out of a sense of justice but rather because he and Dreyfus shared the same foreign "tastes," and because both of them were incapable of venerating the "France" of the French. In other words, Zola, just as much as Dreyfus, embodied the principal traits of the Jew for Barrès, and thus they were both instinctually and culturally traitors, no matter what they actually did. And they were even more dangerous than declared enemies because they presented themselves and were accepted by many as loyal Frenchmen. The importance of the Dreyfus affair for Barrès was that it destroyed all such pretenses and identified the true, rooted nationalist French as well as the deracinated—that is, foreign—traitorous non-French French, so that the battle for France and French culture could continue openly and without the possibility of mistaking friend and foe.

But the cultural definition of "Frenchness" also meant that the problem of national identity would be complicated under the best of circumstances, even without an ever-increasing influx of foreigners. For "the common idea" that Barrès claimed originally linked the French to each other in the past had been lost in modernity and could not be restored. Barrès felt that to attempt to create and impose some other unifying idea on the French—that of race, for example—was equally unrealistic:

> Certain races succeed in being conscious of themselves organically. That is the case of the Anglo-Saxon and Teutonic collectivities, which are more and more on the way to creating themselves as races. (Alas, there is no French race, but a French people, a French nation, that is to say, a politically formed collectivity.) Yes, unfortunately, in the eyes of these rival collectivities, who are necessarily our enemy in the struggle for life, ours has not at all succeeded in defining itself for itself. (62)

If the French could not rely on the concept of race to define themselves, because they were politically and culturally founded rather than biologically formed as a people, then some other means had to be used to avoid their being victimized by those "enemy" nations that had succeeded in "creating themselves as races." Not being a biologically determined people certainly makes the definition and formation of a national identity and a collective Self more difficult, but at the same time, and according to the logic of the Barrésian notion of the Self and the nationalism derived from it, this ultimately makes for a stronger, more deeply rooted, complex Nation-Self, one born and developed out of the struggle to be a Self.

Without a "natural" concept of race to provide an identity for a people inevitably split apart in modernity and continually faced with the necessity of recreating and reunifying itself, some other unifying principle had to be discovered or invented. It was in fact *tradition* that in Barrès's work performs exactly the same function as race in racist theories, enabling the French to be *pre*formed and providing cultural rather than racial typologies of what it is to be French. Tradition enables modern Frenchmen to have roots in a past origin, before separation and division; an origin that all the French supposedly carry within themselves as their cultural endowment—in their spirit, their unconscious, or their soul, rather than in their blood. Tradition thus provides the French with the myth of a homogeneous culture, a spiritual homogeneity, to supplement the absence of racial homogeneity.

Not being a race did mean that the French had to be more attentive to their indigenous traditions than a people preformed as a race. If a race was uprooted, cut off from its traditions and its land (from "la terre et les morts"), oppressed by foreigners, even "decadent," it could still in principle try to remake itself by reaffirming what in it made it what it was in spite of its temporary loss of Self: its "blood" and its racial identity. Tradition, for a strictly racially determined nationalism, might be a sign of the people, a storehouse of the myths that indicated the identity of the people, but it was never the source of that identity. Without the ultimate determination of race, the French could not afford to stray too long or too far from the land and its traditions, or to remain deracinated and thus victim to foreign ideas, traditions, and tastes, for they had nothing else on which to found themselves, nothing "biological" to make them what they were and to serve as the determining principle under which they could remake themselves.

This also meant that the "pollution" or "corruption" of French tradition, culture, and taste constituted as radical a threat to the being of the French as the intermixing of races was for racists. Without a homogeneous culture and purified tradition to carry on as an instinctual endowment and with which to identify, the French people, quite simply, would no longer exist as such and would not be able to remake themselves in the future. Only a closed, integral cultural tradition could guarantee the (re)making of an integral people.

The Aesthetics of the Collective Subject

What exactly roots individuals symbolically in the land? What makes them essentially French, if it is not their blood and if the French nation continues to agonize over its identity, having lost two of its provinces (Alsace and Lorraine) to Germany and being unable to provide the explicit support and energy that would guarantee its own being? What would make it possible for certain individuals to overcome the radical deracination imposed on them by the disruptive forces of modernity, by the military and political losses suffered by their country, and by their education, and to return to "the land and the dead" and thus to themselves? What would make it possible for France, no matter how severe the losses and crises it has endured, to rediscover and remake itself as a unified culture? In terms of the portraits given of the seven young men from Lorraine at the start of *Les Déracinés*, the primary answer to such questions is that it is clearly some specific living link to the past—to tradition and to the land, which persists in them as a living force—that will eventually "save" some of them and provide a model for how France could overcome the crisis of its identity and thus save itself.

The necessary link to the past is narrative and aesthetic, for authentic culture is maintained in the family narratives passed on from generation to generation, in the voices of ancestors retained in the present, and in the aesthetic sensibility and taste inherited from cultural models. The most solidly rooted of Barrès's characters in *Les Déracinés* and other novels all have master storytellers as close relatives and thus have *in themselves*, in their unconscious being, a storehouse of narratives that constitutes what they are or should be. Their eventual return to the land and the dead, and to their predetermined Self, will take the form of a reaffirmation of these narratives and will determine who and what they are. The greatest danger to modern France, a country characterized as being in full identity crisis, therefore, is represented by the alternative counternarratives that threaten to displace the local and national master narratives from their dominant position and make the deracination of the French definitive. In *Les Déracinés*, Barrès recounts the struggle against foreign narratives and in this way provides a narrative model for resisting and compensating for the displacement or destruction of family and national master narratives in general.[12]

In *Les Déracinés*, the first important "foreign, cosmopolitan" threat to the students from Lorraine before they leave for Paris is represented by their *lycée* professor, Paul Bouteiller, a republican and "Kantian," who is described as having "neither soil, nor society, nor, so he thinks, prejudices" (85). Bouteiller is depicted in the novel as preaching moral abstrac-

tions and Kantian universalism to the students as a way of transforming
them into citizens of the Republic who identify with "humanity" rather
than true Frenchmen who have roots in the soil of France and identify
with their own ancestors and themselves. His influence on the students is
not really due as much to the universalist doctrine he teaches, however, as
to his seductive, "poetic" powers and the way he reveals to his students
"the great secrets of poetic melancholy" (76). The narrator describes him
as a "sorcerer of long ago but with a modern appearance" (92), a professor intoxicating his students with "the faraway Oriental perfumes of
death, filtered through a network of German thinkers" (81), transforming them into "citizens of humanity, emancipated, initiates of pure reason" (97), like "captive balloons of varied and brilliant colors . . . who
aspire to fly away, to rise up, to disperse without a destination" (98). Les
Déracinés first exposes the dangers of the "Oriental perfumes" of German thought—German thought that is thus characterized as non-European, feminine, seductive, and deadly—and then provides "authentic"
national narratives and myths to dissipate the scent of the foreign and the
feminine and to reroot the students in the masculine solidity of the land
and the solidarity of an indigenous people.

    Of all the negative figures in Barrès's novels—that is, all those who
embody the foreign and encourage the process of deracination—Astiné
Aravian in this novel is undoubtedly the most interesting and complex,
mainly because she is so seductive and powerful a figure, surpassing all
others through the force of her stories and the power they have to counter
the regional-nationalist tales and myths presented by the novel as a whole
as positive formative models. Astiné, first of all, not only represents in her
stories but also embodies in her person everything that is seductive and
dangerous in "the foreign," in cosmopolitanism. Coming from the
"Orient"—she was born in Armenia—she has traveled throughout the
world, seemingly without roots in any one homeland, and is a hybrid
mixture of cultures and traditions. This kind of uprooted existence is dangerous for anyone, but especially, the highly intrusive and judgmental
narrator reminds us, for women and children: "It is bad to have little
children and the souls of women travel. The best are of one countryside
alone" (130). Women are thus presented as being more susceptible than
men to the attractions of cosmopolitanism, that is, "the dangerous faculty
of borrowing the tone and the allure of each milieu" (131), with the inevitable result that they sacrifice "[their] own manner." And what is even
worse, we are led to conclude, such hybridization of tone and allure is
extremely attractive to young men who have not traveled, for "cosmopolitan" women such as Astiné easily lead astray those who cannot resist
their "exotic" charms.

    In addition, Astiné's stories and the mythical names they evoke both
possess the force of "the origins of history" and are linked to the forma-

tion of her young lover's imagination and dreams: "[Sturel's] imagination was created with stories of these legendary sites"; they represent "a magnificent thread which links him to his past and his first dreams" (157). The stories of "the Orient" threaten the singularity of the Lorrainian-French origin more than any other foreign forces, even more than the abstractions of Kantian philosophy, because they have a powerful seductive power that is related both to a tradition even older than that of France or Europe and to an original, legendary non-Lorrainian origin and past in the imagination of the young Lorrainian himself—to "his first dreams." The imagination of Sturel is thus presented as being divided, and as being infiltrated with foreign legends from the start, which makes the task of reestablishing profound links and identifying with his own "land and dead" a contradictory process in which the imagination must struggle against itself in order to overcome what originally activates and stimulates it. As both stimulus and obstacle, the seductive, imaginative, feminine force of "the Orient" can be neither simply affirmed or negated. It is as necessary to the process of rerooting advocated by the novel as it is excessive and disruptive of it.

On the way to the discovery and (re)creation of self, at the very origin of the imagination, the problem of "the Orient" (and especially "the Oriental woman") is a necessary, internal element of "the Occident's" relation to itself. At the same time, "the Orient" is presented as the culmination of the foreign—so dissimilar from Europe and its "Greek origins" that it threatens the life and identity not just of Sturel but, insomuch as he is presented as being typical of modern youth, of the French nation as a whole. In Barrès, "the West" (and more specifically, France) exists as a unified subject and possesses a cultural identity that is manifest in its master narratives and myths only by means of the suppression, negation, or appropriation of "the Orient"; that is, of all the non-Greek origins that France ("the West") carries in some sense within itself (within its own imagination and identity) from the start.[13]

"The Orient" is thus the imaginary means by which "the Occident" either rediscovers itself or loses itself, a necessary imaginary stimulus that always risks taking the national imagination outside and beyond itself. Astiné's stories and Astiné herself possess all the "prestige of poetry" (171), which is described as being a stronger and more original force or stimulant than philosophy, even when "poetically" presented by a gifted "sorcerer." For the foreign in poetry is even more dangerous than the foreign in philosophy or politics; it always works for the wrong, foreign ends and turns one away from the "realities and interests of French life" (171). It is described as having the same effects on Sturel's consciousness that "a virus [would have] in his blood" (170), as being a "poison" that could be resisted only by a mature, healthy organism, not an "organism in disorder" (171).

The mature, healthy, rooted body (individual or national) would risk very little in having limited contact with foreign poisons and could even benefit from consuming them, for they would stir up the body's own indigenous creative imagination and thus have a positive effect on it. Astiné, for example, is described as "an admirable book," and the narrator of the novel, who intervenes constantly in the narration to explain, anticipate, and judge, clearly sympathizes with Sturel when "he eagerly poisons himself with her words" (173). As a kind of muse, Astiné acts as a catalyst for Sturel's own imagination and creative energies. Sturel thus gains from his experiences with this exotic other because he is ultimately able—or the novel presents itself as being able even if he is not—to neutralize her foreign, poetic toxicity.

Only the body and spirit whose hereditary detoxification system has been weakened or not sufficiently developed, however, is susceptible to the full negative effects of the poison. Thus, positive myths and models are needed to restore the system to health in order to direct all energies to their proper *nationalist* ends and ward off the toxicity of the foreign. *Les Déracinés* presents two model scenes in which the goals of Barrès's aestheticized nationalism are dramatized and which serve as models for the "spontaneous" unification of the French people. The first of these scenes occurs at the tomb of Napoleon. Napoleon is the figure in the novel—and in the imagination of much, though not all, of the extreme nationalist right—who serves for the young men as a model of what could be called a national-aesthetic energetics. It is not strictly speaking the historical-political figure—the great general, the emperor, the absolute ruler or dictator, and certainly not the spiritual heir to the Revolution—after whom the students model themselves, as they all have serious differences with various aspects of his politics and the institutions he founded; rather, it is the imaginary, mythical figure they honor. Napoleon's tomb is described as "the intersection of all the energies named audaciousness, will, appetite. For one hundred years, imagination, everywhere else dispersed, has concentrated itself on this point. . . . Level out history, suppress Napoleon; you annihilate the condensed imagination of the century" (259). In the *figure* of Napoleon, all the disparate and conflicting creative energies of the nation are fused together in the supreme image of a national aesthetic Self, the product of the collective imagination of an entire people.

In creating an image of Napoleon by spontaneously synthesizing and identifying with the different literary and aesthetic representations of him, the students in turn create themselves: "Napoleon, our heaven, by means of a noble impulse, we create you and you create us" (262). The model or type in terms of which they aspire to mold or create themselves is admittedly one they have created (imagined) from the many versions and figures with which art and literature have provided them. In the complicated logic of cultural typologies, the original and the model are each dependent on the other for existence, where culture creates the individual and the group only because both have recreated it, responded to its formative energy, and modeled themselves after it.

In a nation where a universally accepted political idea of unity is lacking, and where race is not a determining factor in the creation of the nation and its people, the legendary figure of Napoleon supplements these lacks. He is referred to as *"the Napoleon of the soul"* (262) and given the title *"PROFESSOR OF ENERGY"* (263). "That is his definite physiognomy and his decisive form, obtained by superimposing all of the figures of him that specialists, artists, and different peoples have traced" (264). More powerful a figure than their *lycée* professor, Bouteiller, as effective as Astiné in stimulating the students' imagination because he is already mixed in their imagination with the work of artists, the *figure* of Napoleon represents nothing less than the guarantee of their own being and that of the nation, the aesthetic foundation, model, and stimulus for cultural unity and self-creation. The mythic Napoleon is thus the ultimate national counterfigure to both the abstract, republican universalism of Bouteiller and the exotic, "Oriental" cosmopolitanism of Astiné.

Around the mythical, aestheticized figure of Napoleon, the young deracinated students become united in a common but still unformed spiritual cause and recognize the common essence they all possess as a reflection of this national type:

> They recognize each other as brothers. They shake hands. Impassioned cries burst from their lips. Subjugated to the play of such powerful forces, stirred up by their admiration and solidarity, they are ready to accept any authoritative speech. . . . They leave Napoleon behind and return to themselves, for whom they are responsible. It is enough to say Emperor; and his grand name, which creates individuals, forces them to say: *I, We.* (273)

When the national umbilical cord has been broken and the young Lorrainians, removed from their land and their ancestors, find themselves in a hostile cosmopolitan environment, scenes of unification such as this are necessary in order to recreate in a new, invigorated form what has been lost through deracination. The legendary Napoleon, his name and title alone, produce the emotional experience of an "I" that is at the same time a "We," thus reestablishing in microcosm the ideal community, its collective energy, and most important, its enthusiasm.

Ultimately, then, in the novel, the enthusiasm felt around the tomb of Napoleon serves to highlight once again the primary and essentially imaginary cultural, aesthetic nature of the national identity. It is not a narrow political identity that can be constituted by the formation of a nationalist party, but a metaphysical-aesthetic identity to be created only through a total transformation of the political realm and of the French themselves. Napoleon, an imaginary composite figure from the already legendary past, inspires energy and unity, but the enthusiasm the students feel at the moment of collective identification is also limited. As the narrator indicates, the purpose of their enthusiastic identification with each other remains undetermined, and thus their energy and unity are easily dissipated.

> Around what? For what end? . . . Something imaginary, like the figure of Napoleon in 1884, cannot give to juxtaposed unities the faculty of acting together. Good for motivating certain individuals, this great legend cannot give any consistency to their group or inspire any resolutions. (277)

The fact that there is no living figure (or idea) around which to rally makes the students' reactions at Napoleon's tomb only a first step in their process of recreating themselves into a collective, truly national "we." The real figure that could give unity and substance to their group and inspire resolute action is still lacking, and "without a national man, . . . a leader" (279), they and France will lack consistency and durability.

The establishment of the national man and leader, however, cannot come before the unification of the group or collectivity. In the context of the novel, the temptation of having the dictator serve as a solution to all the problems of national disunity is rejected. It is considered by the narrator to be a sign of the "illness" of disassociation itself: "When they try to group themselves in terms of the primitive mode of the clan, when they are haunted by the Caesarist idea, it's an instinct of sick people" (283). What must come first, what is the only truly serious problem, "is to reconstruct the damaged national substance" (283), defined as "the true foundation of the French, . . . a common nature, a social and historical product possessed . . . by each one of us" (281). All narrow, political questions have to be considered secondary in terms of this primary, essential question: how to recapture, recreate, return to the "common nature" of the French people, the historical-cultural endowment each "true" Frenchman inherits at birth. The restoration of the "national substance" must be given priority over politics and must determine the truth of the political in general. No nationalist politics, no matter how energetic and absolute, can thus be effective if the cultural foundation of the Nation-Self has not first been restored.

The priority Barrès gives to the cultural does not make his form of nationalism (or the French forms of fascism modeled after it) less extreme or violent than nationalisms that give priority to practical political issues. On the contrary, it makes his nationalism more uncompromising, since the cultural ideal it pursues is presented as being extrapolitical or prepolitical, absolute, and, in this sense, "natural." In this way, culture replaces nature and serves as the justification for the most violent and radical forms of exclusion. In the novel, in the name of the ideal of cultural root-edness and unity, "foreign elements" from inside as well as outside the group are eliminated, and the violence necessary to accomplish the elimi-nation or even extermination of the foreign is presented as inevitable, necessary, and ultimately the responsibility of no one, because it is a product of the absolute "natural" law of the survival of the collectivity.

Not only must the seductive power of those outsiders who have "for-eign tastes" or who "poison" the consciousness of French youth with exotic, foreign poetry and narratives be neutralized, but those within the collectivity who are considered foreign because of their class origins and lack of aesthetic-cultural sensitivity must also be eliminated. From within the group of the principal characters in *Les Déracinés*, the two with working-class or serf origins, Racadot and Mouchefrin, will be expelled and will be driven into a poverty and misery greater than any their an-cestors ever knew, because their origins prevent them from sharing with the others a commonness of feeling: "The totality was held together only by the university serving as a vice. . . . They shared among themselves neither sentiment nor even simple pleasantness. The instinctual mecha-nism of this collectivity tends to expel the Racadot's, the Mouchefrin's, to throw them out into the proletariat, to degrade them" (394). The same aesthetic-instinctual mechanism that unifies also punishes, expels, and does away with those who do not fit, and cannot be made to fit, within the community—those who lack the common substance of Frenchness within their instinctual and sentimental endowment. The community of sentiment is ruthlessly exclusive and uncompromising.

The murder of Astiné that Mouchefrin and Racadot commit in desper-ation justifies their punishment and even serves the ends of the commu-nity from which they must be expelled. The consensus of the group is that they must be destroyed as wild animals are when they offer a threat to a community: "They should not be allowed to multiply to poison every-thing. . . . Society must slaughter them, as it does wolves and wild boars in the forests of Neufchâteau during the winter" (461–62). This is the terrible punishment the community must carry out, but it is made easier by the fact that Racadot and Mouchefrin have by their condition and their act already been reduced to an inhuman state: "Mochefrin is not a man, he's a submerged being, an elusive, creeping thing. . . . He's a rep-tile" (473). One can regret, as Sturel does, that two of the seven Lorraini-ans fail in this way, but their failure is also the possibility of success of the group as a whole. Even Sturel at the end acknowledges this inevitable "fact": "In our little group's attempt to raise ourselves up, it was certain that there would be some waste. Racadot, Mouchefrin are our ransom, the price of our becoming perfect. I hate their crime, but I persist in seeing them in terms of me as sacrificed" (493). The elimination of all those whom the national imagination can figure as sacrificial waste products of the group, as "reptiles," promotes the re-creation and guarantees the survival of the collectivity. The ideology of the Self demands ultimately the sacrifice of all "inhuman," foreign elements *within* the collectivity that interfere with its full realization or implementation.

But there is another and more dangerous foreign element that had to be eliminated, according to what I would call the "natural" law of survival of the national substance and of the culturally fittest: the victim of Mouchefrin and Racadot—Astiné, "the Oriental," the former lover and muse of Sturel. After describing in great detail the agony of Astiné as she is being murdered for her jewelry, the narrator postulates that Sturel, with the wisdom of age, would later come to the correct conclusion that her death was necessary, dictated by her own culture for the realization of her Self, as much as by his culture for the realization of his.[14]

> Sturel will understand later that these tragic circumstances were necessary, atrocious instruments for the perfect biography of Astiné Aravian. He will not admit that any hypothesis could have emerged that would have spared his friend this bloody end. . . . Sturel well recognizes that such a life, unless it is incomplete and contradictory, would allow only for an outcome where there is vice, horror, and desperate tones. (428)

Sturel will come to understand all this when he fully realizes that for a Self—individual or collective—to realize itself, cultural laws, and the typologies and destinies they determine, must be followed.

The determinism that makes Sturel truly French—the cultural tradition and heritage he carries on in him—also necessitates that his feminine Other, the Oriental woman, fulfill her tragic destiny—the one the West assigns to the Orient—and be sacrificed at the altar of the Same: "He realized that he still loved his Asian; however he judged it to be childlike and *against nature* to dispute a destiny for which his unfortunate sister was so clearly marked" (437, my emphasis). Nature itself is thus presented as justifying a form of total cultural determinism, which thus makes the law of Western culture the original and indisputable natural law.

To further emphasize the formative power of culture, the narratives of the assassination of Astiné and the trial and execution of Racadot in the last sections of the novel are constantly interrupted because of another death, that of Victor Hugo. If the national body eliminates its "waste products" and foreign elements in the above scenes, the collective outpouring of national sentiment and solidarity that accompanies the death and burial of Hugo constitutes a positive model for the process of self-identification of the national Subject. Sturel moves from one extreme to the other, a witness first to the early stages of an ignominious assassination and then to the spontaneous outpouring of national sentiment and the expression of the unity of nation and Self through the collective eulogization of Hugo, linking the two scenes together and making the first a necessary precondition for the second. The logic of the novel is unambiguous and brutal; the elimination of the foreign and the construction of the Nation-Subject justify any means used to accomplish them.

The popular demonstrations accompanying the funeral of Hugo are presented as a gigantic aesthetic celebration of collective national identity, a spontaneous transcendence of individuality and divisiveness by means of an identification with Hugo as an exalted version of the national Self:

> In this barely conscious crowd, some, seeing glory, trembled; others feeling death, hastened to live; others still . . . wanted to fraternize. They did better than that, they became one. This prodigious mixture of enthusiasts and debauched people, of simpletons and simple and sophisticated minds, organizes itself into one tremendous unique being, camped at the feet of greatness. Its front, which it turns toward the casket and which funereal torches light up, is made up of a hundred thousand faces, some base, others ecstatic, but none insensitive. Its breathing was like the noise of the sea. (466)

The scene stands on its own as an end in itself, a heightened state of cultural awareness, of increased sensitivity to and worship of the greatness of the Nation-Self and the individual Self identifying with it, regardless of the petty, base characteristics of the individuals collectivized within its image. The base and lowly have been raised up to a higher, collective, aestheticized level after the foreign and the bestial have been eliminated as waste products.

As in the case of Napoleon, the Hugo who is a "mystical leader" and a principle of unity is an idealized figure distanced from his romantic literary interests and republican political activities.[15] The ideal that the masses idolize is an abstract formalist ideal. In loving Hugo, the masses love themselves; they love the figures and types that are the very substance of their ideal (fictional) cultural being as French men and women; they love especially *the words* that constitute their being. For if Napoleon is given the title of "Professor of Energy," Hugo's title is "Master of French Words."

> Above all, words, words, words! That's his title, his force, to be master of French words: their totality forms the entire treasure and the entire soul of the race. . . . It's his legendary side which dominates among the masses and which fills them with love. . . . Yes, it's the mystical leader, the modern seer, and not the romantic, the elegiac and dramatic poet, that the huge crowds accompany. (464–65)

The people of Paris become a collective unity, but one defined linguistically, poetically, and culturally, not biologically; that is, one whose soul and mind are filled with the same words, rather than one whose body is filled with the "same blood."

Hugo, poet and collective cultural ideal, brings everyone back to the origins of the "French race." The force of his poetry is considered essentially mythical, directly linked to the original scene of the emergence of a people:

> One is right to listen to his voice as a primitive voice. Words, as his prodigious verbal genius knew how to arrange them, made perceptible innumerable secret threads which linked each of us with nature in its entirety. A word is the murmur of the race fixed throughout the centuries in several syllables. It is the long echo of the rumbling of humanity when it emerged out of its animal condition. One finds the first mysterious awakening of our ancestor, who, standing up on his hind feet, expressed himself. The individual then differed very little from the species, from animality in its entirety; we had not yet separated the moral world from the material world either. Words worked on, assembled, restored in their youthful splendor by Hugo make us participate in this fraternity, this communion. (467–68)

The role of the national poet, of the master of French words, then, is to facilitate the return to the origin, to the moment before division when perfect communion was a natural state, when the "race" was born not in blood but *in and as words*.

The poetic murmur and arrangement of words in the works of Hugo not only evoke this mythological state of the emergence of the first humans (who are in this scene, of course, already in their essence French), but they *are* this state itself, insomuch as they make it possible to experience this mythical past and the future reunification of the French, *in the present*, as an immediate aesthetic experience. In a sense, the sacred words of Hugo, the poet, and the enthusiastic, collective identification with the *figure* of the poet and his words provide the model for *Les Déracinés* and for what it attempts to accomplish: the aestheticizing or mythologizing of the Nation-Self in general. Barrès's nationalist aesthetics and politics of the Self culminate in such mythical scenes of unification, which are inseparable from the violent purges of the foreign (of internal and external foreigners) that accompany them. Such scenes would also serve as models for the aestheticizing of political experience of Barrès's fascist heirs decades later.

In no precursor of French literary fascism are the forces and energies associated with the aestheticized, totalized Self more powerfully staged than in Barrès's work. Barrès's extremism in the name of the Self may not be an orthodox or a very sophisticated political philosophy of the subject, but its simplicity and dogmatism were undoubtedly part of its aesthetic and political appeal to literary fascists. It constitutes an absolute, unrestrained culturalist version of the philosophy of the subject, one willing—at least in principle—to go to any lengths to realize what is seen as the unbounded potential of the Self, its power to be itself and the world at the same time, to be total if not totalitarian.

Two

The Beautiful Community: The Fascist Legacy of Charles Péguy

> That awful democratic system, . . . the only one
> that will remain in the modern world, the least
> popular, the least profoundly people that has ever
> been or that we have ever seen in the world, and
> above all, the least republican, reigns uncontested
> in history.
>
> Charles Péguy, "Clio: Dialogue de
> l'Histoire et de l'âme païenne"
> (1912–1914)

Aesthetic Socialism

The work of few literary figures has been more at the center of controversy in recent times than that of the poet and essayist, Charles Péguy. The battle over Péguy and his legacy has been primarily about whether his work rightfully belongs in the extremist French nationalist and racist traditions, which in the 1930s and 1940s provided a support for fascism, anti-Semitism, and eventually collaboration with Nazi Germany, or whether it is, on the contrary, diametrically opposed to these traditions. The conflict, in other words, has been over whether Péguy's writing (and because he is often taken to be representative of important tendencies of modern French literature and thought, modern French history and culture in general) should be considered either fundamentally democratic or protofascist; either a privileged example of a profoundly humanistic cultural pluralism and a model for all opposition to totalitarian ideologies and racism; or, on the contrary, representative of dogmatic, totalitarian ideological thinking and a model for nationalist extremism, racism, and anti-Semitism.[1]

What is particularly interesting about Péguy is that he was on the opposite side of the conflict in each of two of the most divisive events in modern French history. Given the ideological use to which his work was put during the Occupation by French fascists and collaborators, it could be considered to have provided an important foundation for French fascism. And yet, while he was alive, Péguy remained a militant and unrepentant Dreyfusard, a severe critic of anti-Semitism, and a staunch defender of a mystical ideal of the Republic, clearly on the opposite side of the battle for the political and cultural destiny of France from anti-Dreyfusard nationalists and other "fathers" of French fascism such as Maurice Barrès and Charles Maurras. The controversy surrounding Péguy (and French culture in general) that continues today has to do with which Péguy and which France emerged victorious in those two most crucial and divisive political and cultural battles for France—the Dreyfus affair and the collaboration of French intellectuals with Nazi Germany.

Writers obviously cannot be held totally responsible for the fate of their works after their death—or even, for that matter, during their lives, although at least while they are still alive they can protest and disclaim uses they find misleading or incorrect, or whose implications they simply oppose. No one controls the legacy of any work, not even the author, for if there is one thing even the "master thinkers" have no mastery over, it is what others will do to and with their work. To take an extreme case, the fact that Nietzsche was used by the Nazis does not make him only or primarily a proto-Nazi thinker. And yet the uses that texts are put to cannot be ignored, no matter how opposite those uses might be to the explicit intentions of their author or the overall and dominant effects of the texts themselves. The uses and abuses of texts become part of their history and thus must be taken seriously, especially if the texts have as a part of their legacy an important totalitarian or racist phase.

It may not be wrong, but it is certainly not enough, to say that certain uses are abuses—that they are partial or distorted readings—in order to save the texts they simplify or distort. It is also necessary to analyze with care and precision *how* texts are used and which figures, arguments, concepts, and strategies are borrowed and mobilized for contexts, causes, or ends far different from those advocated or suggested by the texts themselves.[2] No matter how partial, dishonest, absurd, or grotesque their references to and uses of the name of Nietzsche were, Nazi ideologues were able to find and exploit within Nietzsche's texts elements essential to Nazi ideology—even if Nietzsche's satire and critique of German nationalism and his attacks on anti-Semitism, among many other things, had to be ignored or censored. And this means that the arguments and strategies in Nietzsche's work that should have made it difficult or impossible for the Nazis to proclaim a *German* National Socialism in his name must be analyzed in terms of the National Socialism his texts were called on to support. One could find examples of other work—although none more dramatic than Nietzsche's—to illustrate the difficulties involved in analyzing and understanding the historical-political responsibility of texts for the uses to which they are put, even (or especially) when they are mobilized in the name of totalitarian ideologies and principles to which they implicitly or explicitly are opposed or whose presuppositions they put into question before the fact.

Any reader of Charles Péguy's political writings is faced with a problem similar (though not identical) to the one facing the reader of Nietzsche. On the surface, no one seemed a less likely candidate than Péguy for the "honor" of having been considered by French fascists one of the "founding fathers of fascism."[3] Socialist, republican, Dreyfusard, severe critic of anti-Semitism, Catholic mystic, Péguy, right up until his death in the Battle of the Marne in August 1914, was, at least on the surface, opposed to almost all of the essential elements that would constitute the different versions of fascism in France. The question remains, however, as to how he could have been seen as a precursor and founding father by so many. What exactly did fascist writers see in his work that attracted them to it and made them see it as protofascist? Were the fascist writers and thinkers who refer to him simply wrong, incompetent readers, narrow ideologues ready to make any text they liked, any writer they admired—and especially a militant nationalist writer—conform to fascist ideology? Some undoubtedly were, and the problem would be certainly easier to resolve, but much less interesting, if this were in fact the case for all of them. But in all cases, the questions remain: Why did French fascists admire Péguy in the first place? What did they find in his work, rather than in some other author's work, to praise?

In *Colère de Péguy* (Paris: Hachette, 1987), Jean-Michel Rey tries to disassociate Péguy completely from his fascist legacy and all forms of extremist nationalism. Rey condemns all attempts to "classify" a writer such as Péguy, for he claims that to treat a true writer in terms of ideological or religious concerns always constitutes a strategy for not reading him and moreover justifies why "we," today, *should not* read him. Rey's militant defense of Péguy is thus also a defense of reading and writing as profoundly anti-ideological practices, which means that Péguy's writing *as writing*, no matter what it says and what political effects it actually had, can have nothing to do with the various ideological contexts in which it was placed.

Rey especially emphasizes the way Péguy's writing—always turning back on itself, unfinished, disordered—was open to heterogeneity and what Rey calls the "truly historical":

> Writing as the collection of antecedents, the treatment of the heterogeneous and the diverse, as a discipline without a method . . . the unprecedented opening of the present, even as expenditure, as the negotiation with real forces, seized in their profundity, as what is original in history. (39–40)

Such writing, for Rey (assuming that his description is accurate), in its very form and regardless or in spite of its content, is by nature undogmatic, critical of ideological constructs, and thus truly historical: in other words, anything but vulgar, extremist-nationalist, or protofascist. Thus, Rey argues that it is only by ignoring Péguy's writing as such that his work can be considered to have anything to do with the contexts in which it was used. For Rey, *writing* as such is the antithesis of vulgar nationalism and fascism; in fact, of all ideology. Its heterogeneity and diversity, its lack of method, are always opposed to and undermine the homogeneous, monolithic characteristics of ideology in general. To save Péguy, Rey must thus sacrifice important components of the very writing he claims must be *read* and not censored; he must ignore its various and contradictory ideological effects in order to claim it has nothing at all to do with any ideology whatsoever.

Rey thus attacks and dismisses the political readings and uses made of Péguy during the war and Occupation as grotesque falsifications of Péguy's writing and thought. He argues that when a text by Péguy was published in the first issue of the *Nouvelle Revue Française*, edited by Drieu La Rochelle during the Occupation, this constituted a serious betrayal of Péguy's writing and a serious and highly motivated ideological distortion of his work:

> What did they try to make the work of Péguy say, after the disappearance of the author? It was used for political causes that were fundamentally foreign to it. (Just as was done for Nietzsche.) During the Occupation, they notably looked to make of Péguy an apostle of the most vulgar nationalism. His text was cut up and editings performed on it: well-known operations that attest at the same time perhaps, through a definite bias, to the importance of this work and to its disconcerting character. (102)

Rey is of course not wrong to insist on the way in which Péguy's texts had to be edited in order to reappear in the specific context of the Occupation, when all publications were closely controlled and censored, and when only a certain form of French nationalism—one that did not overtly challenge the Nazi project for a "New Europe"—was permitted. Not only did all anti-German references have to be censored, but all positive references in his work to Jews and Jewish mysticism of course had to be eliminated as well. Péguy's work definitely had to be mutilated to fit into this context, which is to say that Rey is certainly right to claim that Péguy was not "an apostle of vulgar nationalism," if vulgar nationalism is defined as militantly collaborationist, explicitly fascist, anti-Semitic, or National-Socialist in the Nazi sense of the term.

But because Péguy was an apostle—and the word is chosen advisedly—of what I would call a militant spiritualistic or aestheticist form of nationalism, it seems to me (at best) misleading for Rey to claim that the political causes for which Péguy's work was used by fascists and collaborationists "were *fundamentally* foreign to it," or that, as Rey goes on to argue, his work "had *nothing* to do" with the contexts in which it was republished during the war (103, my emphases). Not just during the war but for at least twenty years before, Péguy's work was much cited in extremist nationalist contexts, which, no matter how extreme and dangerous, cannot be dismissed as being simply "vulgar." Too many important writers and intellectuals contributed to the construction and defense of this extreme form of nationalism to dismiss it so easily. In other words, Péguy's contributions to forms of French nationalism that before and during the Second World War were fascist and then collaborationist are much greater than Rey admits. And even though Péguy's texts had to be edited to fit the specific propaganda purposes of some French collaborators and the German censors, they did not have to be edited or cut to have an important influence on most French literary fascists.[4]

Péguy's socialist mysticism or spiritualism was frequently evoked by fascists and translated into a more directly political context; that is, it was freed of its references to Christianity, and then transformed into one of the principal elements of a highly aestheticized or literary form of fascism proposed by numerous writers and intellectuals. When these translations and transformations are performed, Péguy's work does not remain exactly the same, but it certainly cannot be claimed to be *fundamentally foreign* to the extremist nationalist and fascist contexts in which it was used. The question that especially interests me is what roles both Péguy's *writing* and his *concept* of writing played in his fascist legacy, what his notions of art and literature had to do with both *his* politics and the fascist politics his texts were later called upon to serve.[5]

If we read Péguy's texts in terms of the various literary, cultural, and ideological concerns but resist the temptation to reduce everything in his texts to a single principle or idea—either an ideological or an anti-ideological principle—the problem of the cultural and political implications of his work is quite complex. Péguy was a republican who admired ancient France and hated modernity, parliamentary politics, and all political parties. He was a committed socialist, but he broke with the Socialist party and thereafter made it and the Socialist leader Jean Jaurès the privileged objects of his attacks. He was a militant Dreyfusard, but he felt that the politics of those on his side were even more "criminal" than the politics of the anti-Dreyfusards. He was a mystical Catholic who constantly criticized the Catholic Church, a severe critic of anti-Semitism who abhorred what he called "Jewish politics," an intellectual and poet who took every chance he could to attack the "intellectual party" (especially historians and sociologists) and denounce their responsibility for the evils of modernity, political corruption, and the loss of the true (spiritual) sense of the Republic. He was also a radical political theorist who hated politics and theory. Péguy's work on this general level seems to have no unique source or to determine no specific legacy; it opens, rather, at least in principle, onto diverse and contradictory aesthetic, cultural, and political possibilities.

In the name of the absolute ideals of Christianity and the Republic, which he claimed were profoundly intertwined, Péguy constantly called for a revolutionary return to the true spirituality of the French people, the transcendence of democratic, parliamentary, and religious institutions, the unification of the disparate elements of the nation, and thus the end of class divisions and the misery of the poor. Such a spiritual revolution made against modernity would, he felt, bring about the destruction of anti-Semitism as a political position as well. In almost all of his writings, Péguy saw the Jews as the victims, not the masters or beneficiaries, of capitalism and modernity in general. French fascists who referred to his work made similar arguments, obviously not in the name of the Republic or in favor of the Jews, but in violent opposition to both. What they were especially attracted to was the theoretical model for the spiritual transcendence of the politics of modernity that Péguy's work seemed to offer.

Robert Brasillach, for example, constantly referred to Péguy in his work and considered him one of the models for his own commitment to fascism. In an article on Georges Bernanos, Brasillach praised Bernanos by comparing him to Péguy, who, Brasillach claimed, had long before warned against the dangers of "intellectual parties and the materialist civilization, against the power of money and against every weakening of France," and reminded the modern world of "the ancient virtue of poverty, . . . the virtues of heroism and saintliness" ("Georges Bernanos," *L'Action Française* [March 5, 1931]). In an essay written during the Occupation, after reading Marcel Péguy's book, *Le Destin de Charles Péguy*, Brasillach situated Péguy's work even closer to the fascist politics that he, like Péguy's son, supported:

> [Marcel Péguy's] thesis is that Péguy . . . is also a very great sociologist, worthy of being considered the inspirer of the new France, in brief, a French National Socialist. The thesis deserves to be known, and in spite of several important reservations (Péguy, unfortunately, wasn't racist, at least in theory), the thesis is correct. . . . We are here in the presence of a series of sacred texts, a sort of French breviary. ("Péguy ou l'inconnu," *Je suis partout*, no. 547 [January 24, 1942])

Brasillach regrets that Péguy was not a racist, but he is clearly willing to overlook this "weakness," given the importance of Péguy's particular form of spiritualistic "national socialism" and the importance he gives to the nation—the homeland, its people, and its traditions—as the foundation of all spirituality.

What seems most foreign in Péguy's work to the contexts in which
fascists put it, then, are his republicanism, his militant Dreyfusism, and
his respect for and defense of the Jews. French fascist writers like Brasillach usually passed over Péguy's Dreyfusism and his scorn for anti-Semitism as quickly as they could and tried to explain them away, to treat
them as insignificant, or simply to ignore them. Péguy's son, Marcel, for
example, had no trouble separating his father's defense of Dreyfus from
any defense of the Jews in general: "Dreyfus was Jewish. There were men
like my father who took a stand for Dreyfus *even though he was* Jewish"
(*Le Destin de Charles Péguy*, 137). Without claiming in any way that
Péguy's texts led exclusively or inevitably to fascism, I shall argue that the
fascist version of Péguy, no matter how dogmatic and partial, is not *in its
general* lines in contradiction with the major arguments advanced by
Péguy's political texts. In any case, neither his Dreyfusism nor his attacks
on anti-Semitism were considered by literary fascists to be serious problems, given the overriding attraction of his general spiritualistic approach
to politics, which they claimed laid the foundation for a specifically
French form of fascism or national socialism.

In order to better understand the spiritual, aestheticized ideal of the
Republic that dominates Péguy's work, it is necessary to analyze some of
his early essays from the period in which he still considered himself a
socialist; that is, when he still thought spiritual ends could be achieved by
political means. In "Marcel, Premier dialogue de la cité harmonieuse"
(1898),[6] Péguy drew a detailed picture of the ideal socialist city. As the
title of the essay indicates, harmony is its most prominent characteristic.
Harmony regulates all relations within the city and in this way could be
said to be the goal itself of socialism—what distinguished socialism from
all other political ideologies. The real harmony in which people would
live, which socialism would supposedly provide, is given a specific form
and function in Péguy's ideal imaginary community. On the first level, the
socialist harmonious city is profoundly nonexclusive, open to all, regardless of national or geographic origin, profession, class, religion, or ethnic
or racial background:

> The harmonious city has as its citizens all living beings who are souls . . . be-
> cause it is not harmonious, not proper that there are souls who are foreign-
> ers. . . . Thus all men of all families, all men of all lands, of lands that are far
> and lands that are near, all men of all professions, . . . all men of all countries,
> poor countries and rich countries, . . . all men of all races, . . . all men of all
> languages, . . . all men of all cultures, . . . all men of all beliefs, of all religions,
> of all philosophies, of all lives, all men of all states, all men of all nations, all
> men of all countries, have become citizens of the harmonious city, because it is
> not proper that there are men who are foreigners. (v. 1, 55–56)

Perhaps the universalist socialist ideal has never been stated more directly or more powerfully than here; certainly never has it been more inclusive. Nothing is foreign to the city or outside it, given its potential to incorporate everyone into itself. And because everyone is included within it, the socialist city is in the strongest sense of the terms universal, absolute, total, an enormous machinery of the incorporation of differences into a functioning, harmonious totality.

It seems legitimate to query the basis of the harmony of the harmonious city, given the great diversity of the national, economic, religious, cultural, ethnic, and racial backgrounds of its people. What exactly was shared in common to make this city harmonious rather than heterogeneous and conflictual? Péguy's answer was a spiritual commonness, a common soul. The spirituality and perfection of the soul were, for Péguy, the fundamental issues in the construction of the city, and individual beauty constituted the essence of the harmony of each soul.

> In the harmonious city, each soul realizes to the fullest its own personal beauty, each soul realizes to the fullest its degree of beauty, . . . each soul becomes to the fullest what it *is*. In the society that was not yet harmonious, souls did not realize their own personal beauty, . . . they did not become what they were; they did not accomplish their form and lived deformed. (77–78)

The individual beauty of the particular souls—and the possibility the city gives them to realize fully this beauty—is the proof of what would be called today the "cultural diversity" of the city and the basis of the harmony of its collective soul. The soul of the city is thus conceived by Péguy as the collective beauty of the individual souls, each living in harmony in itself and at the same time in a state of immanence or collective harmony with all of the others. Diversity thus leads to and supports the singularity of the collectivity—of the collective soul whose beauty and harmony determine the form and truth of the diverse individual souls.

"The foreign," which in the form of differences of national origin, race, and religion is claimed to be totally incorporated into the harmony (beauty) of the city (and in this way transcended by being included), reappears on the level of the will, where it is this time not incorporated into the totality but radically excluded: "All foreign elements are banished from wills in the harmonious city; the wills of harmonious souls are pure of foreign elements" (86). The price one pays for beauty and harmony is thus the homogenization of will. The foreign and the heterogeneous that can be incorporated into the harmonious *form* of the city cannot be incorporated into the deepest interiority of the *will*, for the exteriority they represent, were it to enter the pure interiority of will, would by this entry alone already have interrupted the pure relation with itself that the will is claimed to have. Even if subsequently excluded, it would be too late: the interiority of will would be divided from itself, open to an other; it would be impure, not itself. It is therefore necessary that the exclusion of foreign wills be original and absolute; the foreign must not even be known: "Thus the citizens of the harmonious city do not know foreign wills, non-living wills" (87). The foreign is equivalent to the nonliving because it is not part of the interior life of the will, its only real life. What is outside the will *is not.*

Péguy's mystical, aesthetic socialism thus has a complex, contradictory relation to the foreign. In terms of the place of "exterior" geographical, national, religious, cultural, and racial factors, it is totally inclusive, incorporating what could initially be considered foreign into the collectivity by making all foreign elements harmonious and functioning parts of the city, with the particular harmony of each being a sign of the harmony of the collectivity. This massive incorporation may be a problem in itself, but at least initially it seems to indicate a definite openness to the foreign and the diverse. But on another and more profound level, that of the pure interior life of the will, the foreign has to be radically excluded as the greatest imaginable menace to will. For a will that does not will itself, a will that is in any way determined or even influenced by factors outside itself, cannot really be considered a living, natural will at all. On this level, the alterity that was seemingly admitted in the first place can now be seen to have from the start been radically excluded.

The radically all-inclusive, internationalist aspects of Péguy's socialism can thus be seen to be rooted in a radically exclusivist voluntarism, one that could potentially be called on, as it was by Péguy himself on the eve of World War I, to support a militant, xenophobic nationalism, or even, as was later the case with French fascists, to support a national socialism that was explicitly anti-Semitic. The mechanisms of exclusion are in place on a very profound level to justify the most radical forms of control or the elimination of whatever is deemed to be foreign to the will of the city, to its harmony (beauty) and that of the "natural" collectivities that constitute it: that is, "the familial wills," "the friendship wills," and the "national wills." "Nothing exterior to the collective souls commands the wills of these souls in the harmonious city. No one has command over the wills of the collective souls in the harmonious city" (89). The collective wills command themselves, and nothing is allowed to interfere with the overall interior harmony of the city's collective will to itself or the harmony of the particular wills constituting it. Socialism's task consisted of creating the city as a beautiful, organic, willed entity and then ensuring that no interference with or disruption to its harmony or beauty would occur.

The most obvious political consequence—for Péguy was also concerned with the practical, political effects of his utopian musings—of the principle of immediacy attributed to the city's collective will was not just that voting was unnecessary but, more important, that it *had to be pro-hibited* because it interfered with the pure expression of the will willing itself. Elections of any sort thus constituted an artificial, exterior, foreign imposition on both the particular and the collective wills of the city. Elections always break up the collective will into competing parties and force both the particular and the collective wills to make specific decisions at specific times, to choose among competing individuals, parties, and interests.

> The decisions of the harmonious individual and collective souls are not made, as we used to say in disharmonious society, *by a majority of votes*, but wills are willed by harmonious souls when they are ready for the souls to will them, when they are in shape for the souls to conform to them. Thus the citizen souls in the harmonious city do not know the weighing of pros and cons of *voting*, comparison by *votes, the law of majorities, the respect of minorities, polls*, because this weighing of pros and cons is based on the calculation of voting. (95)

The will does not calculate; it wills. It is not expressed in votes or in the compromises of parliamentary democracy, which in principle at least give some recognition to and protect minority positions and dissenting wills. It wills when *it is ready* to will and when what it wills conforms to the souls that will; that is, to the harmonious collectivity that the city consti-tutes. The harmonious city is in this sense, then, by its will and as a will, a self-constituting, autonomous, but profoundly anti-democratic willed form: that is, a beautiful art form that incorporates superficial differences into its harmony in order to will itself as a totality and to radically ex-clude what does not conform to its will.

As a political entity, the city is dependent on socialism for its existence, but its deepest truth is not really practical and political but *disinterested*, dependent only on the internal laws of the organic work it is destined to be. In other words, its truth is aesthetic. Even the most willful forms of work in the city are considered "independent and free of everything in the harmonious city, because it is not proper that disinterested work [*travail*] be commanded by anything that could deform its work [*oeuvre*] or ef-fect" (96). Art is treated by Péguy as the most spiritual of the disinterested forms of work—the others being science and philosophy—and the most complete model for the harmonious city, which was on its most profound level "the city of good artists" (99). "Made only for themselves," works of art constitute the ultimate model for all works in which "all foreign elements have been banished," all works that are "pure of foreign ele-ments" (99).

Unlike science, which provides information about the real, works of art provide only information about themselves, information "about the real as it is proposed to the knowledge of artists." The reality proposed to the knowledge of artists is the matter of art, claims Péguy, but the matter of reality in art is not material matter but matter that has undergone an aesthetic *"mise en forme* without having been deformed of its form" (100). In works of art, one "learns" primarily what form is, what the work of the artist has done to matter to make it harmonious form. And because the reality of art is to be found exclusively in art, in its form, the relation of art to reality is internal rather than external.

The real "art of the political" is thus to make the political a work of art. The privilege Péguy granted to art as a model for the political is evident in his "Réponse brève à Jaurès" (July 4, 1900), in which he criticized Jaurès's politicized view of art and especially the idea that under socialism art would be socialist. On the contrary, Péguy argued, art should never serve the revolution, but rather the revolution should serve art and should make it possible: "We are preparing the socialist revolution in order for art to appear—free—to the knowledge of men. . . . The socialist revolution will give us the liberation of art. It will give us a free art but not a socialist art" (v. 1, 543–44). Statements such as these do not represent just a defense of the integrity and autonomy of art against its politicization; they are also indications of the priority given to art in Péguy's notion of the socialist revolution. The purpose of the revolution is to make art free, and the freedom guaranteed art and to be manifested in art would be both the sign and the guarantee of the freedom of society and of the "health" (harmony) of reality itself. In this sense, Péguy's early utopian socialism must be considered a radical aestheticism, for his notion of freedom (in art and politics) is primarily the freedom of the will to will itself without exterior interference and to fulfill its destiny as a harmonious, beautiful form.

Antimodernism and the Spiritualization of History

The question of Péguy's militant Dreyfusism is also more complex than it first seems. Rather than assume that his support of Dreyfus constitutes in itself the definitive proof that he was opposed to *all of the principles* of the extremist nationalism of his anti-Dreyfusard opponents and that literary fascists were therefore completely wrong to consider him in any way a "father" of French fascism, an investigation of the terms in which he defined his own Dreyfusism reveals important links between the underlying spiritualist assumptions of his position and those of literary fascism. The text in which Péguy undoubtedly gave his most extensive interpretation of the Dreyfus affair and the most elaborate defense of the "mysticism" of his own republicanism and Dreyfusism is "Notre Jeunesse" (1910). Because of this, it is also a key text for understanding the major components of Péguy's spiritualistic nationalism, and it is an absolutely crucial text for interpreting what could be called Péguy's "ultrarepublicanism" and for comprehending how it could take on a new life and be given a new *anti*republican sense with fascism. What is clear from the start is that Péguy considered true, heroic republicanism (in his terms, republican mysticism) almost entirely a thing of the past, separated by an abyss from modernity and the politics of the present—that is, from all democratic parliamentary politics and the ideologies and parties of both the left and the right.

Péguy constantly and brutally attacked academic, positivist history, which he considered to be nothing more than a facile justification for and defense of modernity. He saw himself as a militant historian struggling against modernity to resurrect and protect what it had forgotten, denied, or destroyed: its own spiritual roots in premodern or ancient cultures. As a historian, Péguy had a cause to defend, and it was to prevent the religious and political spirituality he associated with Christian mysticism and true republican values from completely dying. He saw himself living at a crucial turning point and a moment of profound crisis in history, a moment in which spirituality itself could be definitively lost if a living link with the past were not reestablished:

> We are literally the last representatives [of republicanism], and unless our children get involved in it, practically posthumous survivors. In any case, [we are] the last *witnesses*. . . . We are the arrière-garde, . . . an isolated and sometimes almost abandoned arrière-garde. . . . We are practically *specimens*. . . . We are ourselves going to be archives, archives and charts, fossils, witnesses, survivors of these historic ages. Charts that one consults. We are very badly situated. In chronology. In the succession of generations. . . . We are the last of the generations that possess republican mysticism. And our Dreyfus affair will have been the last of the operations of republican mysticism. We are the last. Practically after-the-last. (v. 3, 9–10)

But the untimeliness of such survivors and witnesses, the fact that they come after the authentic generation of republicans and before a modern generation indifferent to spiritual values, is also their critical advantage.

For to be "badly situated" is also to be "historically situated at a critical point, at a discriminating point" (11). It is to be obliged to say what no one wants to hear and to be the critical judge of the movement of history itself, to be in an ideal position to see what needs to be done so that the mysticism and spirituality of the past will not be definitively lost, so that the "entire glorious past, the entire honorable past, and what is even more important, closer to the essence, the entire racial, heroic, perhaps saintly past" (12) will not be forgotten. Péguy's view of the true (antiacademic, antipositivist) historian as witness or survivor, archive or specimen, has him holding the fate of an entire people in his hands, a people whose very being is threatened by the movement of history from the ancient to the modern.[7] For without the retention of its "glorious, honorable, heroic, even saintly past," this people cannot be considered to have a history of its own, to constitute a single, homogeneous "race," a race that is spiritually and culturally defined.

Péguy introduces his account of his own participation in the Dreyfus affair and his analysis of its ultimate historical sense by describing the importance of the family archives of the Milliet family, a genuine "republican family" from the previous era. In the tradition of Michelet, he stresses that true history is popular history, not that of the "great men" but of the "troops behind them"; not that of the "premier roles, the grand masks, . . . grand theater and representation," but rather "what was behind, what was below, how this people of France was made, . . . what, in this heroic age, was the *tissue* itself of the people and of the republican party. What we want to construct is precisely an ethnic *histology*" (6). "Ethnic histology" as popular history has more to do with the tissue and texture of daily life than with important dates, objective quantifiable data, unique events, or the theatrical representation of the actions of national leaders. Péguy located spirituality not in the "dressed up history [*histoire endimanchée*, literally history in Sunday dress]" of the official, "professorial" historians he scorned, but in the history of the daily life of a people, the history of "a race in its reality" (7). And this is why he considered the history written by professional historians to have been doubly destructive in terms of the popular values he wanted to preserve. As a defense of technological progress and modernization, it was in the process of totally destroying the way of life "the people" once knew. As the official account of the past, it had already destroyed much of the past by focusing on documents and what could be documented and ignoring the texture of everyday life, what for him was the very *tissue* of the life and substance of the people.

Péguy felt that the papers of the Milliet family represented an entire past republican culture, and his critical goal was nothing less than the undoing of modern history and the restoration of what he considered authentic popular culture:

> People will see there [in the papers] what it was to be a culture, how it was infinitely different (and infinitely more precious) than a science, an archaeology, a teaching, an information, a piece of erudition, and naturally, a system. People will see what it was to be a culture at a time when professors had in no way crushed it. . . . People will see what it was to be a culture when there existed a culture, how it's practically undefinable, an entire age, an entire world of which today we no longer have any idea. (8)

To polemicize and write against (professorial) history is to write for the restoration of a particular form of popular culture, because the "*derepublicanization*," the "*dechristianization*," and the "*demystification*" that

Péguy claims are characteristic of historicized modernity make modernity the enemy not just of French culture but of all culture: "It is in fact the first time in the history of the world that a world lives and prospers, *appears* to prosper, *against all culture*" (11). To write against modernity, science, and erudition is thus to write for the restoration of a particular image of the people as a product of (traditional) culture.

If Péguy's critique of "history from above" can be defended in terms of the way it attempts, after Michelet, to open history up to "the absent" or "the silent" of history, it should also be seen that it is rooted in very particular notions of popular culture and of the people that cannot simply be accepted without critical scrutiny. For history "from below" has to do with "how the men who were our ancestors and whom we recognize as masters lived." It presents "what the people was at the time when there was a people. . . . What a race was at the time when there was a race, at the time when there was this race and it was flourishing" (7–8). The question of the *ethnic* foundation of authentic history and Péguy's use of the term "race" to connote the republican essence of the French people must certainly be read in the specific context in which they appear and not be confused with "biologically" determined racist concepts. But at the very least, it also needs to be said that if race in this context is not a specifically racist term, it nevertheless points to the fact that there are restrictions or limitations inherent in spirituality, differences among peoples ("races") that determine who could be considered to belong to this "spiritual people" and its culture and who does not belong to them. The cultural and religious typology rooted in a "spiritual" notion of race is still *a typology*.

For even if this people is not, strictly speaking, genetically determined, its "blood" is still crucial to its spiritual survival, for when its blood no longer contains any traces of its previous Christian spirituality, as a race it is no longer what it once was, no longer itself. And the principal historical problem Péguy wants to understand in "Notre Jeunesse" and other essays devoted to historical and cultural issues is how this could have happened:

> How of this people who was so profoundly Christian, who had Christianity in its blood (through an infusion, through a so-to-speak metaphysical and overall, unique physiological operation), . . . one could have succeeded in making (of it) what we see, this people we know, (having become) so profoundly un-Christian, so profoundly, so interiorly de-Christianized, . . . this modern people, . . . so de-Christian in its soul, its heart, and its marrow. So de-Christian in its blood. ("Véronique: Dialogue de l'Histoire et de l'âme charnelle" [1909, 1912], v. 3, 645–46)

The "*fault of mysticism*" that had to have been committed to have produced this state—committed, when it comes to Christian spirituality, Péguy decides, in large part by the clergy—is what he calls a "mystical disaster, a disaster of mysticism" (647), having destroyed the very being of a people through the contamination of the people's *spiritual* blood. The ideal culture, or the ideal of culture Péguy holds onto, therefore, is a culture "purified" of all such "mystical faults" and returned to its original integrity, one in which the spiritual ideal remains intact.

What is true of Péguy's ideal of Christianity is also true of his ideal of republican mysticism, the *idea* of the Republic with which Péguy identified and whose last witness he claimed to be. This *idea* provided him with an extrapolitical position that transcended all politics, even and especially republican politics, and made of his own political position chiefly the belief in and impossible pursuit of a mystical absolute, a *total spiritual politics* that was always confronting and opposing political reality, but which was never, which could never be, presented in itself. The idea of the Republic had the status of the lost reality (or fiction) of a people that once was, a unified, laborious people "who in its entirety worked together, bourgeois and peasant, in joy and health, and who had a veritable cult of work, a cult, a religion of work well done" ("Notre Jeunesse," 8). This ideal embodied by the people was all the more powerful a weapon against all types of republican politics because it evoked against such politics the very ideal they were supposed to believe in and embody, that of an integral popular culture that had been lost by being despiritualized.

Because Péguy characterized modernity basically as an era of disbelief, the process of derepublicanization was for him accompanied by and equivalent to a process of de-Christianization. "It is the same, unique, profound movement of *demystification* . . . that this people no longer believes in the Republic and that it no longer believes in God, that it no longer wants to lead a republican life and no longer wants to lead a Christian life" (10–11). Thus, it is not just that Péguy's republicanism can be seen to be profoundly Christian in nature, but also that it functions the same way that Christianity does for him, that these two terms, one nominally political, the other religious, are inextricably bound together in such a way that every true republican must in some sense be a Christian and every true Christian a republican, at least in Péguy's spiritualist sense of the two terms. Mysticism (spirituality) thus defines and binds together the two terms, as well as the political and the religious in general. There are no partial measures when it comes to this dual absolute. One either believes in republican and Catholic mysticism, or one does not; one is either their ally or their enemy, a saint or a sinner, spiritually and politically healthy or diseased and decadent; that is, one has either pure or contaminated "spiritual blood."

The true Republic in Péguy's sense thus has nothing to do with *modernity*, or with democracy and modern republican politics; it has more affinity with traditional France and even with the *ancien régime*. The most fundamental opposition for Péguy, then, because it is spiritual rather than narrowly political, is not between royalism and republicanism: "As I have put it so many times in these notebooks, . . . the debate is not strictly speaking between the Republic and the Monarchy, between the Republic and Royalty, especially if they are considered as political forms" (11). The debate is rather between the ancient and the modern, with the Republic firmly located, along with the monarchy, in the space and time *of the ancient*:

> For the debate is not, as is said, between the *ancien régime* and the Revolution. The *ancien régime* was a regime of old France. The Revolution is eminently an operation of old France. . . . The debate is not between an *ancien régime*, an old France which would end in 1789 and a new France which would begin in 1789. The debate is much more profound. It is between, on the one hand, all of old France together, . . . pagan and Christian, traditional and revolutionary, monarchist, royalist, and republican—and, on the other, facing it and opposed to it, a certain basic form of domination that was established around 1881, which is not the Republic, which says it is the Republic but which lives off the Republic, which is the most dangerous enemy of the Republic, which is strictly speaking the domination of the intellectual party. The debate is between this entire culture, all of culture, and all this barbarism, which is properly speaking barbarism itself. (22–23)

In other words, the Republic, as an ideal, continued to function, at least in part, until modern republican (intellectual) parties came to power late in the nineteenth century to act in its name and in this way to destroy it. Secularizing the state and its institutions, the modern Republic cut itself off from "all of old France together" and thus from what Péguy calls true culture. The modern is thus for him nothing other than barbarism itself.

Republican parties, for Péguy, like all other political parties, act as parasites within the Republic. But he considered some elements of monarchism to be legitimately mystical—though not the monarchist or royalist parties themselves, at least not in terms of their politics. Péguy's relations, for example, with Charles Maurras and the Action Française were more complicated and nuanced than one might at first expect. Their diametrically opposed positions on the Dreyfus affair made them of course *political* enemies, but since Péguy condemned *all* the politics of the affair, this difference was not for him the fundamental issue, since he admitted that there was a mystical side to Maurras's royalism that he claimed to admire. Though he was willing to acknowledge and listen to the mysticism he found at times expressed in the royalist newspaper, *L'Action Française*, he felt that Maurras and those associated with him ultimately cut themselves off from mysticism by "tirelessly comparing republican politics to royalist mysticism" and not admitting the common nature of the two mysticisms: "Our school masters concealed from us the mysticism of old France, the mysticism of the *ancien régime*. . . . Today our adversaries want to conceal that mysticism of the *ancien régime*, that *mysticism of old France that republican mysticism embodied. And notably revolutionary mysticism*" (22). As political parties, therefore, the republican and monarchist parties had nothing in common; but as mysticisms they were rooted in the same mysticism of "old France."

Closer in this spiritual sense to Maurras and royalist mysticism than to Dreyfus himself and Dreyfusard politics, Péguy's mystical republicanism had as many if not more potential allies in the camp of his political enemies as it did in its own political camp, a point certainly not missed by fascists decades later. Those who demanded the restoration of the monarchy and those who worked for the restoration or birth of the true, "national-socialist" community could find a common ground in the spiritualist republicanism of Péguy, which was paradoxically profoundly antidemocratic and founded in an ideal of culture best represented by "old France."

Péguy argued that royalist mysticism shared with the mysticism of the Republic a fundamental spirituality and distance from politics in general:

> Different mysticisms are much less enemies of each other, than the different politics are. Because their task is not, as it is for the different politics, to divide up ceaselessly a temporal matter, a temporal world, a temporal power unremittingly limited. . . . And when they are enemies, they are so in a completely different way, at an infinitely more essential profundity, with a nobility infinitely more profound. (37).

Quite simply, republican *politics* were for Péguy *not truly French*, for they were cut off from all of the cultural values of old France, the culture and spiritual values of the ancient world that both royalist and republican mysticism kept alive. It would not be wrong even to say that monarchist mysticism was for Péguy, on the most profound spiritual level, also an ally of republican mysticism in its radical opposition to politics, for only "a mysticism can to go against all politics *at the same time*" (54). And for Péguy, it was absolutely essential to rise above the historical and political arena and to go against all politics at the same time.

Péguy's hatred for what he calls the "intellectual party" was rooted in his aversion for the so-called domination of the intellect in politics. Péguy's republicanism was in this way "instinctual" or emotional, not intellectual; it had to be felt, lived, and believed in, not hypothesized, deduced, or rationalized:

> Thoughts, instincts, races, habits which for us were nature itself, which were given, off of which we lived, . . . which were more than legitimate, more than

undisputed: nonreflective. These have become what is the worst thing in the world: theses, historical, hypotheses, I mean what is least solid, most inexistent. The undersides of theses. When an organic regime has become logical, . . . it is a regime that is prostrate. Now one proves, one demonstrates the Republic. When it was alive, one did not prove it. One lived it. (14)

No political theory, no political strategy could therefore bring about or guarantee the reestablishment of the Republic in Péguy's sense. On the contrary, political theses, hypotheses, debates, and strategies are all signs of the loss of the true sense of the Republic, of the replacement of "the organic" with "the logical." The only way to return to the true, mystical sense of the Republic was through a total transformation of life that was not primarily or originally political but rather spiritual and cultural in nature—through a reactivation of certain basic *instincts* the French people once manifested and that, for Péguy, still lay dormant in them.

The loss or corruption of the true sense of the Republic through republican *politics* illustrated for Péguy a general political law: "The degradation of mysticism into politics is it not the basic law? . . . Everything begins in mysticism and finishes in politics" (20). And therefore the essential, extra-political task was to struggle against this law to ensure "*in each order, in each system, that MYSTICISM NOT BE DEVOURED BY THE POLITICS TO WHICH IT GAVE BIRTH*" (20). The Dreyfus affair, of course, was itself a prime example of the general political law, for it "was an essentially mystical affair. It lived of its mysticism. It died of its politics. That's the law, that's the rule" (41). Péguy never tired of repeating this law and using it against all political parties and strategies: against republican as well as royalist parties, against nationalist as well as socialist parties, against both the nationalist, Catholic political parties of the right and what he called "Jewish politics" and the "foreign," internationalist politics of the socialist left.

For Péguy, quite simply, all politics were "stupid [*sottes*], . . . pretentious, . . . intrusive, . . . unproductive" (50), if not criminal, especially the politics of the Dreyfusards themselves. What he called the "Jewish politics" and the "republican politics" of the Dreyfusards were even worse than the politics of the anti-Dreyfusards, because the former betrayed the most authentic and profound sense of mysticism and exploited it for their own particular political ends:

> Our politicians, our politics, were the most criminal for they were criminal to the second degree. . . . If they had exercised their profession as politicians, they would only have been criminal to the first degree. But they wanted at the same time to conserve all the advantages of mysticism. And this is precisely what constitutes the second degree. . . . They wanted to play two contrary games together, both the mystical game and the political game, which excludes the

mystical. . . . They decided to profit from *their* politics and *our* mysticism, . . .
always playing the temporal and the eternal together. (90–91)

Péguy's increasing scorn for politics in general and the very harsh criticisms he made of republican and socialist political figures in particular
should be seen as leading to a transcendent or total politics, a politics
above politics in the form of not another ideology contending with others
but rather of an absolute spiritual movement, the total embodiment
and application of the idea of a unified people, a national culture or
community.[8]

In "Notre Jeunesse," when Péguy speaks in the past tense about the
form of socialism in which he previously believed, he considers socialism
less as a political process or ideology and more as a spiritual purification
or decontamination—the word *assainissement* recurs frequently, almost
obsessively in this text—and reunification of the nation. Not only did he
consider purification a profoundly patriotic and nationalist endeavor, because its goal was to restore the French nation to itself, but he also felt
that the process itself was in its essence "French," an indication of the
principal task the French had always performed in history, of what it
meant to be French:

> The purification, the clarification of the world has always been the destiny, the
> vocation of France, the French duty itself. The purification of what is sick, the
> clarification of what is unclear, the giving order to what is disordered, the
> organization of what is crude. . . . Is it necessary to note how much this social-
> ism based on generosity, . . . how much this pure and full generosity is in the
> French tradition—more than in the French tradition itself, more profoundly, in
> French genius? In the sap and in the race itself. In the sap and blood of the race.
> (108)

As Péguy insists on "purification," and as expressions such as "the sap
and blood of the race" recur with increasing frequency in his work, it
should not be forgotten that Péguy saw the spiritual attributes of generos-
ity as being profoundly French, existing in the sap and blood of the race
itself, thus giving the French a spiritual rather than a specifically biological or racial identity.

The French for Péguy were thus considered agents of order and models
of *spiritual* rather than biological purity. And even though it is important
not to confuse Péguy's spiritual notion of race with biological notions, it
is also true that this kind of distinction mattered less and less in the context of extremist nationalisms and fascism. This is the case not because
French literary fascists never evoked the same distinction—they often
did—but rather because of the close alliance of spiritual and biological

racism in extremist forms of nationalism and fascism, and the difficulty if not impossibility of separating conclusively the spiritual from the biological when it comes to the question of race. And can it really be argued that purification advocated in the name of a "spiritual" (cultural, religious, philosophical, or even ethical) race is really potentially less serious, less dangerous than racial purification? The grounds for such an argument seem tenuous at best and ignore how much even the most "biologically determined" racisms also owe to aesthetic, spiritual values, how much race itself is also a "spiritual" or cultural concept.[9]

In Péguy's terms, socialism had to undergo a total spiritual revolution in order to free itself from and rise above politics and in this way become a religion. But religion itself had to undergo in its turn another form of revolution, this time temporal, in order to be restored to itself and be made truly religious. "In the modern world," he argued, "Christianity is no longer the people, which it once was, . . . an immense people, an immense race; Christianity is no longer socially the religion of profundities, a religion of the people, the religion of an entire temporal and eternal people" (100). In order to become again the church of the people it once was, the Catholic Church had to be willing "*to pay the costs* of an economic revolution, of a social revolution, of an industrial revolution, to say it in a word, of a *temporal* revolution for *eternal* salvation. . . . Such is properly the inscription of the eternal in the temporal" (101). Christianity and socialism, Christian mysticism and republican mysticism, thus intersect precisely at the point where the political is raised up beyond itself and becomes spiritual and where the spiritual pays the political costs of its confrontation with, and even subjection to, the temporal.

This double revolution, this total, universal revolution, would in this way constitute, for Péguy, the full realization of the nation and its people, the only way "to found [peoples and nations], to establish them finally, to give them birth, to make them, and to let them grow. It was *to make* them" (104). And Péguy was calling for nothing less than a new founding, a remaking of a spiritual people. This for him was France's destiny, its truth, and its spiritual-racial identity. The call of his early socialist writings to defend the "harmonious city and its beautiful souls" had become in "Notre Jeunesse" the cry for a total revolution and the founding of a renewed spiritual people or race. The synthesis of religious-cultural mysticism and social revolution advocated in the latter work could be seen as a logical outgrowth or application of the idea of the "beautiful city" in the sense that the ultimate purpose of politics was still claimed to be outside of politics, spiritual and "creative": the making of an organic "aesthetic-political work" or the making of an organic people and culture.

Nation, Culture, Race

In a series of essays written near the end of his life, which, like "Clio" and "Véronique," were published posthumously, Péguy radically shifted the emphasis of his spiritualist national populism by defining it less in terms of republican or socialist mysticism and more in terms of an increasingly militaristic nationalism that was even more explicitly Catholic than it was in his earlier texts. The figure most representative of this militant form of nationalism was no longer the "beautiful soul" or the mystical figure of "the people" defined in Christian-socialist terms, but it was now the spiritual-temporal figure of the soldier defined in Christian-militaristic terms. The unity and joy of the people working the land was thus replaced, in Péguy's work, by the unity and joy of soldiers defending the land and the people against foreign enemies. If the spiritual had to be subjected to the temporal in order to be truly spiritual, the most profoundly spiritual "saint," the fullest embodiment of national spiritualism, was, for Péguy (once again), the soldier-saint: Jeanne d'Arc. But she was now more soldier than inspired peasant or saint.

The soldier was considered essential to the making of a spiritual people, for the soldier secured and defended the land and made it possible for there to be a national language, a culture, a people, and a race:

> The soldier measures off the extent of land where a language is spoken, where customs, a spirit, a soul, a cult, a race reign. The soldier measures off the extent of land where a soul can breathe. The soldier measures off the extent of land where a people does not die. . . . It is the soldier who measures off the extent of temporal land, which is *the same* as spiritual land and intellectual land. ("L'Argent Suite" [1913], v. 3, 902)

The land, for Péguy, is certainly not exclusively or predominantly a material, geographic entity, for it is also a spiritual or cultural concept or ideal. But the possibility of the spiritual, and thus the very possibility of a people and a race, nevertheless rests squarely on the shoulders of the soldier who measures off and protects a material, geographic space in which a language can be spoken and a culture can take form.[10] Just as the material is spiritual for Péguy, the spiritual is material, and defending the materiality of the land—especially through war—is therefore as fundamental a concern as purifying and protecting its spirituality. It is the same concern.

The soldier is crucial not just for establishing but also for carrying on the national heritage. For not just the French nation but also Western civilization as a whole owes its development to the soldier. There could have been no continuation of Greek culture, no Western tradition, and thus no France, no French people, culture, or language, without the Roman soldier who spread the spirituality of Greece throughout the world:

> [The Roman soldier] measured off the land for the only two great legacies of man; for philosophy and faith, for wisdom and faith, for the ancient world and the Christian world, for Plato and the prophets. . . . Inside he carried with him the Greek world, that is to say, the first half of the ancient world. And ancient thought would not have been inserted into the world and it would not have commanded the thought of the entire world if the Roman soldier had not accomplished this temporal insertion, . . . if the Roman world had not accomplished this sort of grafting unique in the world, . . . where Rome supplies matter and the temporal and the Greeks the spiritual and even what could be called spiritual matter. (902–3)

The soldier, then, has become the primary force and actor in history, for Péguy, the figure on whose back nations are carved out and through whom cultural and spiritual values are carried on.

Given the increased importance Péguy gave to the soldier as the determining factor in the continuation of the spiritual sense of the nation (starting out with the temporal factor of where French was spoken), Péguy's militarized nation began to resemble more and more explicitly a kingdom rather than a republic, even in the mystical sense of the term. The true soldier was the soldier of the Crusades, or even more, the soldier of Jeanne d'Arc's army: "That is to say that the more a battle is beautiful, militarily beautiful, the more it is similar to the battles of Jeanne d'Arc. He who defends France still defends the kingdom of France. . . . And what Jeanne d'Arc demanded of her men were not virtues, it was a Christian life" (929). Péguy even went so far as to call the Republic "the fourth dynasty" (930), allying himself by such comments with conservative Catholics and royalists even more directly than before.

The war the French soldier had to fight was a holy war, and he had to fight it as a Christian to make it "militarily beautiful," that is, spiritual. More and more, what it meant to be French was defined openly in Christian terms, not just because Péguy associated Christian and republican mysticism, as he previously had, but because his insistence on the temporal dimension of spirituality made the geographic space where French was spoken and where French-Christian values and spirituality were inscribed the focus of his writing, the political-cultural ideal he defended at all costs. Jewish mysticism, because it was not inscribed in a temporal place, and certainly not in the land the French soldier had to defend, had increasingly less significance, except perhaps as part of the prehistory of Christianity.[11]

In his "Note Conjointe sur M. Descartes et la Philosophie Carté-
sienne," Péguy made a number of significant changes in his approach to
the Republic and to the Jews. The Dreyfus affair obviously seemed a distant memory by the time this text was written, and other dangers appeared more menacing than anti-Semitism. France, which he claimed was
the only "successful" civilization the world had known since Greece, was
in grave danger:

> Our two men [the two philosophers portrayed in the essay, the one described
> as Christian and pro-Bergson, the other as Jewish and anti-Bergson, and identi-
> fied only once in passing as Péguy himself and Julien Benda] are melancholic.
> How could they not be. . . . They see the French people threatened from all
> sides, betrayed by all hands, betraying itself. They know that there have been
> only two successes in the world; and in the ancient world it was the Greek
> people, and in the modern world, it was the French people. . . . They know that
> nothing is more fragile, nothing more precarious, than such successes. (v. 3,
> 1288)

The two philosophers thus agree on the serious threat to France and
Western civilization that the impending war presents, and they see that in
such a situation it is necessary to defend at all costs the last successful
civilization to avoid the fate of the Jews, "the race itself of non-success."
For if the success of the French race is lost, they agree that there is "nowhere from which another success can come" (1288). But they do nevertheless have very different attitudes about how to combat the threat to
French (Western) culture, and Péguy chose in this text to characterize
these differences in terms of the differences between Christians and Jews
in general.

Nowhere else in his work are the differences between Christians and
Jews so pronounced; nowhere are their implications so significant and
disturbing in terms of the typologies they produce:

> An anxious tenderness, which the Jew dissimulates and to which he seems to
> resign himself (resigned to dispersion), which remains inexpiable and almost
> frenzied for the Christian, groups them together around ancient culture and
> French culture as if around a relic every day more and more threatened. Here
> the internal difference between the two cultures shines forth. Every Jew origi-
> nates in a certain fatalism. Oriental. Every (actual, French) Christian originates
> in a certain revolt. Occidental. (1288–89)

The "Oriental fatalism" of the Jew may give him strength, but it is the
"Occidental revolt" of the Christian that will save the French (and the
remnants of the Greek) nation and culture. When it comes to the very
survival of the Occident, it is certainly not the best of things to originate

in the Orient or to be fatalistic in the face of serious threats to Western civilization.

Although it is only a very small step to develop the implications of this perspective and treat the "Oriental" origin of the Jew itself as a threat, or the *principal* threat, to the survival of the "Occident," Péguy did not take this step. Such "Oriental fatalism" was not for him the worst of things. The Jew has to accept the misery of his situation because that is all he has ever known, and he (and Péguy) considers misery and suffering to be good:

> The Jew considers it natural to be ill. Son . . . of a race which has been suffering for centuries and centuries and which will gain for having been ill longer than the others, he says, he knows that spiritual work is paid for with a kind of inexpiable fatigue. He finds that just. He finds that things are still very fine like that. (1290–91)

The Jew in fact has made suffering his identity, and his ability to survive while conquered and without a land of his own is his principal force: "The Jew has been conquered for the last seventeen to nineteen centuries: that is his eternal force. And therein also lies his eternal victory" (1292). "His victory" is not that of France or Western culture in general, however, but that of "Oriental fatalism" itself; that is, unending uprootedness and a spirituality cut off from even the possibility of any temporal inscription. It is the victory of survival and acceptance of one's fate, not the remaking and defense of a land, a people, and a culture.

According to Péguy, what was most important for the nation, for the maintenance of French culture, and for Western civilization as a whole, given the strength of what he called the patient "Jewish uneasiness" with the world, was to incorporate this uneasiness into an "Occidental" body and give it the force of revolt. This was what Jesus accomplished and what therefore constituted the essence of Christianity:

> Jesus was able to graft Jewish uneasiness onto the Christian body. That was necessary so that the all-consuming characteristics of this uneasiness, attenuated in an attenuated race, . . . could in a new race, and almost instantaneously, achieve a profundity that was finally incurable. And Jesus wasn't able (or didn't want to) graft Jewish patience onto the Christian body. (1293).

What Jesus supposedly did not want to do, Péguy did not want to do either. The French-Christian nationalist could not afford to be patient when the nation was at risk. He might even at some point have to become impatient about the Jew's patience itself in order not to become part of what Péguy calls an "attenuated race," that is, a "race" like the Jews.

As if this were not enough, there existed for Péguy what he called "an even more subtle difference of race, a split or fissure perhaps even more divisive" than that of Jewish patience as opposed to Christian revolt. It was one that touched the very nature of his vocation as a writer: the double issue of reading and writing and their relation to Judaism and Christianity, on the one hand, and to the identities of the ancient and modern worlds, on the other. "The Jew knows how to read," claims Péguy. "The Christian, the Catholic does not know how to read" (1296). Reading for the Jews was *the* sacred task: "It is reading the Book. It is the Book and the Law. To read is to read the word of God. . . . To read is the sacred operation as it is the ancient operation. All Jews are readers" (1296). Reading, then, Péguy believes, seems to be the fundamental and primary spiritual Jewish operation, what linked pre-Christian man to the ancient world and to the spiritual in general. Without reading, there seemingly would have been no spirituality at all.

Such was not the case, however, for Christianity remained the highest and most complete expression of the spiritual, the supreme model for spirituality. The Christian, unlike the Jew "who has always read," had only been reading, Péguy claimed, using the case of his own family as typical, since the people and true republican/Christian values had been lost in the world, only since modernity had begun to dominate and degrade mysticism and spirituality. Rather than being a handicap, the illiteracy of his Catholic heritage constituted for him a decided advantage over any spirituality rooted in reading: "Perhaps a more profound . . . penetration is reserved for those who do not know how to read" (1296). Freed from the mediation of the written word and the intellect, spirituality was for him situated more profoundly within a people when they had immediate access to it, when their spirituality was lived rather than being merely a function of what and how they read.

Reading was firmly on the side of wealth and political power. Illiteracy was the sign of the poor, whose family ties could not be traced in the property records of *notaires*, which went back for generations and generations to protect the legitimacy of economic and historical inheritance, but only in the meager baptismal records of the parishes, where the identity of the family was quickly lost because it was not necessary for, and even constituted an obstacle to, spirituality: "[The Catholic, Péguy] sees a great division of the world. On one side, the *notaire* (in all his forms), and on the other the miserable records of the parishes. . . . On one side, the entire historical record. On the other, the miserable records of the parishes. That is to say, the book of baptisms" (1298). Literacy, linked to personal inheritance and historical identity, was the modern evil Péguy had always fought against, especially the literacy that supported wealth and political and intellectual power, the literacy synonymous with personal ownership, money, inheritance, and historical records. Péguy's goal was always a higher, more immediate, collective (anonymous) form of spirituality than was possible in a spirituality determined by reading and interpretation.

There is no ambiguity about which side Péguy was on and which side the Jew (along with the Protestant and the rich Catholic) was on:

> Being poor and French, Catholic and peasant, he has no family papers. His family papers are the parish records. . . . Nothing that left any trace in the papers of *notaires*. They never possessed anything. Poor and of the people, they left it to the Jews, the Protestants, and the bourgeois Catholics to have a written genealogy. (1298)

To be Catholic and French—to be truly French was to be Catholic, at least as the poor were Catholic—was to have no papers of one's own, no recorded genealogy, and even no identifiable family of one's own, after a generation or two, other than the common family of the "race." True spirituality depended on one remaining as close to this anonymous collectivity as possible.

After his grandparents, Péguy wrote, "[the Catholic] sees nothing but an immense mass and a vast race, and immediately after, immediately behind, he distinguishes nothing else. Why not say it, he plunges with pride into this anonymity. The anonymous is his patrimony. Anonymity is his immense patrimony. The more communal the land is, the more he wants to grow out of the land. . . . The more communal the race is, the more secret joy he has and, it must be said, the more pride he has to be a man of this race" (1299). The genealogy of the poor Catholic quickly merges into the anonymous, collective identity and immediacy of the people growing directly out of the land, of the communal race. The longer the family has been literate, the more difficult, the more impossible, this journey back to the collectivity constituted by the people will be. The more difficult it will be to achieve the dual goal Péguy assigned himself: to be "a citizen of the communal species, a Christian of the common species" (1299). Péguy is still defining "race" as the spirituality of a people, but the people, through their illiteracy, are more closely linked to the land they work and more clearly defined in terms of their specific religious beliefs than ever before.

But even if his ancestors did not write, Péguy did; and what he wrote about were the spiritual virtues of a particular form of illiteracy. The second in his family to write (after his mother), he wrote against writing and saw his pen at times as a "dangerous instrument," especially when his writing was not going well (1302). But even when it was going well, the purpose of his writing was to evoke, to return to, and to indicate the profundity of the silence and illiteracy of the common and the communal, of the "race" whose identity could not be captured in writing or recorded in official economic or historical documents. For him, a people was opposed to writing in the same way that the mystical was opposed to the political, the ancient to the modern, and culture to history; the same way "the book of creation," which the illiterate of previous times "read" without knowing how to read and the book in a sense they themselves were, was opposed to "the miserable journal" modern man had become (1303). To write is in this sense the antispiritual act par excellence; it is to "harden" everything, to bring it into the light, to take away its mystery. To write is to break "the silence of prayer, the silence of vows, the silence of rest and the silence even of work, . . . the silence of solitude, the silence of poverty" (1304). It is to break the silence characteristic of race and the silence of the spiritual in general.

Péguy, himself a prodigious writer, has the Catholic writer ask himself, "Why does everyone write? What is being published?" He answers such questions by insisting that there are no good reasons to write and an infinite number of reasons to stop: "The man stops talking. The man plunges into the silence of the race . . . and finds there the last prolongation that we can seize of the eternal silence of the first creation" (1305). After the fall from the original silence, writing can do no better than condemn reading and writing and praise the silence of the origin: "How close to the creation this silence and this shadow are. How noble they are. . . . Everything else is industry. Everything else is jumble. Everything else is alphabet" (1304). And yet Péguy continued to write until his death in World War I. He wrote unceasingly and obsessively against the destructive powers of writing, pausing from time to time to listen to the original silence in which he believed all true (Christian) spirituality was rooted. He acknowledged that in modernity, even the Catholic was condemned to write, but his struggle was not that of the Protestant who had been writing for much too long to understand why a struggle was necessary, and certainly not that of the Jew "who has always written" and whose spirituality was inscribed in and defined in terms of reading and writing. For the only option open to the true spiritual (Catholic) writer is a militant writing against writing, a writing that negates and transcends the written and achieves the original silence of the spiritual.

If "the letter kills," as Péguy remembers he was taught, if "the letter is an instrument of murder, and perhaps the only instrument of murder" (1305), then only the Catholic can effectively fight against this deadly instrument or at least rediscover the means of postponing the spiritual death it produces. Only the (poor) Catholic can rediscover the "original silence of the race" and thus of the nation, because only he is close enough to it still to hear it and respond to it. Only he is close enough to the land and the true sense of the nation (of the race) to defend it as it should be defended. Péguy never suggested that either Protestants or Jews should be considered enemies of the spiritual nation or excluded from it. At the same time, he certainly did not present them as allies one could depend on to defend the nation when it needed to be defended: that is, to defend it against the exterior threats of other nations and interior threats to spiritual purity; against history itself, which uses writing to inscribe, objectify, and calculate; against modernity in general as the product of despiritualized history; and finally, against writing itself and its own despiritualizing effects.

Others, though, would have no trouble taking this step, associating the writing of Jews with the evils of modernity; no hesitancy equating the people of writing and of the Book with the enemies of the nation and making anti-Semitism the principal component of their attempts to eliminate all foreign elements from the national culture. From the perspective of the extremist history in which Péguy's texts played an important role, Péguy's most nationalistic texts clearly presented arguments supportive of ideological tendencies whose specific political manifestations he explicitly opposed. It would be impossible, then, to deny that these texts supplied important elements for the foundation of the "fascist city," even though it constitutes a radical transformation and hardening of Péguy's original notion of the socialist "harmonious city." The fascist city owes much to the fundamental unifying, antidemocratic, willed spirituality of Péguy's socialist city, to its foundations in the aesthetic-spiritual cult or culture of the people. It also is indebted to the notion of a spiritual race whose collective identity comes from its intimate and immediate links with the land.

I am not claiming that fascism or National Socialism was the inevitable or unique product of Péguy's spiritualistic, aestheticist nationalism. But I have certainly emphasized how in its broad outlines, and in certain (although not all) of its details, it is not antithetical to fascism. Neither Péguy's concept of writing nor his defense of the spiritual values of a people (race) and its culture can be used to free him totally from his own troubling legacy. His arguments on behalf of the aesthetics and politics of the harmonious city, of spiritualism or mysticism as the transcendence of politics, and of the original spirituality and thus "illiteracy" of the French race were all easily assimilated into both extremist nationalisms and literary fascism. Literary fascists, especially, saw both his early socialist aesthetics of politics and his later nationalism, which was formulated in large part as an attack on parliamentary democracy and the values of modernity, to be attempts to surpass the divisive politics and literary practices of modernity in the name of a new, total spirituality. Literary fascists found in this militant Catholic writer, who wrote incessantly against writing and modernity, an important model for their own aspirations for literature and politics, an "antiliterary," "antipolitical" model for their absolute literary-political aspirations.

Three

The Nation as Artwork:
Charles Maurras and the Classical Origins
of French Literary Fascism

Our France is a work of art. It is a political work
of art born of the collaboration of an obliging
nature and the thought of our kings.
  Charles Maurras, "La Maison de France"
  (1901)

Plato asserts in *The Republic* that one cannot
tamper with the rules of music (that is, of poetry
and taste) without disturbing the fundamental
laws of government.
  Charles Maurras, "Le Centenaire de Victor
  Hugo" (Gazette de France, *February 20, 1902)*

Maurras, who has practically failed in his career
in France, succeeded in Italy and is the father of
fascism.
  Pierre Drieu la Rochelle, Genève ou Moscou
  (1928)

We could find nothing that represented better the
youth of nationalism than the Action Française,
a kind of "pre-fascism" already in the air, the
union of a strong social doctrine and national
intelligence, . . . and the clarification of the fascist
or National Socialist idea has been our grand
quest ever since.
  Robert Brasillach, Notre avant-guerre *(1941)*

Antiromantic Organicism

On February 7, 1941, when the extremist weekly *Je suis partout* began to
be published again under German supervision after an interruption of
eight months due to the war and defeat, the subtitle of the newspaper was

changed from "Grand hebdomadaire de la vie mondiale" to "Grand hebdomadaire politique et littéraire." To change the focus of the weekly from "world life" to "politics and literature" was not, as it might first seem, to indicate that the newspaper had become narrower in scope—no longer directly concerned with the world as a whole—and certainly not that it intended to be in any way less political. On the contrary, the new subtitle was a sign of a renewed, even more militant commitment to extremist nationalist politics, fascism, and anti-Semitism, and even of a desire to collaborate directly with the Nazi occupiers to construct a new European Order in which, the principal voices at the journal hoped, a fascist France would play an important role. Giving literature equal billing with politics in the subtitle was a way of emphasizing the fact that the fascism espoused by the newspaper was rooted in the intimate relation between the political and the literary-aesthetic, that fascism was as much a "spiritual," literary-cultural phenomenon as a strictly historical-political one.

The pairing of politics and literature in its title, similar to the titles of numerous other extremist newspapers and weeklies of the period, indicated above all that *Je suis partout* saw itself as continuing a long tradition of the extreme nationalist right, one in which literature was recognized as being the principal model for and support of politics, the sign that politics was being taken seriously and considered a fundamental, essential problem. Politics was thus treated not just in terms of the programs, policies, and actions of political groups and parties to achieve specific goals, or the conflicts in the world theater among different nations and ideologies, but also as the area in which fundamental questions concerning the ideal form and fundamental nature of the national community and the people were raised. Nothing less than the truth of the political was at stake in the linkage between politics and literature. Thus, at the very moment that *Je suis partout* was increasing its distance from the Action Française by the specific politics it championed and by collaborating with the Germans and continuing to publish in Paris, it was at the same time indirectly acknowledging the great debt it owed to the extremist nationalist literary tradition in France and especially to Charles Maurras and his thinking, particularly to the way Maurras had articulated the fundamental relation between the literary and the political, which a number of his disciples would exploit in the name of fascism.[1]

Maurras, however, was not at all happy with the reappearance of *Je suis partout*, for after supporting and constantly defending the weekly throughout the 1930s as it became increasingly and more militantly fascist—while, it is true, remaining (at least officially) anti-German—he denounced the decision to begin publishing again in occupied Paris. This marked the definitive break between the father of "Integral Nationalism"

and younger followers such as Robert Brasillach and Lucien Rebatet, between a radical form of royalist nationalism and a French form of nationalist socialism or fascism. As Maurras put it when he was asked to approve of the project to continue publishing the newspaper in Paris: "How
can a national journal think about reappearing in Paris and asking for an
authorization from the Germans, under German censorship? It's completely impossible."² Maurras chose to move *L'Action Française* to Lyon
and to energetically support Pétain and Vichy from within "Free France."
Thus he accepted censorship, but only because it was at least nominally
"French." He participated in collaboration, but in a way that was supposedly not dictated by the Germans but developed by Pétain in the name
of the "National Revolution" and to defend "La Seule France" [Only
France].³

What interests me especially in the relation between Maurras and the
French literary fascism, which is best represented by a newspaper like *Je
suis partout*, are the aspects of Maurras's work that provide a foundation
for the very literary fascism he ended up condemning when it took a too
explicitly pro-German, pro-Nazi collaborationist form. The problem of
how the nation can be conceived as a work of art and where the limits, if
any, are to be placed on the aestheticizing of politics turn out to be key
issues in determining both the relation and differences between Maurras
and his fascist heirs.⁴ For whatever innovations French literary fascists
proposed for France, no matter how "revolutionary" and "socialist"
their fascism was claimed to be, most also claimed that fascism was at the
same time the most profound expression of the spiritual essence of
France, not just modern France but also "eternal France." Maurras provided many of the arguments and strategies to back up such claims, even
if the political consequences of the claims in a fascist context were quite
different from and often at times opposed to Maurras's own. Maurras
made a traditional but at the same time radical concept of the nation the
regulating principle of both literature and politics, using terms and arguments that were easily adapted to fascism, in spite of the monarchist,
traditionalist ends they were made to serve in his work. But even the
question of the monarch for Maurras was more complex than it might at
first seem, and Maurras himself clearly indicated the openings in his own
very particular form of royalism through which literary fascists would
move and provided many of the aesthetic and political principles on
which literary fascism in France would be founded.

The chief political and spiritual problem for France, as Maurras and
many others on both the left and the right at the end of the century repeatedly claimed, was that France had been living through a long period of
decadence and had become dangerously weak, or, as Maurras put it, effeminate: "Everything, from the spirit to love, has become effeminate.

Everything has grown weak" ("Le Chemin de Paradis" [1894], in *Pages littéraires choisies* [Paris: Honoré Champion, 1922], 8). Maurras's general project could be defined as an attempt to revitalize the French spirit, make it once again sharp, strong, and energetic—and, in his terms, masculine. This was at the same time both a political and a poetic project, for he saw the weakening of literature as always accompanying a weakening of the political, not because literature is determined by politics in any simple, causal sense, but because both are, or should be, expressions of the national spirit and thus share the same origin and nature. To recover the true (masculine) poetic language of France and to restore the hereditary monarchy—the institution of the original and "true father"—were thus for Maurras one and the same project.[5]

Maurras felt that France had undergone a long and profound identity crisis since the Revolution, experiencing only limited moments of what he called rationality, lucidity, and sanity in which the disintegration of the nation was countered and the only "real" resolution to the long crisis repeatedly indicated. Even more than in the actual restoration of the king, these antirevolutionary values were most fully realized in the work of those rare thinkers and writers who kept alive traditional rationality and classical poetic values. Given that the spiritual crisis was profound, it could not be confined to one area alone but had to be by definition evident in all manifestations of spirituality, especially in what Maurras considered its most important and determining manifestations: literature, politics, and religion. The decadence and impotence of one of these areas were for him always indications of the decadence and impotence of the others, and without masculine "force and energy" both politics and poetry had become nothing more than empty, sterile forms. The general law that links literature to politics—Maurras's reference to Plato in one of the epigraphs to this chapter indicates that for him it was a universal law—has special significance in the modern period, however, for it linked romanticism to the Revolution and thus dictated that "Integral Nationalism" had to be both antirevolutionary and a militant antirepublicanism, and a vehement and polemical antiromanticism as well.

In the "Préface de l'Edition Définitive" to *Romantisme et Révolution* (Versailles: Bibliothèque des Oeuvres Politiques, 1928), Maurras assigns to revolutionary politics and romantic poetics the same identity: "Both the friends and adversaries of Romanticism are in agreement as to its profound identity with the Revolution. . . . Romanticism and the Revolution resemble stems which are distinct in appearance but which come out of the same root" (2). The sources of the Revolution and romanticism were of course all "foreign" and included Rousseau, Luther, German thought in general, and all manifestations of the "Jewish spirit," all of which he, like Barrès, considered "barbarian":

The fathers of the Revolution are in Geneva, in Wittenberg, and formerly in Jerusalem. They all derive from the Jewish spirit and from varieties of independent Christianity which rage in Oriental deserts or in Germanic forests, that is to say, at the different crossroads of barbarism. (4)

Barbarism was thus defined as Jewish, Protestant, and German—in short, "Oriental"; in its essence, everything that was opposed to and destructive of "Western civilization," that is, the classical world and its only legitimate modern heir: Catholic, royalist France.

Even though he is only one name among others on this list, Jean-Jacques Rousseau, to whom Maurras most often referred as "le misérable Rousseau" (5), in fact has a special place. As both a writer of literature and a political theorist, as a Swiss who wrote in French but was influenced by and represented the interests of "Germanic barbarism," as well as someone "nourished on Hebraic revolt" (6), his work and his person embodied all of the diversified evils being denounced. Rousseau's work was the point at which the diversified foreign threats to traditional France intersected, the point from which the dual evils of romanticism and the Revolution grew. Maurras claims that Rousseau "came from one of the parts of the world where, for two centuries, different mixtures of decomposition had been swirling" (5), and thus he was not just a product of decomposition but its culmination, the fusion of all its destructive forces. Rousseau preached and embodied all of the essential traits of what was threatening France and, by extension, threatening the civilized world in general, since Maurras, like Barrès and Péguy, saw France as the unique authentic inheritor of the classical world. "Le misérable Rousseau" was thus the ultimate figure of anti-France.

Having identified Rousseau as the key figure in the dual, literary-political decomposition of modern France, Maurras spares him no insult: "One finds in him almost equal doses of criminal man or savage man and simple madman. . . . This savage, this half-man, this sort of wild animal drenched in its native mire pleased by means of the paradoxical and impossible nature of his primitive apparatus. . . . Savage nations, savage natures therefore followed Rousseau, adopting him as a fellow countryman" (6–7). Rousseau thus occupies the place described as the intersection of what could be called three different manifestations of the spiritual: "the triple literary, religious, and political coincidence" of a number of important "facts" all having to do with the interruption of tradition and the destruction of the authority and hierarchy of its institutions and truths.

In Rousseau, certain habits of the spirit, certain policies of taste, certain customs and traditions of the State are interrupted: his *Héloïse*, his *Confessions*, and the attitude and conduct of his life bring us back (it is a real return) to the

reign of "nature," whose affectation Romantic sensibility will take up; his
"Profession of Faith" reduces religious life to an interior god of Protestant logic
without cult or priest; his politics will subjugate France to the doctrine which
destroys the monarchy and dreams of the republic. (7)

Because the "coincidence is triple"—that is, touching all important aspects of the spiritual—the remedy, if it is to do more than mask the symptoms, must have a triple effect as well.

In terms of each of these converging elements, Maurras defended the restoration of the tradition that had been interrupted. He advocated a return to a classical aesthetics and order of taste in order to restore beauty; a return to the Catholic Church and its institutions and ceremonies in order to restore truth; and a return to the monarchy in order to restore political continuity, harmony, and national unity and grandeur. Maurras's literary and political activism, therefore, was one that combated modernity itself and attempted to restore to literature and politics the forms and truths supposedly established and guaranteed by tradition.

Since literature itself, for Maurras, had become romantic and "effeminate," without force, energy, or truth, it was not a simple matter of turning to literature for a countermodel for the political. In fact, in the modern period, when literature could be considered to have played a determining role in politics, the results for Maurras had been disastrous: "When royal authority disappeared, it did not give way, as has been said, to the sovereignty of the people: the successor to the Bourbons is the man of letters" ("L'Avenir de l'Intelligence," in *Romantisme et Révolution*, 46). Thus, for Maurras, the revolutionary period was "the highest point of literary dictatorship. . . . No government was ever more literary" (47). Obviously not just any aestheticizing of politics or fusion of the literary and the political would do. The dictatorship of a certain modern form of literature rooted in individualism and what Maurras called negative freedoms constituted the very sign of political and literary decadence, of the loss of beauty, truth, and creative energy.

Maurras's most interesting examples of the dangers of such a dictatorship had to do with Napoleon, who, he claimed, "represents the crowned man of letters" (48). Napoleon, the poet-politician, was able at times to create the semblance of order by "drawing from his unreliable daydreams the strong appearance of consistent realities." But this was precisely the problem: a false, fictional order was being presented and taken for a real one, just as a false, fictional "legal France" was still obscuring and being taken for "the real France."

Assuredly, all our misfortunes ensue from these deceptive appearances: they have never stopped thwarting the profound necessities of the real order. However, our phases of fleeting tranquility had no other cause than the very real agreement of the administrative fictions with the literary fictions that agitated everyone's mind and led all astray. From this meeting of these two fictions and of these two literatures, one official the other private, was born the precarious but real feeling of a harmony or relative affinity. (48)

Maurras felt that Napoleon's fusion of literary and political fictions did create harmony and order, then, but he also claimed that unlike the "real" order and harmony exemplified by the monarchy, these encouraged only a *feeling* of harmony without producing *real harmony*. What could be called "the dictatorship of literature" was thus especially dangerous because it induced tranquility, when in fact through its dual fictions it was actually covering over the disorder raging beneath and between the literary and the political. For Maurras, then, a romantic aestheticizing of politics represented the most dangerous opponent to a legitimate, classical aesthetics, the negative form of both aesthetics and politics.

But Napoleon was not just the heir of Rousseau and the Revolution, the creator and administrator of misleading political fictions. He was also the great general, the military genius who inspired and unified an entire people, the true nationalist poet and assembler of the French people:

Nothing is more opposed to this bad political and diplomatic literature than Napoleon commander of the army: nothing is more positive; nothing is more national. Like the generals of 1792, he revives, he stimulates the warrior core of the nation; he brings in all the elements making up the French, assembles them, and hurls their mass against the foreigner. In this way he puts them to the test, unites them, fuses them together. New resources of patriotic sentiment are revealed, are concentrated together, and served by the superior authority of the master; they oppose the ideology of letters with an unexpected system of violent forces. (48–49)

Napoleon thus embodied at the same time the most positive and the most negative elements of the early nineteenth century: its literary-political decadence and its military successes, its internationalist fictions and its nationalist "realities," its weak, sterile ideology of letters and its creative, activist military exploits. Under Napoleon, the violence of the authentic, unified forces of the nation was directed not only against the foreigner outside but against the foreigner inside, against the very "ideology of letters" he had instituted. Napoleon was presented as both the product of the Revolution and romanticism and a violent antidote to them.

Maurras saw "literature" in the nineteenth century as the principal impediment to the implementation of a system of forces, violent as they might be, that would effectively destroy the false fictions of the nation and guarantee the unity and superiority of the true, integral nation: "*Every-*

*thing useful and necessary undertaken by the Force of things, was mis-
directed or methodically contested by literary Intelligence"* (50–51). If,
for Maurras, Napoleon was both the great nationalist military poet and
the failed literary-political poet, nineteenth-century France was a country
in which the creative, nationalist forces were always being countered by
weak literary-political fictions.

The principal literary-political conclusion to be drawn from such an
analysis is that France, in order to realize itself fully, had to activate in the
aesthetic-political realms the same violent forces that Napoleon successfully inspired *and mastered* in the military realm. Maurras obviously saw
his own role as a poet, critic, and political theorist to be the advocate of
such a program. What could be called the royalist, classical-aestheticist
dictatorship of the nation had to replace the dictatorship of romantic/
revolutionary literature in order to restore creative force to literature and
politics and in order to make them truly national. Only then could the
fusion of the literary, the political, and the religious be ensured in a way
that no single field—and certainly not the literary field as such—could
dominate the others and so that nationalism would be "integral"; that is,
actively, militantly *spiritual*. Politics would then become the genuine expression of the *work* of the nation and would also in turn (re)produce the
nation as an *artwork*.

The weak fictions of the Revolution and romanticism were, for Maurras, predominately the fictions associated with the concept of the individual, and he considered none to be more dangerous in its capacity to
misdirect and contest the true forces of the nation than the "fiction" of
individual freedom. "The same body of false ideas which are as inhospi-
table to the human spirit as they are pernicious and deadly to the human
species" (11), ideas which are linked to the fiction of individual freedom,
could be discovered, he claimed, in both literature and politics. The fact
that romantic politics and literature were both rooted in the "fiction of
individual freedom" meant that the two realms could never be separated,
so that to attack the literary movement was at the same time always to
attack the political ideology:

> The two vocabularies of criticism and politics were fused together and com-
> pleted each other: the divine freedom of the Word, the sovereign freedom of the
> Citizen, the equality of verbal themes or of social elements, a vague fraternity
> creating the "right" of everyone and their "right" to everything. These formu-
> las flowing one into the other, exchanged their metaphors with each other. . . .
> The great political error was finally recognized as illustrating the aesthetic
> error, which, having become glaring, served to allow the former to be seen
> more clearly. (11–12)

Because romanticism and the Revolution grew out of the same foreign
roots and were inextricably intertwined through not just the concepts but

THE NATION AS ARTWORK   79

also the metaphors they shared and exchanged with each other, because they were rooted in a common error, the failure of individual freedom in art and literature could be used to attack the principle of individual freedom in the political realm and show, from a perspective that was outside of politics per se, its political shortcomings.

The inflated place that romanticism gave to the individual self was thus the sign that tradition and the "true" community of readers were being devalued. It was also, as Maurras's essay "Le Romantisme féminin" clearly indicates, a sign of the weakness of the movement, an indication of its fundamental "femininity."

> The idea, the precise feeling, the abstract image of the *self* do not offer themselves to virile intelligence with as much frequency and precision as in a feminine mind. To say *I* is practically a part of the character of women. The *self* gushes forth in their discourse at the slightest pretext, not in an auxiliary capacity, not for the convenience of language, but with a rush of blatant, personal impressions that signify quite exactly: *I who am speaking, I and no one else* (191).

The "feminine," romantic "I" brings everything back to itself, makes itself the norm in terms of which all other norms, subjects, forms, orders, and traditions are presented, judged, and understood. The relation of this "I" to any collectivity, even one consisting of other such "I's," can only be conflictual, given that each "I" will be restricted by the demands and interests of all the others. Such an "I" is thus always considered to be a carrier of disorder.

For these reasons, the weak, destructive, romantic self represented a serious threat to "virile," classical French poetics, but it also could be considered in its "femininity" ultimately to be not really "French" at all, regardless of the importance of French romanticism as a literary movement. Only the masculine ideal of the nation was truly French. The dominance of the (feminine) self in romanticism was a foreign aberration, a serious challenge to paternal authority and hierarchy, a disintegrating force undermining the unity of the authentic national community.[6] Maurras constantly attacked Rousseau and Mme de Staël for having attempted to destroy the French language and its literary traditions by introducing foreign elements into both. He approved wholeheartedly of a critic who called them "undisciplined aliens [*métèques*—a word he used to describe all of those he determined to be non-French, especially Jews]," and he said of romanticism in general that "as a foreigner, it loves the foreign" (182–83).

The "foreign" origins of the leading precursors or exponents of romantic ideology and poetics were ultimately less important, however, than what he considered the internal foreign elements in the work of French romantics from Chateaubriand through Hugo and even to Mallarmé, whom he characterized as the last and most extreme inheritor of romantic poetics.[7] He argues in Mallarmé's case that romanticism results not in the "gushing forth" of sentimental, lyrical expressions of the "feminine self," but in what seems to be at the other extreme of poetic form and content, the mechanical manipulation of language governed by no rules whatsoever. The most serious dangers of the freedoms taken by the romantic self are not just solipsism and emotionalism, then, but also a formal, mechanistic poetics and politics that destroy all meaning and value.

In fact, to Maurras, the most *foreign* aspect of romanticism, especially as it is exemplified at its extreme by Mallarmé, is the way in which words are considered entities in themselves. "The foreign" in poetry in this instance is recognized by the fact that individual words are treated primarily as *vocables*, which gives them an "absolute sovereignty, unlimited authority" and in terms of which "meaning itself loses its rights of direction and composition" ("Le Romantisme féminin," in *Romantisme et Révolution*, 150). What is not "French," then, is the devaluation of meaning and syntax, the domination of sound over sense. What is French, on the contrary, is to "order ideas so that they themselves arrange the syllables of words in the reason and order of song" (*De la politique naturelle au nationalisme intégral* [Paris: Librairie Philosophique J. Vrin, 1976], 53). Threatened in the priority given to the *vocable* is the French language itself as a *system* of form *and* meaning:

> From being an element subordinated to syntax, the word has become with Romanticism the principal element. With Mallarmé, words are arranged on the paper according to their mutual attraction and reciprocal exclusions: purely mechanical affinities, calls, contrasts that demand absolutely no operation of the mind [*esprit*] of the poet, neither his choice nor his judgment. . . . The aesthetic theories of Mallarmé would have been unreservedly fitting for a kind of animal lacking the superior faculties of the intelligence. (*Romantisme et Révolution*, 186)

For Maurras, the primary spiritual function of the intelligence is to create order and form. Mallarmé's poetry and poetics fail to measure up to this requirement, and Maurras thus considers what we would now call "the play of the signifier" in Mallarmé's poetry to be not only un-French and feminine but even barbaric and inhuman.

If Mallarmé's poems can be considered to be "arranged" and thus to have a certain exterior, mechanical form, they nonetheless lack the fundamental unity and beauty (and thus form) of true poetry, because they ignore and even challenge the unity of syntax, what Maurras considered the dynamic unifying principle of the French language as such. He who thus challenges and subverts the traditional concept of the French language must be treated not just as an inferior poet but also as an enemy of civilization and the nation—a *sous-homme*, "a kind of animal lacking the superior faculties of the intelligence." Maurras viewed all enemies of the French nation as inferior men—as animals, women, barbarians, or Jews—all those who threatened the masculine identity of French culture and politics. This means, among other things, that Maurras felt no limits should be imposed on the "holy war" that had to be waged against them, a war for the very existence of "civilized man," that is, *French man*.

No matter how limited and dogmatic Maurras's reading of Mallarmé might seem to us today, it clearly reveals the political stakes for Maurras of literature and art and why he so violently attacked any writer associated with romanticism. The political risks represented by Mallarmé were just as great as those presented by increased immigration into France or the growth of German nationalism, because in romantic poetry "language is dishonored, rhythm tortured." Romanticism, along with its political ally, revolution, therefore could be claimed to be leading the spirit, leading rational man, to its/his death:

> The decadence of all the humanities shows that the future, the future of French intelligence and of Occidental spirit as a whole, is still foundering. It should not be dissimulated that one runs the risk of seeing man himself die out in this way, political and rational man, man the artist and man the singer. Anyone who prolongs the double romantic and revolutionary deviation provides the Spirit with the sweeping freedom to die. (24 bis).

In the name of giving renewed life to art and literature, and in this way to the Spirit in general, Maurras proposed a return to or a restoration of the traditional, classical unity of the literary work and the nation. He constantly returned to the concept of "the integral work" as the principal question for the spiritual life of the nation, and thus for both its aesthetics and its politics. Spiritual life, for him, was guaranteed by the unity of the work; nothing less than the death of the spirit resulted from the disintegration or the absence of the work. Such dogmatic support for classical aesthetics made Maurras undeniably the most conservative of the various "fathers" of French literary fascism, at least as concerns his tastes in literature.

Even though he was a militant royalist, Maurras claimed that he was not opposed to the notion of freedom in general, but only to "anarchistic," romantic/revolutionary freedom, which he argued always destroyed the work and the "true freedom" that constituted the work and that was equivalent to art itself:

> Felicitous freedom . . . is the art of life, it is art itself. The freedoms to be discouraged are those that are enemies of the work, either because they keep it

from being accomplished or because they tear it apart as soon as it is formed. If the work in question were allowed to speak and give its opinion, . . . it would undoubtedly say, conforming to the reactions of its vital instinct: "*I love everything that makes me live, and I hate everything that would kill me.*" The interests of the work are the only ones to consult. . . . A positive freedom is given [to the poet], a negative freedom is denied according to the same principles. Freedom to create. Prohibition to tear apart. These are the last works of thought and tradition in the matter of Poetics. Freedom has value by its usage and by its fruits. It is indebted only to good; evil is without rights. Why? Because one makes and the other undoes the Poem. (17)

In Maurras's poetics, then, the work, the poem, is everything. It is the ultimate, determining, unique criterion in terms of which to judge whether freedom is positive or negative, creative or destructive, aesthetic or nonaesthetic. In such an argument, the poem ceases to be an object and becomes a subject. Speaking on its own as a living being, it demands that its own integrity and vitality be protected, that all freedom have as a unique goal the construction of a poetic work. Once it has been established—through a classical poetics—what makes the work/poem integral and vital, then everything else follows logically and dogmatically from this absolute aesthetic (and political) principle.

In speaking of the work in this way, Maurras uses terminology and critical criteria that seem at first glance to be rooted in romantic organicist aesthetic theory—which is largely German and English in origin—in order to denounce French romanticism for not being truly French (for being German) and for its destruction of the vital character of the work. His "organicism," however, is explicitly more classical than romantic, for the "freedom" and vital unity of the work is for him always controlled and determined by rules and tradition, and it is in this sense preromantic or antiromantic. Given that he treats the work as a living unity and the integrity of "the Poem" as a fusion or incorporation of different and even conflicting elements and forces, his antiromanticism and antirepublicanism nevertheless retain a decidedly postromantic tone. The self-declared and ferocious enemy of romanticism thus reveals himself as a romantic of sorts after all, for the notion of the organic nature of the work is one point where neoclassical, romantic, and postromantic aesthetic theories—and perhaps revolutionary and antirevolutionary political theories—overlap and "exchange metaphors" and concepts in important ways.[8]

In fact, Maurras's militant classical poetics constitutes a struggle to take organicism back from the romantics (and the Germans and English) by emphasizing its classical and *French* neoclassical prehistory over its romantic manifestations, a struggle that was at the same time meant to take the state back from republican institutions and return to an earlier version of the "organic nation," united not in terms of the supposedly "fictive" will of the people but in terms of the one "real" institution that Maurras claimed authentically founded and guaranteed unity: the monarchy. Maurras's Integral Nationalism is an uncompromising, dogmatic application of a classical organicist model to poetics and politics, with the nation in the political realm corresponding to the Poem in the poetic realm—the nation as the original community and fundamental political artwork, the artwork of all artworks.[9]

In Maurras's view, the nation is a work (artwork) whose unifying principles were determined in history and thus supported by tradition in the same way that classical aesthetic criteria determine the laws governing the unity and life of the poem. For before there was the French nation, before there was French poetry, Greece already existed and supplied the models and rules for determining what an aesthetic-political work really was or what it should be. France could only be itself by imitating not Greece per se but the aesthetics of Greece, by safeguarding within itself the essence of Greece and Rome, what Maurras saw as the true origin of France, the essence of its identity. France is what it is, France can become what it should be, only because it is first and foremost *the only legitimate heir* to the ancient world.

Because of this lineage, the French embodied for Maurras in their history and in themselves nothing less than the *genre humain*.

> The development of our nationality in the 16th, 17th, and even 18th century [was] so complete, so brilliant, of a humanity so perfect that France became the legitimate heir of the Greek and Roman world. Through France measure, reason, and taste reigned over our Occident: in spite of barbaric civilizations, the true Civilization survived right up to the threshold of the contemporary period. In spite of the Revolution, . . . in spite of Romanticism, . . . one can still argue that civilization displays in this country of France some quite beautiful traces. Our tradition is only interrupted, our capital subsists. It depends on us to make it flourish and bear fruit again. . . . A few of our rivals suspect this. . . . Germans are barbarians, and yet the best of them know this. I won't even speak of the Moscovites or the Tartars. France is the human species, not just for us but for the human species. (*Mes idées politiques* [Paris: Editions Albatros, 1986], 146—originally published in 1937)

In addition to the typically inflated and xenophobic chauvinism of this passage, the other and perhaps more significant point Maurras makes has to do with the form of the aesthetic-political struggle he envisages to bring the French nation back to its glory, to make France more than "the museum" of the beautiful traces of past civilization. If France is to be the living embodiment of "the true civilization," once again bearing the fruit of the aesthetic capital Western civilization has bequeathed to it, it must both model itself after the ancients and make use of the aesthetic tradition originating in Greece, and at the same time it must combat vigorously all other claims—primarily German—to such an inheritance.

Maurras always claimed that his notion of tradition was anything but passive, not a stodgy retention of the past but an activist intervention of the most powerful forces of the past in the present: "Tradition means transmission. Tradition gathers together the forces of blood and soil. . . . True tradition is *critical*, and without these distinctions, the past no longer serves as anything, its successes ceasing to be examples, its setbacks, to be lessons. . . . Tradition is not lethargy but its contrary" (*Mes idées politiques*, 134). The "forces of blood and soil" may be the ultimate ground of Maurras's nationalism, but these forces have little positive effects, and in fact could have serious destructive effects if they are not gathered together, fused, and arranged and made to work together in harmony for the same end. Tradition is thus the means of bringing together and transmitting "natural forces," of providing the *form* these and other forces take that allows them to intervene critically in the present and restore to it what is most successful and "beautiful" in the past. The formative process that Maurras associates with tradition, then, is the aesthetic operation par excellence. It is not just the ground for politics for the Integral Nationalist, providing its model and material, but it also provides the means or operations for achieving political unity and the proper functioning of the nation as an organic artwork.

Maurras defended his own classical aesthetics of politics not just in aesthetic terms but in terms of its "realism" and its alleged roots in nature as well. If organic unity characterizes the form of the nation, the origin of the nation and its model is the *patrie* conceived as the primal family, the original and natural community or society. "The fatherland is a *natural society*, or what amounts to exactly the same thing, a historical one. Its decisive characteristic is birth. One does not choose one's fatherland—*the land of one's fathers*—anymore than one chooses one's father and mother" (*Mes idées politiques*, 278). In the same vein, Maurras argued that "the national community, the Fatherland, and the State are in no way associations born of the personal choice of their members, but works of nature and necessity" ("Dictateur et Roi," in *Enquête sur la Monarchie*, 455). As natural as the origin of the nation is claimed to be, however, the nation does not remain in its original or natural form but is shaped, given a direction and meaning, and transmitted over time. Tradition is natural inheritance given form. In this way, tradition raises nature to a higher level without ever losing its "naturalness." In fact, the highest form of nature becomes the aesthetic form, that form molded by culture and civilization, not brute, "spontaneous," disordered nature in itself, which is the nature of "ignorant men and backward countries"; that is, of Rousseau and the Germans.

The origins of Maurras's nationalism were thus profoundly aesthetic, for his approach to politics and the nation was dominated by the ideal of beauty, rather than by any strictly political, geographic, or racial determination. When he was criticized for having made beauty "Greek" and thus for "subjugating the science of the beautiful to the law of place and race," Maurras replied: "I do not praise the Greeks but the work of the Greeks, and I praise it not for being Greek but for being beautiful. It is not because it is Greek that we go toward beauty, but because it is beautiful that we hasten toward Greece" ("Esthétique et voyage," in *Pages littéraires choisies*, 191). The same argument would then have to hold for his defense of France: neither race nor place (neither blood nor soil) is the essence of the French nation, but as a work (of art) it is rather its beauty and vitality that should make one "hasten to it," defend it, judge it to be superior to all other nations, and see it as the true, modern embodiment of the classical "beautiful nation."

In the same way, Maurras claimed that his defense of the monarchy had nothing to do with the innate superiority of any individual king: "We have said that the hereditary sovereign is in the best position to govern well. We have never said that this good government was a virtue of his blood" ("Discours préliminaire," in *Enquête sur la Monarchie*, LXXXVI). What mattered was the king's place and function within the nation and not his individual worth or even his royal blood. The guarantees of order, unity, and grandeur that *the place* of the monarch had traditionally provided were for Maurras essential to the nation if it were to become an organic work. The dominance of what Maurras called the "functional" aspects of his royalism revealed that on the most basic level he was always ultimately more interested in making the nation work as a smoothly functioning organic entity, a political artwork, than in the actual restoration of the king.

Making beauty rather than geographical location the defining characteristics of the "integral nation" allowed Maurras to reject another seemingly important part of the legacy of Greece—democracy—for not conforming to the dictates of order and beauty, and for destroying rather than accumulating and safeguarding the values and works of the past.

> The brief destiny of what is called democracy in antiquity makes me realize that the essence of this regime is only to consume what aristocratic periods have produced. Production, action demanded a powerful order. Consumption is less demanding: neither tumult nor routine hinders it very much. Of the goods that generations have slowly produced and accumulated, every democracy makes a

huge bonfire. . . . To be a nationalist and to want democracy is to want to
waste and at the same time economize the force of France, which is, I believe,
impossible. (*Pages littéraires choisies*, 193)

Missing from democracy is order, and without order there is no genuine
beauty. As a destructive, disordering, all-consuming force, democracy is
at the same time and primarily an antiaesthetic force, one that lays waste
to the artwork that the nation is or should be and to its "cultural capital."
What Maurras claims he learned from antiquity as much as from modernity is that democracy and the political-aesthetic work do not mix, that
the former is the death of the latter. If beauty draws one to Greece and its
aesthetic and political works, it is also beauty that reveals that democracy
is opposed to the nation-work and in its essence, even in antiquity, is
unaesthetic or antiaesthetic.

The primary and determining principles of Greek aesthetics, for Maurras, are what Nietzsche called "Apollonian" and have to do primarily
with the "quality and perfection" of the work, the necessity for the work
to be constituted by unified, harmonious relations developed from within
the work and not copied slavishly from models: "It was felt [in Greece]
that it was not enough to copy forms, neither to make them bigger nor to
reduce them, and that true [aesthetic] pleasure arose from a harmonious
and appropriate relation" ("La Naissance de la Raison," in *Pages
littéraires choisies*, 247). This is, of course, also the principle that is linked
to the birth of reason in Athens: "Learned men stopped thinking that
knowledge consisted in a mass of known facts; they looked for the order
that determined them and gave them their full value" (247). True knowledge and beauty are thus always limited, arranged, determined by order.
In this sense, true knowledge, like politics, especially a politics modeled
after art, could also be said to have beauty as its principal value. "Politics
is a science," argued Maurras, "because it is a craft or rather an art"
(*Enquête sur la Monarchie*, CXXIII). And if modernity, in the form of
democracy, had forgotten what reason and beauty were, and was dupe to
the attraction of what he called the grandiose and the numerous, it was up
to the art of politics to negate this divisiveness and fragmentation and
transform them once again into the ordered work of the integral nation.

If Maurras emphasized the formal aspects of classical aesthetics, he
also gave force an important, though secondary role in both the aesthetic
and political realms:

Force in itself, . . . force which is not yet in the service of either good or evil,
bare force is by itself a very precious, very great good because it is the expression of the activity of being. One would have to be an imbecile to want to
ignore its benefits. . . . This does not mean it always does good or that there is
no greater good. . . . As it is capable of everything, it needs as a primary safe-

guard a rule and, when serving the best cause, an order. Order contributes to making it entirely and completely efficacious. (*Mes idées politiques*, 110).

To use a Nietzschean vocabulary of which Maurras would not have completely approved but to which he was in fact very close and which his fascist heirs did use, Maurras is arguing here for the synthesis of force and form, of the Dionysian and the Apollonian, but primarily in the name of form. He is in this way defending an Apollonian aesthetics, reversing the principal argument of Nietzsche in *The Birth of Tragedy*, who, as part of what he would later call his "artist's metaphysics," had argued in similar terms for a tragic synthesis in the name of a Dionysian aesthetics of force.

One of the important differences between Maurras's fascist "sons" and their classical "father" was the increased importance the former gave to force in their aesthetics of politics. But it is a question more of degree or emphasis than principle, because they too stressed the necessity for a dialectic relation between force and the aesthetic or political form in which it is manifested. It is also important to note that Maurras himself acknowledged the "great good" that force was. Had he not done so, his aesthetics and politics would have seemed much less attractive to his fascist heirs, much less provocative and violently opposed to democracy and the status quo. He would have seemed much less revolutionary and subversive had his own aesthetics of politics been a pure, mechanical formalism, which for him always constituted a neutralization of force rather than its ordered and thus full realization.

Integral Nationalism, Anti-Semitism, and the Aesthetic Power of the Monarch

The political slogan most closely associated with Maurras, "Politique d'abord" (Politics first), means that the nation—as an organic work—has to come first. "The nation comes before all groups within the nation. The defense of the whole is imposed on the parts. In the order of realities, there are first of all nations. Nations before classes. Nations before business. . . . One joins a party, one is born of a nation" (*Mes idées politiques*, 282). The nation is the "natural unity" one is born into, the family of all families and the class of all classes. The national culture preexists all individuals and gives them their value and even their identity. "The individual who comes into the world in a 'civilization' *finds incomparably more than he brings*" (138). Maurras thus defined "man" as originally and in his essence an inheritor, indebted to his culture for his very identity; and in a manner almost identical to Barrès's definition of the Self, Maurras too rooted the individual in the land and its dead. Maurras's version of the Barrésian "Je suis eux-mêmes" was "We *are* our ancestors, our masters, our elders. We *are* our books, our paintings, our statues" (173). When "we" are not what the nation bequeaths to us, "we" are not what we were born to be. Maurras's militant culturalist nationalism, like Barrès's, was also a call for the "we" to take form, to take the form of a prior "we" of a classical type that serves as a model for all true "we's." It was a call to overcome the divisiveness of individualism, of class conflicts, of party warfare, and become a "person"; that is, in Maurras's terms, an integral function of the whole, supporting and serving the organic unity of the nation and carrying on its authentic cultural and political traditions.[10]

Maurras, like his fellow anti-Dreyfusard, Barrès, was a militant anti-Semite and considered the Jews to be on a par with the Germans as the most dangerous enemies of the French nation; more dangerous, perhaps, in the sense that they were both internal as well as external enemies. And yet also like Barrès, his royalist form of nationalism was not rooted in a strictly biologically determined racism, no matter how violent and crude his frequent denunciations of the Jews. Maurras argued quite insistently throughout his work that "nationality is not a phenomenon of race" (283). His nationalism, like that of most French nationalist extremists and literary fascists, was rooted rather in a cultural, or what I would call an aestheticist, anti-Semitism. For he believed that Jews threatened the integral nation not by their blood but by their own nonlinear history and alternative tradition, by the disruption to integral form their presence within the nation provoked in the nation-work. The Jew is the ultimate figure of the non-Greek or anti-Greek (and thus the non-French or anti-French); and without a "proper heritage," he was considered a disseminating, disruptive antiaesthetic force both without and within the geographic confines of the nation, and more important, a danger to its spiritual integrity, to the very essence of the nation as an organic, classically determined artwork.

Maurras's anti-Semitism was in large part inherited from traditional Catholic anti-Semitism, which became an important *political* force at the time of the Dreyfus affair. It was equally and more fundamentally an essential component of his aesthetics of the nation, for national organicism can exist only if the inorganic elements of the nation are eliminated from the nation-work and the organic elements are incorporated into it. Incorporation or expulsion, this is the only alternative given by the absolute principle of the nation-work. All of the "social programs" proposed by Maurras or associated with the Action Française, whose goal was to overcome class divisions and incorporate the working class into the smooth functioning of the nation, had as their direct correlative the disenfranchisement if not expulsion of the Jews (and other "foreign elements") from the organic community. Anti-Semitism was not, then, an incidental part of Maurras's aestheticizing of politics but rather a fundamental, de-termining element in the construction and operation of the machinery of nationalism. Quite simply, "the work has to be" (270), and for it to be, the political-aesthetic operations of incorporation and expulsion had to be given priority. The integral-nationalist aestheticizing of politics is thus, at least in theory, always uncompromising and totalizing, if not totalitar-ian; its ultimate project is always a total project, one carried out at the expense of the Jew and or as the foreigner.

Maurras claimed that all political, economic, and religious crises—ev-erything opposed to the values, truths, and aesthetics of the "Occident," as well as to the unification and harmonious, ordered operation of the nation—had an "Oriental," Jewish cause:

> All of the important modern crises have an Oriental character to them: Biblical in spirit or Jewish through their personnel in the 16th century, the German Reformation, the English Reformation, and the French Reformation; then, in the 18th and 19th centuries the three French revolutions between the Terror and the Commune; and finally in the 20th century, the convulsions of Moscow, Madrid, and Barcelona display this same trait: more or less vivid, but funda-mental, they express either a intellectual Hebrewism or Hebrew acts in flesh and blood. (66)

Throughout this long history, the nation alone had resisted the constant crises—reforms or revolutions—supposedly provoked by the Jews. The true integral nation before and outside the reach of the Revolution is or-ganized in terms of and represented by the king and supported by the institution of the Catholic Church. Nation, Church, and Monarch thus form an inseparable triad; the antination, anti-Church, and antiroyalist principle of the revolution, represented by the Jew, is nothing less than evil incarnate, "Satan" himself (66).

As vehemently as Maurras polemicized against the destructive work supposedly already carried out by Jews, he was supremely confident that the body politic, the nation-work, still had within itself, no matter how bad its current spiritual health, the aesthetic and political (that is, spiri-tual) resources to resist the foreign and function once again, as it had in the past, as an integral, organic work. The sign of this possibility and the ultimate political counterfigure to the figure of the Jew was for Maurras, of course, the monarch—not so much the actual king or pretender as the ideal or figure (fiction) of the king. In this sense, Maurras's royalism de-pended less on the real king, or even on the historical institution of the monarchy, than on the place, function, and image of the king at the center and as the support of the nation-work.[11]

Even though Maurras was never, strictly speaking, a fascist, he did for a time praise Italian fascism for accomplishing many of the political goals he felt France also had to achieve and could achieve only through the restoration of the monarchy. At times it even seemed as if he were describing a version of his own Integral Nationalism when he spoke of fascism:

> What in fact is *Fascism*? A socialism emancipated from democracy. A trade unionism free of the chains the class struggle had imposed on Italian labor. A methodical and successful will to bring together in a same fasces [*faisceau*] all the human factors of national production. . . . A determination to approach, to treat, to resolve the worker question *in itself* . . . and to unite the unions in corporations, to coordinate them, to incorporate the proletariat into the hereditary and traditional activities of the historical State of the Fatherland. (62–63)

As far as this quotation goes, it would seem that there is no essential difference between Maurras's royalist nationalism and Italian fascism. It reveals that Maurras clearly recognized his own influence on the development of fascism and saw it to be a (incomplete) form of Integral Nationalism.

Maurras even went so far as to call the fascist dictator a "mon-arque" (*Enquête sur la Monarchie*, LXXXIV). In quotations such as these, Maurras clearly indicated why he supported various movements and journals such as *Je suis partout* (at least until the Occupation), which were more fascist than monarchist in orientation but which owed much to his own thinking. The "faisceau" in Maurras's description is simply another name for the organicism of the nation-work, in terms of the operations that bring together the various human factors as well as in the exterior form of the organic unity achieved by their *incorporation* into the traditional, historical State, the Fatherland. While Maurras made the fascist dictator into the reflection of the king, his fascist followers treated the king as a precursor and model of the dictator.

The fascist dictator, however, was not the king; his place in the nation-work might be similar or identical to that of the king, but the figure he represented, or that represented him, was not the same; nor was his function the same over time. This is undoubtedly why Maurras never actually became a fascist, even if he was especially intrigued by Italian fascism. He considered the fascist dictator first of all to be a figure and force of unification, an embodiment of the national unity he brings about through a process of incorporation that is at times violent. The dictator is even necessary at times, admitted Maurras, as the only remedy for the crises dividing and destroying the nation; but he is never sufficient. Because his actual person occupies the position of authority, the dictator can never guarantee stability or continuity over time. The unity he brings to the nation is as tenuous as his own life: "A man alone is little. The life of a man, the heart of a man, the head of a man, all that is quite exposed, quite pervious to a bullet, a knife, to sickness, to all kinds of plots" (*Mes idées politiques*, 294). In a certain sense, the dictator is not enough of a *figure*, not rooted deeply enough at the center of the "faisceau" or work the nation has become or is to become. He is too personal and therefore too exterior an authority, and he thus cannot, *through his person alone*, guarantee the aesthetic-political integrity and continuity of his work over time. He does not have history and tradition to support him; he does not have the assurance of his firstborn son succeeding him to guarantee the future of the nation. The dictator is thus only a temporary and artificial solution—a modern solution—to the divisions of the nation.

Only the king or the figure of the king—because his authority and function are not contingent and dependent on his life but are guaranteed by tradition and by royal succession—could guarantee the integrity and continuity of the nation-work. Because the king's actual person means nothing and his particular capacities are practically irrelevant, his death therefore is without consequence. The family and tradition are the king, the royal institution is the king, not the individual king himself. His power was thus deemed to be natural and eternal rather than artificial and contingent:

> The only rational and sane form of the authority of a single person is the one that rests on the family, from first-born to first-born, following a law that excludes competition. It is a power that is so natural that, comprising that of the dictator and possessing it in a virtual way, the chief who exercises this power is no longer called dictator: he is king (let us understand the word precisely: *rex*, director and leader, functionary of the intelligence), and this royal magistrate, combining the two ideas of command and heredity, is such a supple thing that it never stops being itself when it changes with time. . . . As occurs for very great things, the institution is very much superior to the man. (294–95)

The king, then, is a director and leader (or perhaps a certain kind of "rational" *Duce* or *Führer*) who figures or embodies not just the political unity of the nation, but its historical and spiritual unity as well. Quite simply, *"the King of France does not die"* (*Enquête sur la Monarchie*, CXXVII), and his identity never really changes because his identity is not determined by his person but by his function.

The king's function has always been to create the nation as an organic work of art and to inscribe himself, his image, at the center of the work. A nation, as a single, unique work, can have only one author and one center, and that author and center are and have always been the same *figure*. Julius Caesar, according to Maurras, made France "possible," but the French kings, working as a single author, slowly realized the work as a whole:

> Often [the kings] assimilated [territory] before conquering it. At other times, the smallest conquered domain is subjected to a patient effort of assimilation,

before they take on a new conquest. Such is their art, such is the "admirable result" whose monument France is. . . . Good or bad, weak or strong, none of these princes ever lost sight of the generation of France. One would say that it is the work of a single man. It is the work of an institution, of a tradition, and of a House. (495)

The institution of the king, Maurras claims, is "consubstantial with the history of our State, our nation, and our spirit" (C). In order to be the kind of artwork that the nation is claimed to be, the consubstantiality of "artist" and work is necessary, for ideally there should be no difference between the parts of the whole, the king, and the figure of the whole, no difference between king and nation, king and people. If an aesthetic sense of unity is the supreme political goal, Maurras's Integral Nationalism can be seen to possess a powerful and convincing *logic* within the narrow parameters defined by such an aestheticist project. Fascism, at least the literary fascism proposed by many disciples of Maurras, could be considered the modern, revolutionary version of the same general aesthetic-political program, but a program no longer defined politically in terms of royalism or defined aesthetically strictly in terms of classicism.

Despite its traditional character, then, Integral Nationalism could be considered a fascism before-the-fact, one that claims to have realized (and to be able to realize again) the true—that is, total—project of national unification, not just in the present and for the future but in terms of and for the past as well. To give up the idea of the monarchy is for Maurras to give up nothing less than the idea of the integral nation itself. With the monarchy at its center, the nation "exists by its proper force, *sua mole stat*" (*Mes idées politiques*, 302), self-constituting, unified, and identical to itself, the supreme, sovereign subject. If in arguing against what he considered the dangerous democratic mystification of the popular will and the impersonal, collective subject, Maurras claims that "the sovereign is not subject, the subject not sovereign" (306); it is so because for him the king alone is an absolute subject, the embodiment of the nation as an organic unity. All other subjects are subject to him (it) and to the unity and authority he represents. There is and can be, therefore, only one subject in Integral Nationalism, the royal subject personifying and equivalent to the nation-subject, and in terms of whom the people become one: one people, one king, one nation.

The very aesthetic and political concepts that led many of Maurras's younger followers to fascism and active collaboration with Nazi Germany during the Occupation were, however, at the very same time at the heart of Maurras's refusal to collaborate *directly* with Nazi Germany after the defeat. Unlike Brasillach and Rebatet, he refused to actively support Hitler, whom he had always linked to the romantic, revolutionary German tradition he had constantly denounced:

Germany is the country of the Revolution. The Revolution comes from Germany. . . . If we stick to the essential (which so many critics forget), the filiation Luther, Rousseau, Kant, Fichte, Bismark, Hitler is evident. . . . *The Hitlerian movement, is it really, as so many democrats believe, a reactionary, anti-individualist, and anti-democratic movement? Is it not on the contrary one of the most dangerous forms of democratic individualism: the Cesarian dictatorship?* (*L'Action Française* [September 26, 1933], republished in *De la politique naturelle au nationalisme intégral*, 123)

Throughout the war, Maurras refrained from directly supporting what he called in 1933 the "tyrannical State of Hitler," one which he claimed expressed an "abstract national will, completely metaphysical and religious" (123), and which was unlike what he argued was the "vigorous realism" of Integral Nationalism. He did not keep a distance from Pétain or Vichy, however, and thus could rightly be considered to have collaborated, even if in a different form from most of his fascist heirs, and at a distance and on what he claimed were "his own" and Pétain's terms.

Hitler remained too much a product of democracy and of the "Orient" for Maurras to link National Socialism too closely to his own vision of France, for Hitler's mode of unifying Germany imposed on it "the most rigid, the most sectarian, and the most artificial of unitarisms—a *believe OR die*, a *believe AND die* that makes it resemble and brings it close to the measures of an Islam" (124). Unlike his younger fascist followers, Maurras thought that France had nothing to learn from this "Islamic" model, which represented one of the most dangerous threats to the integrity of France, a model that he considered an extreme product of democracy and the East rather than their opposite. What changed during the Occupation, of course, was that he could no longer write such things; he could no longer overtly attack the traditional enemy of France. Instead, Maurras devoted all his attention and energy to attacking England, which had replaced Germany in his writing as the principal foreign enemy of France, denouncing "the traitor de Gaulle," as he always called him, and defending the integrity of France, now no longer in terms of the king, the divine ruler, but rather as personified by Pétain, "the divine surprise" that resulted from the humiliating defeat.[12]

Maurras defended Pétain in the exact terms he used previously to defend the monarchy, making Pétain the symbolic center of the French nation: "He who wanted no other title than that of *Chief of the French State* personifies our historical and geographic unity. He is their brilliant sign, but also the means of organic and vital action" (*De la colère à la justice: Réflexions sur un désastre* [Geneva: Editions du Milieu du Monde, 1941], 74). Without being able to claim for him the legitimacy of royal lineage, and yet clearly wanting to distinguish him from dictators whose right to govern depended only on force, Maurras gave Pétain another type of "natural legitimacy," that supplied by military *tradition*: "We ask only for the dictatorship of the French Army and of its natural hierarchy" ("Unité française. D'abord,"in *La Seule France*, 18). And what is natural about the army is that, like royalty, it is equated in history with the nation as a whole: "It's out of the *real country*, its heart, its soul and its millenial genius that our army came, in its order and its spirit. The government of the army constitutes the brilliant image of French unity" (19). Pétain is thus presented as the worthy successor to Napoleon, the great military genius who unified France in spite of and in a sense against the Revolution, but without Napoleon's romantic aesthetic-political limitations.

Maurras ensures Pétain's legitimacy by equating him directly with France as a whole, by making him, like the king, represent the unique sovereign subject with absolute authority:

> When the defeat occurred, the nation needed a defender who was devoted only to it, who represented only it, who was interested only in its essential being. . . . Instead of the parts of the nation, its Totality was taken into account, and we looked to the heights . . . where the greatest servants of the nation were—where the best, the greatest was: . . . *PETAIN* who depended on no one, *PETAIN* whose services were of a strictly national order, *PETAIN* who owed his authority only to himself or to his worth, . . . it was *PETAIN* who imposed himself on even the simplest gaze. (*De la colère à la justice*, 78–79)

In this way, "the gift of his person" that Pétain made to France was the gift of itself that France made to itself, since for all intents and purposes, Pétain was France.

The slogan associated with Maurras, "Politics First," became during this period "Unity First," which was equivalent to "*France First*" and then "*France, France* all alone" (*La Seule France*, 37). The survival of France, of a reactionary, traditional, hierarchical Catholic, antidemocratic France, no matter the costs, was the unique principle of Maurras's defense of Pétain:

> National unity morally regained at the appropriate moment around its consecrated chief. Such is the living sense, such is the vital sense of *politics first*. . . . What will allow [France] to exercise its normal life function? It's first *to be, to be with force*, thus to retain its political and moral unity, then its territorial unity. Without this, nothing at all will be of any use to it. . . . To resist eventual misfortunes, there has to be *a* France. (*La Seule France*, 34–36).

Maurras's defense of Pétain and Vichy was characterized, as usual, by its powerful simplicity, and it was driven by the same implacable, dogmatic logic found in his defense of the monarchy. "Only France" and "France Alone" meant that if Vichy's collaboration aided the war efforts of that radical outgrowth of the Orient and democracy called Nazism and

France's traditional enemy, Germany, it did not really matter, for France was the only value that had to be considered. What was good for France, and for its survival, was unambiguously good, and every act of collaboration by Vichy was defended with the same insistence: "the *sovereignty* of France" was the essential and only issue (286). Once Pétain was placed in the role and had the function of the king, the fiction of a free, sovereign France under German Occupation could be constructed and defended according to the same aesthetic-political principles and operations as those for Integral Nationalism.[13]

It was thus in the name of the survival and revival of the integral nation that Maurras enthusiastically supported Pétain's "National Revolution" and his war against "métèques" and attacked "the traitor de Gaulle" (117), who he claimed was working for the English to destroy France and bring about what he called the "Fifth Revolution" in France (*La Seule France*, 123).[14] But such unity had its price, which Maurras was more than happy to have all "aliens," and especially the Jews, pay. In an essay entitled "La France aux Français" (in *La Seule France*)—a xenophobic slogan originally made popular by Edouard Drumont, author of *La France Juive*, and more recently used by the Le Pen's National Front—Maurras claimed that "under the condition of an atrocious national mourning, at a time of glorious resurrection, the government of Maréchal Pétain put the businesses of devastating *métèques* back in their proper place, and he returned to the sons of our land the ownership of their professions and restored the honor and freedom of their work" (190). In "Juifs et Franc-Maçons" (also in *La Seule France*), he defended Vichy's "Statute on the Jews" of October 3, 1940,[15] because he claimed it "has nothing against the religious faith of the Israelites, their blood, or their goods. It wants to save the spirit and fortune of the country, as it has the strict duty to do" (194). For Maurras, the anti-Semitism of Vichy was identical to the anti-Semitism he had always proposed—a "rational," "State anti-Semitism," rather than an "anti-Semitism of the skin," one that reestablished the true hierarchy of the country: "The first act of the government was to say: *France for the French*, priority to the immediate children of the land and blood, the *métèques* would come only after them" (272). If Vichy France went further in its anti-Semitic legislation than the Germans demanded, it was for reasons that Maurras wholeheartedly approved and for a social vision that owed much to his thought.

It is highly ironic that it is when France was politically the least independent and sovereign that Maurras praised its sovereignty and national integrity the most vigorously. The integral-nationalist fiction of the political that he had constructed in his royalist writings was powerful enough, however, to justify the most severe repressions in the name of national sovereignty and to eliminate everything that conflicted with the picture of the nation being presented. The totalizing fiction of organic nationalism that dominated Maurras's ideology from beginning to end made this militant royalist one of Pétain's strongest and most loyal supporters. At the same time, it kept him from moving to the next stage of collaboration and actively supporting the cause of Nazi Germany, as many of his disciples did. Reactionary in his aesthetic tastes and reactionary in his political tastes as well, Maurras nevertheless provided an aesthetics of the nation that was an important foundation for the revolutionary forms of nationalism that French literary fascists championed; and therefore it also provided a basis for the more direct and active forms of collaboration and support of Nazi Germany that he himself condemned.

The political position of Robert Brasillach did not differ essentially from that of Maurras in its general outlines and the overall picture of the integral, organic nation it delineated. Like Rebatet, who distanced himself even more from Vichy and Maurras, Brasillach simply drew different conclusions from such a picture. Brasillach and Rebatet quickly grew impatient with Pétain (and Maurras) and decided that active and direct collaboration with Nazi Germany was the only way to bring about a true national—that is, a National-Socialist—fascist revolution in France. As Maurras was willing to accept Pétain symbolically as king, so Brasillach and other fascists wanted a leader to emerge to replace Pétain. They had in mind a youthful, energetic fascist dictator who would have the same national legitimacy Maurras attributed to Pétain. But the aesthetic and political configuration of fascism that the literary fascists proposed was basically a logical extension and radicalization of Maurras's position, even if the step to fascism and direct collaboration with the Nazis was one Maurras himself had been unwilling to make.

Part Two ————————————————————

LITERARY FASCISTS

Four

Fascism as Aesthetic Experience:
Robert Brasillach and
the Politics of Literature

For the leader (*Führer*), the mass is no more
a problem than is paint for the artist. . . . The
greatest aim of true politics has always been to
form a people out of the mass, and a state out of
the people.
  Josef Goebbels, Michael *(1923)*

[The Nuremberg rallies] are the highest artistic
creation of our time.
  Robert Brasillach, Je suis partout
  (January 29, 1943)

Nationalism, Fascism, and the Defense
of Literature

Many still find it difficult to accept the fact that a significant number of
important French intellectuals and writers were tempted by and committed themselves to fascism during the 1930s and that many collaborated
actively with Nazi Germany during the Occupation. It is as if the violence,
injustices, and crimes carried out in the name of fascism would necessarily make fascism incompatible with an authentic literary sensibility, as if
there were something in the nature of literary texts or speculative and
critical essays that opposed them to totalitarian ideologies. A prevalent
assumption of both revisionists and antirevisionists alike—that is, even of
those intent on condemning fascist writers *for their politics*—seems to be
that if a writer was really a fascist, he could not have been a true writer or
critic; if he was an authentic writer or artist, he could not have been a
fascist.

Those critics whose chief purpose is to denounce fascism, and all those
who were tempted by it, have for the most part refused to take seriously
the literary and critical essays of literary fascists and have been reluctant
to make the effort to understand how their fascism was rooted in and

largely formed by their literary and intellectual interests and commitments. The strictly political condemnation of the activities of literary fascists is thus generally limited by the critics' literary or critical shortsightedness, by their assumption that the politics of literary fascists totally determine their literary activities and that their creative and critical work is thus always a direct and uncomplicated derivative of their ideological commitments—an inferior, politicized, unliterary form of literature and criticism.

It is not difficult, however, to see how a form of revisionism could also root itself in the assumption that the literary and the political are totally separate realms and that one always determines—and in this way reduces significantly the importance of—the other. By simply reversing the privilege given to the political over the literary, the principal argument of those revisionist critics who have attempted to defend fascist and collaborationist writers has been that these writers were not completely (or in any way) responsible for their political actions because they were primarily writers or literary critics. Revisionists thus tend to treat them as naive, impressionistic innocents when it comes to politics, ignorant of the real consequences of their support for Nazism and their denunciations of Jews and all opponents of fascism and collaboration.[1] Emphasizing the major fascist writers' alleged contributions to French literature and culture, revisionists might admit that the political actions of literary fascists and collaborators could be judged to have been "mistaken," but they should not be taken too seriously. For their politics are insignificant when compared to the literary achievements and cultural legacy of these "misguided" poets. Literature and the specifically literary side of literary fascism are thus emphasized in order to ignore, excuse, or explain away various writers' commitment to fascism by linking it to, or deriving it from, a more essential literary or critical sensibility.

When opposing this form of simplistic and dangerous rehabilitation of fascist, collaborationist writers, the temptation is great to take the opposite position; that is, to treat the literary-poetic side of their fascism as inconsequential and to emphasize the unjust and criminal political and human consequences of fascism, which are so significant that nothing can mitigate the responsibilities of those who actively defended fascism and anti-Semitism. For some militant antirevisionists, to take seriously the literary-poetic theory and practices of literary fascists is unequivocally to trivialize, legitimize, or explain away their politics.

One of the strongest antirevisionist statements of this sort is a recent pamphlet written by Jacqueline Baldran and Claude Bouchurberg, *Brasillach ou la célébration du mépris* (Paris: A. J. Presse, 1988), which legitimately denounces recent attempts to transform Robert Brasillach into a literary martyr and whitewash his deep political involvement with fascism and collaboration.[2] The authors, in perhaps justifiable anger, take the following position on the relation of the literary and the political in his work and in terms of fascism in general:

> Robert Brasillach was a writer; no one would deny it. A poet perhaps. A fascist most definitely. Poet and fascist. Fascist and poet. Should the poet make us forget the fascist? . . . Fascism, in its products, was absolute Evil, death. Fascism was not simply poetic reverie. The association of fascism and poetry falls within the category of deception. (52)

Certainly neither fascism in general nor literary fascism in particular was simply or exclusively poetic reverie, if this means a naive form of romantic escapism. But the assertion that all analyses of the relations between literature and fascism are deceptive because they give the impression that literary fascism was merely harmless literary musing, or that in focusing on "the poet" one inevitably forgets the fascist, underestimates the place of the poetic in even the most ruthless and criminal expressions of fascism. When the poetic is evoked as a formative model for and a fundamental operation of the political, "poetic reverie" can have—and in the context of French literary fascism, it did have—totalitarian political consequences.[3]

To argue that the fascism of a writer such as Brasillach was profoundly "literary" is not necessarily to mitigate his political responsibilities. It is not to excuse or explain away anything. On the contrary, it is important to analyze the consequences of the fascist aestheticizing or poeticizing of politics and to determine how a mythic and mystifying notion of literature and culture could and did function as a model for politics and provide an aesthetic justification for some of the worst political excesses, injustices, and crimes. I thus treat Brasillach and the other ultranationalist and fascist writers discussed in this book as both writers and fascists: "poets," writers, literary critics and theorists, as well as extremist political journalists, pamphleteers, and demagogues. The fact that a particular vision or myth of literature and art was inseparable from and supported their fascist politics does not mean that they had only limited responsibilities for the consequences of their writings and actions. On the contrary, their political responsibilities as writers or critics are total, and the destructive effects of their "poetic reveries" are primary among these responsibilities. Antirevisionists rightly claim that politics should not be trivialized, especially when it comes to fascism; but neither should poetics or aesthetics.[4]

For Brasillach and many others on the extreme right, to separate literature and politics was to impoverish each. First, such separation reduced the political to the empty politics of parties and economic influence that they abhorred and constantly denounced. Second, it took away from politics its potential grandeur, its vision of the nation as an organic unity, and its means of creating a radically new social and national "order" in which the true identity of a people could be realized and the creative forces of the nation activated. At the same time, such a separation reduced literature to an irrational, frivolous pastime and cut it off from its tradition and truth, causing it to flounder in what literary fascists considered the empty individualism and decadence of romanticism. The linkage of politics and literature also meant that the literary battles that raged in the pages of newspapers and journals in the 1930s were just as polemical and political as the political battles, for just as much was at stake for both literature and politics *in literature* as in politics.

Revisionists have attempted to rehabilitate Brasillach as a writer by radically separating his literary essays and novels from his politics in order to emphasize his literary achievements and underplay and excuse his political crimes. This not only flys in the face of all Brasillach's work, but it also contradicts important elements of the French nationalist and fascist traditions he so vigorously and relentlessly defended up to the moment of his death. Brasillach himself never made the claim that his literary activities should be separated from or used to counterbalance his politics. Rather, he defended both the literary and political positions he had taken as being those of someone completely loyal to France and working at all times in what he claimed were France's best interests: a true nationalist, a "patriotic" *French* fascist.[5]

Defending France's national interests also meant defending its art and literature *as art and literature*. Brasillach was at times a violent polemicist, a vicious anti-Semite, and a political demagogue, but in his approach to literature and art he was not in every instance a blatant and crude propagandist, for he did not always judge the merit of works solely on the basis of the political affiliations of their author. It is true that the "gods" of the right such as Maurras, Léon Daudet, Jacques Bainville, and Henri Massis—that is, those most closely affiliated with *L'Action Française*— were routinely and enthusiastically praised. And this respect for Maurras and his associates continued even after Brasillach broke with Maurras after the defeat and continued to publish *Je suis partout* in Paris during the Occupation.[6] Works by other extremist and fascist writers, however, were just as likely to be criticized for their literary and political shortcomings as those of moderate or even leftist writers. Brasillach criticized Drieu la Rochelle, for example, just as severely as he did André Malraux; and his reservations concerning Céline's work were more serious than those he had of the work of François Mauriac or even Jules Romains.

In other words, Brasillach's early extremist and subsequent fascist political allegiances did not mean that he considered all fascist or extremist

writers allies or all moderate, republican, or even socialist writers enemies—in terms of their literary writings. The works of "political allies"
could fail to measure up to his critical standards just as easily as those of
"enemies" might in part succeed, sometimes in spite of their political
commitments. A canon dominated by nationalist writers certainly existed
for literary fascists, but it was not as rigid and politically dogmatic as one
might have imagined.

However, Brasillach's desire to respect the integrity and autonomy of
literature, to acknowledge its complexity and the diversity and richness of
its history, and his refusal to always reduce literature to its immediate
political context in no way counter or undo the political ends of literary
fascism. Literary fascism was rooted in a developed and far from simplistic defense of the unity, autonomy, and integrity of literature in order to
consider it an expression of or even a principal support for the unity and
integrity of the French nation and people. French literary fascists all
claimed that some of the important signs that a nation was "alive," open
to the future, and creatively exploiting its "spiritual" resources—and thus
ready to enter the "New (that is, fascist) Order"—were the richness and
autonomy of its culture, the originality of its art, and the disruptive poetic
force and beauty of its literature. These same aesthetic principles were
directly applied to politics, for fascism was defined by Brasillach and others precisely as the "new poetry" of modernity; that is, as the new aesthetics of the political—as politics finding its truth or authentic, "revolutionary" mission in the form of a total (totalitarian) aesthetics.

Brasillach's general approach to literature was derived explicitly from
Maurras, and it retained the fundamental characteristics of Maurras's
extremist nationalist, antiromantic, classical poetics and politics: what I
have called an antiromantic organicism. But unlike Maurras, Brasillach
was not dogmatically antimodernist for either aesthetic or political reasons. Unity and integrity constituted the primary and fundamental principles of his approach to literature; but in the modern period, he felt that
the predetermined, formal unity of classical art and poetics could no
longer be considered sufficient. Instead, he believed that the unity of the
work should be treated as a dynamic, creative process of the will interact-
ing with language and cultural matter, not as an application of predetermined linguistic or rhetorical forms to matter.

In an early article on Léon Daudet, the son of Alphonse Daudet and the
codirector with Maurras of *L'Action Française*, Brasillach stressed ap-
provingly the primary place of the law of unity in both the aesthetics and
politics of Daudet. He admired the way in which aesthetic unity served as
a model for political unity, and the will to unity *of the artist* served as the
model for the will to unity of the political theorist:

In the aesthetic order, the search for concordances constitutes also its own victory. He for whom everything is linked in this world . . . will find that the unity of a work will appear in an even stronger way. He will not construct this work around an isolated fact or a mass of facts without relation, but around a complex totality that great laws bind together. [Daudet] has devoted himself to the search for these laws, even in a world as supple and as variable as the human universe and the historical universe. . . . [He] has thus attempted to discover the laws of identity and relationship necessary for politics. ("Léon Daudet: *La Pluie et le sang*," *L'Action Française* [September 15, 1932])

The search for the poetic or aesthetic unity of the artwork thus leads to the search for an analogous unity in the sociopolitical universe. The laws of identity and relationship are considered the basis for both literature and politics. Even if these laws do not have the same exterior form in each area, they are based on the same organicist principles and the same aesthetics.

The laws of unity should be sought and discovered in the literary or historical material itself; that is, they should originate in and reflect the mass of variables of each universe. The specific form of the law in each case does not preexist its discovery or the process of its formation; what does preexist is only the *will to discover* such a law of unity, for the belief that such a law can and should be discovered makes possible its discovery. This aesthetic will-to-unity would, in Brasillach's later work, no longer be a sign of true, "Integral Nationalism," but it would be defined specifically as the essence of fascism: "It's that we want French unity and that the word 'fascism' does not mean anything else but the union in fasces of all the forces of the nation" ("La Conjuration anti-fasciste au service des Juifs," *Je suis partout*, no. 549 [February 7, 1942]). In this sense, fascism is the form that the radical, absolutist, nationalist poetic organicism of the Action Française took in the hands of younger disciples such as Brasillach when it was applied to the social world as a modern, revolutionary version of Maurras's political will-to-unity. Literary fascism is thus not literary organicism per se but its extension and *application* to the political, its use as *the model* for the national-socialist revolution.

Brasillach argued that the health of the nation (and or as the work of art) depended on the counterbalancing of authority and freedom, but that the counterbalancing and equilibrium should be clearly more weighted on the side of the hierarchy, integrity, and unity of tradition and authority than on the forces that would rearrange the balance in some other way and at their expense. In Maurras's case, the equilibrium was guaranteed by the king and traditional hierarchy and authority. In Brasillach's case, it came to be guaranteed in the modern world by the fascist dictator and the unique party he formed and led. The leader and the party were to have the responsibility of forming, mobilizing, and unifying the nation just as the poet forms the poem. In doing so, they were not simply to perpetuate the past but to give the people a new form; that is, they were to form nothing less than a new work, "a new human type" ("Pour un fascisme français," *Je suis partout*, no. 588 [November 6, 1942]).

There is nothing passive about such an aesthetics, even if the notions of order, hierarchy, and totality dominate it. On the contrary, since the totality of the work is not given in advance, it must be formed as part of the struggle against all those forces that work to destroy it and all the "abstract"—that is, idealist or formalist/aestheticist—totalities ready to act in its place. In an article entitled "Le Polémiste" and devoted to Maurras, whom he calls the "master of French nationalism," Brasillach claims that Maurrasian aesthetics have to do with "beauty itself [la beauté propre]," and that they constitute an *"aesthetics* of combat" (*L'Action Française* [June 16, 1938]). He defends the polemical and even violent quality of Maurras's work by characterizing it as "a well-ordered violence," a fusion of different forces "which come together and stir each other up in the struggle, just as the peak of a beautiful fire rises up from a well-ordered hearth." In the same article, he compares the form of Maurras's polemics to the highest form of drama, to that of Shakespeare and Corneille. He argues that what is felt in Maurras's writing is the "shock that true beauty gives to passion," a "muted tension of the phrase in which the brusque flash of an image seems to explode." What is essential in Maurras's ideological stance, what constitutes even "the truth" of his politics, then, is its *beauty*, defined not in strict formalist terms but as a controlled or ordered violence, which is rooted in and serves both aesthetic and political totalization. The ultimate test and value of political action are not the changes it brings about in society—although these are certainly not irrelevant—but the force and "beauty" of its manifestations and effects, whether they are "politically" successful or not. Beauty not political efficacy eventually turns out to be the ultimate norm for political as well as aesthetic judgment, even where Brasillach's later commitment to fascism is concerned.

Disintegration, fragmentation, romantic individualism, and pluralism all constitute a major obstacle to aesthetic integrity; they threaten as well the political integrity of a people. But in literary fascism it is not a question of just any unity at all, for following Maurras, Brasillach questions the unity projected by "idealism"; that is, socialist, revolutionary idealism, on the one hand, and romantic, literary idealism, on the other. From Brasillach's perspective, one of the most serious criticisms that can be made of any political thinker or any writer is that he is *abstract*, and that the aesthetic and/or political unity or form of his work consists of an application of a preexisting unity—whether formal or ideological—to the specific and diversified material of the historical-political or aesthetic realms. This means that the aesthetics and politics of Brasillach's literary fascism are always twofold: most often, a violent attempt to destroy all abstract, formalist-idealist totalizations, and then, the reunification of the disparate elements of the political and literary-aesthetic realms in terms of their "real," as opposed to their ideal, integrity or identity. In the political realm, this "reality" consists of the (re)fashioning of the identity of a people rooted in the land, tradition, and authentic national values; in the literary realm, it is the expression of the unity and organic integrity of the national language and the creative heritage or genius of the people itself as they are manifested especially in a national literature.

Without ever being raised overtly, the principal questions that haunt Brasillach's work on literature are: How much destruction of tradition can be allowed without risking the destruction of the very bases of nationalism and fascism? How much can a work be constituted by violent forces and disruptive forms and still remain *a work*? In other words, what is the "proper relation" of the "fascist revolution" in literature and in politics to tradition and form? It is first in terms of literature that Brasillach attempted to answer these questions. In an article on the nineteenth-century poet Lautréamont, he defended *Les Chants de Malador* against the possible charge that it might be an example of "degenerate art." He ironically admitted that "Mr. Goebbels, if he knew the work, would probably not like it," but he defended "its immense critical significance" and considered it in no way "barbarian" but, on the contrary, "a highly civilized work, . . . based on the knowledge and parody of an entire literature." Rather than being "the symbol of every disorder," as he said it was considered after the First World War (a reading encouraged, he claimed, by the Surrealists' praise of it), Brasillach argued that it was, rather, "a kind of defense of true classicism by way of the absurd" ("C.-J. Odic: *L'Ombre à la Barraquer*; Lautréamont: *Oeuvres complètes*," *L'Action Française* [April 7, 1938]). Lautréamont in this way represents for Brasillach a model for true literature (and politics): because of his intimate knowledge of the entire history of literature, he is able to parody the modern manifestations and aberrations in this tradition in order to return to a more authentic form of tradition in a renewed, reinvigorated, truly French ("fascist") classicism.

An entire view of history and literature underlies such comments about the nature of authentic literary classicism: what is most radically "new" and aesthetically and politically harmonious for Brasillach is not the simple adulation of the past, but the reemergence of traditional values by means of a revolt against and a parody of the emptiness of the present and the resulting reestablishment of a more authentic link with the past. As Brasillach argues, "Through an irony that I greatly appreciate, the most

revolutionary movements [here, surrealism] need tradition, and everything that the postwar period believed it invented actually dates from *the
other* prewar period."[7] What he calls tradition is the historical continuity
that exists in spite of the imaginary or surface breaks and reversals that
"revolutionary movements" are thought to have inserted into history.
For Brasillach, the true "revolution"—that is, the fascist revolution—ensures both in literature and in politics a profound, historical continuity,
which in fact consists of a constant reawakening and recreating of the
truth carried on in tradition. Such continuity is the work not only of great
leaders with a vision of the future, but also of gifted youth, of "children"
and poets such as Lautréamont, who break with the "present" in order to
provide more substantial and revolutionary links with the past—and revolutionary possibilities for the future.

Literature, then, for Brasillach, should not be considered a simple reflection of historical-political forces, for it has an autonomous history of
its own. Truly "revolutionary" writers always reveal their understanding
of literary tradition and their appreciation of it within their work. They
are not so unduly influenced by the demands of the present, even the most
pressing political demands, that they let them determine the style and
content of their work. It could even be said that for a literary fascist such
as Brasillach, writers on the most profound levels of their work should
resist the exigencies of the present and devote themselves to literature and
not to politics, particularly if devoting themselves to politics means following a party line or a fixed ideology and having it regulate and determine their approach to literature or the form of their writing and its
relation to tradition. The ultimate political sense of literature for literary
fascism would be, then, not primarily what it says explicitly about the
politics of the present but how it relates to tradition and the past; and
more specifically, how it relates to and exploits the resources of the national language and culture to reawaken the creativity and "genius" inherent in them.

Stéphane Mallarmé is an interesting example, for his work represents
a serious problem for Brasillach, perhaps more serious than that of any
other writer he treats. And it is also through his analysis of Mallarmé's
work that the most extreme contradictions of his approach to tradition
and language come to the fore. Brasillach cannot deny the importance of
Mallarmé's poetry and poetics for the history of French literature and for
its future. At the same time, he sees great risks for poetry, for the French
language, and for the nation in Mallarmé's radical experimentations with
language and form. Brasillach is thus led by his own logic into a seemingly insolvable paradox: he approves of and supports the legacy Mallarmé leaves (chiefly as it comes through Valéry), and at the same time he
distrusts and attacks its radical implications for language and literature,

and, more specifically, for the integrity of the national language and culture. Mallarmé's case is one in which important aspects of a writer's poetic practice and his poetics themselves have contributed to the revitalization of the "national tradition" and thus cannot be simply dismissed out of hand if one claims to respect the vitality of tradition. Yet, at the same time, his work radically challenges the notion of a national language and the nationalist politics such a notion supports. There seems to be no way to resolve the contradiction: to save Mallarmé and his poetics, on the one hand, and to save the integrity of the national language, on the other.

Brasillach's solution is really no solution at all. Unlike Maurras, who condemned Mallarmé as the last and most dangerous, irrational, "barbarian" romantic, Brasillach split Mallarmé's work in two, praising the poet while condemning the writer of prose. He agreed that the poet should be treated as part of a long and glorious French tradition, but he maintained that the very same risks Mallarmé took in his poetry, and which served to revitalize poetry and tradition, acted against the unity of language in his prose:

> This "alchemist" of the French language, as Thierry Maulnier calls him, if he is part of a very ancient tradition, he is certainly the most lucid representative. His long effort, his theories on art, his brilliant aesthetics . . . were rewarded by several mysterious, pure, and rich verses which are unique in our language, even without forgetting Racine, Baudelaire, and Nerval. But this reward had its counterbalance, of which Mallarméan prose makes us aware: he really acted against the French language. One is stupefied in reading his letters not by their obscurity but by the sins committed against language.[8]

These sins against language—and the religious vocabulary must be taken seriously—were also considered sins against the nation. If Mallarmé's prose, as Brasillach claimed, is quite simply "impossible," it seems inevitable that its destructiveness would ultimately have to infiltrate his poetry as well. Brasillach decided that the price was too great to pay for such innovations, and that the French language itself (and thus French poetry as well as prose) was being threatened.

Even if "obscurity . . . is one of the *essential* traditions of our poetry," argues Brasillach, "it has to be adapted to the clarity of syntax." A clear, coherent syntax is precisely what is missing from Mallarmé, according to Brasillach, and its destruction is the principal sin he commits. He refuses to adapt the obscurity caused by the "disintegration he patiently pursues, the inversions and finery of his style," to the underlying clarity of syntax. He refuses to adapt the freedom allowed one level of language to its traditional foundation in the order of syntax, to make poetic freedom and even obscurity serve, rather than undermine, the values and structure of the national language and the nation itself. Brasillach believed that this is why Mallarmé, "the magnificent adventurer, the alchemist of language," was also the poet who "most endangered the sense itself of our genius." National genius—and for Brasillach, true genius, no matter how eccentric or seemingly individualistic, is always a product and sign of the collectivity of the nation and national language—is always menaced when its fundamental unity is attacked.

Mallarmé's "sin" is thus the sin of betrayal, for by distancing himself from his own language and culture, he becomes, in Brasillach's view, a foreigner in his own land and by implication a traitor to his language and country:

> But perhaps the attention he gave to words and to the connections of words entails its own dangers: for he ended up setting sounds in place as if they were sparkling, but not always pure jewels, without always being concerned with the real song of our language. Desirous of being the creator of his own dialect, he ended up placing himself even further away from the common homeland, even in order to write the simplest letters, the simplest discourses, and becoming a foreigner in his own nation.

Brasillach thus decides that on the deepest level of language poetry cannot be totally separated from prose, and this results in a condemnation of the consequences of Mallarmé's poetics in general, at least when not held in check by the unity of tradition and syntax. Willing up to a point to acknowledge the importance of Mallarmé's disruptive, experimental poetics, Brasillach nevertheless finds the risks to language to be too great when the order of syntax is not respected. Without the support of this fundamental order, language is threatened with anarchy, by "foreign dialects" that endanger its integrity. "The *real song* of [the French] language," Brasillach maintains, could thus be lost forever if it is corrupted to too great an extent by the foreign, discordant sounds of a poet such as Mallarmé.

Similar nationalist-linguistic criteria are used by Brasillach to judge the work of Louis-Ferdinand Céline, and a similar though inverted contradiction is evident in his analysis. In an article in *L'Action Française* (June 11, 1936), on Céline's *Mort à crédit*, Brasillach again focuses on both the positive function of radical forms of the revolt against tradition in literature and the limitations that have to be imposed on all revolt to keep it from becoming totally destructive. In this light, he considers Céline's *Voyage au bout de la nuit* to be "a strange work, unpleasant and attractive at the same time," a "revolt" that contained elements that were "both new and sincere." And yet, even though Brasillach does not want simply to condemn and exclude this work from the national heritage, he cannot quite bring himself to welcome it into the literary homeland either. He describes it as a "strange monument, an unknown menhir planted in

French soil that for better or for worse one has to explore." *Voyage au bout de la nuit* is ultimately considered a curious attraction whose source is not known (and thus is not truly or originally "French") but is "planted" in the soil of the French language. The nationalist critic is forced to live with it, visit it as a national curiosity, and perhaps even marvel at its strangeness. In this way, it can become part of the national heritage, a kind of prehistoric, "pre-original" exteriority within the territory of the French language, but one, Brasillach still cautions, that should not be visited too often or given too much attention or importance, for fear of fragmenting the territory by opening it up even further to "foreign elements" and thus further disrupting the integrity of the language.

Brasillach is less positive about Céline's *Mort à crédit*, this "monster," which he has to force himself to read. Here, he considers that Céline, encouraged by the success of his previous novel, has gone too far and entered into a "domain where literature is untenable," where he "shamelessly devotes himself to the intoxication of literature." Bored by the monotony of the style of the book, feeling smothered by the "garbage" with which the book is filled, Brasillach claims that his nose cannot take "so much excrement on each page of the book." His judgment is that this work will have no heritage, that it is not art and not French, and therefore that it will be (and should be) quickly forgotten by the French:

> One does not write in order to create such an artificial and false world, even if it is adorned with the colors of reality. I believe that Mr. Céline, who possesses a powerful talent and perhaps a kind of genius, condemns himself more and more by the style he has adopted, by the assiduous decomposition of language and forms to which he abandons himself.

Céline's "sins" are ultimately the same as those of Mallarmé, even if committed in a very different style and linked to very different aesthetic ends. He, too, is condemned for undoing the integrity of language and form, and for being an enemy of true aesthetics and thus of true (nationalist) politics as well. And nothing, or almost nothing, can compensate for the decomposition of the national language and the destruction of its cultural forms.

In 1936, these sins seemed to Brasillach to be unforgivable. Two years later, however, with the publication of Céline's first anti-Semitic pamphlet, *Bagatelles pour un massacre*, which Brasillach reviewed in *L'Action Française* on January 13, 1938, Céline is transformed from a potential enemy of the nation into the author of what Brasillach calls an "enormous book, this magnificent book [which] is the first signal of 'the revolt of the natives'" (la révolte des indigènes). In spite of the fact that its "revolt [could be considered] excessive, more instinctual than reasonable, and even dangerous," Brasillach defends it because, as he says, "after all, we are the natives." Céline is brought back into the nationalist fold not in spite of his excesses against the Jews and against the French language, but because of them. Céline thus provides an image of "the natives" by giving voice to their "original" though far from rational or logical hatred of the "non-native."

Natives are allowed to be excessive in the cause of the native land; natives are even allowed to provide ammunition to the enemy by their diatribes against the enemy. "Reasonable people will tell me"—and Brasillach always argued that he was a reasonable person and that his anti-Semitism was rational and not instinctual, animalistic, or violent— that "'Jews will look for and quickly find in this book the best arguments against those who attack them.' And I am, in principle, of the same opinion." Brasillach even goes so far as to suggest that such a work could easily be imagined to have been written by a Jew, because in its "extravagances," it serves to "discredit anti-Semites." And yet, in spite of all these dangerous excesses and the fact that he feels that Céline's "overview of literature is false"—not an insignificant observation for a literary critic such as Brasillach—he admits to having been "royally amused" by the book and is sure that it will bring "joy and consolation" to the readers of his column. Explaining away and justifying the excessive, instinctual anger and violence of Céline, keeping a distance from it while enjoying it, this was Brasillach's way of putting it to use for the cause of his "more rational" form of anti-Semitism. It was in fact a way of justifying (as being amusing) the most violent forms of anti-Semitism by having them serve a supposedly "rational" purpose. But just as important, it was a way for Brasillach to justify his own anti-Semitism by opposing it to its more violent, "instinctual" ally and by claiming it had a moderating effect on it.

While Brasillach was editor of *Je suis partout*, the newspaper published two special issues on the Jews: no. 386 (April 15, 1938) and no. 430 (February 17, 1939). Both were organized by Lucien Rebatet, and both sold exceptionally well and were reprinted. The first claimed in bold and underlined print next to the title that it was a *"RIGOROUSLY OBJEC-TIVE ISSUE"* and, Brasillach added in "La Question juive," his own contribution to it, that the purpose of the entire issue was to transform instinctual hatred and give it a rational purpose:

> We do not want to kill anyone; we do not want to organize any sort of pogrom whatsoever. But we do also think that the best way to prevent the always unforeseeable reactions of an anti-Semitism of instinct is to organize an anti-Semitism of reason. . . . We would like this issue to serve to discern the motives of this instinctual reaction and to transform it into a rational decision.

Brasillach presented his role as that of a moderate, judicious, almost detached observer, who was simply trying to channel the potentially dangerous (though, for him, understandable and valid) instincts of his people into more rational channels and thus protect his country, and also, he claimed, the Jews, from the worst forms of violence and injustice that instinctual hatred could inspire. His goal was not to negate violence or instinct but give them a "higher" aesthetic and political purpose, to make disruptive, irrational force a component of organic, rational form.

For literary fascists such as Brasillach, the treatment of all Jews as foreigners was a neat, respectable "aesthetic" solution to the threat the Jews supposedly represented to national integrity and identity. Its political consequences could hardly be considered neat or respectable, however, in spite of what Brasillach and others might have argued. In the second special issue of *Je suis partout* on the Jews, Brasillach, in "Les Français devant les Juif," defined in some detail the specifics of the proposal he supported for a special statute for the Jews in France and, more important, outlined how to define a Jew. He first affirmed that the writers at *Je suis partout* were "not at all prejudiced and not racist, . . . not xenophopic," chiefly because they were willing to admit that not everything that individual Jews had accomplished was evil or dangerous. They were capable of acknowledging that certain scientific discoveries made by Jews had served the common good, and they were even willing to applaud Charlie Chaplin (whom Brasillach called a "half-Jew") and Yehudi Menuhin, as well as to admire Marcel Proust (also a "half-Jew"). In spite of his admiration for the achievements of certain "exceptional Jews," however, Brasillach insisted that the fact that all Jews were foreigners "must entail its consequences, all its consequences. There is nothing terrible or vexing about them." This, of course, could be argued only if *the only alternatives* to such a statute were pogroms, massacres, and other even more extreme forms of injustice and persecution, and only if the necessity for the exclusion of Jews was the unquestionable principle from which one started. Brasillach opposed all forms of spontaneous, uncontrolled, "instinctual" violence against the Jews, not because he was concerned with protecting the Jews, but because he feared the consequences of such violence for the nation. "Persecutions have always been the product of peoples who were anarchistic and insecure about their power," he wrote. Order and reason had to reign, even or especially when it came to anti-Semitism.

On June 2, 1941, Brasillach took the next logical step. The Jewish "foreigner," who in his earlier piece was in principle as welcome in the country as any other foreigner, explicitly became—what he or she in fact always was—the declared enemy of France: "We continue to treat the Jewish problem as we have always treated it, without any sentimentalism. We are not barbarians and butchers. . . . It is necessary to resolve the Jewish problem because the Jew is the foreigner, he is the enemy, he pushed us into war, and it is just that he pay" (*Je suis partout*, no. 514). To be free of sentimentalism is to be willing to make the enemy pay for his

crimes, but Brasillach was most often vague as to what he meant by
"pay."[9] But as late as March 19, 1943, in an article entitled "La Guerre
et la paix" (*Je suis partout*, no. 606), Brasillach, who was so well in-
formed about so many other things, seemed willfully ignorant about the
true fate of deported Jews and wrote in support of a statement made by
Goebbels to the foreign press about Germany's desire for a "humane"
solution to the "Jewish problem": "Many will be quite surprised, that is
for sure, to read in this declaration sentences in which Dr. Goebbels
evokes a 'humane' solution to the Jewish problem . . . in order to eliminate the international Jewish poison. That also has its importance."
The reference to the Jews as a poison reveals more about his position,
of course, than any claim to want a "humane solution to the Jewish
problem."

Brasillach claimed, in a text written while in prison, "Lettre à un soldat
de la Classe 60," that when he learned about the "extent of the anti-
Jewish measures" taken by the Germans, he was against them. He added:
"I am anti-Semitic, and I know through the study of history the horror of
Jewish dictatorships, but it seems to me and has always seemed to me
inadmissible that families have been separated, children discarded, depor-
tations organized, which could have been defended if they hadn't had as
their goal, hidden from us, death, pure and simple. This is not the way to
resolve the Jewish problem" (*Ecrit à Fresnes*, 137). Brasillach's illusion—
assuming he was sincere here and not lying to save his own life—an illusion that he certainly shared with many other French fascists, was that
because he did not know or approve of the mass extermination of the
Jews, because he thought it "inadmissible" when he found out about it,
he in no essential way contributed to it. One cannot, however, constantly
denounce the Jews and praise Goebbels for his "humane solution to the
Jewish problem" and not accept some responsibility for the injustices and
criminal actions taken against Jews by the Nazi occupiers with whom he
collaborated and the Vichy government he criticized for not going far
enough in its own anti-Semitic legislation and practices. Even if he had
not even heard rumors of the fate of the Jews after they had been deported—something that is difficult to believe—Brasillach had to have
known of their treatment in camps in France and the conditions on the
trains taking them to the death camps. Quite simply, like many others, all
this did not concern him, and he was satisfied to believe whatever
Goebbels and others said, no matter how much it was contradicted by all
evidence.[10]

Literary fascists like Brasillach, in other words, wanted to have it both
ways. They wanted a nationalist literature that was revolutionary but
that at the same time affirmed the primacy of order and tradition. In the
same way, they proposed a nationalism that was violently anti-Semitic

but that claimed not to propose or support violent, "irrational" solutions to the "Jewish question." They wanted to aestheticize the political while keeping their aesthetics under the control of reason, defined, of course, in terms of political order and authority and modeled after the hierarchy and organic totality of the classical literary work but in a new, modern form. "Instincts," even the most violent kind, thus became "rational" when they served the "New Order"; they were irrational and dangerous when they were destructive of all order, the new as well as the old, and when they were not fashioned into an aesthetic-political work.

Anti-Semitism served the same purpose as the fascist political demonstrations Brasillach admired so much. It constituted an important element in the process of the identification of the "natives" with themselves and was a manifestation of the "revolt of the natives" against the foreign. It was the ultimate sign that one was native. "Reason," especially when it was used to defend or support an extreme form of nationalism, could be violent, animalistic, and instinctual—to use Brasillach's own terminology against him. One of the principal functions of the aestheticizing of politics in literary fascism was to make the identification of a people or a nation with itself (its own image)—as well as the violence against the other necessary for such an identification—appear to be necessary and acceptable, constitutive elements of an ordered, rational aesthetic-political form. Anti-Semitism, nationalism, and the privilege given to a certain form of literature were all inextricably intertwined and served as the very foundation of Brasillach's literary fascism. The Jew, the foreign, and the unliterary or antiliterary all had to be controlled, or even better eliminated, for a true, nationalist form of aesthetics and politics to exist. They were ultimately the same disordering, dissipating, antipoetic, formless enemy.

Fascist Joy and the Aestheticizing of Experience

Before the war, Nazi Germany represented a serious dilemma for most of the younger contributors to *L'Action Française*. They were attracted to many (though certainly not all) of the changes Hitler had brought about in Germany, but at the same time they had inherited from Maurras a militantly anti-German position. The problem for many on the extreme right before the war was how to relate to what seemed positive in German National Socialism without proposing that France ally itself with Germany or attempt to copy it in a servile manner. Brasillach and other literary fascists felt that Maurras's position during the Occupation was unrealistic and even foolish, given the possibilities they saw for France in the "New Fascist Order" that Germany had created in Europe. Preferring the fascism of Italy, Spain, or Portugal to the National Socialism of Germany,

Brasillach, after the Montoire meetings during which Pétain pledged collaboration with Hitler, nevertheless moved to an enthusiastically pro-German position. The transformation in his politics was especially evident in his judgments of the aesthetic dimensions of German politics, specifically of the particular form of the Nazi aestheticizing of politics and its possible relation to the aesthetics and political form of a truly indigenous French fascism.

In an article in *L'Action Française* of December 13, 1934, Brasillach agreed with the position taken by Henri Massis in *Débats*, the book he was reviewing, that France (and the West in general) had to defend itself against German influences, against the "ancient German paganism [still found in Spengler, Curtius, and Sieburg] that Charlemagne did not undo, any more than the legions of Varus before him." He suggested that the principal faults and dangers of German thought—and this accusation ran throughout the work of all of the contributors to the newspaper—were abstraction and irrationalism:

> It is a philosophy, an abstract concept of the world that dominates. . . . This possession by a force without reason, or rather beyond reason as it is beyond good and evil, we find it described by philosophers before being embodied by Hitler. These dangerous types of music are for other peoples, and we will never understand them.

Brasillach's insistence on the strange and dangerous nature of the "music" he heard coming from Germany should not be taken lightly or treated as a simple metaphor. Since he considered German thought and German aesthetics irrational, this meant that German nationalist politics (socialist or not)—especially if aesthetics was alleged to be the fundamental truth of politics—also had to be irrational, disordered, and even anarchistic.

The German aestheticizing of politics represented a threat not just to French nationalism but to aesthetic-political order and unity in general. The French had no ear, Brasillach asserted, and would never have an ear for such discordant, unstructured, emotional music. Thus, French nationalist politics could never be modeled after or dominated by German aesthetics or the German form of the aestheticizing of politics. French literary fascism should not in any way then duplicate German National Socialism but should continually insist on its differences with it. Just as in the case of Mallarmé, the "real song" of the French language was threatened when it was confronted with discordant music of this type.

In an article in which he criticized *La Gerbe des forces* of the Germanophile and Hitler fanatic, Alphonse de Chateaubriant, Brasillach claimed that it was "puerile" to give oneself over—with a kind of absolute, religious, one could even say in this context, aestheticist respect—to the charm of forces or forms of authority simply because they are powerful or attractive. "I would be the last to deny that [Hitlerian poetry] has its *charm* in the exact sense of the word. But the distinctive feature of man is precisely to be able to resist charms" (*L'Action Française* [July 8, 1937]). Brasillach admitted that he respected and was attracted to the explicit manifestations of "the origins of authority, the national organization of human labor, the love of youth, and the sense of honor" that he found in Hitler's Germany. At the same time, he emphasized how Germany had to be resisted, not in spite of but *because of* its charms, in order for France not to become in any way its slave, not even a slave to its aesthetic charms. French nationalism meant above all the construction of a French "moral force and national force," and in this context, the creation of a French political "poetry" to rival Hitler's. Brasillach's politics and aesthetics, his literary fascism, were thus anything but slavishly German or Nazi in origin. On the contrary, at least until after the defeat, his political position was overtly anti-German and intent on developing an effective counterforce to German authority and domination. Thus would also mean neutralizing the charm and force of German poetry and aesthetics, for these were in an important sense the basis for both the authority and the charm of National Socialism.

It could be said that Hitlerian poetry and the charm and authority of Germany were easy to resist as long as they were considered to be profoundly *German* and remained confined to German soil and culture. The principal goal of Brasillach's articles on Germany before the war was to ensure that the French did not succumb to the charm of Hitler's "poetry" and try to import it into France in a German form. "When Germany in its turn accomplished its revolution, it gave to the revolution its own personality, which it is not a question of transferring elsewhere," wrote Brasillach. He acknowledged what he called "the sovereign beauty" of Nazi ceremonies, but stressed that they "originate first of all in the consuls of the German land, in old German demons." And if this is not bad enough, he condemned them by associating them with "the lively and barbaric festivities and ceremonies" of Russia ("Introduction à l'esprit fasciste, Part II," *Je suis partout*, no. 397 [July 1, 1938]).

After the defeat and during the Occupation, Brasillach no longer proposed any significant resistance to Germany or to the "alien" nature of Germany's aesthetics. On the contrary, his chief argument was that France could learn much *about itself* by appreciating the beauty of the German aestheticizing of the political. In "De la cité de Goethe au nouvel 'axe' de Berlin," a long article published in *Je suis partout* (no. 507) on November 8, 1941, after he and six other French writers had attended the European Congress of Writers at Weimar as part of the official French delegation, Brasillach claimed to have discovered something more than the "New Germany" during his travels: "It is not only Germany, in fact, that we went to find over there but also our entire age, the unity of our age." In Germany, he now found all of the important elements of the "New European Order," the political and aesthetic unity that was to determine the future of all of the various European nations.

Brasillach also saw in the German manifestations of its own identity the signs of the possible unification of France—the possibility of creating a "New France," one not modeled slavishly after Germany, but a France that had discovered the beauty and power of its own identity and that would thus find its rightful place in the "New Order" of Europe:

> One has the right not to like certain forms of the contemporary aesthetic in Germany—for my part, I admit to being extremely sensitive to the beauty and the power of the national festivities—but one cannot refuse to understand the vitality that it embodies, the continuity with the vitality of the past that it symbolizes. And that, we can make it ours, not by a useless copy or imitation but by a more developed knowledge of who we are.

National identity could thus be realized (fashioned and manifested) if the French learned from the vitality of Germany's aesthetics and made such aesthetics their own. An appreciation of and sensitivity to the German aesthetics of politics, Brasillach argued, would not make the French more German, but more French. Rather than the content and form of the images (fictions) of self, Germany offered the model for an aesthetic *operation*, an aesthetic-political strategy for the self-fashioning of a people, that France could emulate. Only through such an aestheticizing or "fictioning" of politics would France finally be able to form, *on its own*, the images of itself with which its people could identify and by means of which it could have the sense of being at one with itself.[11]

One of the principal goals of Brasillach's articles during the Occupation was the creation of a French national aesthetics of politics. His concept of French fascism, his initial support of Pétain and then his criticism of Pétain for not going far enough, his constant praise of Germany, and his various public acts of collaboration (such as speeches given in support of Germany, trips made to Germany, and articles written for German publications) were all related to this goal. More than anything else, it was the aesthetic *experience* of fascism, the supposedly unmediated sense of community that fascism produced, that interested and attracted Brasillach. This did not make his writings in any way less political; on the contrary, it moved his literary fascism closer and closer to National Socialism and its own aesthetics of politics. The fascist aestheticizing of politics is a profoundly political and totalitarian act in its ends and in the means it proposes to achieve those ends. The means for achieving the ends of the self-formation of a people are in fact already the ends: the process of the "fictioning" of a people *is* the identity of the people.

Politics during the Occupation thus became the quest for a "French form" for the aestheticizing of politics, a search for a nationalist aesthetics that would serve the same function as the German forms Hitler gave to what Brasillach claimed were the "universal truths" that National Socialism embodied ("Devant l'équivoque," *Je suis partout*, no. 570 [July 3, 1942]). He felt that the ceremonies of Nazi Germany had lost their "irrationality," their "foreignness" had become less threatening and "strange," and they now represented nothing less than "the highest artistic creation of [his] time." That is why the chief political question for France was how to translate such creations into the French national idiom, how to give a French form and style to the images and identity of a unified people, one already created in Germany but still to be created in France *in French* terms:

> These [aesthetic] elements are definitely Germanic, but they are beautiful because they are supported by universal ideas, the idea of the fatherland, of fidelity, of youth. One will never make me believe that these ideas are foreign to my country and that it cannot also translate them into images in its own style. For there is no great doctrine, no great exaltation of a people, without these quasi-religious visions. The calamity of democracy is to have deprived the nation of images, images to love, images to respect, images to adore—the Revolution of the twentieth century has given them back to the nation. ("Les Leçons d'un anniversaire," *Je suis partout*, no. 599 [January 29, 1943]).

Brasillach's literary fascism focused on images because the fashioning and the unification of a people were its goal, and there could be no successful unification that did not manifest itself in images, in the fictions of a people that would become synonymous with the people. He believed that democracy had failed to produce images worthy of respect and adoration, and thus had quite simply failed to produce, or "fictionalize," a people.

Literary fascism was thus an art of image-making, for it constituted the transformation of a conflictual diversity of singularities into a unified whole that a people could recognize as itself and identify with. Above all, politics was the aesthetic experience or appreciation of such images, with the people both participating in and observing the process of image-making. Thus the "ideas" of fascism and the aesthetic *operations* that produced the images and ideas were both claimed to be universal. The question of how a nationalist movement could at the same time be representative of universal ideas—that is, how fascism could be a nationalist movement specific to each country and still represent the unique future of all of Europe—was thus resolved by making the style and form of the images of self autonomous, nationalist problems, while attributing universal truth to the ideas at the foundation of all nationalism and conferring universal beauty on the general aesthetic operations necessary to produce such images.

For Brasillach, it could be argued that the aesthetic experience constituted the most profound level of politics. Whether a political movement succeeded or failed, whether the transformations wrought on the body politic lasted or not, was ultimately less significant to him than the *intensity* of the experiences of unity. In fact, like a powerful symphonic or dramatic presentation (theater was always a special interest of Brasillach's), a painting, or a film,[12] the aesthetic experience of the political constituted *an end in itself* and had no necessary duration beyond itself. It could be recalled with nostalgia and reevoked in memory, but basically all truly intense, full aesthetic-political experiences were destined to be "lost" in time. Because of this, Brasillach's discussions of politics and his writings inevitably were a "recherche du temps perdu." His form of literary fascism (and perhaps all forms of French literary fascism) was fatalistic and nostalgic. The most fully realized and most beautiful aesthetic-political experiences were for him always in some sense lost, even as they were being experienced—signs or models of what could be or should have been.

The primary aesthetic experience of fascism was the feeling of unity, the feeling of being at one with one's immediate group and, by projection, with the entire nation: "A youth camp at night, the impression of forming one body with one's entire nation, a totalitarian celebration, these are the elements of fascist poetry" ("Lettre à un soldat de la Classe 60," 142). Such experiences, Brasillach felt, were not only at the very foundation of the production of the "new fascist man," which was the goal of all fascist poetry and politics, but they also produced a feeling of intense joy that was self-fulfilling. This joy was the joy of youth and the outdoors, of participating in collective experiences typical of scouting, armies, sports teams, and youth camps (and even prisoner-of-war camps), the joy of songs and marches. After the joy had ended, what was undeniably left was the memory of *the experience itself* and the joy it had produced.

In *Je suis partout* of July 8, 1938 (no. 398), in the third and last part of his series entitled "Introduction à l'esprit fasciste," Brasillach focused on what he called the "new human type" created by fascism, and he characterized this new type primarily in terms of its experience of joy:

> The outrageousness of the adversaries of fascism is found above all in this total misunderstanding of fascist joy. . . . The young fascist, supported by his race and his nation, proud of his vigorous body and his lucid mind, scornful of the abundant goods of the world, the young fascist in his camp, with his comrades

in peace who can become his comrades in war, the young fascist who sings, who marches, who works, who dreams, he is above all a joyous being. . . . I do not know if, as Mussolini has claimed, "the 20th century will be the century of fascism," but I do know that nothing will keep fascist joy from having existed and from having expanded minds through feeling and reason.

Brasillach's emphasis on the experience of fascist joy, which can never be denied or taken away, no matter the success or failure of fascism as a strictly political movement, was not so much a sign of his political cautiousness in 1938 as a statement about what he found essential in fascism and in politics in general: the intense aesthetic experience of immediacy and of being-at-one with others, and actively acknowledging the immanence, commonness, or identity of the collectivity.

In *Je suis partout* on November 6, 1942 (No. 588), under very different conditions than in 1938, in an article entitled "Pour un fascisme français," Brasillach concluded by quoting his comments on joy from 1938. By the end of 1942, optimism about the formation of a fascist Europe, which for at least two years had been supported by German military victories, was becoming increasingly difficult to sustain, and it was less certain every day, even for committed fascists such as Brasillach, that the twentieth century would be fascist or National Socialist. What Brasillach held onto, in spite of the worsening conditions in Europe for the continued domination of Nazi Germany, and thus for fascism, was something that could not be denied or reversed because it was a strong aesthetic, personal, though at the same time collective, experience. Quite simply, fascism had been lived as an intense aesthetic experience and that was and would always be its value. It mattered less whether the century would in fact be fascist or whether fascism would produce structural changes in France or Europe of any duration than whether fascism could be said to have produced joy, whether it had affected and moved the individuals who participated in its theatrical-political productions, whether individuals had experienced the totalitarian feeling of "being of one body with the entire nation."

An event even produces a more complete, a more powerful, and a purer aesthetic-political experience if it "fails" in its specific political aspirations, if it is not forced to maintain itself, to institutionalize itself, to give itself a less than ideal form—that is, if it remains as much as possible a purely "spiritual" and aesthetic experience. The violent demonstrations and failed coup d'état of February 6, 1934, which resulted in twenty-six deaths and served as the sign for Brasillach and other French fascists of what could have been, are an excellent example of such an experience:

If the sixth of February was a failure as a conspiracy, it was an instinctive and magnificent revolt, a night of sacrifice which remains in our memory with its odor, its cold wind, its pale running figures, its human groups occupying the sidewalks, its unconquerable hope in a national Revolution, the exact date of birth of social nationalism in our country. No matter that, later, every part of this blazing fire, of these deaths who were all pure, was exploited, by the right and the left. One cannot keep what was from having been. (*Notre avant-guerre*, 161).

The purity and intensity Brasillach attributed to the actions taken and the sacrifices made by the victims of the failed coup meant to him that the events of February 6, 1934, represented a collective, tragic experience which could not be prolonged in history as such but which had to be memorialized, and perpetuated as myth: "Every year we go to the Place de la Concorde and place violets in front of this fountain become cenotaph . . . in memory of the twenty-six deaths. Every year the crowd diminishes, because French patriots are forgetful by nature. Revolutionaries alone have understood the sense of myths and ceremonies" (161). The memory of the event in the form of memorialization would ensure that the emotive purity of the events remained intact as a purely spiritual, aesthetic experience.

Maurice Bardèche was not wrong to argue, therefore, even if his reasons for doing so are highly suspect, that Brasillach never admired Germany more than in the moments preceding its defeat: "If Germany was great, it was not during its period of conquest but by the courage it showed in disaster" ("Introduction," *Ecrit à Fresnes*, 33). For at the moment of defeat, National Socialism came closer to the imaginary state of total spirituality of the purely aesthetic experience of politics than at any other moment, precisely because at the moment of its destruction as a sociopolitical phenomenon, it could be considered to have achieved a "tragic destiny" and be retained in consciousness as a pure memory or myth. In "Naissance d'un sentiment" (*Révolution Nationale* [September 4, 1943]), written after leaving *Je suis partout*, Brasillach admitted that he had been grieved by all that the German army had recently suffered, and that "from [being] a collaborationist of reason, [he had] in addition become a collaborationist of the heart." This led him to write in the same newspaper several months later that "he had been having an affair with German genius that [he would] never forget. The French of different persuasions have all more or less been sleeping with the Germans during these last years, not without quarrels, and the memory will remain sweet" ("Lettre à quelques jeunes gens", *Révolution Nationale* [February 19, 1944]). Although Brasillach wrote that he had been "astounded by the destiny of a people who, twice in twenty-five years, saw the entire world join together against it," Brasillach's own "love affair" with the Germans was never more intense than when it was about to end and when he could begin to reexperience it in memory and write about it as a lost plenitude.[13]

Brasillach lyrically stated that "the last days in Paris under the German Occupation were extraordinary. I shall conserve all my life their memory as that of an unreal landscape" ("Journal d'un homme occupé," 47). For him, the approach of the end only added intensity to the experience, regardless or rather because of its unreality: "We went from restaurant to restaurant in a sweet euphoria of catastrophe, saying to ourselves that tomorrow, we would no longer be there" (50). The literary-fascist aestheticization of politics revealed itself in this way to be not just nostalgic but catastrophic and, as we shall see in the case of Drieu la Rochelle, even suicidal, memory being the only place the plenitude of its "spirituality" could be experienced fully. This also meant that the realization of fascism's true spiritual plenitude could come only after its demise, as it was reconstructed and perpetuated in, and as, art and literature.

The nostalgic, catastrophic aspects of Brasillach's literary fascism are especially evident in his accounts of the liberation of Paris, given that the undeniable experience of euphoria of the people of Paris was denied him, not just because he had to hide to avoid being arrested and could not participate in it, but also because their joy was the negation of his own experience of fascist joy:

> Alone, in my room, I experienced a strange emotion. I was now totally cut off from other men. I considered the joy [of those celebrating the liberation] to be naive, tainted with lies. . . . However, this naive people was happy, and this naive people was my own. I did not participate in their joy as I should have. I was not one with them, and I felt strangely dispossessed, heretical, separated. . . . I ought to have been happy, . . . and I remained there, alone and unjustly punished. ("Journal d'un homme occupé," 61).

Obviously feeling sorry for himself because of the "unjust punishment" of solitude, Brasillach, as a nationalist, could not abandon "his people." But he could not participate in their joy or feel at one with them either, for they had abandoned him. Heretic as he was to the religion of the Resistance and the Republic, he could only await his martyrdom to prove by his own death that his heresy was the true nationalist religion and that the people were wrong not to have manifested their unity and joy in fascist aesthetic-political celebrations.

With the defeat of fascism, Brasillach still defended it as a profound experience, for he claimed that "*the* poetry of the twentieth century" had allowed him to participate in the "exaltation of millions of men, . . . the friendship of the youth of all the revived nations." This, he wrote in prison, is what "cannot die," what "little children who, later, when they are twenty-year-old boys, will learn in somber wonderment" ("Lettre à un soldat de la classe 60," 140). This ultimately was also what he would claim was the universality of the fascist aesthetic (and political) experience, its most important claim on the future. He believed that fascism, which he called in *Notre avant-guerre* "ce mal du siècle," always succeeded, because even if it failed as a political movement it succeeded as an aesthetic experience that could always once again affect the youth of the future. He considered fascism a political "fleur du mal" waiting in memory (and in literature and art) to be transplanted, to be nurtured, and to bloom again under the right conditions.

Even if naive, aestheticist, and puerile statements can be found in almost all of his essays describing and defending fascism and National Socialism, this juvenile naïveté is misleading. For at the same time he was capable of the harshest attacks against enemies, especially against Jews, Gaullists, and communists; in fact, against any group that opposed fascism or that was judged to be a threat to his fascist concept (fiction) of the nation. In an article entitled "Pas de pitié pour les assassins de la patrie," which perhaps more than any other article Brasillach wrote was responsible for De Gaulle's refusal to commute his death sentence, he demanded that those who in any way supported the Resistance be considered traitors to their country and given the most severe punishments:

> What are we waiting for to shoot the communist leaders already imprisoned? And these important bourgeois who at night, discretely cut up metro tickets in the form of Gaullist insignia? For there are not just the communists. . . . Against those who want the death of peace and the death of France, *EVERYTHING* is legitimate. . . . No pity for those who want to assassinate the country, whatever they are or whoever they are. (*Je suis partout*, no. 535 [October 25, 1941])

The "boy-scout" and aesthete could at the same time be a vicious polemicist and demagogue. Brasillach's aestheticizing of politics thus revealed its fundamentally violent and vindictive nature, for he considered "everything" legitimate against those who stood in the way of not just the implementation of fascist politics but also the aesthetic experience of fascist joy.

To read Brasillach today is to be struck by the way in which the "high" and the "low" aspects of his aesthetics and politics—the aesthetic ideals and the political violence and vindictiveness—are intertwined. There is no way to separate the two aspects of his writing; nor, I would argue, should one try, either in an attempt to condemn him or in a futile effort to defend him. A sophisticated aesthetic and literary sensibility and a violent, insensitive, and unjust political sensibility are both part of the same mythical and totalizing assemblage of a people, the same process of production and formation of an exclusive national identity that literary fascism attempted to promote and exemplify at the same time. Brasillach's writings help explain why, for many writers and intellectuals of his generation, this mixed and contradictory aesthetics had so much affective and intellectual attraction.

Brasillach's essays also help us understand why fascism must be considered a product of modernity, a fusion of classical and modern aesthetics, rather than an irrational aberration from or a simple reaction against modernity. This means, among other things, that it is not something we dominate or transcend today; it is not something that is simply *of the past*. In a similar vein, Lacoue-Labarthe argues that something essential about the modern conception of the political is revealed in fascism:

> It would be better to learn to stop considering fascism a "pathological" phenomenon (from what extra-social position, asked Freud, would it be possible to make such a diagnosis?) and recognize in it not only (at least) one of the age's possible political forms—and one no more aberrant or inadequate than any other—but the political form, even today, that is best able to enlighten us to the essence of the political in modernity. (*Heidegger, Art and Politics*, 107; translation modified)

What literary fascism especially reveals is the formative role of art and literature in both the conception and the practice of fascist politics, and the profound interconnection of the aesthetic and the political in the totalitarian process of the formation of a national identity.

Even if we could be sure that the specific content of Nazi and fascist racist mythology is truly a thing of the past—and we obviously cannot be—one of the things that still links us directly today to the issues raised by literary fascism is that there is no guarantee, as Lacoue-Labarthe also argues, that this was the "last aestheticization of the political" (86). We cannot be certain that the identificatory techniques of the aestheticizing of politics, and the exclusions, repressions, injustices, and crimes that accompanied them, will not reappear in some form or other in the politics of the future, or that they are not in any way still a part of the politics of the present. If this is even a remote possibility, then a critical approach to fascism would necessitate not just that we condemn fascism as a totalitarian ideology, but that we also attempt to understand its aesthetic and political attractions. We should examine how and for what ends it was formulated by writers and intellectuals such as Brasillach as a totalizing aesthetics of the political—as both an alternative to and the extreme culmination of the aesthetics and politics of modernity.

Five

The Fascist Imagined Community:
The Myths of Europe and Totalitarian Man
in Drieu la Rochelle

Certainly, the figure of Europe, like all
geographical figures, is only a myth.
  Drieu la Rochelle, Journal *(November 23,
  1942)*

I wish for the triumph of totalitarian man over the
world. The time of divided man is past, the time of
reunited man is returning.
  Journal *(June 10, 1944)*

My only connection to the Occident, but it is a
strong one, is the connection of art. The Occident
is artistic and political; it's the same thing.
  Journal *(October 17, 1944)*

Let the ruins of European culture be ruined.
  Journal *(July 27, 1943)*

The Modernist Political Imagination

In dealing with the difficulties involved in defining and understanding the
nature and attraction of nationalism, not just in the history of Europe and
the developed nations, but for the emerging nations of the Third World as
well, Benedict Anderson has claimed that the "cultural artifact" called
"nation or nation-ness" should be treated primarily not as a historically
or geographically defined material reality but as an "imagined community" (*Imagined Communities: Reflections on the Origin and Spread of
Nationalism* [New York: Verso, 1991], 4). This means that what for a
committed nationalist such as Barrès or Maurras is the "natural" product
of specific geographical, historical, linguistic, cultural, or ethnic factors—
a collective sense of self that emerges out of one or a combination of such
factors as an unquestioned irrefutable given—is for Anderson and a number of other contemporary political theorists a construct of the political
imagination, a projection or fiction of community.[1]

Anderson argues that to say that the nation is "an imagined political community" is not to imply that there are more authentic or real communities of other types that the imagined community has replaced or obscured. Rather, all communities are in some sense imagined (fictional constructs) and therefore "are to be distinguished, not by their falsity/genuineness, but by the style in which they are imagined" (6). In fact, as an extreme, uncompromising "style" of imagining the national (or "racial") community, as a style that subordinates all differences and alterity to the organic totality called the nation either by transforming them into functioning parts of the totality or by radically excluding them from it, fascism could be argued to constitute the most extreme, aestheticized form of the imagined community. In the fascist imagined community we see above all the way in which a particular form of imagining, or a logic within the various mechanisms and operations involved in imagining community, when followed to its logical but extreme end, culminates in a totalitarian view of community and the nation. The (political) imagination could even be said to contain within it as a defining characteristic this tendency toward totalizing and totalitarian constructs. Or as Paul Valéry once put it, there is something fundamentally dictatorial in the spiritual faculties themselves, in their need to impose harmony, order, and form on chaos and diversity.[2]

But just as in the notion of the Kantian sublime—where the imagination is conceived not only as both form-producing and embodied in the forms it produces (its aesthetic-formalist and, in a political context, nationalist characteristics), but also as capable of being pushed beyond itself to present the unpresentable, what is beyond form and the aesthetics of the beautiful—so the political imagination of community can also be pushed beyond and outside the confines and form of the nation to project other, less well formed, undetermined "forms" of the communal. If the faculty of the imagination is fundamental to all nationalisms, as Anderson argues, and if the nation is always in some sense a formed or fashioned fiction, then it should not be surprising that for a writer or theorist intent on emphasizing the potentially unlimited powers of the imagination and the restrictive nature of form, the nation would be considered too narrow and restrained, and too monolithic a context for, or product of, the imagination. The notion of a community beyond form would necessitate a less politically or geographically defined—and thus a more fully fictional, "spiritual" imagined—community than the formed nation, and thus also one even more open to the possibilities of unlimited, unfinalized imagined totalization.

Pierre Drieu la Rochelle stands out within the diversified group of French literary fascists treated in this book because he came to fascism from a decidedly extranationalist position. Except for a limited time, and for strategic reasons having to do with his support of Doriot's ultra-nationalist, fascist party, the Parti Populaire Français, he remained a proponent of a fascism that was more European than nationalist in form. In Drieu la Rochelle's work, the myth of Europe could be said to realize its full, contradictory imaginary potential, to be the ideal or absolute fiction of a community beyond all formed, determined communities. The attraction of fascism to him was precisely that of the unbounded force of the creative imagination as it works to destroy and transcend the limitations of both aesthetic and political *form* in order to realize a European spiritual community beyond and of a different type than all national communities, which are determined by the more restrictive and "material" limitations of language, geography, politics, and national culture and tradition.

Drieu la Rochelle's fascism was rooted in a radical critique of all nationalisms, in a refusal to accept the nation as the ultimate origin and end of either politics or aesthetics. To emphasize what he claimed was the *socialist* side of National Socialism (no matter how badly defined and naive his socialism actually was), however, even to the point of replacing it with a term like Fascist Socialism, certainly did not make him less of a fascist. Rather, he constantly attacked the national community and even proposed that the nation be destroyed *in the name of fascism*—as long as "Europe," a less determined, still to be formed, and therefore supposedly more fully spiritual community, would replace the nation and function in its place as a totalizing spiritual model and force.[3]

Drieu la Rochelle did share with the other literary fascists in this book a distrust if not hatred of many aspects of modernity. For he too felt that modernity (and its political expression, democracy) had brought about the devastation of heroic values, of traditional culture and forms of community, and of the geographic and political entity of the nation or homeland (*la patrie*). He considered this to be an undeniable truth, one neither politics nor art could ignore, for it affected the foundations of both. As regrettable as this devastation was, however, he also saw it as the opportunity for the emergence of more radical forms of art and literature and more revolutionary forms of politics. The death of the art and literature determined by the aesthetics of form would make possible the birth of a new, total art, just as the death of the nation would make possible the birth of a new Europe, and the death of "democratic man" would make possible the birth of "totalitarian man."

In his eyes, nothing manifested more dramatically the death of the nation, and all the myths and "gods" traditionally associated with it, than the devastation of World War I. Specifically, he made the return of a soldier from the war *the primal scene* of all of his early political and literary texts. It was a scene of the origin of the general feeling of uneasiness, uncertainty, and radical homelessness that he saw as characteristic of modernity. In numerous poems, essays, and works of fiction, he described the French soldier returning "victoriously" from the war to realize not only that the fields of his homeland had been "trampled" and his homeland destroyed, but also that he no longer belonged to it, that he had nothing to fall back on, his homeland having become a place where his "flesh no longer [held] its own" ("Le Retour du soldat" [May 1920], *Mesure de la France* [Paris: Grasset, 1964], 26). Both spirit and flesh were presented as being irremediably cut off from the land that was supposed to support and nourish them, and the spirit, now homeless, was thus forced to find another home and another "land" and also to take on another form, one not linked to any specific geographical or political site.

The French soldier who for Péguy and Barrès went to war to save the homeland and the spiritual values of France and Western civilization returned from war in Drieu la Rochelle's work only to find that he had saved nothing, that all of the nationalist myths for which he had fought were empty. Everything in fact was reversed, for the nation and people who were in principle victorious had achieved a victory that was "anonymous," not really theirs, a victory "forsaken with shame like a defeat" (29–30). The soldier's country was no longer his, no longer even French; it was a foreign land occupied by foreigners: "The abandoned space was filled with the flesh produced by mothers of other countries. Behind us, in each house, in the place of someone who died or someone who was not born, there was a foreigner. He was alone with the women" (26–27). To return home was to return to a place where "the land and the dead"—and even the unborn—were foreign and where the values of the homeland no longer had any real function. Drieu la Rochelle made of this radical homelessness a process of deracination even more extreme than that depicted by Barrès, and one that in fact could not (and should not) be reversed or overcome, at least not within the narrow geographical and cultural parameters of the nation itself.

In *La Comédie de Charleroi* (Paris: Gallimard, 1934), a collection of short stories depicting his experiences in the war and containing perhaps his best writing, Drieu la Rochelle insists on a theme that recurs constantly in his work: that modern warfare is inhuman and devastating rather than heroic, and that in it there can be no victors. War itself, rather than providing the means for overcoming modernity and reasserting traditional values, manifests the worst aspects of modernity. The "warrior" of the past, standing up for and defending his nation and his people, carrying the values of Western (Christian) civilization on his shoulders— the figure of the soldier that, for example, Péguy constructed and in a sense died for—no longer had any meaning. For the soldier of modern wars spent most of his time flat on his stomach: "War today is to be lying down, sprawled out, flat on one's stomach. Previously, war was men standing up. War today is all the postures of shame" (40). To stand up and fight in a modern war was immediately to die, not as a hero but as one of the millions of anonymous casualties annihilated by modern technology.

In modern war, men never see the enemy that kills them and never meet in the hand-to-hand combat that for Drieu la Rochelle characterized the essence of true war and the true, mythical warrior.

> Men did not rise up in the midst of the war. . . . They did not meet, they did not collide, become entangled or embrace each other. Men were not human, they did not want to be human. They tolerated being inhuman. They did not want to transcend this war and rejoin the eternal war, the human war. . . . They were defeated by this war. And this war which defeated men is bad. This modern war, this war of steel and not of muscles. This war of science and not of art. This war of industry and commerce. . . . This war made by everyone except those who were making it. This war of advanced civilization. No one won this war. . . . I sensed that. I sensed Man dying in me. (71–72)

With the soldier, the ideal itself of Man thus died in the first completely modern, profoundly inhuman war. Science, technology, industry, and commerce had all made it impossible for war to be "human," for its violence and destruction to be transcended and reach the level of the eternal war of "Man," the "war of art," that is, of myth. Drieu la Rochelle's war against war is directed here not against the myth of war but against the reality of war that he discovered was so far removed from the myth, so foreign to it, that the myth of a human war and the notion of Man it supported no longer had any status except to indicate a mythical past from which one was irremediably separated.[4]

In *La Comédie de Charleroi*, as in all of his work from the period before 1934 and his conversion to fascism, Drieu la Rochelle dramatically presents modern war as the sign that the myth of nationalism had ceased functioning positively. And within the general category of nationalism, he includes fascism, which he claims conceives of war as the privileged way of unifying the nation and resolving internal and external conflicts. He thus attacks fascists for misrepresenting war: "War is no longer war. You will see this one day, fascists of all countries, when you have thrown yourselves flat against the ground, with shit in your pants. Then there will be no more plumes, gold medals, spurs, horses, trumpets, or even words, but only an industrial odor that eats out your lungs" (81). But if nationalism and the myths associated with it were already dead, Drieu la Rochelle was clearly searching for alternative myths that would be able to replace those that had died and that would embody once again the warrior values no longer present in war or in the nation. Clearly he did not see fascism at this time as a real alternative, because it was still primarily determined by nationalist myths. He was thus proclaiming the death of fascism soon after its birth, portraying it as old and outdated even before it had reached maturity.

In spite of all the critical comments he made about modern war in his texts, the experience of war for Drieu la Rochelle cannot be considered totally negative. For war also produced exceptional moments of self-realization that continued to serve as models for the actualization of the positive myth of "Man." At very rare moments, in the midst of death and destruction, the soldier, as if drawn out of and beyond himself by a superior force, is able to get up from his prone position and be miraculously transformed. He is no longer an anonymous, isolated, defeated inhuman entity but is now full of force, exalted, fulfilled, pushed to the limits of human experience before being pushed beyond them. At these moments and these moments alone, the soldier becomes truly human and alive, initially not even recognizing that he has acted, but eventually becoming fully conscious of himself and his force:

> All of a sudden, something extraordinary happened. I got up, got up from within the dead, within the larvae. I knew what grace and miracle meant. There is something human in these words. They mean exuberance, exultation, blossoming—before meaning exudation, extravagance, drunkenness. All of a sudden, I knew myself, and I knew my life. This strong man, this free man, this hero, so this was me. So this was my life, this thrust that was never going to stop. . . . Who was this who suddenly burst forth? A leader. Not only a man, a leader. . . . A leader is a man at his fullest; a man who gives and who takes in the same ejaculation. I was a leader. (67–68)

No matter how anonymous, horrible, and degrading war could be, it could also produce an individual who was not a passive victim but a leader, a man free of all constraints and having the most intense experience of the force of life, a unifying force that through the man's actions creates a community of action around him.

The experience of exultation of the hero-leader, no matter how brief in the general experience of war, serves in Drieu la Rochelle's earliest works as the principal characteristic of the ideal human type, even as the reality of war is being denounced. Man at his fullest, man truly realizing his force and spiritual capacities, man knowing himself in action with others, this is the myth of total man that remains a constant in Drieu la Rochelle's work, no matter what his specific political affiliations or his relation to fascism were.

The idea of total man is thus born in the death of the traditional myth of the nationalist warrior in the First World War, just as the idea of Europe as a spiritual community is born in the death of the nation as a political-cultural community. At the end of the war, in the "unique anguish" each country confronted with the realization of its narrowness (*Mesure de la France*, 98), in the absence of any spiritual authority able to resolve or even situate effectively the conflicts, divisions, and decadence of the modern world (104), Drieu la Rochelle saw modern man facing fundamental, profound dangers, which politics alone could not resolve:

> From now on, there is only one total problem. The man who thinks and whose spirit transcends all the distinctions that are no longer alive, perceives only one danger but it is immense, made up of all the evils that can induce decadence in all parts of the human being. Behind all these petty political or social questions which have become obsolete, we can see appear a great questioning of the foundations of everything, of our customs, of our spirit, finally of our civilization. . . . It is here that [one of the countries] must stand up and pronounce the words that will resolve the enigma of the "modern" and assure common salvation. (97–98)

Drieu la Rochelle is here clearly calling on France—and if not France, then some other country (Italy, Germany?)—to take on the role of the hero and leader, as the soldier did in *La Comédie de Charleroi*, and ensure its own salvation by transcending itself as a nation, and by its actions overcome the isolation of all nations by creating a European spiritual community. He is demanding a change more profound than either a political revolution or restoration: what he called another Renaissance (115), the rebirth of Western man in modernity. For only such "total, spiritual solutions" could possibly overcome the death of man and the total devastation of the present.

The Ideal of Total Art

Drieu la Rochelle looked to literature and art rather than politics for models for such total solutions. He was especially attracted to theories and practices that he considered autonomous and, as he said, that had not lost "the sense of the absolute"; that is, that did not follow or were not determined or limited by any particular political ideology or aesthetic theory. The most profound and authentic spiritual model was necessarily the least practical, least directly political model. In his three letters to the Surrealists, the first published in 1925, the second two in 1927 (collected in *Sur les écrivains* [Paris: Gallimard, 1982]), Drieu la Rochelle revealed both what had originally attracted him to the revolutionary literary movement of surrealism and what had also eventually led him to denounce it. What he admired most was the Surrealists' unwillingness to compromise with outdated literary doctrines, nationalist sentiments, or political determinations. What he attacks in these letters is their choice of a political position, communism, and also of a defined aesthetic strategy: "Now you double your *art poétique* with the support of a political line according to a procedure periodically used by literary hacks in France" (47). Drieu la Rochelle argues that art should remain autonomous, free of all formalist and political determinations, in order to realize itself fully. Politics should follow art in order to fulfill itself spiritually, not the reverse. The only thing as bad for the writer as serving a political cause was following an *art poétique*.

The only hope Drieu la Rochelle saw in the Surrealists' political affirmations had to do with a statement they made that directly contradicted their adherence to communism: "For us, salvation is nowhere." He held that the sense of the absolute in literature could only come from the recognition that there was no salvation, that no "little literary doctrine" and no little or big political doctrine could do more than exacerbate the decadence of the contemporary situation by accepting passively one of its determining aesthetic theories or ideologies and thus adding to its divisiveness. On the contrary, Drieu la Rochelle demanded that the writer plunge into the empty decadence of modernity and assume it fully, for only in the rejection of all "little" or partial solutions, only through a negative metaphysics or aesthetics, could an absolute, total spiritual solution be envisaged. Only if salvation is nowhere can salvation be found outside all the places politics and aesthetics had previously located it: neither in art nor in politics as distinct entities or fields but in their fusion in a total Art. For it is only in such an Art, and not in life, he claims, that one truly lives: "The arts, Art in general, exist so that man can live, so that he can realize life. . . . Art for me is the most forceful way to live" (56–57). Art is a higher form of life, one in which force is not limited by restrictive forms but is potentially infinite, creative of form rather than dependent on it.

The attraction of surrealism had to do solely with the destructive forces it produced, for it was only out of an initial destruction of all political and aesthetic limits that affirmative forces had the possibility of emerging: "Your way is the denunciation of literature, of art, because of the need you see to recharge literature, art, with their full moral and human sense. . . . I have always thought . . . that you were opening the way for future affirmations. And I put a lot of hope in that pending fecundity" (78). The Surrealists, in a sense, were not surrealist enough, however, for he argued that they settled for much too little in both the aesthetic and political realms.

In a text from the same period, *Le Jeune Européen* (1927), in *Le Jeune Européen suivi de Genève ou Moscou* (Paris: Gallimard, 1978), Drieu la Rochelle claimed to be looking for alternatives to what he called the sterile collectivization offered not only by communism and fascism, two political movements that he saw as following the "same atrocious ideal" (98), but by surrealism as well. Fascists, communists, and Surrealists were all considered to be "impotent" in terms of the fundamental threat posed by modernity: "Narrow fascisms, babbling communisms, hysterical surrealisms, . . . you are the feeble harbingers of a terrible weakness" (99). The Surrealists' choice of a political commitment to communism simply reflected their literary commitment to questionable aesthetic practices and theories, especially "automatic writing," which were already indications of their willingness to compromise with the politics and aesthetics of modernity.[5]

If he saw the Surrealists as being mistaken in their choice of communism, Drieu la Rochelle at this time did not see fascism as an alternative. As he argued in *Genève ou Moscou* (1928), where fascism came up short was in the way it remained rooted in and limited by its own nationalist foundations. In rejecting fascism for democratic socialism, Drieu la Rochelle was assuming that democracy could overcome its own nationalist foundations, and that it would accept what he called the "nomadism of money and of the spirit from which no one can escape" (154) and resist the temptation to try to recreate the mythical grandeur and integrity of the nation before nomadism.

Drieu la Rochelle repeatedly claimed, against all forms of nationalism, that "there is no fatality" in the relation between man and place, no rational necessity for what emerged out of such a relation. What occurred at the origin of nations was rather the result of a "fortunate encounter" (157) that should be celebrated inasmuch as it initially produced powerful creative forces. These forces were not a defining characteristic of a people, but rather indications of the energy of the act of creation itself, the unrestricted, boundless interaction of spirit with matter and place. Unlike Barrès, who made of the instinctual origins of a people in the land the destiny or fatality of the individual; or even Péguy, who made the "silent" relation of the people with the land the origin and end of all spirituality; Drieu la Rochelle argued that the chance encounter with the original homeland represented a stage to be overcome. All nationalisms that made of the homeland an end rather than a beginning were restricting the very energies and creativity the homeland had originally produced. Only a spiritual *patrie* beyond the national homeland could once again be the site of such original creativity and force.

He believed that as long as a homeland was not yet determined as a nation and its boundaries and identity remained fluid, as long as its force was unrestricted by identifiable cultural norms, it would remain a purely spiritual, creative force. "The homeland breathes fully in the men's souls and they do not know it yet. They do not name it, or if they do, its name designates a growing, receptive reality. It calls to everything, nothing is excluded" (159). The force of this unnamed, unmeasured, and unmeasurable homeland was the force of the unformed as well, the moment before form when force reigns and forms have not yet achieved finality. It was the moment before art and politics, therefore, the "Dionysian" moment of pure explosive and chaotic invention. All true art and all true politics, for Drieu la Rochelle, have their ultimate origin and end in this moment before the institution of the nation and before the determination of aesthetic form. Drieu la Rochelle was thus an antinationalist for the same reasons that he was an antiformalist, for nationalism and formalism were for him two sides of the same coin—each in its own way restricting and repressing; that is, *forgetting* the creative force of the origin. He believed that all great art and all great politics should recall, open onto, and renew this original, disruptive force of the origin before the actual formation and determination of the nation and the work of art.

The only positive act a homeland (and the nation) could perform, in fact, was to die—that is, become mythical—in order to retain the "magic" and spiritual force of its birth and infancy, and this is what Drieu la Rochelle wished for France: "I dream of a France that will soon be in heaven: its essential lesson can no longer be to teach me to be French but more than ever to be a man" (163). France must die as a political entity, as a nation, in order for it to achieve its true spiritual place. The only good nation is thus a dead, spiritual homeland. Europe represents the death of nations, their entry into a higher form of spirituality, a more fully imaginative imagined community. Nationalism, even in its fascist form, had no future, for not only was it an ideology from the previous century, but it was, like Marxism, based on antispiritualist premises, even when it claimed to be defending spiritual values.[6]

In *Genève ou Moscou*, Drieu la Rochelle's polemic against nationalism also leads him to raise the question of race. Given the anti-Semitism of his later works, it is interesting to see that in this work he links racism to nationalism and criticizes it on exactly the same grounds. Racists, he argues, "if they think they escape from the overwhelming belief in the determinism of place, are deluding themselves. What they take away from place, they transfer to blood. They accomplish only a futile displacement within the limitations of the same determinism" (166). In fact, he even claims that racism is not just *a* form, but *the most restrictive* form, of the determinism characteristic of all nationalisms: "Formidable doctrine, that of race, which is in appearance more supple than that of homeland but which excludes all hope even better than it" (167). In *Genève ou Moscou*, Drieu la Rochelle argues that racism is nothing less than the most serious obstacle to the realization of the spiritual entity called Europe.

As this work calls for the end of nationalism, it foresees and demands the end of race and racisms as determining spiritual and political factors as well. Drieu la Rochelle argues that all peoples, no matter how separate they might seem to be, would eventually lose their integrity and be fused together, and the proof he gives of this is the case of the Jews: "The Jewish race is going to founder with all the other races and all of the concerns of the nineteenth century. . . . Homelands are only encounters in the immense adventure of the spirit. Freedom opens up before us" (168). The fusion of all races and peoples is thus the very sign of the freedom of the spirit, for no people or race can resist the inevitable mixing and exchange of places. Freedom is what always opens up outside of the restrictions of place and race, and the spirit dies when it is confined to either. The nomadism of the spirit is thus its greatest strength.

In *L'Europe contre les patries* (Paris: Gallimard, 1931), Drieu la Rochelle even argues that racial purity never existed: "Celts, Germans [*Germains*], these are words to designate almost identical groups in which for already thousands of years primitive races were mixed together. Races, they already did not exist in those days, which is all the more reason for this to be true today" (61). To base any theory on the singularity of a people or the purity of a race is thus to project a regressive myth of the origin that restricts rather than fosters the freedom of the spirit. The new Europe could be made only if what he calls the "old doctrines" of nationalism and racism were first defeated, for it could be built only on their ruins.[7]

Drieu la Rochelle provocatively asserts that "France [and by extension, all other nations] should be allowed to die. Stop covering it with flowers" (29). And addressing Germans he proclaims, "I don't care about France; if you still care about Germany, too bad for you" (24). He goes on to warn Germany, however, that any project to dominate Europe, to unify it by force under the control of one nation, would be doomed to fail:

> You will never have hegemony over Europe. No one was ever able to have it. . . . Europe is made up of courageous peoples. Every attempt at hegemony, the day it is declared, immediately provokes a coalition. And if the impossible occurs, if you were to conquer, your victory would immediately provoke a terrible recurrence of all the various nationalisms. One cannot kill nationalism through the triumph of one of them. (15–16)

For a future collaborator, statements both about the death and rebirth of France and the warnings to Germany are highly significant. Even if the warnings would seemingly make it difficult to support German hegemony in Europe, the desire for the death of France certainly offered a justification for collaboration long before the fact, a justification that had nothing to do with the presence of Nazi troops in France, with National-Socialist ideology, or with fascist politics as such, but rather with the inevitable course of history, which was allegedly in the process of eliminating a used-up political remnant of another era, the nation-state. He could even rejoice in the defeat of France, because it was seen as the deathblow to the "old civilization" and the myths associated with the traditional notion of a national homeland.

The Fascist Imagination and the Myth of Europe

What changed with Drieu la Rochelle's explicit commitment to fascism? At first, that is, in 1934, when he declared himself to be a fascist, nothing essential in terms of his model of the imagined spiritual community and his overall project for the creation of a unified Europe. Nothing, or very little, in terms of his critique of nationalism and by extension his critique of racism. Very little, surprisingly enough, in terms of his attitude toward Italian fascism and German National Socialism. But everything changed in terms of the specific political *means* to be used to create the new Europe, and thus in terms of his own relation to a French form of fascism that would supposedly differ in important ways from both its Italian and German counterparts by being less nationalist and more "socialist." Fascism, first of all, provided him with the schema of a historical process in which the movement toward European unity was seen as a natural necessity, the next step after the full realization and then death of all nations.

"Unité française et unité allemande" (in *Socialisme fasciste*) illustrates this dialectical logic by constructing a Socratic dialogue of sorts between a professor and a student, with the student—who in a curious, ironic reversal of roles occupies the position of Socrates—serving as the spokesperson for Drieu la Rochelle's own views concerning the limitations of all forms of nationalism and the possible basis for the destruction of nationalism and the unification of Europe. The student succeeds eventually in convincing the professor that there is no real natural or biological basis for the delineation of the boundaries of a nation, and that a nationalism based on "blood and language" (Germany) is no better and no worse than one based on "natural" geographical boundaries (France). Both are ultimately justifications for the fact that every state needs limits for its own nationalist political reasons, and that these limits are always fabricated and arbitrarily and often violently imposed, consisting of restrictive imagined constructs rather than natural or historical realities.[8]

The student's point is twofold: on the one hand, he argues that the French, and any other people, if they recognize the arbitrary nature of their own borders and the imaginary characteristics of their national myths, can feel no superiority over other peoples and other forms of nationalisms. And on the other hand, he asserts that were they to accept the principle of the arbitrary nature of all national boundaries and myths, they would see that they had nothing to fear from a Germany that was simply trying to establish itself as a nation and accomplish what France and other modern nations had already accomplished. "The Germans are in the process of accomplishing their national unity. . . . The Germans are late, because they are in the middle of Europe, enclosed on all sides, and thus for them it is more difficult, but it is the same principle, the reason of State. An irrational reason" (198). No nationalist principle, therefore, could be considered a solid base on which to found a total, that is, European politics; none constituted an end with which to orient a true fascist socialism; none was sufficiently imaginative. And what nationalisms lacked in imagination, they always made up for with violence. But arguments such as these are now no longer being marshaled against fascism but are rather being presented from a perspective that views it sympathetically. In its "foreign" or nationalist forms, fascism is seen as a necessary stage in the fulfillment and then disappearance of the nation. In its "French" or European form, fascism is presented as the stage *after* nationalism.

This text indicates that Drieu la Rochelle was in principle willing, or at least he found it amusing to imagine and assert that he was willing, to pay almost any price so that European unification could be accomplished. If "linguistic imperialism is the limit of Germany, the Alps of Germany," then Germany should be allowed, should even be encouraged to establish its borders in this fashion, for the *Anschluss* itself could be considered a positive step in the direction of not only German but also European unification: "I am for the *Anschluss* and, if need be, for the suppression of Belgium and Switzerland. After that, we will see more clearly in Europe. . . . And Europe will not be far from being made" (197). If Drieu la Rochelle could make such a statement in October 1933, the original publication date of this essay, it means that in a sense he had already made his decision to collaborate. For to him, any force that suppressed borders, no matter the costs to the people caught in the *Anschluss*, was a positive force, because it was helping to realize the general project of a unified Europe: "All means are good; I can just as well make use of the means that the Hitlerian revolution offers me as any other means to proceed toward the suppression of borders in Europe" (199). The myth of Europe had now taken on its most radical and terrifying implications, for it meant that potentially everything was possible. European federation was anything but a modest proposal.[9]

In "Mesure de l'Allemagne," written in March 1934 after a trip to Germany, Drieu la Rochelle claimed that what disturbed him most about

Nazi Germany was not the extremism of its political project, or the dangers it posed for surrounding countries, but rather the moderate, aestheticist, formal character of its entire enterprise:

> What I saw in Berlin penetrated me with a kind of terror and despair. I saw confident and brave youth but committed to very feeble goals. . . . At bottom, they are heading toward a spiritual, aesthetic conception of society. Everyone must work to make Germany a harmonious totality, a closed limited whole which satisfies itself, which revels in itself. Everyone lives only to take pleasure in the whole. It's certainly a civilization that can develop under the sign of cinema. It's a static ideal. Listening to the Germans speak of their dynamism doubles me up with laughter; no, it rather makes me smile bitterly. . . . In reality, Germany is in the process of becoming completely static, it is in the process of finding its stasis in finding its national foundation. (*Socialisme fasciste*, 210–12)

These comments, as reassuring as they tried to be concerning the potential threat to France posed by Nazi Germany, indicate clearly that Drieu la Rochelle saw his own version of fascism, and his own spiritual conception of society, to be much more radical, dynamic, and uncompromising than the Nazi version and the "feeble goals" it established for its youth.

To focus too intently on the whole is to sacrifice the dynamism of the parts for the whole, to sacrifice the productive conflict of forces for formal, "aesthetic" national integrity. It produces an integral but static civilization, and Drieu la Rochelle even claimed that it produced a formal, aestheticized totality, a surface aesthetics of the image under the sign of the cinema, rather than the dynamic "total" aesthetics of force he associated with literature in his critique of surrealism and nationalism. Unlike Brasillach, film was not for Drieu la Rochelle a positive metaphor for politics, or a model for the experience of immediacy, or for the dynamic fusion of the individual and the group. More "conservative" than Brasillach (and Rebatet) in his misgivings about the technology or "art" of cinema, he was at the same time less classical and more "radical" in his literary and political aspirations and tastes.

Along with his declaration of fascism in the various essays collected in *Socialisme fasciste*, Drieu la Rochelle began to soften his critique of radical forms of French nationalism and to make anti-Semitism and racism important components of his vision of Europe. To think like a European would soon mean for him to think like a racist and an anti-Semite, and even like a nationalist. It would mean that anti-Semitism and racism for Drieu la Rochelle could be separated from the fatalism he attributed to nationalism and could be considered dynamic rather than static aesthetic-political principles—and that a certain nationalism with socialist, European ends could be as well. If all means were good, then even nationalism, racism, and anti-Semitism could be used as important strategic weapons for achieving the European ends to which he was committed, as long as they could now be made to serve those ends rather than constitute narrow and conflicting ends in themselves.

In principle, he was still against race as the foundation or determining idea of his ideal imagined community, whether it was the French nation or a unified fascist Europe; so much so, in fact, that he made racism a sign of Jewishness and the foreign. The determination of race by "blood" was pertinent only when it concerned Jews: "There is a *biological, anthropological fatality* which broadly differentiates Jews from Europeans" ("A propos du racisme" [July 29, 1938], in *Chronique politique* 1934–1942 [Paris: Gallimard, 1943], 156), but no such fatality supposedly existed when it came to "true Europeans," whose strength resulted from intermarriage among various European groups and from the overcoming of narrow racial, regional, or national determinism. Drieu la Rochelle implied that his principal goal was to keep the "fatality of race" that he associated with the Jews outside of the European and French spiritual communities—which of course was to found those communities in racism.

Another important change in the way in which he imagined community and the political strategies he derived from it was related to the continued success of National Socialism in Germany, and the lack of any signs that Germany was "exhausting itself" in its nationalist efforts toward reunification. The increasing political and military power of Nazi Germany was, for Drieu la Rochelle, as it was for the overwhelming majority of French fascists, at the same time a sign of the success of fascism and a threat to France, the proof that France had to go through its own fascist revolution not in sterile imitation of Germany or in order to become its ally but in order to limit the hegemony of Germany and defend itself against possible German aggression. The alternative was presented once again, as the title of another essay indicates, as being the choice between life or death: "Mourir en démocrates ou survivre en fascistes" (October 28, 1938), and the chief justification for France becoming fascist was, paradoxically, that fascism constituted "the only method capable of blocking and diverting the expansion of fascist countries" (*Chronique politique*, 193). The best reason for becoming fascist was to divert fascism from a narrowly nationalist course and make it more socialist and more European; that is, less German and in this way *more fascist*.

Aesthetic Ideals and Collaborationist Politics

With the defeat of France by Nazi Germany in 1940, the reasons for defending a specifically French form of fascism disappeared. The nationalism that was evident in Drieu la Rochelle's essays for Doriot's Parti

Populaire Français thus faded into the background, and fascist Europe reemerged as the most complete form of the imagined community, but now also as a justification or pretext for collaboration with the Germans. Drieu la Rochelle was certainly not unique among literary fascists in the way he associated the birth of a new fascist order in Europe with the birth of a "new man," a man who was at the same time warrior, athlete, artist, and thinker, a *total man*. He, like other collaborators and fascists, presented the victories of the German army in the early years of the war (and even the conquest of France) as the accomplishment of this European spiritual project. All means were good if they could be said to lead to this end.

The details of his argument for the reunification of Europe under Nazi Germany were more complicated, however, than the general picture just presented. One of the principal questions that Drieu la Rochelle felt needed to be answered, since German domination was for him and other collaborators an undeniable and unchangeable *reality*, was what place France would have in a unified, German-dominated, fascist Europe. Another question had to be answered first, before the place of France in the new Europe could be determined. It was, What is France, or rather, Who or what are the French?

To answer such questions, Drieu la Rochelle always argued that France was not an isolated, singular entity and that the French did not have just one identity or one cultural, geographic, and ethnic background. Rather, they had at least three: Nordic-French, Central-French, and Mediterranean-French. He claimed in "Nouvelle Mesure de la France," for example, that there existed "the properly Frank, Nordic, Germanic France," where at the time of Caesar "Germanic laws and customs ruled." Even though he argued that the contributions of this northern and eastern area had been slighted in the history of France and needed to be recognized, the danger existed that after the Armistice Germany would "extend its racist demands here" and make only it and not the rest of France part of a "Europe reunited around a Germanic core" (*Chronique politique*, 238–39). In order to prevent this, France had to recognize that Nordic influences were an important part of its identity and that French literature and art were in great part Nordic. In affirming the fundamental French nature of "Germanic," Celtic France, France would acknowledge its profound links with Germany and at the same time its own originality.

Second, Drieu la Rochelle felt that the influence of southern France, had been inflated, especially in the arts. In this way he continued a polemic with Maurras, who he claims had "systematically stifled the importance of the Nordic element" (242). Drieu la Rochelle went so far as to claim that if poetic form could be considered to have been developed in the south of France, the essence of French poetry, its lyrical *force*, had from the start not been Mediterranean but Nordic:

> To deny the Nordic inspiration, as it shines forth through romanesque language and form, would be absurd. . . . The necessity of a Nordic influence in French poetry is unquestionably illustrated by the fact that lyrical force declined in French literature as overly direct Italian or Latin influences became more pronounced. . . . The current of true lyricism . . . begins again only with the poets freed of the influences of the South and who feel the lyricism of the Seine come back to life in them with the contact with Nordic literatures. (241)

In the name of the importance of the Nordic, Germanic component of France, Drieu la Rochelle argued against German racial hegemony and for an idea of France as a mixture or fusion of the various ethnic and regional elements, a play of forces, a balance of force and form, which constituted the true genius and originality of France—as opposed to Germany.

The key to who the French were was "the France of the Seine and Loire," the area where "the profound and original mixture of the Mediterranean contributions and the Nordic contributions was produced" (239). Nothing less than "French genius as it is known emerged from this mixture," he argued, but with its emergence, there was also "the progressive forgetting of the Nordic element and the more and more boisterous recognition of the Mediterranean influences" (240). French genius, therefore, was precisely in the process of losing its greatness and its "Frenchness" by emphasizing one of its components at the expense of the other.

Such an argument was nothing less than a defense of Germany's role in righting the precarious balance that constituted the "genius" of France. "In a Europe largely re-Germanized, the genius of the Seine and Loire can survive and come back alive only in taking full consciousness of the equality of the three elements, that is, in restoring its value to the Germanic, Frank element that had been for too long underestimated, forgotten, and bullied" (240). By conquering France, Germany had given France the possibility of becoming itself once again, of becoming the mixture of the Nordic and Mediterranean that was also the model mixture for the construction of the new Europe. "Re-Germanized Europe" would be a Europe in which German racial laws would not govern and which would consist not of "one *Volk*" (people) but which would be a fusion of different peoples; a "re-Germanized" France was to be a France not dominated by either Nordic or Mediterannean forces but one in which Germanic elements and Mediterranean elements fused with each other and existed in equilibrium. Drieu la Rochelle's Europeanist strategy of collaboration was certainly evident in such a position: praise, cooperate with, and give due respect to the greatness of Germany and the Germanic components of France, but in the name of a France that "must come alive again in a new Europe" (246), and not in the name of the purity of the German people or the French people per se.

Drieu la Rochelle made another argument in this text to justify his collaboration with the Germans. It was a realist argument based on the historical necessity of revolution: "Germany, in the present century, is one of the incarnations of the revolution just as France incarnated it in an other century. . . . This revolution that Germany proposes to some and imposes on others is necessary for all, just like the French Revolution. The people who fought or who are fighting against Germany need this spiritual reform and this social reform that it represents no less than Germany" (248). With no less conviction than Hegel arguing for the historical necessity of the French Revolution, and of Napoleon who carried it across Europe on the backs of his army, Drieu la Rochelle attributed to the German army and to Hitler the same historical mission: "All this is in the armed mission of Germany. . . . Germany incarnates the necessity of the century" (249). To be against Nazi Germany was then to be against historical necessity itself; to fight against Germany was to fight against the very rebirth that all people needed to undergo in order to become active participants in the new Europe. To be against Nazi Germany was to be against Europe and even against oneself.

The tragedy of the situation in which France found itself, then, consisted not in the defeat itself, but in the fact that the leaders of France did not prevent the war by "making the nation the immediate collaborator of this destiny, rather than making the nation its victim" (251). German hegemony and the National-Socialist revolution it proposed for all of Europe were thus treated as historical inevitabilities—as the destiny of Europe that fascists like Drieu la Rochelle claimed they were able to foresee but which the leaders of France could not or would not admit. Because he argued collaboration with Germany should have started before the defeat, to collaborate after the defeat was simply to try to correct a serious political error and to make up for lost time. He claimed that collaboration should be done out of a sense of history and out of strength, not out of weakness and submission to an enemy.[10]

Apocalyptic Fictions

By the end of 1942, the optimism associated with the feeling that he was on the side of history gave way to the pessimism and despair of seeing that version of history thwarted and fascism in Europe beginning to be countered and then destroyed. The images that began to dominate Drieu la Rochelle's writing at this time, rather than of a victorious, unified, rejuvenated Europe, were not surprisingly those of failure, civil war, and vengeance—of a final destruction and a last judgment from which no one would escape. The titles of three essays included in *Le Français d'Europe*, but originally written for *Révolution Nationale*, after Drieu la Rochelle had given up the directorship of *La Nouvelle Revue Française* and with it many of his illusions about the inevitability of a fascist Europe, indicate clearly how a feeling of increasing doom pervaded his writing at this time: "Prose morose" (July 10, 1943), "Fatalité française" (July 31, 1943), and "Toujours amer" (September 25, 1943). He seemed to be feeling as much morose pleasure in the impending failure of fascism as he had felt overwhelming joy in its apparent success in the first years of the war.

In his journal, he went even further than in his articles in assigning blame, claiming that "Germans aren't much more fascist than the French" (*Journal*, [March 15, 1943], 338), and that "[he had] been dead since 1943, when [he] had fully recognized the insufficiency of the Germans, the proof of the exhaustion of Europe" ([March 18, 1944], 373). As was the case before the war, insufficiency rather than the plenitude of force had once again become the dominant theme of his writings, but it now directly concerned the insufficiency of fascism and the fascists' responsibility for the failure to construct a fascist Europe and for the destruction of totalitarian man. In another essay from *Le Français d'Europe*, "Entre l'hiver et le printemps" (April 1942), Drieu la Rochelle assumed for himself the only function seemingly left to the committed French fascist writer and collaborator. It was to become the prophet not of the historical necessity of fascism but of its pending demise, not of the birth of a new European man but of the death of the fascist, totalitarian man.[11]

Drieu la Rochelle's model writer was now no longer the revolutionary writer who fused together life and art in a total work but the writer as the prophet of doom and destruction, best exemplified by the biblical prophets. He not only quoted extensively from Isaiah in his essay, "Entre l'hiver et le printemps," but he also situated himself in the place of the prophet predicting the downfall of his own land. He referred to Isaiah in especially glowing terms, calling him a man "who loves and knows force, who sees where it is and where it is not"; these were characteristics, of course, that he constantly attributed to himself. In fact he described all the prophets as the only exceptions to be found within an otherwise decadent people:

> These prophets, these are men who have the sense of force among an introverted and weakened people. They are only priests and poets who lament, who insult, who make literature of the defeat of their country, because they know they will not be heard; they do not even want to be heard because they know

it is too late and that the time of empires has come. . . . They bury their country and the idea of a local country under a heap of imprecations and execrations. . . . A strange and sorrowful man, the prophet, always hounded in the present and joining together in his detestable words the past and the future, which are, each one, a mockery for his country, occupied, invaded, trampled on by History. (132)

The prophet thus represented the ultimate model of the poet who was considered a traitor to his country, because as a prophet of doom he was never listened to, even though or because he spoke the truth. The writer who wished for the death of his nation and projected the imagined community of Europe as his spiritual homeland had thus become once again the poet isolated from his land and its people, but now without even an imagined spiritual community for which to write. He had become the isolated and scorned poet of the Apocalypse, the only authentic figure of courage and the last remaining witness to the beauty not of birth and poetic force but of destruction and death.[12]

In his journal, Drieu la Rochelle presented the last months of the war and the Occupation as the negation of everything; nothing had value for him anymore except destruction. He gave a litany of dead or dying ideals in which he had once believed or at least which he had once imagined he could pursue and achieve. Love, politics, and literature had all become things of the past for him. He wondered how he could have wasted so much time on the first two, given that the ideals or myths he had pursued had always been infinitely removed from the reality he had lived. And yet he admitted that when his faculty of imagination had failed him or had been rendered inoperable by the pressure of external events—that is, when he could no longer imagine "the body of a beautiful woman" or "an ideal political state" (*Journal*, [October 18, 1944], 425)—then literature also had died for him because it no longer had any spiritual force. He asserted that "the time of literature and art is close [*sic*]," and that he did not "believe in literature and [he thinks] the time of literature is gone" ([December 31, 1944], 438; [January 27, 1945], 446—in English in the original). In his mind, the death of both fascism and the myth of Europe had induced the death of art and literature as well, for the ideal of literature as a total work, a myth of literature homologous to and supportive of the fascist myth of the "New Europe," did not survive the death of the community imagined or modeled after it.[13]

"The total man" he always wanted to be ([February, 3, 1945], 447) also died with the myth of Europe, but because he believed that myths in totalitarian schema do not die without being replaced by other myths, death itself replaced birth as an absolute, as the last myth, the myth of all myths: "Oh death, I do not forget you. Oh life truer than life. Oh unsayable thing that is beyond life and truer than life. Not beyond but within. It's the core of my being I want to attain" ([October 23, 1944], 426). It could be argued, then, that Drieu la Rochelle never really gave up his fascist totalitarian project, even in his journal when he announced its aesthetic and political deaths—the death of Europe, of fascist man, of art, and finally his own death. Rather, he characterized his literary fascism openly in terms of the apocalyptic project it had always contained within itself, not just because of his own "suicidal" tendencies but rather because the totalitarian aesthetic-political project for both the self and the community was itself destructive and suicidal, bringing the threat of extinction of everything if the ideal of totalitarian man could not be realized.[14]

In his peroration in the last section of "Exorde," a text included in *Récit Secret*, Drieu la Rochelle made his final political statement. In the name of the transcendent ideal of Europe, he demanded to be judged and found guilty by the Resistance, for he acknowledged proudly that he (like Judas) was a traitor; and he asserted boldly that in being condemned he would still escape the judgment of those condemning him:

> I put myself at your mercy, completely sure of escaping you, the moment past, in time. . . . Be faithful to the pride of the Resistance as I am faithful to the pride of Collaboration. Don't cheat any more than I cheat. Condemn me to death. . . . Yes, I am a traitor. Yes, I had secret dealings with the enemy [*J'ai été d'intelligence avec l'ennemi*]. I brought French secrets [*l'intelligence française*] to the enemy. It wasn't my fault if this enemy was not intelligent. I am not an ordinary patriot, a fervent nationalist: I am an internationalist. I am not a Frenchman, I am a European. You are one too, either knowingly or unknowingly. But we have played our cards, and I've lost. I demand death. (99)

Not only was the position of traitor to all forms of politics the only position that did not betray the ideals of the European spiritual community that were still being evoked, but martyrdom was the only way left for him to realize these ideals, to escape from the punishment to be imposed on him, and to transcend all politics. The desire for a death as the traitor who saw himself really as the true European or internationalist, rather than nationalist patriot, was the last scene in this totalitarian scenario, the last possible attempt to perform a transcendent aesthetic-political act.

In the work of Drieu la Rochelle, the ideal of total art and the myth of the unformed spiritual community it supported come before and model, if not determine, his political involvement with fascism. This does not make him less of a fascist or mitigate his political responsibilities; if anything, it makes him, as he wrote in his journal near the end of the war, more of a fascist than the most militant political fascists, more of a Nazi than the Nazis, ultimately even more faithful to Hitlerism than Hitler himself: "I condemn not only the Germans of Paris, cowardly and deceitful liberals, who had always cheated and betrayed those of us who believed in the Hitlerian European revolution, but Hitlerism itself, fascism, organically incapable of engendering that revolution" (*Journal* [July 29, 1944], 410–11). Fascism, even in its most racist and totalitarian form, thus proved itself *organically* incapable of giving birth to the total spiritual revolution that Drieu la Rochelle had posited as its fundamental project.

All that was left for the writer who would have liked to have been "great" and to have produced a true, organic work of art but had failed to do so, who would have liked to have acted as a warrior for the fascist cause but was too weak to do so, was to bring about by a final, solitary act the mythical fusion that had been accomplished in neither literature nor politics: "I have always regretted that man is never complete and that the artist cannot be a man of action. . . . I consider it therefore good fortune to be able to mix my blood with my writing and to make the function of writing serious to all points of view" ("Last Letter to His Brother" [August 10, 1944], *Journal*, 505). In taking his own life, the failed writer and political activist would succeed and ensure that his writing, no matter how flawed, decadent, and insufficient, would be taken seriously as an authentic force.

This particular attempt at death failed, but a later attempt at suicide (March 15, 1945) succeeded, thus guaranteeing Drieu la Rochelle the place he has held in the minds of many ever since: the place of the mythical, heroic, tragic, and thus authentic French fascist. Drieu la Rochelle is the fascist writer many militant antifascists are the most willing to excuse, because he supposedly refused to compromise his principles and took his own life at the end. His is the place of *the suicidal writer*, the significance of whose politics can eventually be overlooked or at least minimized, not just because the essence of his activities was *literary* but, more important, because he was willing to pay the price for his political illusions and acts by killing himself.[15]

Drieu la Rochelle accomplished by his suicide what he had failed to do in his life or his writing. In death he finally became the "complete man"— and thus the complete artist—whom he regretted never having been in life, and whom he felt fascism should have made possible. Having mixed his blood with his writing and made it *serious*, he thus became for many in death the embodiment of the myth of the heroic writer, a myth that in fact perpetuates the myth of a spiritual "literary" community at the very basis of his political commitments. Fascist man is thus truly born only in death, but the suicidal aspects of literary fascism do not mitigate in the least its totalitarian ambitions. Instead, they confirm them.

Six

Literary Fascism and the Problem of Gender: The Aesthetics of the Body in Drieu la Rochelle

> Pederasty and the Jews, they go well together. What a sorry decadence. . . . The entire world is in decadence. The "Modern" is a planetary catastrophe.
>
> *Drieu la Rochelle*, Journal *(November 18, 1939)*

> I hadn't understood that man gives form to woman, but she brings him her substance, her life, that magnificent brute matter of her spirituality which calls for the chisel [of man].
>
> Journal *(December 23, 1939)*

> More than ever I understand that for me lust, the confusion of bodies of so many women, was a way of subordinating the feminine element in my life to the exigencies of a masculine spirituality.
>
> Journal *(February 27, 1940)*

The Gender(s) of Fascism: Sartre, Adorno, Theweleit

To put the question of gender as it applies to fascism as directly as possible: Can fascism be assigned *a* sexual identity? And if it can, what is gained by focusing on the gender implications of fascist ideology? That fascism, with its cult of (masculine) youth, of the soldier-warrior, of virile and most often aggressive and violent athletic values in general, has become a topic of gender-oriented studies is certainly not surprising. Because fascist texts such as Brasillach's or Drieu la Rochelle's are in their general lines unapologetically rooted in what has come to be known as masculinist ideology, they seem to cry out for analyses concerned with gender differences. And in terms of the question of gender, it is certainly not difficult to show how a totalitarian masculinist ideology such as fas-

cism—the ideology of masculine superiority radicalized or even absolutized—is itself a symptom of a deep fear of women and results in the violent rejection of all nonsubservient or nonidealized women, all those who
threaten masculine superiority and male values, values that are considered masculine because they are phallic, aggressive, and destructive of
women and of all those considered to be less than totally *masculine* males.

A problem of a very particular kind must be dealt with, however, when
it comes to gender-oriented studies of fascism. It is not the problem facing
any theory or critical methodology when confronted with the complexity
of material that resists analysis and forces the critical approach to develop
more flexible strategies to deal with such complexity, but the opposite
problem, that of self-evidence. In terms of fascism, the work of gender
analysis appears much too easy. The distinctions between masculine and
feminine, aggressiveness and sociability, domination and freedom are
seemingly so clearly drawn within fascist texts and politics that the delineation and denunciation of this absolute form of the masculine, and the
analysis of the dangers of such an extreme form of "masculinism," do not
themselves need to be either nuanced or complex. It may also be that the
crassness and rigidity of the form of gender differentiation found in most
fascist texts encourage the application of models and procedures of analysis that themselves accept rigid distinctions between the masculine and
the feminine. The goals of such analyses are of course praiseworthy: to
attack all expressions of fascism and undermine the sexual hierarchy blatant in all of them. The risk, however, is that of demonizing or patholo-
gizing fascism in order all the better to distant oneself from it, of making
fascism exclusively the expression of the "sick," overly aggressive, overly
masculine male, or even of the pathological nature of maleness itself.

But if Freud got himself into trouble—as well he should have—asking
the question, "What does a woman want?", we should perhaps learn
from his mistakes and not be too hasty in asking and answering Freud's
question and questions like it, whether we ask them of women or of men.
For if we are or if we should be extremely critical of such questions when
they are addressed to women, should not we be as vigilant and critical
when it comes to men? Are we really so sure that we know what men
want, what they are, and what their so-called "subject position" is that
we are able, not just to show that fascism is violent, aggressive, and dogmatically hierarchical and exclusive in its communitarian aspirations,
and in this sense "phallic" or "masculinist" in its dominant traits and
essence, but also to argue or imply that "the masculine" is *in its essence*
already fascist or protofascist, and that "the feminine" is thus privileged
as the antifascist principle or force par excellence?

It is not as if such arguments are wrong. On the contrary, as concerns
fascism, they seem self-evident and irrefutable. But what might appear to

many as self-evident today, was not always so, because the history of the study of fascism is divided on the issue of the masculinist foundation of fascism, and nowhere more so than as it concerns French literary fascists and collaborationists. It seems evident to us now that the warrior mystique, the ideal of male bonding at the heart of fascist youth groups, fascist movements, and political parties, and even the cult of the dictator/ leader, should all be considered products of the all-powerful, antifeminine male ego ideal; but from the very beginning, there have been those who have accused fascists in general, and those French fascists who were the most enthusiastic collaborators with Nazi Germany in particular, not for being overly masculine, violent brutes and male supremacists, but rather for failing to be masculine enough. In this way, collaborators were portrayed as being particularly weak and feminine, feminized males or homosexuals, not true French *men*. In other words, what would be taken by most critics today as evidence of an absolute masculine ideology has also frequently been treated as the failure of certain men to be "men," to live up to even a moderate version of "maleness."

The latter position cannot be simply dismissed, no matter how homophobic it might be, for it may not turn out to be any more (or any less) problematical than the position that simply equates fascism with the masculine. The most well known of the accusations against French collaborators that treated them as failed men, as "women" and/or homosexuals, was of course made by Jean-Paul Sartre in his essay "Qu'est-ce qu'un collaborateur?", originally published in August 1945.[1] In trying to explain French collaboration and at the same time distance himself and other members of the Resistance from it as much as possible, Sartre took an extreme patriotic and militantly nationalist position, treating collaboration as an "illness," a social pathology similar to criminality and suicide, "a phenomenon of disassimilation," a "fixation through foreign collective forms on elements badly assimilated by the indigenous community" (*Situations*, III, 46). Collaborators were considered by Sartre to be exactly what they (and, in fact, extremist nationalists before them) accused their own enemies of being: dangerous "forces of disintegration" (47) within the nation, social "waste" (*déchet*; 48, 49), a group that supposedly refused to be or could not be integrated into the legitimate political traditions and culture of France and that had to be rejected and discarded as waste in order to purify and maintain the authentic nationalist traditions, whether they were claimed to be republican or antirepublican in form.

Sartre claimed that collaboration was something the collaborator carried within himself long before he actually collaborated—an antisocial tendency, a fundamental choice, or a "vocation" (44) that could be said to constitute the "nature" (43) of the collaborator and that simply awaited the proper circumstances (the defeat and the Occupation) before manifesting itself fully. In a sense, Satre decided, these men were never really "French" to begin with, for they had "no real links to contemporary France" (48), and so their choice of the foreign coincided with their true foreign nature. This was the very same accusation that Barrès and others had made of Dreyfus and the Dreyfusards, and the identical claim that the anti-Semitic fascists and collaborators had made against the Jews. Sartre claimed that one should not confuse collaborators with fascists and that he was chiefly interested in describing the former. And it is certainly true that some French fascists refused to collaborate, while many nonfascists were in fact militant collaborators. But Sartre's portrait of typical collaborators, the "interior emigrants" who had always refused the democratic traditions of France, "royalists of the Action Française and fascists of *Je suis partout*" (48), coincides with the profile of the group of literary fascists being treated in this book. It is as if the most developed form of collaboration, the fullest realization of the state of the social waste product, is the *fascist* collaborator.

The French fascist collaborator is not only a disintegrating, foreign element within the authentic French tradition—"supported by foreign armies, he could only be an agent of the foreign" (50)—but he is also weak and effeminate. His chief characteristic is submissiveness, accepting and giving in, first of all, to historical events and, second, to what he perceives to be the most powerful forces of the present. The collaborator has been weakened by what Sartre calls "the ideology of our time, . . . stricken with that intellectual disease one can call historicism" (52). Such a disease weakens the political immune system, the system that allows one to resist the foreign and then question and even oppose the domination of historical events that may *seem* at any one moment to have already determined the course of future history. Without the force to say no to what exists, to resist *what is* for what could be, and moreover justifying "what is" as what should be, the collaborator—and here Sartre equated the collaborator directly with the fascist (61)—poses as a realist. But his realism, Sartre claimed, simply "covers over his fear of doing the job of man," which is "to say yes or no according to principles" rather than passively accepting a future forged by the present (53). The fascist collaborator is no man at all, for the effects of his historicist disease have rendered him incapable of fulfilling his obligations as a man.

Sartre denounced what he called the collaborator's hastily conceived "ethics of virility," in which "the submission to facts" was considered "a test of courage and of virile toughness" (56–57), in the name of an activist ethics and the true courage and virile toughness of the resistant. Writing after the defeat of Nazi Germany and the destruction of fascism in Europe, Sartre had the "force" of the present historical moment on his side, as he condemned the collaborationist's less than virile privileging of and submission to historical events. But more important, Satre's own anti-historicist "ethics of virility" depended on the fascist-collaborationist ethics being destroyed through nothing less than a test of force in man-to-man philosophical-political combat. His purpose was to show that the better "man" (the better concept of man) would always ultimately win in history; and, in fact, with the end of the war and the liberation of France, the better man had already won.

The fascist collaborator, "this priest of virile potency and masculine virtues," who believed in force and posited it as the ultimate moral concept, was for Sartre really a false man, for he acted like a woman and used "the weapons of the weak, of women," that is, "intrigue, trickery which is supported by force, . . . even charm and seduction" (58). Sartre highlighted in the writings of major fascist collaborators, such as Alphonse de Chateaubriant, Drieu la Rochelle, and Brasillach (whose name appears in his text as Brazillach), references to the relations between France and Germany that were characterized as "a sexual union in which France plays the role of the woman." For Sartre, this indicated that in the collaborationist relation to power, there was "a curious mixture of masochism and homosexuality. The Parisian homosexual milieu, moreover, supplied numerous and brilliant recruits [for collaboration]" (58). Sartre thus generalized from a limited number of references in the work of noted fascist collaborators, and from a limited number of cases of homosexuals who had collaborated, to make the collaborator a feminized male and collaboration a profoundly homosexual act. He alleged that homosexuality was not just the sign of "femininity" but evidence of the masochism of men who in the name of virility destroyed their own virility. The man-to-man combat thus was no contest, for one of the combatants had been disqualified from the start, with his virility, but not virility itself, so seriously put into question that he could not possibly defend himself against the stronger virile force of the true republican.[2]

In the name of completing the work of the French Revolution of 1789 through a new revolution, Sartre argued that "it is necessary to accomplish as much as possible the unification of French society," which meant that the primary element of disintegration, the collaborator—the "enemy democratic societies perpetually carry in their womb [en leur sein]"—had to be assimilated into democracy or eliminated; "the breeding-ground [pépinière] of fascists that democracy has always been" had in the future to be closely monitored and controlled by "restrictive laws" (60), so that fascism would not be born again. For only in this way would the failure of "every political realism" (61) of this type be guaranteed. Assimilation or expulsion, that was the only alternative open for the feminized, masochistic internal enemies of France. It is as if Sartre were also condemning the feminine side of democracy, for if democracy had not always carried in its womb such misformed, feminized males, then the unification of France would seemingly have already taken place long ago—among "true men." Only the harsh and restrictive laws of the authentically virile male could guarantee that the breeding ground of fascism constituted by Mother Democracy would be less fertile in the future, with "her" offspring being less masochistic, better formed, and more fully in conformance with the ideal, integrated male.

Sartre was certainly not alone among important political theorists of the left in characterizing the fascist as a "failed male" or homosexual. Theodor Adorno, in a section of *Minima Moralia* (translated by E.F.N. Jephcott [London: Verso Press, 1985]) written in 1944 and entitled "Tough Baby," made the sweeping claim that "totalitarianism and homosexuality belong together." His claim was based on the "observation" that so-called "he-men" or "tough-guys" were in fact "masochists," their lives based on the "lie [which] is nothing other than repressed homosexuality. . . . In the end the tough guys are the truly effeminate ones, who need the weaklings as their victims in order not to admit they are like them" (46). Thus, Adorno continued, the more exaggerated and active the implementation of the male principle of domination, the more "totally passive, virtually feminine" it actually becomes. In other words, the total realization of the he-man in, or as, totalitarianism amounts to the creation of what could be called a "she-man," a man who is not really a man because he is too much or too exclusively a man and admits of no alternate principle to the masculine, a subject that "negates everything which is not of his own kind" (46). The exclusion of the woman, and of any other principle opposed to an absolute, masculine one, was in this way paradoxically seen as a sign of passivity and effeminacy, and thus of the homosexual. At its limits, then, the opposition masculine/feminine reversed itself, with one term becoming its opposite, and in this way the attack on fascism as the cult of the masculine principle constituted an attack on the feminine principle that represented the culmination of the masculine. It was only, then, in not being masculinists, that men could become men; it was in realizing absolutely the masculine principle that they would show themselves to be passive women.

Adorno thus left the hierarchy determining the opposition between masculine and feminine in place, but his concept of the way one term reversed itself and became the other seriously complicated the delineation of male and female. What was clear, however, was that the homosexual and the feminine remained negative terms, a destiny that the masculine was to avoid at all costs. Even though this was not Adorno's explicit intention, the process of reversal that he described was so radical that a blurring or ambivalence of sexual identity did occur at the limits of the distinction between the genders, for no matter how many negative connotations were attached to the process, if the masculine at the moment of its fullest, most exclusive culmination was necessarily transformed into the feminine, into a feminized version of the masculine, what really was left of the masculine and the feminine as distinct entities? Was not the masculine as such just as negative as the feminine, even in the masculinist terms of Adorno's argument, and was not the feminine just as positive as the masculine? The confusion of one gender with the other that Adorno's analysis produced did not neutralize in any way the "virile ideology" in which it was rooted, but it did reveal the contradictions at the core of the process of dialectical reversal in which the realization of sexual identity culminated, no matter which term was privileged and which one devalued.

To attack the limitations of gyno/homophobic approaches to fascism such as Sartre's and Adorno's may be an important step in the process of understanding better both the attractiveness of fascism to so many male writers and its aesthetic and political complexity, but it is not in itself sufficient, especially if the attempt to undermine the masculinist hierarchy evident in their work ends up instead simply reversing it. This is the case with Klaus Theweleit's freewheeling study of fascism, *Male Fantasies*.[3] No study of the fundamental masculine identity of fascism has been more unrelenting, radical, and unorthodox in its *chasse à l'homme* than Theweleit's, but at the same time the problems and limitations of this work are many. They range from its major premise that fascism is primarily a question of the rigidity and violence of male *desire*, to its often superficial and confused treatment of both politics and psychoanalysis, to its mystification of the pleasure principle and gross simplification of Freud's notion of the death drive, and finally to its rambling and very subjective analyses of the political issues and texts it treats and the arbitrary or "free" associations it makes among very different issues. In spite of these and other limitations—its avoidance of any developed discussion of the racism and anti-Semitism at the core of Nazi ideology, for one—*Male Fantasies* does succeed in demonstrating the polemical force of the equation of the masculine with fascism, as well as of the resulting equation of the feminine and feminine desire with nonfascism or antifascism. It also reveals the problems with such equations, even if they were to be more systematically developed and were not connected to an idiosyncratic approach such as Theweleit's.

The primary problem has to do with the opposition itself between the masculine and the feminine, even or especially in the realm of desire, a problem Theweleit indirectly acknowledges at the very beginning of his two-volume study and to which he returns again near the end of the second volume. It is the issue of homosexuality and where it should be situated in terms of the opposition between repressive and violent male desire and male bonding, on the one hand, and what he depicts as open, non-restrained, flowing female desire, on the other. Everything he says about men's fear of women and of the images he associates with female desire seems to implicate the male homosexual as much as, if not more than, the male heterosexual in fascist desire. This leads him very close to both Sartre and Adorno in the question of the latent homosexuality of masculine desire in general and of the soldier male or the fascist male in particular. His repeated and energetic refusal to accept such a consequence of his own argument indicates, in my mind, the fundamental flaw within the argument itself, one that is explicitly denied but nevertheless functionally present in all of his analyses. For if the major premise is that desire is fundamentally *either* masculine *or* feminine, restricted or free, then there can be no ambivalence between or complication of these principles or of the identity of either sex. There is no place, therefore, for principles and forms of desire that are neither simply masculine nor feminine, that are both pleasurable and destructive or free and restrictive at the same time.

Theweleit uses the journals of the German Freikorps as his principal examples of the fantasies of the soldier male and thus, even though their actual participation in the German National Socialist party could hardly be called representative or conclusive, as examples of the fantasies of the fascist male in general. He not only equates the soldiers' political fears and hatred of communism with their imaginary fears and hatred of sexually active, free women, but he argues that the former are always rooted in and ultimately derived from the latter. He believes that fascist politics and ideology are always derived from and are a function of male desire, and that they are ultimately connected to the everyday desires and experiences of *all men*. For those who might not want to generalize as quickly as he does, for any man who is unwilling to call the specific desires and fears of the soldier males (or the male as soldier) essentially masculine and thus identify himself with them, Theweleit's response is simply that such a man is either lying to himself or has repressed what all men desire:

> Any male reading the texts of these soldier males—and not taking immediate refuge in repression—might find in them a whole series of traits he recognizes from his own past or present behavior, from his own fantasies. (Any man who categorically denies this might want to verify it by asking the present, or past, women in his life.) (89)

Theweleit is thus claiming that a denial that the violent examples of male desire are typical of all men makes one, paradoxically, if not less of a man, then at least a man who does not know himself or his own fantasies. Theweleit, on the contrary, *knows* what a man wants, what he desires and fears, and how he acts with women, for he has listened to women, who are presented in this work as the ultimate and irrefutable authorities on what men desire, and how.

The man who knows what women know about men and admits that he too has these same desires and fears has a chance of no longer being as masculine or as patriarchal as before, a chance of fearing less and desiring more; that is, of desiring in an unbounded way—not as a man but *as a woman*. For as Theweleit puts it, "The pleasure principle . . . is in no way patriarchal" (201), and thus all true desire and pleasure are by definition feminine. The inverse, of course, Theweleit believes, is also true: all radical restrictions of "the flow of desire" or malformations of "productive" desire, its transformation into "nonproductive" desire, the work of destruction and the death drive, are thus masculine in their essence and fascist in their ultimate implications and applications.[4] And fascism is nothing less than an attempt to eradicate pleasure and to control and thus "eradicate" the woman: "The core of all fascist propaganda is a battle against everything that constitutes enjoyment and pleasure" (v. 2, 7).

Theweleit insists that he is talking about the "social nature of such 'gender-distinctions'" (v. 1, 221), not the nature of the male and the female as such, and not the natural attributes of either or both sexes in themselves. In this vein, he argues that "the sexuality of the patriarch is less 'male' than it is deadly, just as that of the subjected women is not so much 'female' as suppressed, devivified—though sustaining less damage from its own work of suppression, it also contains the more beautiful possibilities for the future" (221–22). But in other instances and more frequently, he identifies the sexuality of the patriarch with male desire and destruction, the sexuality of the nonpatriarch with female desire and with the unbounded "productions" of the pleasure principle. These are the "beautiful possibilities" to which he refers. In the same vein, he also claims that "female chauvinism is a contradiction in terms" (v. 2, 87), which is to say that chauvinism is always the attribute of the male, even when practiced by women

The implementation of fascist economic and political policies was, according to Theweleit, on its deepest level the answer "to the fascist's need for activities to satisfy his *psychic compulsion* to domination" (v. 2, 406). In this sense, "the type of man who contributed to fascism's triumph" could be said to have "existed in essence long before the beginning of the war in 1914" (v. 2, 351), perhaps even from the beginning of time. Structurally similar to Sartre's version of fascism and collaboration—but the reversal of it in terms of the hierarchy of gender values it proposes—Theweleit's position on fascism in general, his denials notwithstanding, is that it constitutes the masculine essence or nature of a certain type of man, or of man *as a type*—of the man whose essence and destiny are to be fully male. Fascism originally "develops from his feelings [those of this type of man]; he is a fascist from the inside" before being one on the outside (380). The implication is that fascism will truly be a thing of the past only when the masculine type is destroyed from the inside, only when male-female relations are totally recast because the male has been totally *re-formed* or remade, and only when his desire also becomes productive (female) and cut off from all restrictive and destructive masculine forces. Arguing against the destructive norms of male (fascist) desire, Theweleit's radical alternative is itself strongly normative and restrictive, advocating a free and creative, unbounded desire as the ideal nonfascist principle and a new masculine type to replace the patriarchal fascist type: a superwoman to replace the superman. Theweleit not only acts as if he knows what men desire; he also acts as if he knows what desire in general should be.

Theweleit thus considers fascism to be primarily the struggle against desire: "Fascism, then, waged its battle against human desires by encoding them with a particular set of attributes: with effeminacy, unhealthiness, criminality, Jewishness—all of which existed together under the umbrella of 'Bolshevism'" (v. 2, 13). It is a battle in which the woman pays the heaviest price because, Theweleit claims, it is always against her—the woman in, or as, the Jew; the woman in, or as, the communist; the woman as disease and decadence—that the war is waged. Fascists hate women, hate the way they desire, and the pleasure principle they embody and live, and their fascism is primarily an expression of this hatred and the attempt to dominate and destroy any feminine threats to their own rigid, destructive, phallic identity. And inasmuch as all men are claimed to desire, fantasize, and act in their relations with women with the same fears and hatreds as those of the Freikorps and the fascists, all men, as men, are at the very least latent fascists.

And this is where the question of homosexuality comes in. In fact, it comes in everywhere, in all those places left empty by the suppression of the woman, everywhere men desire their own phallic rigidity and themselves to the exclusion of women. It is difficult to see how it could be argued that the logic of Theweleit's analysis does not imply that an imagined community consisting exclusively of men and determined by men, a world of masculine bonding and love, would in its essence be homosexual, and that the total realization of the masculine ideology in the male type then would necessarily be homosexuality. But Theweleit repeatedly rejects such implications. The first time he mentions the issue, it is to oppose the notion proposed by various writers (he refers directly to Reich and Adorno) that homosexuality is an essential component of aggression among soldier-males (that is, in his terminology, fascists) and group ties in general, as Freud argued. Such notions, he claims, cannot be sustained, given that we lack "any sort of theoretically grounded understanding of what the term 'homosexuality' might mean," and that there is no "agreement about the form of social behavior, love relationships and preferred activities, possibilities for satisfaction of drives, forms of pleasure and unpleasure, . . . that might be expected from the type of person who is labeled homosexual, or latently homosexual" (v. 1, 54).

Theweleit wisely advises caution in this area, therefore, because the differences of opinion indicate to him that the opinions advanced even among analysts constitute a "series of prejudices, false ideas, and personal-defense mechanisms" (54–55). To label something or someone homosexual has always been to treat (and reject) him as *other*. In what Theweleit considers a very cloudy area, and in order to avoid all anti-homosexual (masculinist) biases, he initially refuses to speculate and link the homosexual to the soldier-male, a concept for which he obviously feels a consensus (at least among women) already exists as to what this type of man desires and what forms of pleasure and unpleasure might be expected from him. In this sense, it is the lack of knowledge of homosexual desire that all the better highlights what for Theweleit is the known, representable, and theoretically grounded nature of nonhomosexual, masculine desire.

Near the end of the second volume, when he returns to the question of the relation between fascism and homosexuality, it is in order to separate "true" homosexual desire and sexuality from asexual, encoded sexual practices between fascist men, which he considers in fact not to be homosexual:

> As a homosexual, the fascist can prove, both to himself and others, that he is "nonbourgeois," and boldly defiant of normality. His "homosexuality" is strictly encoded; and for this very reason, it never becomes sexual. Like the opposite from which it flees, it is rigidly codified. . . . [The fascist male's] escape into homosexuality ultimately functions as reterritorialization: as an act prescribed by the social order, it never opens new outlets; it simply reinforces dams. (323, 324).

In other words, when fascists act as homosexuals, their "homosexuality" is encoded in the same way as the sexuality of fascists who act as heterosexuals. Their fantasies and desires are, therefore, *male* rather than, homosexual; their flight from women (and "true" female desire) is identical to that of the nominally heterosexual soldier-male, who fears and flees women in the same way. The fascist male is not homosexual, then, even when he is a homosexual, because his desires do not meet the rigid standards of the norm Theweleit applies to them.

Theweleit, therefore, does act as if he also knows what homosexuals want, and consensus or not, he distinguishes what they desire, their true sexuality, from the homosexual practices of fascists, thus putting "true" homosexuals on the same side as women as representatives of the other of masculine (fascist) desire, on the side of true desire and pleasure. Desire itself is the sole property of *the other* of men: of women and men who desire as women do. The fascist, on the other hand, is a fully realized, extreme example of the male in general, of "a body incapable of the experience of pleasure in any form" (195). Fascism, as the negation of pleasure, is thus the most extreme form of repression, the fullest manifestation of *the pathological*.

Desiring, fantasizing, and having sexual experiences like a woman thus provide the only alternative to and cure for fascism, and in this way female desire is presented by Theweleit as the unique nonfascist, nonmasculinist norm.[5] In the end, Theweleit's radically normative, "feminist" approach to fascism, which treats fascism as the supreme masculinist ideology, turns out to be just as restrictive and normative (in the name of liberation and female desire) as Sartre's or Adorno's traditional homophobic characterization of fascism as the work of "lesser men." Such is the risk—and it is a risk rather than a necessity—run by any critical endeavor that attempts to radically overturn the hierarchy of gender differences. It is the risk of reversing and in this way perpetuating the hierarchy, the risk of undoing the existing norms but in the process imposing new (or the same) norms that are linked to and dependent on the rejected norms through a process of radical opposition.

Sartre's, Adorno's, and Theweleit's analyses and condemnations of fascism all have as their goal the identification and isolation of the sexuality of the fascist and of fascism itself, so that we can all finally distance ourselves from or free ourselves of him and of it. Whether fascism is considered *the supreme* expression of the masculine or *the less than masculine* expression of an "inferior," feminized male is ultimately of less importance than the characterization of the fascist as a foreign or pathological *other*, as representing what is radically different from the ideal political or libidinal norm.

The Fascist Aesthetics of the Body

It would be impossible to deny that there is an important gender component in fascist imaginary constructs in general and in the construction of the figure of the fascist type in particular. But as much as we can learn from Sartre, Adorno, and Theweleit about pitfalls inherent in all attempts to determine *the* gender of fascism, it will take a more critical and less normative approach to the problem than theirs to deal with the question of "the gender(s) of fascism" in its contradictory complexity. It will take an approach that does not pretend to know what or how men and women (either heterosexual or gay and lesbian men and women) desire, one that does not know what authentic desire is or should be and that does not have as its ultimate goal the imposition of either a norm for desire or of desire itself as the ultimate norm.

Alice Kaplan has indicated some of the problems inherent in the determination of fascism as an essentially or exclusively masculine ideology.[6] Unlike Theweleit, she insists on the radical ambivalence of fascist writers toward both the masculine and the feminine and the paternal and the maternal components of fascism, because, she argues, "sexism is highly interactive," and the various masculine and feminine categories are "so unstable" (*Reproductions of Banality: Fascism, Literature, and French Intellectual Life* [Minneapolis: University of Minnesota Press, 1986], 11). This leads her to conclude that "one can't 'decide' between the mother-bound and father-bound elements in fascism. They get bundled up in fascism's totalizing machinery and offered up in fascist language to appeal at different emotional registers at different moments of fascism's history" (24). Her own references in this context are primarily to Brasillach, but in much the same spirit I would argue that Drieu la Rochelle's writings constitute an even more complex, contradictory example of the instability and ambivalence of masculine/feminine, paternal/maternal distinctions within the "virile ideology" constituted by fascism. Just as his aesthetics contain both modernist and antimodernist elements—as Robert Soucy has argued in "Drieu la Rochelle and Modernist Anti-Modernism in French Fascism," *Modern Language Notes*, v. 95, no. 4 (1980)—and his politics both nationalist and antinationalist principles, an argument could be made that his fascism was as much if not more rooted in the ambivalence of gender as in dominant masculinist, homophobic values alone. His fascism thus consisted of a fusion (or confusion) of genders as much as it did of a fusion of different and even opposing ideologies and aesthetics.

This in no way denies that Drieu la Rochelle's aesthetics of politics were sexually charged, but it seems legitimate to ask with which sex(es) his politics were "charged," how they were "charged," and what relation they had to sexual difference(s) in general? It is not that masculinist values, including antifeminine and violently homophobic statements, are missing from his literary and political writings or his journal; it is just that an approach which focuses exclusively on the strictly masculinist side of his form of "male fantasies" would, like those insisting on the "feminine" or homosexual nature of fascism, fall short of understanding the importance of gender ambivalence in his aesthetics of fascism. This ambivalence certainly does not make him less of a fascist. It rather reveals the complexity of the question of gender in fascism and why fascism cannot be treated simply as the discourse of the *other*, whether the other is defined as foreigner, monster, or madman, or as either the "feminized," less than virile male, or as the fearful and violently repressive, gynophobic soldier-male.

Drieu la Rochelle consistently characterized the decadence of modernity in terms of both gender and race, associating decadence and the loss of productive virility primarily with women, homosexuals, and Jews. He considered force and creativity, on the other hand, to be aspects of the ideal character of the true male, even if rarely if ever achieved by real men. In this sense, his sexual and political fantasies of the ideal totalitarian community seem perfect examples of fascist "male fantasies." And yet a rigid opposition between the masculine and the feminine does not determine Drieu la Rochelle's approach to fascism in its entirety. For as he shows in his novels, and as he frequently indicates in his essays and especially in his journal written during the Occupation, the new fascist man and fascism itself are counterforces *within* rather than forces existing outside the general decadence of modernity: "As a good decadent, I have the taste for willed and conscious force due to a lack of spontaneous and inborn force. Believing in decadence, I couldn't believe in anything other than fascism, which is proof of decadence because it is the conscious resistance to decadence with the means determined by that very decadence" (*Journal* [November 25, 1942], 312–13). He presents the fascist "new man," therefore, not so much as being opposed in his very nature to the decadence of nonvirile or antivirile forces as using the means determined by the decadent figures themselves to resist the very decadence they represent. This seems to be the only way for him, a modern, decadent male lacking in "spontaneous and inborn [masculine] force," to achieve any relation to force at all. Because fascism, as he sees it, is willed, constructed, and aesthetically formed, it constitutes a relation to force that in Drieu la Rochelle's own terms could be said to be as "feminine" as "masculine," as aesthetic as political.

His form of literary fascism proposes an aesthetics and politics of the body, a way of forming the body in terms of the dual ideal of beauty and force. In *Notes pour comprendre le siècle* (Paris: Gallimard, 1941), Drieu la Rochelle made his most developed statement concerning the place of the body in the new European spiritual community allegedly being created by Nazi Germany. He moved in this work beyond slogans such as "Better soccer matches than war" or "The France of camping and kayaking over the France of cocktails and cinema," which were typical of his writings for the Parti Populaire Français, to construct an entire history of the body.[7] This history of the body was of course at the same time a defense and an illustration of fascism.

To return to the body is first of all to return to the theme of fascism as a transcendent movement of youthful energy, the most profound expression of life itself, of pure force. The body is a political and *aesthetic* figure, material and spiritual at the same time. If the individual body is weak, badly functioning, divided against itself, so will be the body politic, the people, and the nation. If the body is healthy, vigorous, and the support of spiritual and cultural values and energies, the people will also be healthy and united. The fascist cult of the body was thus not just an eccentric curiosity; it was at the very foundation or center of fascist aesthetics and politics. In fascist discourse the body functions as a metaphysical concept in physical form, the spiritual embodied in flesh and blood. Fascist discourse on the body and on such things as sports, camping, and hiking should thus be taken very seriously, no matter how naive and sophomoric it might at times seem in the work of writers such as Drieu la Rochelle and Brasillach.

For Drieu la Rochelle, the Middle Ages, the imaginary model for the new Europe, was first and foremost a time of youth and physical force: "Youth triumphed not only in everyday practices but in the arts, poetry, philosophy, religion. . . . It was an era of physical force" (9). In this way, the Middle Ages was modeled after what, following Nietzsche and the German romantics, he called a first antiquity in Greece, an antiquity before force was tamed by form, before the Dionysian was subdued by the Apollonian, before body and soul were separated by philosophy (Plato); that is, before the body was "isolated under the false light of aesthetics" (8).[8] Aesthetics in its narrow (Apollonian) sense isolates and divides; the body aestheticized is already the body in the process of losing its dynamic force. Drieu la Rochelle's continued insistence on force to counter the aesthetics of form led to a demand for a total aesthetics before the division of force and form. Such an aesthetics claimed that with fascism the body reemerged as it was before the long separation that originated in the second antiquity, which was developed in the Latin world, reborn in the Renaissance, and then finally became institutionalized in French neoclassical aesthetic theory. The body reunited with itself and the spirit thus became the principal sign of the new fascist *man*.

Drieu la Rochelle argued that the most profound sign of the catastrophic state of the body in modernity was not just the sorry, divisive state of politics in parliamentary democracies like France before the war. It was also the absence of genuine art in those countries, for with the disembodiment of modern man, the hands needed to create art were incapable of doing so. He believed that the decline of spiritual life and artistic creation always accompanied the decline of physical activity:

> Today, what are hands good for? Hands, poor hands which hang down at our sides. How do you expect there still to be painters born, when our hands our dead? And musicians as well. And even writers. Because style, for the latter as for all the others, is born of the memory of the entire body. (84)

For Drieu la Rochelle, style was man, but man was nothing spiritually if he was not first corporally sound. The weakening of the body, and the lack of physical development and fitness, indicated also the end of art. Just as modern man, when he became urban and lost contact with his body, ceased "to be a peasant and a warrior, [which] is again for him a way of losing the sense of every work, every thought" (85), he also ceased being able to produce works of art—and thus to produce the political as a dynamic, Dionysian work of art.

A body that is not healthy but not yet dead still functions in a reduced sort of way. In modernity, active, productive man is reduced to what Drieu la Rochelle called the semi-impotency of eroticism: "Man no longer walks, no longer runs, no longer jumps. He barely moves his organs and his members. He eats and drinks too much. The only movement left to him is eroticism" (78). In eroticism, to deal with a theme that runs throughout Drieu la Rochelle's political essays and novels, no child is produced. The exclusively erotic act, which is barely an act, has no purpose outside itself; it is unproductive. This results in its being excessively repeated with fatigue, passivity, and "inversion" as the inevitable result: Man "makes love too much, he tires himself out, he becomes passive. Inverted with women, he might just as well be with men. And women caressing men can just as well caress women" (86–87). The figure of the productive body in Drieu la Rochelle's work is thus, not surprisingly, both homophobic and gynophobic, for the man who "barely moves his organs and members" for purposes other than erotic pleasure and the woman who caresses men (and women) for the same purely erotic ends are (along with Jews) the principal figures of the unhealthy body. What he called the decadent "urban syphilis" of modernity was indicated most dramatically in Drieu la Rochelle's work in such images as "nonproductive" sexuality, a sexuality that did not produce a child (a work).[9]

In literature, Mallarmé represents the disembodiment of art, having written poetry in which Drieu la Rochelle claims there is only impotent, aesthetic "eroticism" rather than genuine creative force, a form of writing that produces no work:

> No longer a body but no soul as well. . . . No longer any passion, neither carnal nor spiritual. . . . No faith, except in art, but what is art if it no longer ejaculates life? An allusion to what was, to the ancient monument of creation; a delicate, fine, piercing gesture, the fleeting sway of an impotency that imitates the rhythm of coitus. An apology for sterility and mental onanism in *Hérodiade*; an analysis of physical as well as mental impotency in *l'Après-midi d'un Faune*. (98)

In the eyes of a Maurras or a Brasillach, Mallarmé also was invested with many of the attributes of what they considered the ultimate form of romantic decadence and sterility, because his poetry and poetics were seen as foreign to the French, a betrayal of France, and a destruction of the

French language. For them, Mallarmé was situated in the place of the foreigner and the Jew. For Drieu la Rochelle, Mallarmé occupied the same decadent place, but in his argument it was primarily the place of the homosexual (of the Jew as homosexual), the allegedly onanistic, inverted, "feminized male."

If art does not "ejaculate life"—that is, consist of an outburst of energy that *produces a work*—if it is onanistic and thus in Drieu la Rochelle's terms impotent, then it cannot be considered true art, just as the imitation of the rhythm of coitus cannot be considered "authentic" coitus. The ideal (of) art is thus also an ideal (of) coitus, which admits of no imitations and determines a norm of pure force and productivity. The ideal of art as an original, productive corporal force thus determines a dogmatic aesthetics and normative sexual politics that support Drieu la Rochelle's condemnation and exclusion of the onanism of a Mallarmé and the "homosexual" onanism of all those whose erotic and aesthetic pleasure could also be deemed "nonproductive." *Notes pour comprendre le siècle* thus represents an indictment of decadent or degenerate art as being a manifestation of the physical and sexual decadence or degeneracy of the culture that produces them.

Drieu la Rochelle points to Paul Claudel as the contemporary poet who represents the opposite values from a Mallarmé and who has miraculously been able to produce once again an authentic and complete poetry: "In this last romantic, this last symbolist, there is no more romanticism, no more symbolism at all. The circle is closed, man has reconstructed himself; body and soul, after such a long separation, are joined together" (115). "Claudel is the only truly healthy writer since the Middle Ages who is also truly great. A bizarre and miraculous reawakening of force in this exhausted France" (124). Claudel, along with a few other exceptional writers—he names Péguy, Bernanos, Bloy—has rediscovered nothing less than the "mystical foundation" of the French spirit, its true foundation, which a long history of rationalism had covered over and whose loss romanticism, symbolism, and naturalism each in its own way had exemplified and mourned.

This brief history of literature is also, of course, explicitly a history of politics. The reappearance of the mystical in literature is presented as the rediscovery of the true spiritual source of the political. "Can one consider as a negation of politics," Drieu la Rochelle asks, "what is a just and preliminary absorption into the sources of mystical thought? It is necessary to understand, because these sources have been blocked from the beginning of the eighteenth century and always more or less obstructed since then, that this has made all politics futile" (127). The rediscovery of the mystical source of literature and art by a limited number of writers constitutes nothing less than the sign of the possibility of a total political revival and provides as well the model for that revival. Literature leads the way back to the origin and creates the spiritual foundation for the political revival that fascism was to provide. Fused with the rediscovery of "athleticism," which he called a "science of the total body" (134), the return to mysticism in literature, while he described as "the reawakening of spiritual athleticism" (139), Drieu la Rochelle pointed the way to the creation of the total human type, to fascism as the revolution and restoration of the body (153) and the birth of a "new man."

The Trouble with Gender and the Ambivalence of Desire

Drieu la Rochelle's novel *Gilles*[10] has rightly been called a "fascist parable," for, as Michel Winock argues, "better than most theoretical texts, it presents . . . a rich catalogue of fascist ideas as they had been expressed within a French context" ("Une parabole fasciste: 'Gilles' de Drieu la Rochelle," in *Nationalisme, antisémitisme et fascisme en France* [Paris: Seuil, 1982], 349). But given the importance of the series of portraits it presents of the various women with whom Gilles (the principal character of the novel) is involved, and the relation of those portraits to his political aspirations and disappointments, the novel could just as rightly be called a sexual parable of the fantasies of a fascist male and their fundamental relation to his politics.

In those rare instances when Gilles's relationship with a woman is presented in positive terms, it is because the woman has fulfilled the function assigned to women by the novel as a whole: that of manifesting the beauty and intensity of force in itself. Alice, a nurse with whom Gilles has a brief but intense affair while a soldier during World War I, is described by the narrator as bringing to Gilles "a magnanimity of the heart to which he had believed his destiny was devoted, . . . a force completely developed and completely released" (210). Her recognition of his potential force transforms him into the warrior he desired to be but could not be in war: "She recognized in Gilles a man who . . . presented himself as being of her race, given how direct he had been" (207). For it is in *response* to the intensity of her desire and force that his own soldierly force is stimulated and returns: "He loved Alice with all his war force having come back" (210). In *Gilles*, the soldier-male needs a woman equal or even superior to his alleged force in order to be equal to (his ideal of) himself.

This presentation of force and desire is certainly determined by masculinist values, but it defines a world in which all active women are not feared for being passionate, forceful, and even warriorlike but rather desired as both the stimulant and reflection of man's alleged force and virility. Alice herself is presented as a warrior-woman, the perfect double for the soldier-male, the ideal reflection in fact of what he is or would like himself to be. She exists so that he can prove himself worthy of the "force" that she seems to possess naturally and that she evokes spontaneously. If the "warrior-male" realizes himself through a woman equal or superior to himself, then the "warrior-female" in turn is fulfilled only by *his* self-realization: "The greatest joy a woman can have, that from which she can draw the most profound sensual effects, is the certainty a man gives her of his moral virility. Gilles, just back from the front, could supply this certainty" (207). Man's moral virility remains the ultimate and dominant value in this universe, but its certainty and confirmation depend as much on the warrior-woman, the woman of "race," as on the warrior-man.

Only the exceptional woman (like the exceptional man), however, can achieve this warrior status and be considered to belong to *his* race, a term that has more to do in this context with gender than with blood. In almost all other instances in this novel and elsewhere in Drieu la Rochelle's work, race is used in an explicitly anti-Semitic sense. For the "race" totally opposed to the warrior-race is the "Jewish race," and the figure presented as the psychological, political, and sexual enemy of Gilles in the novel is Rebecca, who is not only Jewish, born in Russia, and a communist, but is also interested in psychoanalysis. As important, if not more important for the politicized aesthetics of the novel, she is ugly: "Rebecca was small, with an ugly face and figure" (405). At the top of the "racial" and aesthetic hierarchy is the forceful, sexually liberated warrior-woman; at the bottom is the ugly, deceitful, corrupting Jewish communist.[11]

The sexual (and racial) characteristics and implications of the aesthetic ideals at the basis of Drieu la Rochelle's fascism are manifested most completely in the portrait of an American woman named Dora, for it is Dora, more than any of the other women in the novel, who embodies the beauty and force of the "superior race" and manifests in her body the possibility for the (re)birth of superior man:

> Dora was not beautiful if you looked at her face. . . . But her body manifested the beauty of a race. . . . In this American, with her mixture of Scottish, Irish, Saxon blood, were crossed and multiplied several characteristics of the Nordic peoples. It was exactly this side that attracted all of Gilles's emotions. . . . When he took this big body in his arms, he embraced an idea of life dear to him. A certain idea of force and nobility that he had lost. . . . Why look for it anywhere else but here? Why look for it in the masculine world, in the spells of ambition? A woman is just as much a reality as the crowd is. A plague on the hierarchy of passions. One passion is worth just as much as another. (271)

Dora's body—and it is only her body that represents the pure, formal beauty and force of classical art—induces in Gilles a strong temptation to retreat from what he calls the world of men (of politics, ideas, and war) and be satisfied with embracing the aesthetic ideal of life and "a certain idea of force and nobility." Dora thus represents the material manifestation of Gilles's aesthetic and political beliefs as well as the further temptation to live in exile away from "men" in order, paradoxically, to remain in contact with that most manly of ideals, force, present in modernity not in the politics of men but in the beauty of a woman's body.

The extreme opposite of the racially and aesthetically determined beauty of the idealized body of the woman is not only the Jewish communist, however, but also the ugliness and impotency of the masculine body politic in democracy. In the third section of the novel entitled "L'Apocalypse," the political project devised by Gilles for a new "national-social party" is presented to the congress of the Radical party, where the diseased body politic is fully on display. The spectacle sickens Gilles but confirms what he already believes: "This public resumed all French publics. . . . France was nothing more than senility, avarice, and hypocrisy" (557). There is no real contact between orator and public, and therefore no "living" force is experienced or produced. As a political experience described in sexual terms, leaders and public were both satisfied with their private pleasures and took no interest in anything else: "The orator no more wanted to take hold of the public than the public wanted to be taken hold of. Instead of a holy and fertile sexual encounter, one saw two onanisms approach each other, brush against each other, and then slip away from each other" (556). Such mutual masturbation will, of course, produce no healthy political offspring and indicates that there is no chance that modern France—decadent, senile, and sterile, if not "degenerate"—could once again become young, virile, and productive.

Only fascism and a politics of creative force are presented in the novel as the negation of the politics of parties and sects and of all noncreative, nonproductive forces: of the masturbatory politics of democratic politicians and the masturbatory aesthetics of Jews and homosexuals, and finally, of all women who fail to measure up to the ideal of beauty represented by Dora and who love without reproducing and thus fall within either or both of the categories of decadence. Drieu la Rochelle's homophobia and anti-Semitism are thus intimately interrelated and important components of his fascist aesthetics of politics, for the Jew and the homosexual represent the extreme opposite of both the fascist male and the idealized, aestheticized woman, whose body displays the creative, aesthetic force from which the male is in fact separated and which he must "repossess" to realize himself fully as a man.

But the ideal woman must also be a fertile mother to ensure that death and sterility no longer dominate and that France will no longer be without children, without force, and without art; the "new man" without heirs.[12] Fascism could be seen as the figure of the perfect fusion of the "fascist man" and the "aestheticized woman," a man who becomes a man only by first embracing and "possessing" the beauty and force of the woman. The man admires, desires, and cultivates the force of her beauty, which *he* no longer possesses in himself, before being able to become that force. The aesthetic (woman) in this sense is always the model and foundation for the political (man). The man must first "possess" the woman and assume or usurp her place, before fully taking on his function as a virile man. He cannot give birth to or become such a man by himself because he does not possess force in himself. He can possess and be at one with force only outside of himself, in or as a woman.

Drieu la Rochelle, militant fascist, is also clearly on the side of the beauty and creative, productive force he attributes to certain exceptional women. But which side that is may not be as easy to determine as it first might have seemed, especially when he becomes an active collaborator and must justify his fascism predominantly in terms of collaboration. In "A Certains" (August 1941), originally published in *La Nouvelle Revue Française* while he was its editor,[13] he denounces the weakness of those reluctant to commit themselves to collaboration and compares them to Jews who are "horrified by guns" (58). Abruptly, he shifts from their supposed lack of courage in war to Jewish women who, he claims, considered it "disgusting to be pregnant" and "shameful to suffer in giving birth." Addressing them directly, he asserts: "However, you still allow for coitus. But undoubtedly your son will be a homosexual and no longer allow for it" (59). If the French do not act—that is, collaborate—then they will end up like Jews: fearful, sterile, impotent, and ultimately "homosexual." At the end of the essay, when he finally accuses "certain Frenchmen," those who passively resist collaboration, of being *neutres*— that is, neutral and neutered—he is accusing them also of not being true French *men*, of being Jews and homosexuals.

Drieu la Rochelle's most detailed justifications for his collaboration, besides the argument that Germany was in the process of creating a new unified Europe—"L'Allemagne Européenne" (January 1942) is the title of one of his essays from the *Nouvelle Revue Française*—were made on the basis of what he called his respect for and even *love* of force, no matter how and where it manifested itself. In "Entre l'Hiver et le Printemps" (April 1942), one of the essays on which Sartre based his claim that collaborators were all feminized males or homosexuals, Drieu la Rochelle presented himself as a member of a very select group as a lover not of his nation, but of an ideal European body soon to be created: "We are not very numerous, those who love Europe with a carnal love, a concrete love, a patriotic love" (*Le Français d'Europe*, 124). The state of a Frenchman who loves Europe and its force is never easy, because he finds himself

almost entirely alone in his own country and a foreigner to the force he
desires in others and for himself: "Alas! It is atrocious to love force, to be
profoundly inhabited by the desire to live in its midst and to be for one's
whole life excluded from this sacred resource" (119).

A true lover of force is therefore driven to look for force where it exists,
even at his own expense and that of his country:

> A man worthy of this name cannot look only within the limits of his own
> people. . . . I saw peoples stronger than the French. I was upset and rejoiced at
> the same time. He who loves force follows its scent, recognizes it wherever it is.
> And if force manifests itself against him and his people, he still has to rejoice.
> He rejoices in mourning. (120)

The carnal lover of force must be willing to follow "its scent" wherever
it leads him and collaborate in the forms and political structures it insti-
tutes and in the destruction it brings about. His pleasure may never be
simple, for it is always divided: it is not only the restricted pleasure of "a
man" but also the limitless pleasure of "a woman," not only the pleasure
of a man who "is" force in himself but also the pleasure of a man who
desires or wills force in or as a woman, not only joyful, productive pleasure but mournful, destructive pleasure as well. It may even add to his joy
that he, his country, and the women he at the same time idealizes and
scorns always pay a price for such pleasure.

It may be legitimately asked at this point whether, within the context
of French literary fascism, to love force in this way is to love as a man or
a woman, and whether what one is loving in, or as, force are its masculine
or feminine attributes, assuming one can still distinguish conclusively
between them. Despite his condemnation of sterile, allegedly homosexual eroticism throughout his work, Drieu la Rochelle—as if anticipating
Sartre's criticism and agreeing with it before the fact—also acknowledges
in his journal what he calls his own "homosexual tendencies," which he
relates not just to his sporadic impotency but also to his love of force: "I
started very young being sporadically impotent. An introverted, inverted
nature, but with women. Masculine in spurts, often Narcissus dreaming
of possessing while being possessed. I was hopelessly masochistic and
naturally sadistic in my spare time. . . . My enemies often sensed, it's
visible enough, the feminine, inverted character of my love for force"
(*Journal* [June 1944], 393). Such an admission, however, does not make
Sartre's (or Adorno's) analysis any less problematical, but rather indicates the masculinist biases Sartre and Drieu la Rochelle had in common:
a homophobic and gynophobic equation of homosexuality with femininity and masochism and the *love* of force, as opposed to masculine
potency in itself, which is thus equated with the *being* of force. Drieu la
Rochelle's admission of his own "homosexuality" in no way diminishes

his scorn for "sterile" women and his condemnation of homosexuality throughout his work as the opposite of fascist (virile), productive force. It rather constitutes an admission that he himself never measured up to such an ideal but worshiped it from what he called an inferior "feminine" position, that he was in his own eyes less than a total man, and finally, that the decadence and "femininity" he denounced were important components of his own being and of the fascist aestheticizing of politics that he proposed.

In fact, one finds in the writings of Drieu la Rochelle the same ambiguity and ambivalence concerning the "gender" of fascism that were evident in Adorno's condemnation of the fascist masculine ideal for being homosexual. For what is not being acknowledged in such admissions is that the masculine ideal of force has, even in its own terms, an important feminine dimension. At the same time, the "subject position" of the lover of force is as much the man's as the woman's, the heterosexual's as the homosexual's. The denunciation of homosexuality and the devaluing of or scorn for the feminine must thus be read in more than one way. They are signs not just of the affirmation of the masculine but also of the contradictory, *internal* relation to the feminine of even the most masculinist of masculine ideals, that of the fascist male. And to love the force of Nazi Germany would then also be to love "as a man" the feminine side of fascism, and the failure to be that force oneself could also be seen then as the failure to attain aesthetic totalization, to be the ideal embodied by the aestheticized woman. The failure to be sufficiently virile is thus also the failure to be sufficiently womanly, the failure to be equal to the force manifested in the beauty of the woman.

In such a configuration, the woman is of course still being defined in terms of the man, with her place and function being determined by his desires and in terms of his ideals. But even within these serious constraints, the fascist man is not simply masculine or virile (nor the opposite); the woman, whether idealized or scorned, is not simply excluded, repressed, or feared by him but also desired and desiring. The notion of the "total man" is dependent on the idealized aesthetic totalization of the woman, and it is this dual process of totalization that defines Drieu la Rochelle's literary fascism more than the dogmatic and violent desires of the soldier-male.

Gender ambivalence is most definitely limited by such demands for totalization, but while fascism in general can still rightly be considered an extreme masculinist or virile ideology, in the case of Drieu la Rochelle, the goals of the literary fascism he desired but failed to realize could more accurately be defined as an extreme manifestation not just of the ideology of *the man* but rather of the ideology *of gender* as such, whether dogmatically masculinist or nominally "feminist." Such an ideology is constituted by the project to establish both genders as distinct and totalizeable identities, to make man as such or woman as such either an ideal type or the representative of absolute negativity, of a pathological deviation from and threat to the norm or ideal represented by the other. If this is so, no approach that accepts such distinctions and the hierarchies they impose, no matter which term is privileged or how vigorously the masculinist ideology of fascism is opposed, can effectively undermine the ultimate gender ideal of literary fascism: to be "total."

Seven _____

Literary Anti-Semitism: The Poetics of Race in Drumont and Céline

> The most diverse races—Celtic, Gaulois, Gallo-
> Roman, Germanic, Frank, Norman—melted
> together in this harmonious totality that is the
> French nation. . . . Only the Jew could not enter
> into this amalgam.
>   *Edouard Drumont*, La France juive *(1885)*

> Art is only Race and Fatherland!
> Salvation through the Arts!
>   *Céline*, Les Beaux Draps *(1941)*

The Aesthetic Totalization of the Other

No one today should need to be reminded that France has a long anti-Semitic tradition, which took on an ever-increasing importance as both a political and a cultural phenomenon throughout the nineteenth century. As Léon Poliakov has put it, "If one wanted to gauge the strength of anti-Semitism in a country by the amount of ink used up on the Jewish question, France would win top honors in the nineteenth century."[1] What interests me especially is what could be called the literary side of this history; that is, the specific role played by literature and literary figures in the formation of a national identity that is rooted in the representation of Jews as foreign, menacing Others.

Michel Winock, in *Nationalisme, antisémitisme et fascisme en France* (Paris: Seuil, 1990), argues that it was the writer and journalist, Edouard Drumont, who was the first truly popular best-selling anti-Semitic author in France, and it was he who laid the foundation for the modern, *political* use of anti-Semitism:

> In establishing anti-Semitism as the system of universal explanation, [Dru-mont] made the Jew the negative pole of nationalist movements: it is in relation to the Jew, against the Jew, that the nationalist will define his French or German identity, proud as he is to belong to a community and to know clearly the adversary who threatens its unity and life. (137)

The *figure* of the Jew in this sense became the support of and the privileged access to national identity; it was on this negative figure, this figure of absolute negativity, that the positive figure of the Frenchman would be constructed. As Winock puts it, "The Jew found his function. He is, through the effect of repulsion, the revealer of national identity. To be French, it was said then, is, par excellence, not to be Jewish" (81). The fabrication of the figure of the Jew as Other thus played an essential role in the fabrication of the figure of the Same, the image or representation of what one was not, crucial to the representation of what one imagined oneself to be. Not only could Drumont's work then be considered the foundation for the modern political use of anti-Semitism, as Winock argues; it could be considered the foundation or model for its modern literary use as well.

But as the *political use* of anti-Semitism increased at the end of the nineteenth century, there was nothing in the negative representation of "the Jew" in literature that differed substantially from previous representations. In fact, in general, nothing is ever really invented, said for the first time, or original to one author or group, or even to one time or place, when it comes to the representation of "the Jew." To draw a portrait of the Jew as the menacing other, because of the long tradition already supporting anti-Semitism, was to draw on a wealth of resources, images, clichés, slogans, stories, fables, "facts," and documents, all irrefutable in the mind of the anti-Semite because they were irreducible components of the national heritage. Nowhere more than here are we in the realm of the "already said" or the "already represented," the common knowledge that everyone—that is, every "true Frenchman"—is supposed to recognize as true.

The anti-Semitic writer in general could be considered the most traditional of all traditionalists when it comes to the question of Jews, and the most outlandish collections of anti-Semitic clichés were always presented as "historical," which in a sense they were, because as myths or fictional representations they already had had a long history before being brought back to life in the modern period. In fact, read in the context of the long anti-Semitic tradition, the typical anti-Semitic writer is at best a petty collector of sayings and stories, a second-rate scribe, a crass imitator of other anti-Semites, a self-proclaimed vulgarizer of supposedly scientific data and theories, and quite often an outright plagiarist.[2] To make something new of this tradition, and to do something other than what had already been done many times before, turned out in almost all instances to be an impossible task. Dominated by the clichéd image or portrait of the Jew, anti-Semitic writing was generally as pathetic and clichéd as the hateful themes and portraits it conveyed.

To read the anti-Semitic literature from the late nineteenth century through the 1930s and 1940s in France is thus to be struck not only by its viciousness and crudeness but also by its horrible repetitiveness, by the way in which writer after writer repeated in a kind of litany the same clichés and myths, and the way in which the portrait of the Jew was repeatedly constructed in order to be contrasted with the "national type." To read one anti-Semitic writer is seemingly to read them all. Nowhere do the effects of ideology, the determination of all thinking by a single unifying *idea*, seem more evident than here; nowhere do attributes normally associated with art and literature—formal invention and experimentation, imagination and creativity, nuance and complexity—seem more absent. The anti-Semitic writer would seem to be condemnable, therefore, not only on moral and political grounds, that is, as an anti-Semite, but also on literary grounds, as a writer.

And then, along came Céline, who in his three anti-Semitic pamphlets—*Bagatelles pour un massacre* (Paris: Denoël, 1937), *L'Ecole des cadavres* (Paris: Denoël, 1938), and *Les Beaux draps* (Paris: Nouvelles Editions Françaises, 1941)—committed his creativity and imagination, and his "poetic genius" and original style, to the cause of anti-Semitism. In doing so, Céline not only once again confirmed that anti-Semitism was an undeniable component of an ongoing French literary tradition, but he also placed anti-Semitism at the core of his own highly "original" if not revolutionary literary-rhetorical legacy and thus made it an essential element of the modernist revolt against tradition as well. In order to understand better the "accomplishment" of Céline in this area, and his "literary" originality in terms of this issue, it will help to look first at the work of Drumont, the "founder" of modern political and, I would argue, modern literary anti-Semitism in France. Author of *La France juive: Essai d'histoire contemporaine* (Paris: Marpon and Flammarion, 1885) and founder of the Ligue Antisémite and the extremist, nationalist, anti-Semitic newspaper *La Libre Parole* (whose motto was "La France aux Français"), Drumont in a sense set the stage for Céline and made it possible for him, in his revolt *against* tradition, to realize the full modern literary potential of traditional anti-Semitism, which also constitutes its political potential as well.

To highlight the importance of the literary legacy of Drumont before Céline, I would point to two references among many. In 1902, Maurice Barrès dedicated his novel *Leurs Figures* to Drumont, his mentor in anti-Semitism, acknowledging the debt he owed to him and in this way proclaiming once again the fundamental link he himself had established between nationalism and anti-Semitism, between the images and figures of the Nation-Self and the war against the ultimate figure of uprootedness and decadence, the anti-Self: the Jew. Decades later, Georges Bernanos referred to Drumont affectionately as "my old master" and called *La*

France juive a "magical" work.[3] What Drumont had in fact accomplished in *La France juive* was not the development of a coherent theory of anti-Semitism that others would apply after him, or the construction of an argument on behalf of its "scientific" or historical legitimacy. Rather, he had provided an enormous literary storehouse of figures and stories for others to refer to, collecting and embellishing on the "historical evidence" linking the Jew to the decadence of modernity, to the transformation of traditional life and values, to the ever-increasing importance of capital, and to the decline of the influence of the Catholic Church—in short, to nothing less than the material destruction and spiritual decadence of France. What makes Drumont's work different from other anti-Semitic pamphlets and works is the ambitiousness of his project, the abundance of references he gives, and the diversity and apparent completeness of the tableau he draws. *La France juive* pretends to give nothing less than *a total picture* of the Jew, to constitute a kind of organized, structured encyclopedic definition of the identity of the Jew and a dramatic demonstration of the entirety of his "crimes."

Drumont's work consists of a series of vivid images, pictures, fragments, and stories of the "evil" represented by "the Jew." As Drumont put it in his response to critics of his work, "The result of my book . . . was to bring the Jew well to the fore, to make him leave his vague and feigned humanitarianism in order to show him as he is" (*La France juive devant l'opinion* [Paris: Marpon and Flammarion, 1886], 11). His work is an attempt to demonstrate, through the presentation of a seemingly inexhaustible supply of cases, caricatures, and stories, the single, obsessive thesis of the book: "Everything comes from the Jew; everything comes back to the Jew. There is in this a conquest . . . of an entire nation by a boundless but cohesive minority" (*La France juive*, vi). The figure of "the Jew" represents for Drumont an absolute, metaphysical force of evil, the source of everything that is destroying France, the one negative figure to which everything decadent can be traced, and the one group (in anti-Semitic terminology, the one "race") that supposedly profits from such destruction. If this is so, writes Drumont, then the only path open to the French, if they are to regain possession of their nation and themselves, is to wage a total war against the Jews in order to bring about the destruction of this vicious cycle in which they are being conquered and losing everything to the Jews, even or especially their sense of self. It is for these reasons that the picture Drumont draws must also have the appearance of being total, of encompassing every aspect of French social, economic, political, religious, and cultural life.[4]

In his response to critics of his work who argued that he had not gotten all his facts right—his "Essay of Contemporary History," as his subtitle reads, was anything but historical in the usual sense of the term—

Drumont himself admitted that he had "undoubtedly been mistaken in several places." But this too was for him only an indication of the superior truth of anti-Semitism in which the work is rooted:

> No matter what some have claimed, *La France juive* is a truthful book. . . . It is true, of that superior truth which, as Alfred de Vigny in his preface to *Cinq Mars* says quite rightly, lives on no less in spite of certain inexact details, of that *truth [la vérité]* which, in history as in art, is sometimes different from what is *true [du vrai]* of facts. (*La France juive devant l'opinion*, 50)

Evoking in this way the distinction Aristotle makes between history, the contingent, factual realm, on the one hand, and the higher, universal truth of poetry, on the other, Drumont roots the "truth" of anti-Semitism in the metaphysical universality of the poetic. At least in principle, everything could be historically false in the picture, but as long as the portrait of the Jews had a formal, rhetorical coherence and force, then the work could be considered more true than if it were factually accurate. As the number of editions of *La France juive* indicate, his anti-Semitic "art" was incredibly popular, and the work not only found the true believers it was looking for but also created a whole new and appreciative audience for anti-Semitism that had not existed before.[5]

The struggle against the foreign in anti-Semitic nationalist literature is inevitably portrayed as an eternal war, as if it were a question of two natural, antagonistic principles that were fated to struggle against each other for all times: "The Semite and the Aryan, these two personifications of distinct races, irremediably hostile to each other, whose antagonism filled the world in the past and will trouble it even more in the future" (5). Even more basic than the conflicts between nations and peoples, then, Drumont recounts in a pseudo-Darwinian manner, is a war in and of nature, a war of survival among antagonistic forces and species, only one of which, the "naturally" weaker force, is actually responsible for it, because it is always looking for revenge for having lost previous battles, always looking for a way to weaken and thus defeat the "naturally superior" force:

> From the very first days of history, we see the Aryan in a struggle with the Semite. . . . The conflict perpetuated itself throughout the ages and almost always the Semite was the instigator before being the vanquished. . . . Today the Semite believes that victory is certain. . . . The Jew has replaced violence by ruse. (7–8)

The fittest, in the general scheme of nature, ought to survive, but the tactics of the weaker force are such that the plot, supposedly guaranteed by nature as the "true," predetermined course of history, is anything but certain.

The "natural" differences between the two "races" are of course crucial to understanding the nature of the war. Since the superiority of European culture over all others, no matter its current state of decadence, is taken as a given—there can be no anti-Semitism without it—the term Aryan, for Drumont, connotes this superiority, "the superior family of the white race, the Indo-European family" (5), while Semite connotes, term for term, trait for trait, the opposite. The lists of characteristics opposing the two terms are always long and seemingly endless; it is as if one can never say enough to ensure that the differences between the "races" will be recognized, that Aryan and Semite will be established as fundamental opposites:

> The Semite is mercenary, greedy, scheming, subtle, sly; the Aryan is enthusiastic, heroic, courtly, disinterested, frank, assured, to the point of naïveté. The Semite is of the material world, seeing hardly anything beyond present life; the Aryan is a son of the heavens, ceaselessly preoccupied with superior aspirations; one lives in reality, the other in the ideal. The Semite is by instinct merchant; . . . the Aryan is farmer, poet, monk, and above all soldier. The Semite has no creative faculty, while in contrast the Aryan invents; not the slightest invention was ever made by a Semite. (9).

Anti-Semitism can be seen in such quotations as the means by which the European attempts to found and support his own ideal, heroic identity, an identity that is nothing but the fiction of his superiority, a construct or image whose shape is determined in opposition to the negative myth of the Semite. The more inflated the portrait of the evil other, the more elevated and totalized the portrait of the identity of the people formulated as the other of the other becomes.

More basic than any of the sociopolitical crimes Drumont attributes to the Jews throughout history are the *cultural* inadequacies ascribed to the Jews, above all their supposed lack of creativity. As we have seen for Barrès, Maurras, Brasillach, and Drieu la Rochelle, all of whom were influenced by Drumont, and as will also be the case for Céline and Rebatet, the Jews, for the literary anti-Semite, quite simply are not and cannot be poets or artists, for they supposedly lack something *in their being* that is necessary for the creative act. "The truth is that the Jew is incapable of going beyond a very low level. Semites have no men of genius of the stature of Dante, Shakespeare, Bossuet, Victor Hugo, Michelangelo, Newton. . . . In art, they have no original, powerful or moving figure, no major work" (26–27). This "deficiency" of Jews in art and in the creation of original work, and the resulting superiority of Europeans in this area, is the basis for all of Drumont's other claims of superiority; it is the primary sign of why Jews ultimately should not be considered Europeans, or in this instance, French. "We cannot name one Jew who is a great French writer," claims Drumont (29), a judgment that will be repeated by anti-Semitic writers in France after him as a kind of nationalist rallying cry. Once it is "established" that Jews have not made any positive cultural contributions to France, then the next step is to claim that they play a completely negative role, constantly interfering with the natural creativity of the French themselves, constituting a threat to French art and culture, which is seen as the natural expression of national identity.

Drumont argues then that it is necessary to "contemplate, study, dissect, scour, analyze [all works of art], if one really wants to see the Jew" (202), because antiaesthetic, Jewish traits are often mistakenly taken as genuinely aesthetic. The meticulous "search for the Jew" in art is thus necessary because what is Jewish is not always the most evident aspect of a work, but when found, it immediately reveals in even what are considered the highest artistic achievements some unaesthetic characteristics that limit and even destroy them as works of art. For the literary anti-Semite, this is the danger of the Jew in general: the destruction of the highest cultural achievements of Europe. This is why everyone must learn "to see the Jew" everywhere he is hiding; the future of art and the future of Europe depend on it.

For Drumont and literary anti-Semitism in general, Jews have not achieved greatness as writers in France and cannot ever become great French writers because, quite simply, they supposedly cannot speak the French language "properly" or write in a natural, spontaneous, "essentially poetic" way: "Speaking French is something else," claims Drumont. "To speak a language, you first have to think in that language." And what this ultimately means for him is not the ability to speak grammatically correct French with a proper accent, a skill that of course can be acquired even if one is not born in France, but something that supposedly cannot be learned or appropriated, something the truly native French have as a birthright. Speaking and thinking "like a native" in this sense is the essence of the question of national identity. "Your discourse has a taste of its native land drawn from a common source of feelings and ideas" (30), Drumont says, in directly addressing his audience, the true French natives. Nonnatives are always deficient in such "taste" and therefore cannot share the deepest feelings and ideas of the native French that history has buried not only in the depths of the land but also in the nuances, accents, tones, and rhythms—the poetry—of the native language. Literary anti-Semitism has as one of its principal didactic goals to teach the French how to see and hear the foreign; that is, how to develop the faculty of taste they are said to be born with, and by doing so, distinguish themselves from the Jews. The cultural politics of anti-Semitism is thus in Drumont first and foremost a politics and policing of language and culture.

In terms of the ideal of an indigenous national culture, diseases of the nervous system of a people are even more dangerous than imperfections or diseases of the blood. For example, neurosis, which Drumont calls "the implacable disease of Jews," and which he claims has been prevalent for so many years among the Jews that their "nervous system ended up being altered" (105), also risks corrupting the French psyche and thus radically changing the relation of the French people to their past, to their culture, and to themselves. "It pleased the Jews, this perpetually agitated people," asserts Drumont in his discussion of the disastrous effects of the French Revolution, "to destroy the bases of ancient society" (136) and in doing so threaten French culture in its entirety. The real threat of "Jewish neurosis" (105), for him, is that when this intellectual, commercial, political agitation spread to the French themselves, they would continue the work of destruction against themselves and their culture begun by the Jews: "This neurosis, the Jew ended up, and this is strange, communicating it to our entire generation" (108). No drug or operation can cure such a disease, for it is not in its essence physiological; political action alone is not sufficient either. Rather a total psychological and metaphysical cure is necessary, one in which literature, art, and philosophy all have a large role to play in bringing the French back to themselves and reuniting them with traditional culture and society. Cure the mind and the spirit, and the rest will follow; if not, Drumont claims, all of France will soon become neurotic and "Jewified" [enjuivé], un-French.

Long before Céline, Drumont thus painted a picture of modern France and modern French history dominated by the negative influence of Jews. Because his anti-Semitism was not, strictly speaking, biologically determined, it could be directed anywhere and at anyone, at all of history and all "negative" or "decadent" aspects of culture and society. For "the Jew," freed from the restrictions imposed by a strictly racist definition, can be anywhere and in everyone, and no individual, group, class, or religious community, no matter how "pure" their blood, can be considered before-the-fact to be resistant to the Jewish neurosis. Everyone is at risk, and in fact, it is a relatively small step to assert, as Céline will, that almost everyone has already been "Jewified," and has become in his values and means of expression a "foreigner," a "Jew."

Anti-Semitic "history" is in this way, of course, written in terms of these determining factors: whether Jews were defeated or victorious, and whether the Jewish neurosis was contained or had its way and exploded onto the historical scene as a kind of madness. Wars, internal political conflicts, and revolts and revolutions, regardless of the particular individuals, groups, or classes explicitly involved in them, all dramatically reveal the same struggle of the nation against the Jews, even within revolutionary forces themselves: "The Commune thus had two sides: the first, unreasonable, impulsive, but courageous: the French side. The other, mercenary, greedy, thieving, basely calculating: the Jewish side" (401). Underneath events, therefore, lies constant political plotting and the manipulation of power that will result in victory or defeat of the Jews, and in the health or sickness of the nation. The unique law determining history for anti-Semitism is unambiguous and totally determining: "When the Jew is rising, France is falling; when the Jew is falling, France is rising" (515). To make France rise up again, the message is clear: the Jew must be made to fall.

By succeeding in raising the myth of the Jew to the "level of an ideology and a political method," as Michel Winock claims (132), but also, I would argue, to the level of a "total art," Drumont in *La France juive* laid the groundwork for generations of anti-Semitic nationalists after him. In his own words, however, as he defended *La France juive* against his critics, Drumont stressed another side of his discourse, one that led even more directly to modern literature and to the anti-Semitic and fascist writers that will take up his legacy: the particular function he gives himself as author in this work. He presents himself as a simple spokesman, a vehicle through which popular sentiment can directly express itself: "I was the spokesman for all sufferings that did not have a voice, for all muted sorrows, for all passive victims, all the resigned, all the exploited, and all the duped who do not have it in them to fight and who don't even dare cry: 'Stop thief!'" (*La France juive devant l'opinion*, 6). The rage of the populist anti-Semite, no matter how personal, is the rage of all those who can be led to believe they have suffered at the hands of the Jews; all those unwilling, unable, or supposedly kept from testifying on their own behalf to the injustices they imagine have been inflicted on them by the evil forces associated with Jews, who are of course also accused of controlling newspapers, the publishing and culture industries, and the universities. Anti-Semitism always gives this nationalist anger a place, a name, and a figure against which to direct itself.

Drumont's anti-Semitism, then, presents itself as nothing less than the collective expression of a suffering people, a people whose country and identity are being stolen or destroyed. In this way, Drumont defends his work as being deeply populist and "nationalist," an authentic, spontaneous expression of strong feelings of the people, an unmediated, unreflective (anti-intellectual) popular art that at the same time maintains its formal integrity and poetic consistency: a spontaneous, popular outburst that is at the same time the highest form of art. Built into literary anti-Semitism is the internal necessity to strive for "poetic" (and political) totalization; that is, the formation, exposition, and demonstration of a single idea or image, and its exhaustive, dogmatic application to every aspect of life. Moderation, compromises, and half measures are in fact antithetical to anti-Semitism; a little anti-Semitism, a moderate form of anti-Semitism, is already the basis for absolute, unbounded, generalized anti-Semitism. Cultural or literary anti-Semitism can even be applied more extensively than biologically determined, strictly racist anti-Semitism, which is ultimately limited by the restriction of having to bring everything in the last instance back to "blood." Literary anti-Semites are limited only by the capacities of their imagination.

Style and Race

Much separates the more expository, syntactically orthodox, classical language of Drumont from the wild, seemingly unstructured, often vulgar, popular language of Céline. But in many respects, it is as if Céline were simply taking up where Drumont left off, giving a new language and style to anti-Semitism and thus fulfilling, and taking to a more extreme limit, a process begun in Drumont's *La France juive* and dictated by its logic. In his pamphlets, Céline readily admitted his debt to all previous anti-Semitic literature, acknowledging that there was nothing original in what he had written in his pamphlets: "All that is written down. I discovered nothing. Absolutely no pretension at all. Simple, virulent, stylized vulgarization" (*L'Ecole des cadavres*, 33). Céline thus saw himself as a vulgarizer of what he called the "science of Judeology," and yet the stylistic "nothing" that constituted his discovery and his chief contribution to the history of anti-Semitism ended up being everything. For Céline's "stylized vulgarization" of anti-Semitism was not just incredibly successful in its turn, but it also raised even more directly than *La France juive* the question of the literary-aesthetic dimension both of Céline's particular form of anti-Semitism and of French anti-Semitism in general. It made his style an important part of the controversy surrounding the publication of his pamphlets, and it has made his poetic theory a problem that had to be analyzed in order to understand the ideological implications of his work.

Because of the controversial and yet elevated position held by Céline's novels in the history of twentieth-century literature, especially his early novels, *Voyage au bout de la nuit* (Paris: Denoël, 1932) and *Mort à crédit* (Paris: Denoël, 1936), the problem of the relation between his novels and his pamphlets—that is, to put it starkly, his "art" and his anti-Semitism— has been much debated. It has often meant that his novels are treated as being radically different in style, form, and effect from his anti-Semitic pamphlets, that literature and anti-Semitism, poetics and politics, are treated as separate and distinct issues in dealing with his works, as if his anti-Semitism ended where his art began, even in the pamphlets themselves. And the question of style has almost always been considered the key to understanding what separates his racist ideology and politics from his "revolutionary" poetic and narrative innovations.

After the war, Céline's insistence on the problem of style was clearly a way of obfuscating his anti-Semitism and his fascist political preferences. In numerous letters to Milton Hindus, and in interviews and texts in which he defended his activities before and during the war by casting them in the best light possible, Céline argued that he was never really an ideologue but rather "a stylist," a *writer* not a political militant. In a letter from Copenhagen (April 16, 1947), which summarizes all of the statements he made at various times on this subject, Céline describes his own rhetoric and style in the following way:[6]

> The fact that you consider me a stylist makes me happy—I am that above all—in no way a thinker, God forbid! nor gr writer but stylist I believe I am—my gr—father was a professor of rhetoric at Le Havre—I take from him without a doubt this skill in emotive "rendering." [. . .] I follow emotion closely with words I don't give it time to dress itself in sentences . . . I seize it totally raw or rather totally poetic—because the core of man in spite of everything is poetic[. . . .] Still it's a trick [*truc*] for making spoken language pass into the written—the trick I'm the one who found it no one else—all in all it's impressionism—To make spoken language pass into literature—it's not stenography—It is necessary to imprint on sentences, on intervals a certain deformation an artifice so that when you read the book, it seems as if someone is speaking in your ear—That is accomplished by the transposition of each word[. . . .] To render on the flat page the effect of spoken spontaneous life it is necessary to twist all of language, rhythm, cadence, words and it's a kind of poetry which provides the best spell [*sortilège*]—the impression, the bewitchment, the dynamism. (*Cahier de l'Herne: Céline*, 383–84)

No matter how "spontaneous" his writing might seem, no matter how much it might seem as if he wrote without literary pretensions or style, Céline always insisted that his writing was rhetorical and poetic in the strongest sense, a working on language to produce powerful effects. He was especially interested in the *rhetorical effect* of spontaneous, unreflective—that is, for him—purely poetic language and authentic, unmediated emotion. And his stylistic goal, he repeatedly claimed, was nothing less than the expression of the being of man, what he called man's "poetic core."

Céline made no hard and fast distinction between his pamphlets and his novels, for he considered his style and rhetoric to be the same in each.

He was especially proud of his rhetorical skills in the pamphlets, stressing already in *Bagatelles pour un massacre* the difficulties involved in pulling off the "trick of style":

> Nothing is more difficult than to direct, dominate, transpose spoken language, emotive language, the only sincere language, usual language, into written language, to fix it without killing it. . . . Try. . . . It's the terrible "technique" in which most writers collapse, a thousand times more difficult than what is called "artistic" writing. (*Bagatelles*, 218)

In this way, Céline, and by no means inaccurately, defined himself as a master of the "trick" of making the written come alive, as a master rhetorician whose goal was to twist written language and turn it against itself in order to destroy its conventions and make it better cast its poetic spell. In other words, all of his work, his pamphlets, his novels, and his plays, in his own terms, could be considered a "simple, virulent, stylized vulgarization"—a vulgarization, however, that reveals certain fundamental truths obscured or destroyed by conventional language and rhetoric and what he called "artistic writing." Céline's is an antipoetic poetics, a poetics that assigns itself the total metaphysical project of capturing the essence of the poetic itself, which is also the essence of the political.

In the same letter from Copenhagen to Hindus, Céline admitted that his rhetoric or style was not appropriate for all subjects, or rather that all subjects were not appropriate for it: "It is also necessary to choose one's subject—Everything is not transposable—subjects 'with life' are needed—hence the terrible risks—in order to read all the secrets" (384). A radical form of rhetorical work on the appropriate subjects, then, would supposedly reveal "the poetic core" of man, the secrets of life itself. As a vehicle for revealing profound secrets, secrets that are deemed essential to the survival of European ("Aryan") man *and his poetry*, the war against the foreign, which is most fully realized in anti-Semitism, must be considered to be *the primary subject* at the very foundation of Céline's poetic ideology in general, even when it is not explicitly present as a dominant, obsessive theme or a determining component of an extremist political ideology.

In this sense, given the way it is linked to the question of style in his work and construed as the principal support for his poetics in general, anti-Semitism must be considered not a momentary aberration in his thinking but a logical direction for his writing to have taken. Céline's "stylized" anti-Semitism is ultimately rooted in and dependent on the metaphysical poetics he constantly evoked to justify his writing in general, for he not only made race the determining element of his poetics, but at the same time he proposed the realization of a poetic ideal as the ultimate purpose of his racism.

In order to save Céline from himself and to defend the originality and force of his subversive literary practice or style, some of the best-known readers of Céline have attempted nevertheless to make the anti-Semitism of his pamphlets insignificant or irrelevant to his "art" by treating his rhetoric and style, abstracted not just from politics but even from the poetic ideology supporting them, as the only questions worthy of consideration.[7] In sharp contrast to approaches that separate the poetic from the ideological stands Julia Kristeva's analysis of Céline, which attempts to explain the profound connection between Céline's anti-Semitism and his commitment to fascism, on the one hand, and his radical form of writing, on the other—how the worst forms of totalitarian ideology and anti-Semitic and racist diatribes are *linked to* what, for her, is a revolutionary and radically antitotalitarian poetic practice.[8] Kristeva's basic argument seems difficult to dispute on both poetic and political grounds: that the pamphlets should not be isolated from the rest of Céline's work because they have the same style of writing as the novels:

> [Céline's pamphlets], in spite of their stereotyped themes, carry on the savage beauty of his style. Isolating them from the totality of his texts is a defensive or accusatory act of the left or the right; it is at any rate an ideological stance, not an analytical or literary procedure. The pamphlets provide the phantasmatic substratum on which, otherwise and elsewhere, the novelistic works were built. (*Powers of Horror*, 174, trans. modified)

Whatever questions one might want to raise concerning Kristeva's reading, her analysis of the way in which Céline's entire literary-aesthetic project is rooted in the recurring phantasms explicitly revealed by the pamphlets is crucial for an understanding of the "political" effects of style and of the poetic or aesthetic nature and function of anti-Semitism in Céline.[9]

Quite simply, Kristeva considers Céline's "politics" to be an internal rather than an external problem for all of his writing:

> His adherence to Nazism, as ambivalent and derisive as that action was, is not one that can be explained. It becomes integrated into the whole as an internal necessity.... His hateful fascination with Jews, which he maintained to the end of his life, and the simple-minded anti-Semitism that intoxicates the tumultuous pages of the pamphlets are no accident. (136, trans. modified)

This may very well still be, as Alice Kaplan claims, a complicated way of saving Céline "from fascism without having to deny his fascism or apologize for it" (*Reproductions of Banality: Fascism, Literature, and French Intellectual Life* [Minneapolis: University of Minnesota Press, 1986], 109), a way of being able to deplore his fascism and still "love" the Céline "whose style might liberate us from the dangerous rigidity of empirical thinking" (108). For Kristeva does "save" Céline and a certain modern literature from falling completely into the abyss opened by his and its fascination with the primal and the mythical (rhythms, music, and the presemantic, which Kristeva associates with the mother), what she calls after Bataille "the abject," whose political manifestations, she argues, are fundamentally totalitarian.[10]

Kristeva's analysis leads us repeatedly back to what could be called the art of the primal in Céline: the presemantic murmurings, rhythms, songs, dances, obscenities that are for her also presymbolic (actually metasymbolic or "ur"-symbolic), antitranscendent manifestations of a libidinal energy in its purest, freest form; that is, under the sign and protection of the *maternal*, in the uninterrupted, undifferentiated (I would add, illusory) proximity if not presence of the mother. This original site, the site of all sites, is at the same time the best and worst of sites. It is the site of total freedom, beauty, and pleasure (read, the poetic), and the site of absolute enslavement, repulsiveness, and horror (read, totalitarian politics). The former meets its limit in and necessarily reverses itself into the latter in this site:

> [Céline's style] persuades us that the pleasure [*jouissance*] of so-called primary narcissism's immanence can be sublimated in a signifier that has been recast and desemanticized to the point of music. Furthermore, it is impossible not to hear the liberating truth of such a call to rhythm and joy. . . . And yet, both the enchantment of the style and libertarian spontaneity do not exist without carrying along with them their own *limit*: at the very moment they seek to escape from the oppression of thinking, from ethical or legislating Unity, they prove to be tied to the deadliest of phantasms. (179–80, trans. modified)

Led on by the promise of *jouissance*, the pleasure of "natural" rhythm and unbounded joy, Céline pushed to the limit his pursuit of "liberating truth" and was willing to take the risks involved in such a total poetic/political endeavor, explicitly assuming the hatred against difference and the Other that such an endeavor ultimately implies. Unrestrained, the poetic pleasure principle leads to death.[11]

The primal, therefore, for Kristeva, could be seen as the ultimate form of the poetic sublime, the irresolvably conflictual realm of love and hatred, beauty and horror, freedom and enslavement. In a sense, all "poetry" is inevitably drawn back to this site if it attempts to realize itself fully *as poetry*. For, as Kristeva acknowledges, "all literature is probably a version of the apocalypse that seems to me rooted, no matter what its socio-historical conditions might be, in the fragile border ('borderline') where identities (subject/object, etc.) do not exist or only barely so— double, blurred, heterogeneous, animal, metamorphosed, altered, abject" (207). This means that Céline for her is just "one possible example among others of the abject" (207), and the real subject of her study is what his writing exemplifies: literature, "the privileged signifier" of the horror of being, as well as of the poetic sense and power of this horror (208).

The chief problem with Kristeva's analysis lies with the metaphysics of poetry that supports it, an (in large part negative) idealization of the poetic as rooted in and equivalent to the primal. Her powerful analysis of Céline's anti-Semitism and fascism and their intimate links with the primal phantasms buried in all his writing, and which orient his style, is thus limited by the privilege she assigns to literature and to the poetic language she claims defines literature. The privilege of the poetic consists in it being considered the original and ultimate form of revolution, of the resistance to transcendence. For this reason, poetry for her *always* approximates both psychosis and totalitarian ideology: "Poetic language, the only language that consumes transcendence and theology to support itself, poetic language, knowingly the enemy of religion, by its very economy borders on psychosis (as for the subject) and totalitarianism or fascism (as for the institutions it implies or evokes)" (*Desire in Language*, 125). For Kristeva, fascism and psychosis, then, haunt all literature, and it is certainly not the least gifted writers who give in to either or both of them, but rather those who risk the most. Kristeva's own fascination with the poetic as *the* original, presemantic language, which has become in her work equivalent to an insistence on the libidinal, maternal, pre-Oedipal characteristics of the ambivalent (read "poetic") subject, leads her with Céline back to the primal. The issue for me is how she and he are led back to this primitive, original site, and what concept of the poetic occupies or constitutes the origin.

Kristeva is certainly not wrong to focus on how Céline's radical attempt to make written language (and literature) more "emotive" is implicated in his hallucinatory diatribes against the Jews, or on how the return to a more "primitive," presemantic poetic level of language mirrors the attempt to return to an impossible, original social site, with the goal of destroying the Symbolic and the transcendent, but at the expense of the figure to which all forms of otherness have been assigned. My question is whether it is sufficient to analyze critically the link between anti-Semitism and literature (the poetic) in Céline's work, if the ultimate goal is to point out the dangers of the one while defending the privileges of the other and "saving it," even if it is in its ultimate form or in the last instance, from fascist contamination.

If a critic fails to challenge the privilege Céline grants to the ideal of an original "native" poetic language as the model for his radical notion of style, if the critic fails to question and undermine the ideal of "literary primitivism" and the immediacy to which his style aspires as fundamental and determining elements of his anti-Semitism, it can legitimately be

asked whether the critic has really succeeded in the crucial task of analyzing the interconnection of poetics and politics in Céline's work. Kristeva
certainly avoids the most common pitfalls of Céline criticism, which come
from initially and totally separating Céline's novels from his pamphlets,
and his poetics from his politics. But she reintroduces a similar separation
on another, deeper level, when she continues in her own approach, in the
name of a critique of fascism and anti-Semitism, to give a very risky,
unstable, but still privileged position to poetic language and literature in
general, as the alternatives to and the enemies of the transcendent, the
Symbolic, and the religious.[12]

  If in Céline the poetic is destructive of what Kristeva calls the Symbolic,
and of all forms of religious and political transcendence, it is precisely
because true poetry constitutes in its own right the only genuine alternative not only to politics and religion but also to all existing forms of literature and art. Poetry is for Céline the only authentic and total form of
transcendence. To understand Céline's anti-Semitism and his politics,
therefore, it is necessary to concentrate not just on his "writing as such"
but also on his *poetic* theory, the way in which his proposals for what I
would call a total poetics serves as the foundation on which his particular
form of hallucinatory, totalitarian politics of race was built. His totalitarian political views and anti-Semitism, in this sense, should not be seen
as representing a retreat from his poetic principles or as a result of his
crossing the border supposedly existing between the poetic and the political, but rather as constituting the most extreme political manifestation of
those poetics.

The Politics of Language and the Poetics of Race

In trying to situate Céline's "racist politics," traditional political categories are not completely adequate. Unlike the majority of French fascists
and anti-Semites with whom he is usually associated, Céline, like Drieu la
Rochelle, was not strictly speaking a nationalist and had little sympathy
for even radical nationalist movements. In *L'Ecole des cadavres* (1938),
Céline denounced even French extremist, anti-Semitic nationalist movements for not being anti-Semitic enough, for not making anti-Semitism their first and only principle: "Our national rectifiers, men like La
Rocque, like Doriot, Maurras, [. . .] they rectify nothing at all, because
they never speak first and foremost of getting rid of the Jews. [. . .] They
are all in all accomplices of the Jews, poisoners, traitors. [. . .] The Jew is
the flesh of their flesh. [. . .] They don't want them to be smashed" (174).
Later in the same text, he attacks nationalism in general for being "still
another Jewish gimmick [. . .] to get us better to kill each other" (223)

through the wars waged in its name. Throughout this pamphlet, Céline argues for the solidarity of the "Aryan race" against the Jews, for an anti-Semitism and racism that would put an end to the divisions and wars among European nations and, above all, make an alliance with Hitler possible and necessary. As a politics, anti-Semitism represented for him the possibility of achieving a unity more basic than any form of political unity based on nationalist principles, the possibility of returning to the origin and the mythical unity of the "Aryan race."

Céline even boasts in the preface to the reedition of *L'Ecole des cadavres* that was published during the Occupation (1942), that "the *Ecole* was the only text from the period (in a journal or book) to be *at one and the same time* anti-Semitic, *racist*, collaborationist (before the fact) up to the point of an immediate military alliance [with Germany], anti-English, anti-freemason, and predicting an absolute catastrophe in the case of conflict" (in *Cahiers Céline*, no. 7, "Céline et l'actualité [1933–1961]" [Paris: Gallimard, 1986], 174). His political ideology, founded firmly in anti-Semitism, seems, at least explicitly, to have had little to do with defending the French nation per se and more to do with collaborating with the Germans in the name of an international "Aryan alliance" and a total war against the Jews and "their allies." In terms of most definitions of what it is to be a nationalist, Céline certainly would not qualify.

But such definitions are much too narrow when it comes to someone like Céline. For if Céline was against nationalism as a narrow political ideology, it was because he claimed it did not go far enough in its defense of the nation, nor penetrate deeply enough into the essence of the French people, but ultimately led to their destruction. In his pamphlets, Céline took the position of what could be called a primary nationalism or an ultranationalism, elaborating the mythical project of reviving and saving the French in their very being as a people, prior to any specific political expression of that identity. His "nation" is a nation before the State, an original identity of the people in nature, one that can be revived not by political doctrine but through a return to a primary, spontaneous emotional "poetic" state, which, though lost, would still be possible to evoke or reproduce through a particular practice of art and literature.

Through arguments stressing the original poetic nature of the French people, Céline explicitly linked the question of the form and style of his own writing to the political project of saving the French people from being completely "Jewified," their poetic essence lost in the unnatural and superficial jargon and rhythms he associated with the Jews: "Rediscover a confidence, a rhythm, a music for this people, a lyricism that takes it out of Jewish gibberish" (*L'Ecole*, 93). Even if it were true, as Céline claimed once again after the war in his fictitious interview with Professor Y, that he was never a political man, never a man of ideas—"I never had any ideas, not me! not one! and I think that nothing is more vulgar, more common, more disgusting than ideas!" (*Entretiens avec le Professeur Y* [Paris: Gallimard, 1983–; originally published in 1955], 19)—the political implications of his poetics would still have to be analyzed. For even if we accept that he was primarily a "poet," a man of language, of the rhythm and lyricism of popular, "spoken" language, it must also be acknowledged that this lyricism itself was governed by a poetic ideal that was inseparable from a political idea of the people, of a purely poetic, musical people, a people of art.

Céline's ultranationalist poetic ideal—an ideal he defended in his pamphlets, as well as after the war, when he was attempting to dismiss or explain away his fascist and anti-Semitic *ideas*—is that of the unity and identity of an original people. Rhythm, music, and lyricism represent the essential elements of this primary poetic reality. "In reality, it's the return to the spontaneous poetry of the savage. The savage doesn't express himself without poetry, he can't" (Letter to Milton Hindus [March 15, 1947], in *Cahier de l'Herne: Céline*, 386). Céline's "primitivism," as a style and as an idea, is in this way intimately linked to the anti-Semitism in terms of which it was explicitly articulated and defended in his pamphlets. For to evoke a state of being before "Jewish gibberish" has had the chance to interfere with the spontaneous, musical poetry of original, "savage man" is to make the Jew not just the historical enemy of the French but also the aesthetic-metaphysical enemy, *the* antipoetic force that destroyed the original state of being and that interferes with the possible return to that state—the force outside of history that inaugurated history as the struggle for survival between poetic and antipoetic forces, between the Aryan and the Jew.

This characterization of the evil ascribed to the Jews as an absolute, metaphysical evil—an aesthetic evil—one that threatens the very souls and being of the French, makes it necessary to bring every political, economic, cultural, and aesthetic question ultimately back to this original site and to this figure. Wherever there is no rhythm and lyricism, there is the Jew; wherever there is rhythm and lyricism, that is, poetry, there the Jew and his gibberish are absent or have been eliminated, and there the "savage," the original and authentic form of the Frenchman, can be himself and can spontaneously express himself in his native music and tongue. The law governing the ultranationalism of Céline is, as he acknowledged in *Bagatelles pour un massacre*, that of the jungle: "The great secret of the jungle, of all jungles, the only truth of men and beasts and things. 'Be conquered or conquer,' the only dilemma, the ultimate truth" (60). In politics and in literature, as in the original, mythical jungle, Céline demanded nothing less than that the war between poetic and antipoetic principles and "races" be explicit, that the enemy be known and openly fought and destroyed. The racial-poetic law of survival was thus presented by Céline as being absolute and uncompromising: "It is necessary for us, humans, to yield to this law, to this tendency or disappear. No compromises at all. 'Develop or Disappear,' the natural law of biological 'development' "—which of course must lead to the conclusion that "the Jew must disappear" (*L'Ecole des cadavres*, 109).

Céline, like Drumont and the other literary anti-Semites, represented "the Jew" as being unpoetic or unaesthetic in his very being, without the gift of aesthetic creation and reduced to the lowliest state of mimeticism: "[The Jew] sings any song you want, dances to all types of music, wriggling with monkeys, howling with the lowly wolves, . . . imitating all animals, all races. . . . He's a mimetic [un mimétique], a whore" (*Les Beaux draps*, 142). To compensate for his lack of creativity, according to Céline, the Jew is forced not only to mime but also to reason rather than feel. The passage that follows summarizes all of the anti-Semitic clichés of the non-original, parasitic, antiaesthetic characteristics projected onto the Jews in order to contrast them point by point with the people endowed with the capacity to feel and create, the people of art:

> Jews are rather poorly gifted for the arts, biologically, at the very foundation of their nature. They try in Europe to create art, nevertheless they manage it badly and at cross purposes. . . It is necessary for them to supplement this lack, to cheat, to ceaselessly plunder, to suck out the life of their neighbors, the natives, to sustain themselves. . . Jews disastrously lack direct, spontaneous emotion. . . They speak instead of experiencing. . . They reason before feeling. . . Strictly speaking, they experience nothing. [. . .] They are condemned if they inhabit our climate to waste their energy on grimaces, tom-toms, in imitations, like Negroes and like all monkeys. . . They feel nothing directly and assimilate very few things profoundly . . . from which comes [. . .] all this pompous, doctrinaire masturbatory material, instead of direct humanity, true inspiration. (*Bagatelles*, 69)

"The Jew," without the gift of art, produces critical treatises and servile imitations of art and in this way acts as an aesthetic and political parasite, threatening true art and authentic artists by sucking out their life and force.

Céline's pretense of being a "man of style," a writer who worked to "render the emotive" in written language, to twist written language so that the spontaneity of feeling came through it, and the related admission that he had never had any ideas, can both be seen, then, not just as statements of poetic principle but also as ways of continuing to claim: I am not a Jew. I am a genuine, poetic Frenchman. I give a true, unmediated, authentic picture of "direct humanity" of which I and my work are representative. This evocation of the primal, emotive force of an original, spontaneous poetic language and the figure of a poetic people cannot be separated in Céline's work from the force and figure to which they are opposed: the apoetic or antipoetic force of servile mimesis and the figure of the Jew as the unfeeling, uninspired mime.[13]

For Céline, the danger represented by the Jews for art and culture in general was not just that they constituted the inauthentic, the nonoriginal, the mimetic—that is, the antiaesthetic extreme—but also that they had succeeded in corrupting the taste of the "Aryan masses," who, because of their influence, could no longer distinguish between the authentic and the false, the original and the copy:

> The immense astuteness of the Jews consists of progressively removing from the standardized masses all taste for the authentic, and then from all indigenous artists every possibility of expressing, communicating their sensitivity to their racial brothers, to reawake in them any authentic emotion. The Jews, the revenge of the Abyssinians! have inverted the taste of Whites so deeply, to the point that the French prefer in the present the false to the authentic, the grimace to sensitivity, imbecile mimetism to direct emotion. (187)

The danger of mimesis is that it is difficult to contain, and if left unchecked it contaminates everything. The revolution in art, like the revolution in society and politics, therefore had to be total in order to counter the corrupting effects of this "inversion of tastes." The capacity to feel, the basic taste for the authentic and the direct, had to be restored, and centuries of the corruption and inversion of the emotive and the aesthetic had to be reversed. Nothing less than the identity of the French (of all Europeans) as "Aryans," which was postulated as being rooted in their capacity to feel and create, was argued to be at stake.

This meant that the "Aryan" had to rediscover his native poetic rhythm in order to fend off the alien rhythms of the "tom-toms" that had been imposed on him and that imprisoned him, making him radically other than he originally was or should be, a robot following the directions of foreign forces, languages, and rhythms:

> The only defense, the only recourse of the White man against robotism, and undoubtedly against war, [. . .] is the return to his proper, emotional rhythm. The circumcised Jews are in the process of castrating the Aryan of his natural emotional rhythm. The Negro Jew is in the process of making the Aryan tumble into Communism and robot art, into the objectivist mentality of perfect slaves for Jews. (191)[14]

Céline considered political enslavement to be inevitable unless an effective resistance to the corrupting poetics of the unnatural could be found. To castrate the Aryan of his natural rhythm is to castrate him of his poetic being, to reduce him to the state of a poetic and political mime or robot; in other words, to make him a Jew.

Not to have the gift of art, of inspiration and feeling, was ultimately not to be totally human, and Céline's anti-Semitism and racism—of both the prewar and the postwar periods—were rooted in the presumption that the "non-Aryan" lacked these gifts.[15] For there was always a poetic purpose behind such racial hatred and ideological "madness." Because "the Jew" was defined as being entirely mimetic rather than original, authentic, or creative, the obsessive, hallucinatory representation of the Jew in Céline's pamphlets could be considered to be his attempt to represent mimesis in itself; that is, to represent the unrestrained process of mimeticism when it is cut off from any original source or referent. It constituted Céline's poetic-political effort to neutralize and overcome the mimetic in its most extreme form. This explains the exaggerated, unrestrained characteristics of such representations, their tendency to take over the entire field of representation, given that they were ungrounded, cut off from any specific reality or referent, and at least in principle infinitely variable. What is consistent in Céline's work, therefore, is not the form given to the Jew (to the mime or mimetic process), but rather the will to overcome all forms of mimeticism and return to the immediacy of pure poetic expression and rhythms. Anti-Semitism, in this context, thus has the form of a radical, primitive poeticism; the total negative representation of the Jew serves as the means for (re)instituting the poetic being of "Aryan man."

Céline's apparent shifts of opinion about whether particular individuals or groups should be characterized as being Jewish or "Jewified" have presented problems for readers looking for a logic or coherence on the referential level of his anti-Semitism. Such apparent contradictions are resolved, however, if they are analyzed in the light of the extreme, antimimetic, poeticist logic at the foundation of Céline's anti-Semitism, for there are no passages in any of Céline's works that *contradict* specific anti-Semitic passages, and certainly none that contradicts his anti-Semitism as a whole. Racine, the pope, or whomever else he called a Jew may not consistently and in all places be presented and denounced as a Jew, but the representation and denunciation of Jews and the "Jewified" as being responsible for the corruption of "Aryans," and the characterization of the entire process of "Jewification" as one in which mimeticism destroys "native" art and the spontaneity of authentic poetic rhythms, are invariable constants of his work. Céline's unrelenting, terrifying, but nonetheless logical poetic and political project was always to reverse this process and overcome mimesis, and in doing so to put an end once and for all to the "Jewification" of the French people and their art.[16]

There is thus an underlying logic to the contradictions of Céline's anti-

Semitism, for he presents both the Jews and the literary and political groups with which he associates them as manifesting the same lack of spontaneous feeling and creativity and representing the same threat to the poetic being of the "Aryan":

> Sur-realism. Nothing more to fear from it! No emotionalism necessary. Take refuge in it, proclaim oneself a genius in it, anyone who wants. Any eunuch whatsoever, any sticky kike in a frenzy of deceptiveness can place himself at the pinnacle. All that is necessary is a little understanding, very easy to achieve, with the critics, that is, among Jews. [. . .] The Jews [. . .] are accomplishing at present, under the same banner, their conquest of the world, the monstrous crushing, the degradation, the systematic and total annihilation of our most natural emotions of all our essential arts, instincts, music, painting, poetry, theater. . . . 'Replace Aryan emotion with the Negro tom-tom.' Sur-realism, the prolongation of naturalism, art for hateful robots, instrument of despotism, of swindling, of Jewish deception. [. . .] It's the cadaster of our emotive degeneration. (*Bagatelles*, 170–71)

The Jew *is* being represented and identified by Céline in this and other passages as the supreme anti-poetic figure who is capable of taking on an infinite number of diverse forms and identities because he lacks an authentic poetic origin and the national-emotive identity of the "Aryan."[17]

The reason the Jew is everywhere is that he is everything the "poetic savage," the natural Frenchman ("Aryan"), is not, everything that is unnatural in the state of nature and after and outside of nature. Of course the Jew has an endless number of diverse, though not (at least not on the level of the poetic logic at work here) contradictory forms—he would not be as dangerous a parasite, as corrupting a mime, as inhibiting a cerebral force, as powerful an enemy, if he were not so heterogeneous in form. This is the most dogmatically ideological and the most ruthlessly logical and least contradictory of positions. It constitutes an excellent example of what Hannah Arendt has called "the tyranny of logicality" (*The Origins of Totalitarianism* [New York: Harcourt Brace Jovanovich, 1973], 473), the determination and evaluation of everything in terms of the same poeticist-racist principle.

Céline's pamphlets are also performances in anti-Semitic rhetoric and representation, as well as teaching devices to aid precisely in recognizing and *identifying* the Jew, wherever he is, whatever form he takes on, whatever antipoetic practice he uses:

> It is necessary to learn [. . .] to recognize the mark, the trace, the grip, the initiative of the Jews in all the upheavals of the world, there where they are carried out. [. . .] It is necessary to learn to decipher in daily practice the color and the tone, the chatter of Jewish imperialism, of Jewish (or freemason) prop-

aganda, it is necessary to learn to pierce through, to determine at the base of all the shadows, [. . .] behind all the grimaces, the universal lie, the implacable conquering Jewish megalomania. (124)

If the Jew is everywhere because he is nothing in himself and has no natural origin to which he can be linked, then nothing and no one is exempt from his influence and from the possibility of being "Jewified," and no hint or trace of Jewish influence is too obscure to identify, no manifestation too insignificant to denounce.

So when Céline rants and raves that wars are Jewish, that the high rate of alcoholism among workers is the fault of the Jews, that democracy, communism, royalism, and nationalism, newspapers of the right and left, all politics, all business, film, theater, and literature, the Catholic Church, the pope, and the Apostles are all Jewish or "Jewified," he must be taken seriously, not just as a dangerous racist and ideologue, but also as a radical, extremist theoretician of the poetic. Which means that his theory of poetics and its totalizing logic must be understood not exclusively in poetic terms but in connection with his hallucinatory political and racist ideas as well. For the only force that remains uncorrupted, outside of the destructive effects of mimesis, is the authentic poetic voice itself, the voice of Céline-poet crying out and denouncing all forms of antipoetic "Jewification" before it is too late, giving to this cry a style and a force it never had before, and refusing to limit it in any way in order to make it less contradictory or more "realistic" in its aims or representations.

Thus, Céline's "revolution in poetic language" can never be taken as simply "liberating," even on poetic grounds alone. For the war he waged against grammar, syntax, and lexical restrictions, against the state of French language in modernity, the dead language French had become in the hands of bourgeois and "Jewified" professors, journalists, and writers, was the same war he waged against the Jews. It was a war fought *on behalf of* another, more primitive, more authentically French, emotive, poetic language, a war to make French literature and the French language truly *French* again or perhaps even for the first time.

To defend the natural poeticity of "native French," he therefore has to denounce all formal, rhetorical, and grammatical limitations imposed on the French language, everything that transformed authentic, emotive French into the falsely "literary" French of the bourgeoisie, of professors, robots, and Jews:

> The delicately French, "stripped down" French language, adapts itself marvelously to this design. [. . .] The "French" of the *lycée*, decanted "French," filtered French, stripped-down rigid French, scrubbed (modernized, naturalist) French, muzzled French, Montaigne, Racine French, Jewish French for baccalaureates, the French of Anatole the Jewified, Goncourt French, the disgusting

French of elegance, molded, Oriental, unctuous, slimy as shit, it's the very epi-
taph of the French race [. . . .] It's the ideal French for Robots. (166–67)

Céline wrote against this French and against the "Jewification" or de-
poeticization of his people; he proposed another "purely poetic" form of
French and another way of being French that were in themselves the sign
that all was not lost, that the "savage poetry" of the original French had
not been totally destroyed and could be restored or recreated once again.
Winning the battle against mimesis and the Jews ultimately meant, then,
restoring to the French language its original, purely poetic qualities. And
even after the war, when he ceased his anti-Semitic diatribes, Céline never
gave up this totalitarian poetics of language.[18]

Whatever the inconsistencies of Céline's explicit political positions,
whatever the absurdities, exaggerations, and contradictions of his racist
claims, this poetic ideal remained consistent and unchallenged throughout his work. To claim that Céline, after Drumont, Barrès, Maurras, and
many others, but in a very different style and context, made of anti-Semitism a profoundly aesthetic, literary phenomenon, is not to say that his
pamphlets had no political effects. Quite the contrary. It is to claim,
rather, that their political effects were rooted in and inseparable from
their poetic premises and rhetorical strategies. Céline could be considered
the writer who most completely realized the anti-Semitic literary project,
who through his unrestrained representation of the Jew as the original
mimetic, antipoetic force demonstrated how anti-Semitism was not just
rooted in an ideological principle or racist idea, but was also the product
of a radical poetic theory and in this way was also a problem of style and
rhetoric. Céline's pamphlets reveal that the mad but brilliant "humor-
ous" lyricism of this poet of popular language, and the poetic theory developed to describe and justify it, are inseparable from his anti-Semitism
and are the foundation of his totalitarian political vision.

I am certainly not suggesting that all radically antimimetic theories of
literature are essentially totalitarian or that an insistence on poetic
rhythm leads inevitably to anti-Semitism. I am arguing, however, that *in
Céline's case* his antimimetic poetics and anti-Semitism, and his poetic
and political visions, were inextricably linked together and that no critic
can afford to ignore the one in order either to praise or condemn the
other. It seems to me important for both poetics and politics to understand how Céline's absolute form of anti-Semitism was in fact profoundly
poetic or literary in form, and how a revolutionary theory and practice of
narrative gave form and style to a racist and totalitarian politics.

This does not mean that all of Céline, every line of every novel he
wrote, must be considered racist and therefore condemned or censored.
On the contrary, it means rather that the fundamental poetic problems

raised by his work, such as the impact of his "revolutionary style," the nature of his poetic theory and practice, and the implications of his break with narrative conventions and lexical restrictions, can never be treated completely in themselves as exclusively poetic problems. Rather, the questions of anti-Semitism and totalitarian politics must always be raised in connection with his poetics and as poetic problems, even when they are not present as explicit themes in the works being treated. A critical understanding of his poetics cannot afford to ignore or deemphasize in any way the monstrous forms his poetic principles took in his pamphlets and the specific destiny the pamphlets gave to the style Céline practiced and defended. In his case, the totalization of the poetic and the political, which is typical of literary fascism in general, is pushed to its extreme limits, revealing in this way the terrifying implications of the absolute poetics of race.

Eight

The Art of Anti-Semitic Rage:
Lucien Rebatet's Aesthetics
of Violence

[*L'Action Française* before 1914] was an
incomparable newspaper, the finest, without a
doubt, ever published in Paris. Everything in it
was new. . . . The violence of its language was
in perfect harmony with the violence of its
thinking. . . .

. . . Who was [Céline], then, really? An anarchist?
. . . No. A poet who had the courage to lend his
Apocalyptic voice to our most righteous but most
dangerous fits of rage.
    Lucien Rebatet, Les Décombres *(1942)*

Finally, always righteously irritated, the most
obstinate and the most violent among us, Lucien
Rebatet. What an astonishing young man! . . .
Always in a rage against men, things, the weather,
food, the theater, politics, he established around
himself a climate of catastrophe and revolt that
no one could resist.
    Robert Brasillach, Notre avant-guerre *(1941)*

Aesthetic Sensibility and Anti-Semitism

Lucien Rebatet, the author of *Les Décombres*,[1] which had the highest
sales of any book in France during the Occupation, was without a doubt
the most virulent anti-Semitic voice at *Je suis partout*. He was also a sophisticated connoisseur of the arts and an accomplished film, theater, and
music critic. Some might naively ask how a man with obvious critical
skills and refined tastes could have been at the same time a violent anti-
Semite and militant fascist. Should not his often proclaimed love of Rembrandt and Mozart, for example, have kept him from being a crude and
vicious anti-Semite? Should not his appreciation of the nuances of Ver-

meer have prevented him from responding as positively as he did to the vulgarity of the Nazi demonstrations, no matter how grandiose? Should not his aesthetic tastes and critical talents have given him some sense of justice and made it impossible for him to defend fascist totalitarian politics and the crimes committed by the Nazis?

I call such questions naive—although understandable, given the way that fascism and anti-Semitism are usually presented as irrational aberrations from the Western political tradition and its cultural norms—because rather than having constituted obstacles or counterforces to his anti-Semitism and political extremism, Rebatet's aesthetic tastes, critical skills, and even what he himself called his dilettantism were necessary and determining components of his commitment to fascism. Even if he claimed at times that an aesthetic appreciation of the political was an impediment to action, even if he committed himself enthusiastically to the "perfunctory," imperfect, inferior art of politics and was willing to make all sorts of compromises in its name (*Les Décombres* [1942], 660), Rebatet's politics were nevertheless firmly rooted in his aesthetics. The question to be asked of the relation of politics and aesthetics in his writing is not, then, how Rebatet could have loved not only Rembrandt and Mozart, but also Pissaro, Proust, Charlie Chaplin, and Bruno Walter's interpretations of Mozart, and still have been a fascist and anti-Semite; rather, it is how his love and critical appreciation of art, literature, film, and music initially led him to fascism and how they continually pushed his fascism and anti-Semitism to increasingly extreme limits.

Few have ever confused Lucien Rebatet with Céline, but perhaps with the incredible success of the publication of *Les Décombres*, Rebatet might have thought that he could some day hope to be considered on the same level as the one writer he had ever met whom he considered to be a true genius. Of course, that never happened, and the long novel (1,312 pages) Rebatet wrote during the last years of the war and completed and published while he was in prison after the war, *Les Deux étendards* (Paris: Gallimard, 1951), has been by and large ignored since its publication.[2] Rebatet made a name for himself first as a film and music critic and then as an anti-Semitic demagogue. But his rage against the Jews, like Céline's, was supported by and organized in terms of the same poetics or aesthetics that he applied to literature and art as a critic. In his case, as well as in that of Céline, the "spontaneity" of violent feelings, especially of hatred and rage against the Jews and against democratic institutions—Rebatet claimed that he never had in his veins "a single globule of democratic blood" (*Les Décombres*, 19)—was not as "mad" as it might at first seem. Like Céline's ravings, his "instinctive" hatreds and rage had a definite aesthetic rigor and coherence to them, and it is that coherence that interests me in this chapter.

As was also the case for Brasillach, Rebatet admitted that the coherence was initially provided by Maurras and the Action Française: "Right after leaving college, I had found in Maurras, in Léon Daudet and their disciples, an explanation and a confirmation of many of my instinctive loathings" (19). Rebatet's constant rage against everything, as his friend and colleague Brasillach described it, was aimed primarily at the limitations of politics. It was a manifestation of his frustration that the social and political worlds—groups, classes, professions, parties, and individual men and women—continued to resist being ordered or formed according to what he argued was the only coherent aesthetic-political vision of the twentieth century: fascism. But unlike other literary fascists such as Brasillach—who Rebatet claimed "came to fascism by way of poetry, which was not, he was going to prove, the worst way to understand it" (44)—Rebatet never seemed to be at ease with the relation between what could be called his aesthetic values and his political convictions. Politics constantly took him away from what he always claimed were his first loves—literature, art, music, and the cinema; and literature and the arts in general were evoked as unblemished ideals when the world of politics continually proved limited, frustrating, incomplete, and unsatisfying to him. In the hands of fascists such as Rebatet, such a mystification of literature and art was indeed a dangerous thing, for it was the motor force of a totalitarian political vision.

In *Les Décombres*, Rebatet described a trip he took to Germany in 1938 ostensibly to report on the political situation there, and in a scene that reappeared in many different versions throughout his memoirs and in his journalism, he first evoked how attracted he was to what he witnessed in the streets, especially to the energy and spirit of the Nazi youth groups: "Nothing called out for friendship more than the rise of an entire generation of youth who were themselves creating their own order" (71). As attractive to him as Nazi political demonstrations of unity were, this hardened, demagogic, fascist ideologue described immediately after what for him was the high point of the trip: the return to another and deeper friendship and to a place of refuge from the world, which provoked a more profound aesthetic experience of fulfillment and joy:

> I had a rendez-vous at Dresden with some illustrious friends: [various paintings] by Vermeer, Rembrandt's from the happy and fruitful years, which are poems of the splendor and blossoming of the senses, scarcely less sublime than the tragedies and meditations of his solitary old age, . . . *The Hunt* of Reubens, lyrical like Wagner and truculent like Brueghel. The museum guards always chased me out much too soon for my liking from this serene and sumptuous universe. . . . This was certainly dilettantism for a professional journalist, miles from a border whose fate held the world breathless. But I only felt a small

amount of remorse. The smile of Saskia and her pink dress spread over the knees of a loving Rembrandt seemed to me far more important than the problem of the Sudetenland. (71–72)

The dilettantism he denounced elsewhere in this same text was in this passage if not defended, at least indulged with few if any regrets. Aesthetic pleasures clearly had to be indulged, for the "joys" of fascist politics and the political demonstrations supporting them were ephemeral by comparison.

For how could Rembrandt and Vermeer not be considered more important than the passing, regional issue of Czechoslovakian national sovereignty and the expansion of the German Reich? How could even the friendship and sympathy felt for the Nazi youth compare with that felt in the presence of Rembrandt's paintings? The problem for Rebatet, given how much he was also passionately involved with political issues, was how similar aesthetic effects of intense pleasure, serenity, and fulfillment could be produced in the political realm, how the two realms could be fused and the same satisfactions found in each; in other words, how historical-political conflicts could be transcended to produce a higher form of politics—politics as a total art.

Given the resistance of the world, the inability and unwillingness of his countrymen to build the fascist city according to what he felt were the best, even if not perfect, plans available, as well as the eventual failure of Nazi Germany to realize the hopes he had for it and himself, Rebatet repeatedly turned back to art and literature for solace and as a way of pursuing the "perfection" found only in them. Throughout his essays, he constantly returned to the solace and beauty offered by art to the connoisseur and critic, even at the risk of "sinning" by dilettantism (*Les Décombres* [1942], 660). But rather than ever leading him to abandon or retreat completely from politics, this constant evocation of the ideal of art made Rebatet demand at each stage an even more uncompromising form of fascist politics, no matter how "unrealistic" and unrealizable it might have seemed to even the most committed French fascists at the time. Literature and art might have led him into politics, but the limits of politics led him back to literature and art, in terms of which he always projected another, more extreme form of politics.

The lesson of anti-Semitism, learned like many other lessons in "the school of Maurras," became for Rebatet the core of his political and aesthetic education. But a commitment to a more radical form of anti-Semitism eventually distanced Rebatet and others at *Je suis partout* from their mentor, Maurras, especially after Céline gave anti-Semitism a new life and an entirely new literary form with the publication of *Bagatelles pour un massacre*. *Les Décombres* clearly expresses Rebatet's commitment to collaboration and an activist fascist politics; it also testifies to his rejection of Maurras and the classical aesthetics of politics associated with him. What this also meant is that anti-Semitism had clearly become the essence of Rebatet's fascist politics. Rebatet's nationalism was certainly not as developed as that of many other French literary fascists, and his notion of socialism was superficial and practically inconsequential, even when compared to the socialism of other literary fascists. What made him a committed French fascist was predominantly his anti-Semitism, for his deep antirepublicanism had at its base the proposition that democracy was *the* political system of the Jews. His admiration for the strong leader as the effective means for unifying and stimulating a people to collective (and most often, vengeful) action ultimately made of him an anti-Semitic demagogue on a par with his hero Céline.

However, even as late as 1942, when Rebatet clearly had already made a name for himself in the fiercely competitive area of anti-Semitic diatribe through his political journalism and especially the publication of two special issues of *Je suis partout* devoted to the "Jewish Question," he warned against the dangers of making the Jews too central, too obsessive a concern, of inflating their power, their capabilities, and the threat they posed for Europe:

> It is neither normal nor healthy for a Christian to confine himself to the study of an inferior and exotic race, to live indefinitely in its intimacy. Most anti-Semites end up by falling into Jewish hyperbole. There is no undertaking, no matter how outlandish, of which they judge Jewry incapable. Anti-Semitism is teeming with hallucinating maniacs who see a thousand Jews for every single one. They announce with haggard eyes the invincibility of this minuscule people of cowards and misshapen individuals, all their limbs trembling at the very sight of a gun, barely twenty million Hebrews scattered throughout four continents, of which more than half are stagnating in their ghettos. (*Les Décombres* [1942], 108)

Unlike Céline, who hallucinated with great lyrical force and saw Jews everywhere, Rebatet argued for a more restrained, "rational" anti-Semitism. Even so, he was just as intent as Céline on resolving the "Jewish Question" once and for all, insisting at the same time how easy it would be to do.[3]

Rebatet willingly and enthusiastically followed the logic of anti-Semitism to its extreme limits, all the while claiming his anti-Semitism was different in kind and form from that of "hallucinating maniacs." The figure of the Jew was not for Rebatet all-powerful and everywhere, in or behind every writer and group, but the "Jewish Question" was at the core of the most crucial cultural, social, and political problems, and in this way was the founding element, the essence of his fascism. But even his uncompromising politics of race were intimately linked to his desire for a detachment from and a transcendence of politics and the emotional plenitude he claimed to experience in the contemplation of art. Such plenitude could only be realized in the political realm through the destruction of all political limitations, resistance, and compromise; that is, only after the destruction of the political as such. The desire for the total political work of art thus went hand and hand with the desire for the end of politics, for it was only in the atmosphere of total destruction, collapse, and hopelessness, only among the rubble (*les décombres*) when all political alternatives had failed or been exhausted, that the fascist nation conceived as a total work of art could emerge as the only remaining alternative to destruction, justifying after the fact and compensating for the violence that had completed the process of destruction.

As Rebatet recounted in his memoirs, and as his political writings constantly asserted, the national, fascist revolution he claimed to be assisting was effectively begun in the ruins of both democratic and traditional (royalist) France: "France is covered with ruins, ruins of things, of dogmas, ruins of institutions" (*Les Décombres*, 9). Since there was nothing left intact from the past to perpetuate, France could emerge from the ruins only with a radically new beginning (with fascism). Rebatet's memoirs proposed to analyze how France had come to be in this state, to identify and denounce those responsible for it—democrats of all sorts, all political parties whether on the right or the left, but behind all of them, the Jews— and finally to outline the form of new life that would emerge after destruction, the way in which a new fascist France could be built.

But the last sentence of the original edition of the book ironically suggests another end, one that would remain within the ruins and rubble and add to them, one that would be without redemption, the end of everything, the end of the end. Such a scenario would make of the person who remained faithful to "the logic of his principles" (*Les Décombres*, 10), as Rebatet claimed he had always done, "the last of his species," something he also admitted would indeed be a "strange adventure" ([1942], 664), but one that would certainly have its own compensations. To be the "last of the species" is the only remaining "hope" when the desired political or aesthetic ideal cannot be realized. It is the destructive wish the uncompromising fascist is unable to repress when the national revolution proves to be a failure and a fascist state is not constructed out of the rubble of the past but whose plans are destroyed before the building can be constructed. In this configuration, a total art and a total politics are inseparable. Total victory and total destruction are as well.

Rebatet's apocalyptic political rage resulted most often from the frustration of his desire to have the whole social mess cleaned up at once, with one sweeping total action. This meant that those responsible for the mess had to be identified and the actions necessary to get rid of them had to be undertaken immediately and as efficiently as possible—at least in principle. This was obviously the attraction of anti-Semitism. The figure of the Jew could stand for all enemies of the nation and all those responsible for its decadence, and the elimination of Jews from society and politics could represent and serve as a model for all total political solutions. As Rebatet admitted, or rather boasted, in the original edition of *Les Décombres*, he believed in 1934 (and one could say until at least the end of the war) that the best and most effective form of political action was either to execute or deport all Jews and Freemasons, the internal "enemies" of France:

> I was convinced that at the point which we found ourselves only one form of politics would be capable of getting us out of the mess: sign up two hundred thousand guys, the unemployed, communists, kids, dare-devils, stick a uniform on them, give them corporals and submachine guns, get the support of a certain number of officers, execute several thousands of Jews and Freemasons and deport just as many. At fifteen, I advocated summary execution as the only way to purge the world of its grossest insanities and worst bandits. I was quite seriously coming back to this system. ([1942], 32)

Like wiping out a errant brush stroke from a painting, or a nonrhythmic line from a poem, or a discordant series of notes from a symphony, the master artist/political thinker purges the world of the discordance and disharmony he has attributed to all insidious "foreign," antiaesthetic elements. The more violent and total the political solution imagined, the more evident the aestheticist characteristics of the politics. In Rebatet's words, "All it would still take would be a corporal and four men to lead to the galleys, whenever we feel like it, our four hundred thousand moaning and trembling Jews" ([1942], 110). With such a "final solution," the true French nation would finally be created.

Before the war, the differences between Rebatet's form of French literary fascism and German National Socialism were by and large the same as those of the other contributors to *Je suis partout*. They were all attracted to certain aspects of Nazi Germany but still considered it a potential threat to France; they admired Hitler and appreciated the staged demonstrations of national unity, but at the same time they resisted what they all argued were the overly systematic, overly romantic aspects of German National Socialism. They thought they had much to learn from Germany, especially in terms of its anti-Semitic principles and policies, but they still felt that Nazism was profoundly foreign to French political and aesthetic tastes. This is revealed in an article from a series on Alsace that Rebatet wrote in which he even called the members of an Alsatian pro-Hitler political group "the enemies of [his] country," even if he shared many beliefs with them. He also argued that "these citizens of the French State are guilty of high treason" ("Que se passe-t-il en Alsace?: Chez l'ennemi," *Je suis partout*, No. 395 [June 17, 1938]). A fascism that was more German than French was thus in 1938 still unacceptable to him.

In another article written in 1938, Rebatet forcefully distanced himself from other French admirers of Hitler and from racially based theories of anti-Semitism and argued, as Brasillach and other graduates of the "school of Maurras" also did, for a more "rational," French form of anti-Semitism:

> There are in our country a half-dozen imbeciles and naive people, numb with admiration before German force, who imagine that some sort of international of the swastika could save Europe. That's to misunderstand the Germans who punish their Jews for the greatest benefit of their own country but who aren't at all unhappy to see them carry with them into our country their corruption and will not hesitate to use them against us if they have the occasion. . . . It is desirable that anti-Semitism remain less instinctive, more measured than that on the other side of the Rhine. ("Vienne sous la croix gammée"—Les Juifs ont voulu l'Anschluss: C'est à cause des Juifs que les Viennois l'ont accepté," *Je suis partout*, No. 406 [September 2, 1938])

The stupidity and naïveté of those people who before the war simply admired Hitler without seeing the danger his policies presented for France, and the problems that would come with an overly instinctive, un-limited anti-Semitism, of course were replaced after the defeat by an ever-increasing acceptance or even admiration on Rebatet's part of these very attributes. It was a change that had been taking shape in Rebatet's work for quite some time, well before the debacle of the war and well before it was acknowledged openly. The notion of a controlled, "rational," or-dered violence was transformed into that of total "aesthetic" violence, just as Maurras's classical notions of art and politics were rejected for a more modern version of totalizing aesthetics and totalitarian politics.

When Céline's *Bagatelles pour un massacre* appeared, Rebatet re-sponded with great enthusiasm in his review of the text, admitting to having read it aloud and recited it in chorus with friends at *Je suis par-tout*. Rebatet was clearly fascinated and moved by the brutal force of Céline's words, and he attempted not only to experience them more fully by reciting aloud passages from *Bagatelles*, but he sought also to capture some of their force in his own style of writing and speaking. One could easily imagine why someone so attracted to violent polemics and the power of words and the voice might also be interested in the power of the radio to broadcast political invective, and this might very well explain why Rebatet accepted a position at the Journal de la Radio at Vichy at the beginning of the Occupation.[4] But as important as the use of the radio might have been for the rise of fascism, Rebatet and other French literary fascists were still much more men of the printed word, the musical composition, and the painted or filmed image than of the radio, which Rebatet in fact called "a strange animal" (*Les Décombres*, 552). Literary fascists greatly preferred the printed page to the airwaves for making their voices heard.

In fact, Rebatet admitted that he was disillusioned by his experiences with the radio at Vichy and had been mistaken in believing that a radio voice could be the authentic (fascist) voice of France: "Radio, when one hears it from afar, possesses a singular eloquence. I had thought I heard in it the voice of a new France, quite feeble but honestly oriented. I arrived at the source of this voice. I found a service surrounded with enemies" (*Les Décombres*, 547). The eloquence and political authenticity of radio, then, was just another political illusion and not what it seemed to be from afar. At its source, it was as corrupt and unreliable a tool as the Vichy government itself, which pretended to speak for the National Revolution and the New Order but came to represent more and more in Rebatet's eyes the continuation of the politics and corruption of prewar, republican France. Rather than amplifying and broadcasting his authentic, revolutionary voice in an effort to help "remake the soul of the French" (554), he claimed his voice was severely constrained and his invectives censored, or as he put it in describing what he was forced to say: "We had already diluted our wine with so much water that it been turned into weak jug wine" (555). He felt that radio constrained the violence and thus the authenticity of the fascist voice to such an extent that it weakened and distorted it rather than amplified it. "Radio talk" was not for Rebatet, because it was just *talk*; he wanted something more substantial, more composed or "aesthetic," to be produced by and as his voice.[5]

The scene of reading Céline's pamphlets aloud in a group is, of course, a tribal scene, one more closely linked to clans or primitive societies chanting their founding myths and denouncing their enemies. It is also a scene of the mythic constitution of a people, one whose implications Jean-Luc Nancy analyzed in *La Communauté désoeuvrée*—a scene, as Nancy shows, which had profound links to the myth of literature and to literature as myth.[6] In terms of the specific issues raised by the work of Rebatet, the technologies and techniques (and myths) of film, music, art, and literature were much more pertinent to his aesthetics of politics than radio was. Rebatet was very proud of the force of his voice and his ability to stir up a crowd, and he often boasted that he had "the biggest mouth" of all the members of *Je suis partout*. This was undoubtedly why he was chosen to end the meetings and rallies they organized during the Occupation and to cry out with all the anger and force his voice could convey at the end of his speeches: "Death to the Jews! Long live the National-Socialist revolution! Long live France!"—as he did in a meeting at the Salle Wagram organized by *Je suis partout* in January of 1944 (reported in *Je suis par-*

tout, No. 649 [January 21, 1944]). But his pride was in a voice that needed no amplification, no modern technology, to be effective and to reach its listeners, a voice that emanated directly from him, and that political cliques and tepid collaborationist governments could not censor. The fascist voice Rebatet wanted to "broadcast" was one that ideally would not need the airways to be disseminated, one that filled up whatever space it was emitted in and was immediately received by the crowd that made it its own, a voice that spoke for and represented, that brought together and thus formed, the National-Socialist collectivity by giving it a figure to hate—the Jew—and an alternative figure with which to identify—Hitler, or the speaker or writer (Rebatet) as his replacement—and most of all, a model, a style (a tone), and a form for its rage.

In spite of his profound admiration for Céline's anger, Rebatet nevertheless frequently acknowledged before the war, perhaps in part in deference to Maurras, that he had reservations about Céline's form of writing and what he called its "foreign" rhythm, thus using an argument against Céline that Céline himself frequently used against the Jews: "I dream of a Céline more profoundly penetrated with the ancient Latin cadences, still having the radiant health of the Rabelaisian verb" (*Je suis partout*, No. 374 [January 21, 1938]). He considered Céline's discourse to be at times too "Nordic" in its cadence, not quite measured or musical enough for his French (Latin) ear, not aesthetic (classical) enough for his French tastes.

But he also felt that this unmeasured quality was also the force of Céline's discourse and therefore should not in any way be constrained, even for aesthetic reasons: "You don't debate with the elements, you don't ask a storm to have the rhythm of a symphony; a purer and more dependable Céline would not have projected the incredible cries of *Bagatelles*." The absolute principle of force at the basis of literary-fascist aesthetics and politics thus, as in the case of Drieu la Rochelle, pushed art and politics beyond the constraints of form. Rebatet's dilemma was how to retain art as the model for politics without diminishing the seemingly extra-aesthetic force and violence of anti-Semitic cries such as Céline's (and his own), how to conceive of and practice a pure, unrestrained *aesthetics of violence*. Céline's work tipped the balance for Rebatet and moved him far enough away from Maurras and the Action Française that there could be no return to what he had come to believe was their ineffective, overly "rational" anti-Semitism and their classical and restrictive aesthetics of politics. It also moved him for similar reasons closer to Hitler and to a deeper admiration for and acceptance of what he called the "eloquence" of "total solutions."

In the article from *Je suis partout* (No. 406) on Austria after the *Anschluss*, which I have already mentioned, Rebatet described in essence the dilemma faced by French literary fascists before the war, and in doing so he also provided the aesthetic solution to the dilemma. The problem of the military threat posed by Nazi Germany to France and other Latin countries was represented figuratively as the problem of how the sound of the boots of the German soldiers marching through the streets of Salzburg interfered with what ideally was and could still be a perfect aesthetic synthesis of the Germanic and the Latin; that is, if the presence of Jews in the city had not in large part already corrupted this city and its art:

> In this ravishing place, which reconciles by its light and by the art of its most illustrious son the Latin spirit and the Germanic spirit, one hears today the noise of boots that have come from the north. This is not the ideal accompaniment for *Eine Kleine Nachtmusik* or *The Marriage of Figaro*. But one cannot forget that Israel, corrupting everything it touches, was in the process of Judaicizing Salzburg. . . . The relative Hitlerization of Salzburg, is it worse than its Jewification?

The answer for Rebatet, of course, was that the "relative Hitlerization" of Salzburg and all of Austria was necessary. And if this was true in Austria, one could ask why it would not have been the same for France, if France too was being "Jewified." No matter the threat posed by Hitler's armies to France, when the choice facing a country was between Hitlerization and "Jewification," an anti-Semitic fascist such as Rebatet would obviously choose the former, so that the synthesis of the Germanic and the Latin that had been achieved in the music of Mozart and was present in the light of Salzburg could be appreciated once again with a minimum of interference, and so that the synthesis they represented could be recreated on the political level as well.

Jews thus represented for Rebatet, following a long nationalist literary tradition, the destruction of the ultimate form of art and the politics modeled after it. Hitler, on the contrary, was presented as only a momentary interference in the aesthetic harmony of Salzburg, which was necessary in order to eliminate an even more radical interference. In order to be a French Hitlerian—and not what Rebatet called an "imbecile" and a traitor—a situation had to exist or be created in which all political choices could be limited to these stark alternatives. For Rebatet and the most extreme French fascists and collaborators, this meant taking a "pacifist" stance before the war and pointing out the folly of war, and then during the Occupation claiming that a total commitment to the Nazi cause was the only way to save Europe and France from an even worse fate. The price for *not* becoming "relatively Hitlerian" (and then totally Hitlerian) was the destruction of France; the price for total collaboration was always presented as being minimal.

The restoration of Salzburg's special light and the "de-Jewification" of its music accomplished by the *Anschluss* had for Rebatet only one somewhat regrettable consequence: the loss of one conductor of merit. "The departure of Mr. Bruno Walter, Jew, talented Mozartian, is unfortunate, but there are in the Reich ten batons equal to his and who have proven it." If Mozart's music could survive the loss of Bruno Walter, then Austria could survive the sound of Nazi boots in its streets—and by implication, France could as well. In a similar vein, in a series of articles on Germany written in 1937, Rebatet defended Nazi anti-Semitic legislation and attacks on "decadent art" by claiming that the loss to the arts was minimal:

> Germany lost a half-dozen original films, two or three fairly considerable novelists. But at this price it was able to rid itself, through a truly exemplary operation of the moral and aesthetic police, of all the trash of substandard Freudism, of the most corrupted expressionism, of pseudo-naturalism. . . . Racists have held that it is incompatible with "German honor" that innovations in the five-year Judeo-Russian style, . . . pathological monstrosities of Jewish-surrealist painting, . . . have been able to pass as expressions of the German soul. . . . The racists are absolutely right" ("L'Allemagne a-t-elle faim?" in *Je suis partout*, No. 325 [February 13, 1937])

The supposed resolution of the "Jewish Question" in art and in politics could in this way be used to justify any political action, no matter how violent, because it was always considered to be for the greater good. The injustices it produced could be ignored, because in purely aesthetic terms they were considered inconsequential.

The Aesthetic Final Solution

At a time when the explicit politics of *Je suis partout* were militantly anti-Semitic, hypernationalist, and fascist, but at the same time anti-Hitlerian, articles such as Rebatet's revealed that the seeds for the change to a pro-Nazi politics had been planted long before the war: in the name of the survival of art and with the model of the arts as a support, and with anti-Semitism as the driving force.[7] Anti-Semitism was Rebatet's principal *political* contribution to the paper, the area outside of art, music, literature, and film where he claimed expertise and began to be acknowledged as an authority and a power with which to be reckoned. In the two special issues on the Jews that he put together for *Je suis partout*—"Les Juifs," no. 386 (April 18, 1938), and "Les Juifs et la France," no. 430 (February 17, 1939)—Rebatet attempted to carve out a space for an anti-Semitism located somewhere between (or bringing about a synthesis of) Maurras's and Céline's versions of anti-Semitism, at the same time "rational" and extreme, aestheticist and activist, ordered and violent.

In his article on the Jews and Germany from the first of the two issues,

Rebatet insisted especially on how the Jews after World War I had supposedly invaded the intellectual and cultural life of Germany in the same
way that they had taken control of the revolutionary movements.

> Jews had monopolized, in the space of twenty years, all of the intellectual activ-
> ity of Germany. In publishing, the theater, film, music, holding almost all of the
> levers of control, they themselves made reputations, and there were reputations
> made only for Jews. . . . They had the moral and financial control of almost all
> of the cinema. Only the so-frequent incapacity of the Jew for original artistic
> creation does not allow us to cite in music or painting any names known to the
> general public. ("Les Juifs et l'Allemagne")

Time and time again in his writings, Rebatet came back to this same
point, the abyss between the absolute control Jews were accused of having over the arts and culture in general, on the one hand, and their incapacity to create, on the other.[8] Like Drumont and Céline, he made of this
incapacity the essence of the entire "Jewish Question." Accused of being
incapable of originality, the Jew was placed in the role of the parasite,
exploiter, and ultimately destroyer of the original and the creative. In
politics, this translated into an equation between Jews and communism in
terms of political oppression and control, and between Jews and democ-
racy/capitalism in terms of economic oppression and control.

The one talent Rebatet begrudgingly attributed to the Jews was that
"in the field of music [they were] excellent interpreters. That was one of
the rare domains in Germany where they held a place that was justified,
although still too exclusive." As long as there were strict controls on the
Jews' participation in the arts, rather than so-called Jewish control of the
arts, Rebatet, in 1938, would have been willing to let Jewish musicians
play for his and others' enjoyment. A strict division had to be maintained,
however, between creativity and imitation, invention and exploitation.
The place of Jews was clearly to serve, and nowhere had they served better than in performing the great music of the Western—that is, for the
anti-Semite, the "Aryan"—tradition. Nowhere were Jews less threatening
(less "parasitic") to art and more its ally than in the field of music; that is,
as long as they submitted themselves totally to the music they played and
interpreted it faithfully. In almost every other area, Rebatet believed that
their gift for interpretation and imitation had led to the corruption of
politics and culture, a loss of taste, and the replacement of true aesthetic
values by artifice and mimicry.

Serving the works of "Aryans" meant interpreting them either as a
musician or as a critic. Each of these functions Rebatet considered derivative but positive, while at the same time dangerously close to the negative
function of corruption. He argued in the second special issue on the Jews
that there were in fact two kinds of imitation: "successful imitation,"

which protected and dramatically demonstrated the beauty of the work, and a decadent form of imitation, which corrupted it by offering artificial facsimiles in the place of the real thing and by encouraging these second-hand creations to be taken as original. He wrote, "[Jews] are more or less skilled imitators, often excellent commentators and interpreters, or unfortunately formidable corruptors. The Jew imitates well, criticizes with subtlety the works of other people, but he realizes very few original creations, and above all he corrupts a great deal" ("La Corruption des esprits," *Je suis partout*, No. 430 [February 17, 1939]). The contradictory logic at the heart of the anti-Semitic denunciation of imitation is nowhere more evident than it is in this essay. The more successful the imitation, the more dangerous it is to the original because it can be confused with it, and thus the more threatening its powers to corrupt, to have commentary taken for originality, mere performance for genius, criticism for creation, and ultimately artifice for art. True art, for the literary anti-Semite such as Rebatet, always began where imitation ended, even in the form of skillful Jewish interpretation and artifice.

According to Rebatet, "The agility of [their] mimetism" had supposedly permitted certain Jews to perform definite services for German music, which indicated that they deserved to be granted exceptions from Hitler's policy of total exclusion. But this same mimetic agility made them dangerous enemies of art and of the people of art, for the unrestrained, uncontrolled mimetism that eliminated all distinctions between the original and the copy would eventually bring about the destruction of art and the originality and integrity of the people through universal *métissage*. In the sociopolitical realm, this meant that Jews were not always recognized for what they were but were indistinguishable from "true Aryans." For this reason, on June 6, 1942, a day before the edict was to go into effect, Rebatet applauded the Nazi decree requiring that Jews in the Occupied Zone wear the Star of David to identify them in public:

> Between the Aryan and [the Jew], it's a decisive struggle. Aryans cannot leave such an enemy free to conceal themselves. The yellow star imposed on them is a national consequence of Judaic duplicity. . . . The Jewish star serves to correct this oddity, which is that a human species radically opposed to peoples of White blood, from all eternity unassimilatable into this blood, is not always discernible at first glance. ("L'Etoile jaune," *Je suis partout*, no. 566 [June 6, 1942])

He acknowledged that the decree and a supplementary, visible sign, a yellow star, were in fact necessary in order to distinguish the indistinguishable, to mark the limit between the original Aryan (and his "White blood") and the Jewish mime (and his "non-White" blood). In art as in society, a visible border had to be drawn in order to protect the original, which was not in itself and on its own, "at first glance," any different from its "inferior" copies.

Rebatet used the supposed destruction of French art by Jewish painters as an example of the destruction of the "French spirit" in general and as an analogy for the destruction of the French nation. What happened in art inevitably happened in society: the disintegration, the decomposition of the authentically French elements of both tradition and of modernity:

> [Modigliani, Pascin, Kisling, etc.] come together in the same involuntary task of disintegration. Their colors are a decomposition of the French palette, their form is dismantled or fugitive, their intellectual ornateness takes the place in their work of plastic intelligence. Their pseudo-stylization, its contact with life, is no more than a arbitrary deformation, and ends up as caricature. . . . Nothing is further from the admirable line of French arts, from Chartres to Auguste Renoir. The Jews of the "Paris School" lived off its remains. They invented nothing. They demolished Cézanne, ruined his colors, coolly pastiched the Douannier Rousseau, grossly aped the ingenious Van Gogh. ("La Corruption des esprits")

The danger of this form of imitation—pastiche and caricature—consisted in its great seductiveness, especially for those, like Rebatet himself, who had rejected academic art and were looking for revolutionary alternatives. Hitler's mistake was to have gone too far and condemned all modern art, even Impressionism, as decadent and degenerate; that is, "Jewish." In the field of music, Hitler had also erred in not recognizing the service musicians such as Horowitz had made and could continue to make on behalf of German music. Rebatet drew the same line as the Nazis did between authentic and degenerate or decadent art; he simply drew it *within* the realm of modern art, not between modern and traditional art. In fact, when it came to art, he was a more rigorous anti-Semite than Hitler, since he wanted to restrict the use of the term "decadent" to those modern paintings that actually were painted by Jews or were from schools or movements dominated by Jews, those that in the eyes of the connoisseur, not the politician, deformed and demolished art.

Until the outbreak of the war, countering Nazism by offering a better, French version of fascism and anti-Semitism was an unquestioned principle of the politics of *Je suis partout*, and for a brief period—the time of the Hitler-Stalin pact—even the "Hitlerites" of the journal, such as Rebatet, openly attacked Hitler not just as a potential threat to France but as an enemy and traitor to the West. In "Pour un art occidental" (*Je suis partout*, No. 471 [December 1, 1939]), Rebatet claimed that it was the Jews associated with what he called "Bolshevik art" who had done the most damage to French art by attacking "all the hierarchies, all the traditions that are the humus where a national art grows. . . . All that is demolished, thrown into the fire, at the same time and in the same way as all the truths of politics," to be replaced by "grimacing apings, unformed daydreams, abortions." He asserted that by making a pact with the communist devil, Hitler had put himself in the position of the ally of the "invaders from the Orient" and thus of the enemies of Western art. In this way, Hitler had become, in spite of his anti-Semitism, an ally of the Jews.

Rebatet also asserted in this article that "the inexpiable fault of Germany is to have betrayed the Occident, our own as much as the admirable German Occident of Holbein, Bach, and Mozart, by bringing barbaric Europe right up to the Rhine." In an attempt to "save the West, whose heart is [France]," Rebatet thus attacked the barbarism of Hitler on two fronts. The first concerned Hitler's foreign policy and his new links to Soviet art and politics and thus to the nihilistic destroyers of Western aesthetic values. The second had to do with German internal affairs and Hitler's removal of all modern art from Germany's museums, which Rebatet called an effect of Hitler's "neo-Academicism." In both cases, Rebatet's defense of art meant clearly separating himself from Hitler's cultural politics, which he felt could have the effect of destroying German art and thus its people, in the name of what he considered more radical and consistent aesthetic and political anti-Semitic principles.

By the time of the war, however, his extreme cultural anti-Semitism was for the most part indistinguishable from the religious, metaphysical racism he had constantly opposed. With the defeat, he easily transformed his Maurrasian-influenced nationalism and anti-Germanic stance into active collaboration with and unmitigated support for Nazi Germany. As he asserted in the concluding section of *Les Décombres*, the continuation of the war had made it impossible for him, for all of those in France who truly believed in the national revolution, not to work actively for a German victory:

> I wish for the victory of Germany because the war it is waging is *my* war, *our* war. . . . I don't admire Germany for being Germany but for having produced Hitler. I praise it for having known how . . . to create for itself the political order in which I recognize all my desires. I think that Hitler has conceived of a magnificent future for our continent, and I passionately want him to realize it. ([1942], 605)

The conditions producing the stark, ultimate choice between survival and extinction—that is, between Hitlerization and "Jewification"—had now been realized in history, and there certainly was no doubt as to which alternative Rebatet had chosen.

In *Les Décombres*, Rebatet no longer had any reservations in proposing that France imitate Nazi Germany's racial policies and even go further than them. He argued not just for the removal of Jews from public functions but also for the violent destruction of their works, even, as a last resort, those he himself loved:

> Jewish spirit is in the intellectual life of France a poisonous weed that must be pulled out right to its most minuscule roots. . . . Auto-da-fés will be ordered for the greatest number of the Jewish or Judaic works of literature, paintings, or musical compositions that have worked the most toward the decadence of our people. . . . There would be no objection, in my opinion, to a great musical virtuoso from the ghetto being authorized to come play for the entertainment of Aryans, as exotic slaves did in ancient Rome. But if this were to become the pretext for an encroachment, no matter how small, of this abominable species on us, I would myself be the first to smash recordings of Chopin and Mozart by the marvelous Horowitz and Menuhin. . . . I am partial to Camille Pissaro, the only great painter Israel, that incredibly anti-plastic race, has produced. I would be ready to decree the incineration of all his canvasses, if it were necessary, so that we would be cured of this nightmare. ([1942], 568–69)

To save true European art, some art would have to be destroyed and some artists excluded—to save one people, another people would have to be destroyed. The logic was that of extermination; the "dilettante" in politics and connoisseur in art had followed the logic of his hyperaestheticism up to the point where the survival of an entire people was at risk, especially given that pages before in the same work he had claimed that "Jewry offers the unique example in the history of humanity of a race for which collective punishment is the only just kind" ([1942], 566). And until he fled France with the retreating German army, Rebatet's cries of vengeance and destruction were made with ever-increasing frequency.

By 1942, Rebatet had come to consider the war against the Jews to be total, without limits on the battlefield or within French society itself. It was no longer primarily an ideological war or a war of national defense, but it had now become a war between the forces of *métissage* (mixed breeding)—that is, Jewish or communist, or Jewish-communist forces—and the forces of the "White race," with nothing less than the survival of the latter at stake.

> The divisions of American Negroes and the Kalmouk divisions were spilling out over Europe. Among the hordes, the swarm of Jews. There would soon be millions of half-breeds [*métis*], which is the dream of the Jews, all of the Occident similar to the Jews, the White race condemned to die. Yes, an entire race can thus be attached to a few threads of destiny, when it has multiplied diabolically its sins against itself. The German has not only saved European civilization. He has perhaps also saved the White man. (622)

The material costs of the war were inconsequential, the loss of lives irrelevant, as long as the "White man" could be said to have been saved, his spirit and his blood restored to their original "purity," and the threat of *métissage* overcome once and for all. In this vein, National Socialism had become for Rebatet "Aryan Socialism": "National Socialism or fascism is the advent of true socialism, that is, Aryan Socialism, the socialism of builders, opposed to the anarchistic and utopic socialism of the Jews" (651). Fascism and anti-Semitism in this way had fully realized their aesthetic-mythical function and had become not just political options but metaphysical obligations.

If Rebatet never tired of reading Céline aloud in chorus with his friends, he also never tired of writing about the dangers of an immanent apocalypse, of claiming over and over again that unless drastic actions were taken immediately, the end would be in sight, always closer than it was before: "France is in danger of dying, even more today that two years ago on the Meuse River" (650). And as the end of National Socialism approached, the severity of the actions he proposed increased proportionately:

> But one shouldn't forget, revolutions are not baptized with holy water. They are baptized with blood. . . . Death is the only punishment that the people understand. Death alone imposes forgetting on the enemy. . . . He who would tomorrow shoot five hundred agitators, generals, tight-fisted employers, and Gaullists of high rank, would provoke, he can be assured, the most satisfying psychological shock imaginable. This useful operation was not taken right after the armistice. But the iniquities accumulated by Vichy, even more than those of 1940, call out for the scaffold and the gallows. ([1942], 654)

In fact, almost everything called out for the scaffold and the gallows, because the only chance left for the success of the national revolution, for the victory of Nazi Germany, for the implementation of fascism in France, for the defeat of the Jews, was the elimination of *all* enemies, both military and cultural, political and spiritual. And the number of enemies continued to grow every day. Demands to punish, kill, execute, and make them pay dominated Rebatet's writing until the end of the war. The demands overwhelmed the little political analysis contained in his writings; he had explicitly become what he had always implicitly been, given that the distinction between his own position and that of the militantly pro-Hitler, "maniac" racist and fascist was from the beginning specious and practically irrelevant. He had become the caricature of the Hitlerian imbecile he had previously denounced.

As the war began to go badly for the German Army, Rebatet enlarged the scope of the apocalypse in a series of articles in the early months of 1943. No longer was it simply a question of the survival of France, but now for him it was all of Europe, the entire "Occident," that was menaced if the German army failed: "It would be for our continent, the annihilation of order, the end of everything" ("Découverte de Berlin," *Je suis partout*, No. 601 [February 12, 1943]). For Nazi Germany to be presented figuratively as the champion of the Occident, England and the United States had to be dismissed—"The triumph of the Anglo-Saxons on the European continent is a Mother Goose fairy tale"—and the war had to be represented as a bloody drama ultimately between communism and fascism, between the East and the West:

> On one side, then, there is the force of the West, the countries in the world who, by their social structure, are the closest to ours. . . . On the other side, it's a terrifying unknown, the Asia of the Steppes with its cruelty and serfdom, a regime that we know could only have been built through terror. . . . It's the Red International. Behind it, there are legions of Jews, the creators of Marxism. . . . We are in fact at the threshold of the Apocalypse, . . . this war of continents is moving to an apocalyptic scale. . . . Western civilization . . . has only one protector, the German army. ("La civilisation devant la guerre," *Je suis partout*, No. 603 [February 26, 1943])

Rebatet continued in this vein up to the very end of the war, and after the debarkation of the Allied troops in Normandy, he referred to the Battle of France, in an article fittingly entitled "Au delà de la Bataille," as "The Battle of the Occident. . . . It's a last act, the one in which the peripeteia are being accelerated to bring on the denouement" (*Je suis partout*, No. 672 [June 30, 1944]). The last act, like the previous acts and peripeteia leading up to it, was now cast as tragedy, the fall of "the West" becoming a noble, meaningful act that contradicted or transcended history and gave meaning to it "beyond" any battles or the outcome of the war as a whole.

Living the apocalypse of the West (over and over again) had become the ultimate sign of fascist political correctness; that is, the indication that one's principles were right and just, even if, or rather, *because* one's cause was being defeated. For even if Rebatet pretended to the end that he believed Germany would not, could not, lose the war, in his articles the way for giving transcendent meaning to loss had been prepared from at least the end of 1942.[9] Certainly by the end of 1943, in articles such as "L'Espoir est fasciste," Rebatet had already begun to prepare the way for the last act and the "triumph" of fascism *in its defeat*:

> Were we, at the end of a European catastrophe, to perish, our arms in our hands in the last battalions of the Occident or by drinking fearlessly the hemlock of the just, we would take along with us the conviction of having fought for the only principles that were reasonable and redeeming. (*Je suis partout*, No. 631 [September 10, 1943])

In fact, when the time came to die in battle or drink the hemlock of the just, Rebatet did nothing of the sort, but fled for his life. His own "triumph" would have to come as a novelist, not as a martyr to the fascist cause he had served and for which *he claimed* he was prepared to die.

In *Les Décombres*, Rebatet described a visit he took to the Leopold-stadt ghetto and his reaction on seeing the miserable condition of the Jews living there: "I was floating in a vengeful joy. I was breathing in the revenge of my race. That hour paid me back for two years of humiliation" ([1942], 62). The anti-Semite took great joy in seeing the Jews humiliated and reduced to absolute misery, in witnessing with his own eyes the spectacle of the use of brutal, total power over the Jews, a power with which he identified, and in breathing the same air as that of the Nazi avengers and their victims. The spectacle itself, not what it portended for the future, was what interested him, moved him, and gave him joy and a sense of power and self-fulfillment in the present. As was also true in the case of Brasillach, what moved Rebatet was a perverse aesthetic satisfaction that came from assisting at a powerful theatrical or cinematographic experience, the illusion that the spectator was at one with force itself—in this case, with the forces of oppression and humiliation of the enemies of one's "race." The joy of the collective sense of self that was revealed in such scenes was nothing but the joy of vengeance.

There was always an important audience in France for such theater, whether acted out, written down, or orally presented. Rebatet had learned long before, and the great success of *Les Décombres* had simply confirmed it, that what his audience wanted to hear from him was a violent denunciation of Jews—that no matter what was happening in the world, the "Jewish Question" could never take second place to historical or political events. He narrated in *Les Décombres*, for example, that just after the German invasion of Czechoslovakia, he was supposed to give a speech on the Jews before a group of members of the Action Française, but because of what had just occurred, he had tried to change the subject:

> I thought it good, honest Aryan fool that I was, . . . to announce that I could no longer do [the planned speech], that the case of the Jews moved onto a secondary level in the face of the news I carried with me. I saw disappointment come over all their faces. . . . [They] had no desire to confront the divisions of Hitler. The hunt for the Jewish enemy seemed to them much more convenient and fruitful. (141)

"The hunt for the Jewish enemy" always replaced the more difficult political questions and offered a seemingly easy solution to the problems faced by France. The hunt covered over and presented immediate solutions for the disastrous political and military situation of France. By the time *Les Décombres* had been completed, Rebatet's own position had also made the "Jewish Question" the unique foundation of all politics, in fact as well as in principle.

The continual refusal of Vichy France to actively engage in the war on the side of Germany, what Rebatet called Vichy's "restrained" policy concerning the Jews, and the failure of the National Revolution to be truly revolutionary all fueled Rebatet's anger. Until the end of the war he continued to make increasingly extreme political and anti-Semitic statements, as if in defiance of any sort of political realism. It was almost as if this was in fact what he had wanted from the start: for all politics to fail and for him to be practically alone in still demanding a total Nazi victory and the creation of an anti-Semitic, fascist, French state. Politics during the Occupation seemed to be his overriding and unique passion, his "joy" coming exclusively from political theater—from both victory and defeat—rather than from literature, music, cinema, or art.

And yet, in another scene from *Les Décombres*, which is practically identical to the one discussed at the very beginning of this chapter, Rebatet described his constant desire to flee the world of politics for that of art. In 1939, just after Germany had invaded Czechoslovakia and Italy had invaded Albania, he narrated how, disgusted with the impotent reaction of the French government, he had retreated once again into the worlds of literature and art in an attempt to blot out the real world:

> I had had enough. I no longer felt the need to write even a single political line. I took up books that spoke of an other time, other men. . . . I went back to unfinished manuscripts, and I felt like spending entire days strolling through the Louvre before Corot and Cézanne, writing a long story on love and God. What a really fine revolutionary! I agree completely. (143)

The sporadic indifference toward politics manifested in such scenes was, however, the indifference of a *political* dogmatist, of someone interested only in ultimate questions, total solutions, and aesthetic-political perfection or totalization. After the publication of *Les Décombres*, and as the war dragged on, the "long story of love and God" was in fact written (*Les Deux étendards*), and in the last years of the war and while he was in prison, it served the same function as his strolls through the Louvre and other museums at moments of great historical crisis. Writing provided Rebatet with the illusion that he was pursuing an ideal, transcendent perspective on life and politics in an imaginary realm in which the failures of the political could be negated, compensated for, and overcome—or at least forgotten.

In *Les Mémoires d'un fasciste*, II, left unfinished at his death in 1972, Rebatet repeatedly emphasized the solace he had found in writing *Les Deux étendards*, especially at the moments of the worst political crises. "Wouldn't this be the most fruitful way to rise above confused, disappointing or unpleasant events?" (11), he rhetorically asked himself at the start of the second volume of his memoirs. In the context of the bitter split between Brasillach's faction and his own at *Je suis partout* in 1943, he retrospectively referred to his novel as "his only passion, his only ambition" at the time (131), which of course allowed him to follow the ultra-Nazi hard-liners at the newspaper, but "reluctantly." Compared to the Normandy invasion and the ever-increasing danger for all "collabos," he admitted that his pursuit of his novel was "frivolous," but this literary frivolity allowed him "to keep his wits in the midst of events about which he could do nothing" (166). And finally, in an article entitled "On ne fusille pas le dimanche" [They don't execute on Sunday], included in *Les Mémoires d'un fasciste*, II—the article originally appeared in the journal *Le Crapouillot* (June 1953)—Rebatet described writing furiously on his novel on what he thought would be the night before his execution: "But by God, I was a writer. I had still a few hours ahead of me to blacken several memorable pages. I had to get to it" (255). The project of the novel and the constant struggle to produce it, if not the reality of the novel itself, permitted him to retreat from the world of events and give meaning and form to himself and his struggle, even at the moments of total political defeat and immanent death.

Rebatet had often praised the "robust and tenacious realism" of Hitler's politics and defended his own commitment to fascism on pragmatic, realistic grounds as well: "The twentieth century would be that of dictators and National Socialism. It served no purpose, except to be left behind, to place ourselves at odds with a current against which we wouldn't have the force to swim upstream. Wisdom was to follow it, in our own way" (*Les Décombres*, 58–59). By the end of the war, that supposed realism had become something very different: a total faith in a cause that even if lost—and he refused to acknowledge publically that the war was being lost by Germany until the very end—would still prevail and determine the future. His penultimate column for *Je suis partout*, written after the failed assassination attempt on Hitler, was entitled "Fidelité au National-Socialisme" and was accompanied by a sketch of Hitler, a swastika, and a sketch of German soldiers. Rebatet finally admitted that Hitler was going to lose the war, but he declared that this was in fact the sign of his greatness and the guarantee that Hitler, and not the victorious Allied forces, would influence the future more, and that Hitler and National Socialism would by losing ultimately triumph:

> Let's admit that Hitler is on the point of being defeated. But think then of the monstrous efforts under which he will have succumbed: six years of a latent, ferocious war, conducted by a practically universal financial blockade, by a planetary propaganda system, by incessant diplomatic machinations, by all the churches, all moral systems, all philosophical systems, all the universities; . . . then the real, total war, setting the four biggest powers in the globe . . . in a heterogeneous but monstrous coalition, and at least five years of this infernal

war, fought with the most savage and disgusting means, twenty million dead, a continent razed. . . . In such cases, you can be sure . . . it is the vanquished who leaves the most profound traces, who puts his mark on his century, . . . who has a political, spiritual posterity. (*Je suis partout*, No. 676 [July 26, 1944])

No "realism" (or historicism) dictated such statements, for the current of history had clearly and for some time reversed its course and flowed massively against fascism and National Socialism. Only a total commitment to an aesthetic-political vision that transcended historical-political realities could withstand the current, because it was located in a spiritual or aesthetic realm outside of history.

Rebatet had retreated into his imaginary museum once again, creating an entirely fictional figure of Hitler as a heroic victim and clinging to the illusion of National Socialism as the only ideology "that remains on a human scale and leaves to the life of the individual his prerogatives, his personality." For him, no facts could ever refute such a vision, for it determined the entirety of historical reality in terms of an ideal, imaginary transcendent construct. He believed that if the responsibility for the war and the destruction it had caused could be assigned entirely to the Allied forces, if National Socialism could be argued to provide the best protection of the individual and thus be the only existing authentic humanism, then the defeat of Hitler and Nazism could certainly be argued to be irrelevant and the future of twentieth-century Europe still claimed to be fascist. It was out of formal, aesthetic necessity—that is, because National Socialism was on the scale of and had the *shape* and *figure* of man—that Europe would eventually recognize itself in such a figure once again. This was not just political ideology working but rather a hyperideological, ultraaestheticist faith in the formative and transformative powers of a vision that in itself needed to have no direct relation to historical reality to retain its force. Like Brasillach and Drieu la Rochelle, Rebatet's aesthetics of politics were manifested in their most radical form at the moment when the practical politics they had supported had failed.

But even before the defeat of Nazism seemed possible to him, Rebatet always claimed he wanted to be known as a great writer more than as an ideologue or spokesperson for fascism or anti-Semitism. In "Confessions de l'auteur," written shortly after the publication of *Les Décombres*, Rebatet explained a large part of the unexpected success of the book and his own satisfaction at that success in terms of the care he took in writing it: "I really took a lot of trouble with my *Décombres*, and especially with the finish, the final touches given to languishing or limping phrases. . . . It's a matter of professional honesty which counts too little today and of which I would like to remind beginning writers" (*Je suis partout*, No. 588 [November 6, 1942]). Comparing himself immodestly with Flaubert and that writer's concern with style, Rebatet spoke as if he had already entered tradition, as if he were already a recognized great writer giving advice to the young. He described himself as nothing less than a hero of the French language struggling as a writer, just as he had struggled in the political realm, to defend his country and its native tongue, not by imitating Céline (an impossible task, he argued), but by using "the traditional resources of the French language":

> Like so many other things in our country, the French language is going to hell. It's time to go back over all its nuts and bolts, to bring it the care not of grammarians . . . but of a good worker, a good artisan. It is necessary to learn or relearn to love this admirable language, as a carpenter loves and caresses a beautiful piece of wood.

Flushed with the success of his book, Rebatet thus attempted to justify the politics of his writings, his outrageous diatribes against the Jews, and his enthusiastic support of Hitler and Nazi Germany, in the name of writing and style. He mentioned the care he claimed to have taken with his own manipulation of the French language, even when it had been necessary "to speak very loud" and "not even be afraid to scream" in order to be heard in the general din. The then unfinished novel, to which he referred in this article as "a work that has so little to do with current events" that "it goes without saying that, . . . with the times as they are, it is on the lowest level of [his] preoccupations," was in fact symbolically the core and support of all his preoccupations.

When he wrote an article in 1944 on the occasion of the centenary of the birth of Drumont, he stressed what he claimed was Drumont's importance as a writer as much as his contributions to the history of French anti-Semitism, and in doing so Rebatet clearly drew a portrait of a best-selling anti-Semitic journalist and pamphleteer that he would also have liked to have seen applied to himself:

> We would not be celebrating the centenary of Drumont if he had not been first of all a superb writer. . . . There is not one of his pages where a stroke of inspiration does not shine forth, in which one recognizes the artist. . . . Drumont possessed exclusively a humor, a good-naturedness of a Rabelaisian giant, which, linked to his constant faculty of indignation, gave to all his pamphlets a human weight of which we still haven't seen the equivalent except in Céline. . . . Every great pamphleteer has a core of vast goodness in him. If he jumps with fury into the fray, it's through altruism, because he *loves* his fellow men, his country, because he can't really see them founder, perish, without screaming a warning, without grabbing onto the collar of their robbers and assassins. ("Drumont parmi nous," *Je suis partout*, No. 663 [April 28, 1944])

This was clearly the scenario Rebatet saw for himself—not that of the tragic political hero dying for his principles and proving their worth and truth by his death, but rather that of the great writer who supposedly never dies but through his writing continues to be remembered, read, honored as a lover of men, a patriot, regardless of, or rather because of, his fury against particular men, groups, religions, or races.

As he placed Drumont in an authentically French literary tradition that ran from Rabelais, to Saint-Simon, to Balzac and then Céline, he was clearly making a place for himself at the summit of that tradition after Céline. The respect for French literary tradition that initially led him to the Action Française and then to fascism and anti-Semitism would in this scenario await him and keep a place open for him. The end of the war was thus, on this imaginary level, anticlimactic and melodramatic rather than tragic, for his long novel still was unfinished and needed to be polished. His true, absolute mission in life still remained to be fulfilled.

Rebatet, the ferocious enemy of all communists, democrats, and Jews, in fact proceeded to take on God and the Catholic Church in his novel with a violence similar to the violence he had used to attack his enemies in his political writings. Michel Croz, the main character in Rebatet's novel *Les Deux étendards* attacks the Catholic Church in terms similar to those that Rebatet used to attack the Jews, demanding *vengeance* for the way the Church had allegedly deformed him spiritually, emotionally, and physically: "I hate the religion into which chance had me be born. This hatred is my backbone, my only tonic. If I no longer had any other reason for being, I would want that hatred to be enough for me. . . . I am the cripple who seeks his vengeance and who succeeds at least in reformulating for himself one rule: work at that vengeance, obstinately, toward and against everything" (738). Unlike the version of the novel given by Etiemble and Steiner, who defend it for its "universality" or "classical beauty," and thus for being entirely opposed to the violence and hatred at the basis of Rebatet's fascism and anti-Semitism, in the novel Rebatet simply redirects his anger and finds an expression for it that is not directly political or racist. But as in the case of Céline, the aestheticist principles that supported Rebatet's political anger have not changed. The most striking similarity between his political writings, his memoirs, and his novel is that the spiritual battle in each is absolute, a matter of either life or death, and the ultimate value of the struggle is the struggle itself, regardless of whether one wins or loses. In fact, spiritual (aesthetic) victory is best ensured by political and personal failure, which justifies cries of unlimited vengeance.

The aesthetic-political ideal in question in Rebatet's work was perhaps best and most succinctly described not in his essays on art or politics, but by Michel Croz, his fictional spokesperson in *Les Deux étendards*, after seeing an especially moving performance of Mozart's *Marriage of Figaro* (the exemplary work of art for Rebatet): "What was sublime was the agreement of everything: the genius of the music, the orchestra that was beating as a single body, the set, the costumes, the purest of acting, the voices without a single flaw. An instant of beauty that leaves us not with joy but only with an eternal regret. We caught a glimpse of perfection, but only to know that it disappears right away" (230–31). The immediate disappearance of aesthetic (or political) perfection after it had been glimpsed, of aesthetic-political (and sexual) plenitude after it had been experienced, was precisely what Rebatet was unable to accept and what provoked his greatest anger. Someone had to be responsible for such a loss; someone had to be made to pay for it. In the novel, it is the Catholic Church and its priests; in his literary and political essays, it is, of course, the Jews.

The violence of Rebatet's writings against the Jews during the war is of course blatant, persistent, and undeniable; but what should not be overlooked in the haste to criticize and condemn it is that it was not an isolated trait or peculiarity of Rebatet's work but an integral component of the dogmatic aestheticist values at the very basis of literary fascism in general. Rebatet's form of fascist aestheticism expressed itself both as a sporadic detachment from politics, or a retreat into the aesthetic domain or the "museum," *and* as an extreme expression of violence *in the political sphere* that supported absolute, totalitarian political ends. In the case of literary fascism, total aesthetic perfection constituted, therefore, a dangerous totalitarian political ideal.

Nine

A *Literary* Fascism beyond Fascism: Thierry Maulnier and the Ideology of Culture

> It is necessary to restore to philosophy the taste for
> blood. It is necessary to restore to metaphysical
> systems their cruelty, their power of life and
> death.
> *Thierry Maulnier*, Nietzsche *(1935)*

> *Combat* [an extremist journal cofounded and run
> by Maulnier] had its place in our friendships, . . .
> in the quite fascist, anti-liberal, and at the same
> time national and socialist atmosphere of those
> times.
> *Robert Brasillach*, Notre avant-guerre *(1941)*

> [Thierry Maulnier's] journal will fail because it
> does not take a clear position. Kléber Haedens
> and Blanchot have been devoured by surrealism.
> Maulnier by radical and Jewish moderationism.
> *Drieu la Rochelle*, Journal *(May 3, 1940)*

> Thierry Maulnier cannot be overtly Gaullist near
> Charles Maurras. . . . But it is clear that Thierry
> Maulnier tends toward Gaullism, that he is
> flirting with it. . . . It is not for us to know for
> what reasons Charles Maurras tolerates this
> individual in his newspaper, any more than it is
> for us to judge. But for us, Maulnier, . . . traitor to
> his best friends, is from now on disqualified. . . .
> It is to be hoped that rogues like Maulnier will be
> mercilessly chased from the French press.
> Le Cri du Peuple *(November 27, 1940;*
> *reprinted in* Je suis partout *[February 7, 1941])*

> [The fascism of the journal *Combat*] was a fascism
> of people who do not die the violent deaths of
> agitators and rabble-rousers but end their days
> as members of the Académie Française.
> *Zeev Sternhell*, Neither Right nor Left

Classicism, Humanism, Fascism

Of all the writers and critics closely linked to Brasillach and contributing to the *L'Action Française*, *Révolution Nationale*, *Je suis partout*, and other journals of the extreme right published in France in the 1930s, Thierry Maulnier is perhaps the most difficult to categorize. In terms of the two principal political movements with which he was most closely associated—the royalism or integral nationalism of the Action Française and the anti-Semitism and fascism of journals such as *Je suis partout*—he was considered an independent, if not, eventually, at least as concerns *Je suis partout* and other collaborationist journals, a dissident and traitor to the cause of fascism. He himself cofounded two journals, *Combat* and *L'Insurgé*, in an effort to define and promote the "National Revolution," which was to take the form, as the title of his book from the same period indicates, both of a hypernationalism, a nationalism "beyond nationalism,"[1] and a radical spiritualistic socialism, a socialism beyond socialism, at least in its various Marxist forms.

But Maulnier, unlike Drieu la Rochelle, Brasillach, and Rebatet, never directly collaborated with the Germans. Instead, he continued to write literary and philosophical-political articles for *L'Action Française* during the Occupation. Also, unlike most of his fascist friends and associates from the 1930s, he never overtly declared himself to be a fascist, but he consistently criticized the totalitarian politics of fascist Italy and Nazi Germany and the attempts to create fascist parties and movements in France, even as he wrote (until the defeat) for journals supporting or sympathetic to such attempts. And although he frequently contributed to militantly anti-Semitic journals, such as *Je suis partout*, and remained publicly loyal to Maurras and the anti-Semitic principles of the Action Française until the end of the war, he repeatedly pointed out the limitations and dangers of all biologically determined nationalisms and the folly of making the "Jewish Question" central to any nationalist politics. For these reasons, Maulnier has been ignored or treated only peripherally by almost all studies of fascism and fascist intellectuals in France. For almost all analysts of the period, he is quite simply not considered a fascist at all.[2]

Maulnier's extreme form of nationalism, which represents a very particular and radical form of literary fascism, possessed what could be called a *classical* purity. Its radical nature consisted not in striving to implement more extreme totalitarian principles than other nationalisms or national socialisms but rather in claiming to be more consistent, basic, and decisive in its defense of the nation. The "au-delà" or the "beyond" of nationalism often evoked by Maulnier was really a return to first principles, to what he considered to be the origin or essence of both true nationalism and socialism, as well as authentic, "spiritualistic" fascism. His fascism could be considered, then, at the same time an "en-deça" or zero degree of nationalism, a form of fascism that was largely intellectual and uncompromisingly *literary*. For to a greater degree than any of the other literary fascists treated in this work—except perhaps, and for the opposite reasons, Céline—literature is the key to understanding his politics. It is not just the founding element and model of his entire political-spiritualist enterprise, but it is also the ideal he was unwilling to compromise for any politics, even fascist politics.

Maulnier's politics, no matter how extreme, were in fact firmly rooted in classical humanism. His first major work, *La Crise est dans l'homme* (Paris: Librairie de la Revue Française, 1932), consists of a series of essays whose main purpose is to redefine and defend classical humanism, to give it such a radical, "modern" form that it could be evoked as an alternative to and cure for the repeated political crises and spiritual decadence of modernity. In this text, Maulnier presents himself as a militant culturalist, writing not on behalf of any specific literary or philosophical movement or political ideology, but on behalf of the spirit itself. Because the ultimate origin of the crisis afflicting modern man and society is not political but spiritual, not outside of man but *in him*, the combat he calls for to defeat an enemy that is not even being recognized as such cannot be that of an army waging war but that of intellectuals "waging thoughts" (8). Before engaging in politics, then, before undertaking specific social or economic analyses of problems and the political actions necessary to resolve them, a reactivation of the mind and a pure form of thinking are necessary in order to educate the self and understand that the real enemy to be fought is first and foremost the enemy of the spirit. Nothing less than the rediscovery of what it means to be human on the deepest spiritual level constitutes the core of the intellectual-political task that was the aim of Maulnier's first book.

As an essential part of this general project of rediscovering "the human," art and literature have to be rediscovered in their turn, and returned to their "true mission," which is, "in a world liberated from the world, to trace a figure of man limited to his eternal traits" (14). This "figure of man" constitutes the key to Maulnier's radical form of humanism. Man in crisis is always man divorced from this ideal figure or type; it is man divided by multiple and contradictory figures, man defined and determined by less than eternal figures. Man in crisis is man reduced to partial figures, figures determined by social, historical, political, or economic forces, man whose future seems to be already determined by material forces outside of *his* control.

The first step to recovery is to be conscious of the insufficient nature of this future and to revolt against it: "He who fixes his eyes on the future that is being forged and who can discern in it the denatured, monstrous figure of this future brother whom he will have to resemble can react only with an egoism ready to do anything" (17). Such a revolt will supposedly bring about the eventual return of the one, genuine "figure of man." This is what Maulnier calls "a total defense of man," one that only artists and writers can undertake, because only they can deal with and show the way out of a crisis that both "comes from the spirit and threatens the spirit" (18). Anything less than a total defense of man, anything other than a defense that is primarily spiritual and thus that would not be undertaken in an "absolute way without any possible restrictions" (21), would, for Maulnier, only deepen the crisis. The writer or artist who takes on such an absolute defense, rather than the writer who has his writing serve a specific political cause, represents the true political militant, the militant of the spirit.[3]

Maulnier was a humanist because classical humanism provided him with a total, ordered figure of man that he held was universal and aesthetic, rather than historical and political in nature, a cultural ideal honed and perfected through time and not just created out of the necessities of the moment. Curiously enough, insofar as it is profoundly aesthetic, such a humanism could also be considered authentically national and social in nature, providing a figure or model for the unification of a people on the most profound, interior level of their being:

> Genuine humanism moves toward a constructed and ordered figure of man; it constitutes for us an idea of life and a mode of being with things in which relations are harmonious and stable. . . . It renounces the intelligible perfection of philosophers, and it directs its illuminating efforts toward an aesthetic and moral unity, toward a harmony conscious of interior life. . . . It founds our perfection on integral results, it imposes discipline on us, it is national and social, and it gives us our figure only in uniting us with others. (34)

The aesthetic and moral unity of the figure of man proposed by genuine humanism thus becomes the basis and model for authentic nationalism and socialism, even for their fusion in nationalist or even national socialism.

"The humanist schema of our destiny," claims Maulnier, is "more true and alive" than that provided by contemporary society "because it has been freed from a vulgar subjectivity." The humanist schema or aestheticized figure of man in itself transcends all class divisions, which means "that on a certain level of consciousness words like bourgeois and proletariat can be forgotten" (40). Maulnier's notion of humanism, one that is also "beyond common humanism which does not reach the total truth of our essence" (41), thus restores man to himself and provides a model for total man. The "new man" suggested by the classical humanist schema has the decided advantage over the "new man" projected by the "common," that is, subjectivist, humanism of liberal democracy or the materialist "new man" of communism, because it allegedly has all of Western history to support it. It is the oldest, most carefully fashioned and thus universal (spiritual) of all "new men."

Maulnier argues repeatedly that humanism is the only genuine alternative to both Marxist collectivism, which he calls "the barbaric name of a barbarity" (183), and democracy, which "devours man body and soul" (193). He believes that both reduce man to material, economic forces at the expense of his unity and spirituality and thus are equally dangerous. He asserts that "democracy is a collective Caesarism," while "socialism is a collective capitalism," with the only hope of successfully opposing these "monstrous menace[s]" being a complete "intellectual recovery. It is a question of imposing a notion of complete, non-disfigured man, of recognizing the proper place of the individual and society in reality and to restore them ideally in their order, a question of restoring them positively in their unity" (194). The intellectual, spiritual recovery Maulnier is calling for thus cannot take place unless the classical humanist model for man is given priority over all "disfigured" democratic and socialist models. This also means that a form of classical *aesthetics* should be given priority over all forms of modern *politics*.

Maulnier's spiritualistic nationalism was French only insomuch as "Frenchness" could be equated with the figure of the universal and the truly human, which, in classical humanist terms, means with Greece. The more a civilization resembled Greece, the more it retained the beauty and truth of Greece, and the less disfigured and the more human it was. Like his mentor, Maurras, Maulnier thus privileged the classical concept of art and literature over all others, but his notion of the classical or total vision of man, and of Greece as the origin of Western civilization, was as much if not more indebted to Nietzsche than it was to the father of the Action Française and Integral Nationalism. His vision of Greece and the aesthetics he associated with it were more Dionysian than Apollonian, an aesthetics of force and violence more than of formal, fashioned, Apollonian beauty.

In his *Nietzsche* (Paris: Gallimard, 1935), Maulnier treats Nietzsche both as the great modern theorist of classical tragedy and as a supreme tragic figure himself. Nietzsche is tragic (and poetic) in his attempt to "resuscitate the drunkenness of the Greeks, not their moderation," but only as long as he opposes "the morality of affirmation, . . . the only tragic morality, the tragic ideal of purity, . . . a Racinian purity" (47), to the divisions of life. The authentically *tragic* (French) Nietzsche is "the model tragic thinker in whom passion alters thought, in whom the path from flesh to metaphysics is the shortest. He gives us miraculous access to the precise and fatal point of our being where body and mind seem to be

hardly separated at all" (23). And this lack of distance or opposition between the material and the spiritual serves as a model for what in Maulnier's mind is the primary "political" (aesthetic-metaphysical) problem of
his time: "It is necessary to restore to metaphysical systems their cruelty:
their power of life and death" (24). "It is important to create a world
where tragic existence is possible" (55). The seeds for a Nietzschean or
"tragic politics" are thus in place.

The tragic (anti-German) Nietzsche is presented by Maulnier as the antinationalist thinker par excellence, but his is an antinationalism that represents at the same time a more demanding, more radical, "cruel" form of
nationalism, a European nationalism beyond sectarian nationalisms.

> Nietzsche no longer recognizes the homeland as anything except a form of
> suffocation. This European does not search for the means for communion and
> peace in the destruction of all homelands. He doesn't condemn in homelands
> their tragic reality, the possibility of fighting, the demand for sacrifice. . . . He
> doesn't ask them to be less demanding or hard; the new homelands he reserves
> for men are perhaps even more demanding and hard. (69)

Thus, in Maulnier's reading, which closely resembles that of Drieu la Rochelle in its attack on the restrictive, suffocating spiritual effects of the
nation or homeland, Nietzsche's criticism of existing, "common" nationalisms is that they do not demand enough of the nation or its people, that
they are too self-contained and self-satisfied in their claims to be homelands. Starkly put, "common nationalisms" are not tragic, not really nationalist enough, because they are still too much under the influence of
political forces foreign to the authentic spirituality of man. They are not
sufficiently human.

In a manner that recalls Barrès's war against the foreign and the barbarian in the name of the Self, but also Drieu la Rochelle's myth of Europe, for Maulnier, the "superior," or tragic, individual must "occupy his
part of the universe without taking on or weighing himself down with
foreign values" (70). This helps explain why superior "European man" is
at the same time destructive of existing, compromised nationalisms and
radically alone: "To destroy national communions is to isolate oneself
and not unite oneself with others. . . . European man is tragic man opposed to man linked to and assisted by national cultures: he is man alone"
(70–71). The "beyond," as concerns the nation, is thus a state of radical
isolation from all immediate, historical and cultural supports and obligations, a radical, total freedom that seems on the surface, as in the case of
Barrès's early work, to be diametrically opposed to any concept of nationalism, even the most extreme.

The tragic individual moves toward the destruction of all values, spiritual as well as material, individual as well as collective. This destructive,
individualist "nihilism," however, does not constitute an end in itself but

rather clears the stage for a radical confrontation of the individual with the irremediable and catastrophic foundation of his being: "Genuine tragedy demands that the world be freed from invented values, that the scene be empty for beings liberated and bound only to themselves, for irremediable acts, unavoidable catastrophes. Nietzschean nihilism is nothing other than a heroic humanism" (82). The more violent and destructive that tragic nihilism becomes, the more heroic and humanist it is considered to be.

Nietzschean "superior man" is beyond good and evil precisely because he is aesthetic and tragic; that is, in Maulnier's terms, unwilling to compromise when it comes to the integrity of passion. According to Maulnier, the truth of classical art and all "great art in general" for Nietzsche is that art is

> a mode of expression different from life, more perfect than life whose awkwardness, insignificances, and stammerings it ignores. No one, perhaps, got closer to defining the lively value of classical discipline, which claims to make passion more ardent and more intelligible, not mutilate it or moderate it. A style of life, a classical style consists thus not in restraining life but in maintaining it, by a skillful and severe constraint, at its height and the point of its most expansive intensity. Such a constraint allows for a more exposed, more essential, more violent existence. (169)

Maulnier thus argues that passion, desire, and will are more intense and violent, and more essential, when they are constrained or *formed*, and that this type of formal constraint and intensification of force constitutes the defining characteristic of the classical. In this sense, the Nietzschean notion of a pure and extreme aesthetics of force can be realized as a maximum of intensity or violence only within the constraints of classical form—the Dionysian realizing itself fully only through the Apollonian.

Nietzsche's own "tragic fall" consists precisely in his having chosen at the end of his life what Maulnier calls primitive barbarism over classicism and civilization, which amounts to having chosen the wrong form of unification and model for the synthesis of force. In this way, he prepared the way for a limited and inferior form of nationalism or fascism, a German National Socialism rather than a truly classical, tragic, French-Greek ultranationalism.

> Tempted by a new synthesis, this German mind, unbalanced in its essence, doesn't resist the temptation to reunite in a *faisceau* the forces that are the enemies of destiny and man and, for tragic combat, magisterially opposed to them. Innocence is now his goal. In this way the image of the great civilized man of the Caesar type tends in the last works of Nietzsche to disappear before barbarian instinct. . . . The barbarian type triumphs, even the idea of civilization is progressively reduced to that of degeneration, . . . the idea of culture is

replaced by the idea of corruption, as that of purity is replaced by savagery. A naive romanticism attempts to discover superior human types in primitive societies. (237–38)

This point where Nietzsche retreated from the tragic is also in Maulnier's political schema where National Socialism can be linked to Marxist and fascist forms of socialism. Maulnier's principal criticism of both fascism and communism can thus be seen to be rooted in his critique of the later Nietzsche. He considered neither to be a genuine nationalism—a true fascism or socialism—because neither was classical, that is, tragic or humanist enough—having rejected tradition for myth, rationality and order for primitivism, classical purity for savagery.

Nietzsche's retreat from the aesthetics of tragedy into German romanticism thus also constitutes the fall of classical humanism, and this fall is characterized by a loss of intensity and violence within both the aesthetic and political realms. If, as I have suggested, this is the point where Nietzsche's work can be used to support German National Socialism, then it is clear that an important aspect of Maulnier's subsequent critique of Nazism is that it was not combative, not violent enough, at least not on the spiritual level. Its aesthetics were so "monistic" that they practically destroyed creative force and conflict, reducing the intensity of true combat to an empty, formalist notion of communion.

> Humanism is in fact sacrificed for a monistic aesthetics of the world, tragedy for cult, combat for communion, and the authentic tragic ideal, founded on the existence of an irreducible human value in conflict with nature, has been resolved. . . . We have already remarked how German this all is, as is German everything that unbalances two irreconcilable experiences toward synthesis. (254)

Maulnier is unwilling to give up the principle of combat, even for "perfect" communion, unwilling to give up a tragic aesthetics of conflicting intensities for the aesthetic-political resolution of forces. In theory, at least, Maulnier's criticism of fascism was that it did not go far enough, that it accepted romantic mythology for "the authentic tragic ideal," and by being in this way too aestheticist—and thus not "fascist" enough—it failed to awaken the nation and Europe to their authentic tragic destiny.

Tragedy, Violence, and the National Revolution

Maulnier's *Racine* (Paris: Gallimard, 1936) develops further the notion of tragic humanism presented in his *Nietzsche* and reveals with more precision how a radical form of classical aesthetics can have a founding, formative role in the elaboration of a nationalist politics "beyond nationalism." In his introduction to *Racine*, in a double and contradictory strategy, Maulnier both separates Racine from the French nation as an existing political entity and roots him profoundly in "tradition," the ground that supports any true national culture or civilization. Racine's theater, strictly speaking, is not French, then, because it has none of the trappings of the French nation and therefore no value as a nationalist symbol or rallying cry. "It is not possible," Maulnier asserts, "to drape Racine's characters [unlike Corneille's] in any national costume, to give them the hair, or the build, or the profile of a people or a race, to put in their hands flags or emblems" (14). Literature and culture, on the one hand, and nationalist politics and social concerns, on the other, are completely separate things, located on entirely different levels: "Racine is not social. France can consider him as an incomparable success of its culture, not as a stimulant of energy, a national guide, a worker of its unity. If France is one day enslaved, it is not a tragedy of Racine that will give birth to an uprising for independence" (13). In order for Racine's theater to be treated on its own terms, it must in fact be cut off from all explicit trappings of the nation, from all immediate social influences, and from politics as such. On this level, Maulnier's is one of the least directly political approaches to drama imaginable.[4]

At the same time, Maulnier asserts, Racine is also the most profoundly nationalist of writers, the best representative of the nation, "the purest of our writers, . . . a national genius" (25). Maulnier's *Racine* constitutes his attempt to save Racine, French classicism, and thus a certain idea of France, from being classified as formalist, aestheticist, or abstract; that is, from being treated as irrelevant to modernity and its political and cultural crises. Maulnier criticizes what he calls the "stupid worshipers of French clarity and French order" for having "done the greatest harm to France, the greatest harm to the spirit" by equating what he calls a "mutilated, abstract, formal classicism" with France and thus acknowledging that French civilization was and is "incapable of authentic experience and creative virtue" (23–24). Above all, he wants to put an end to the "legend of an Apollonian France" and replace it with that of a "Racinian France." His notion of the "new Racinian man" is critical of formalist classicism but remains nevertheless profoundly classical, with authentic classicism defined as the moment when "the greatest vital fervor and the supreme blossoming of creative energies coincide with the triumph of formal perfection" (24).

Maulnier's analysis of Racinian tragedy sheds much light on why he felt it was necessary to pursue the question of the nation and of the national culture "beyond nationalism." For beyond the geographic, political, and cultural limitations of France lies the truth of France and all other European nations: Greece. Beyond the exterior trappings of French culture, French society, and the French people, can be found (Western) civilization and Man as such. Ultimately Racine is considered a national genius, the purest, example of French genius because he is not French but "Greek": "Faced with the simplicity of Racine, one should not think of how French he is but how Greek he is" (155). This means that no nationalism that defines itself entirely in terms of existing nationalist practices, myths, institutions, or values can do any better than repeat the mistakes of those who reduce French classicism completely to formal order and the law of the three unities and thus give a truncated version of the nation and of man. Maulnier the literary-critic and Maulnier the political-theorist demanded something more from both literature and politics, from both classicism and nationalism.

What Maulnier's aesthetics demand and what Racine provides him with is nothing less than a model for the perfect, dynamic unity of form and force, of the Dionysian and the Apollonian, of "inspiration and technique, . . . the delirium of creative energy and the order instituted by the intelligence" (20). Classicism in this sense is a radical aesthetics of force, an uncompromising, delirious plunge into the abyss of madness, excess, instinct, and pure energy, which at the same time is lucid and rigorous self-consciousness, order, and mastery. Classicism is the extreme culmination of civilization, the telos or ultimate destiny of all cultures, which is at the same time a return to the origin, to *being* in itself before it is separated, divided, dispersed, an origin where "fervor and the formal principle, from their birth, . . . form each other, penetrate each other, coincide with each other." Classicism constitutes an origin presided over by a classical god who is simultaneously "an invigorated, humanized Apollo, present at the very source of energies, desires, lyricism, and a Dionysus who, during orgies themselves, knows his form and law" (23). The force, energy, or instinct of classicism is what Maulnier calls a "civilized instinct" (26), a force that has realized its full intensity by being formed.

The model of an ideal tragic culture, as we have seen, is Greek culture, the culture of "the only people in the world that was naturally and instinctively poetic," a people who had "the secret of living its poetry, the secret of a constant and diffuse poetry, qualifying and transfiguring its daily life" (156). In Maulnier's Nietzschean sense, the highest, the absolute political calling of a people is thus to become a people of art. But a people of art is not, however, a people of aesthetic pleasure, tranquil harmony, or naive innocence. A people of art is first and foremost a people of force, of poetic possession in the mystical or demonic sense of the term:

Poetry is one of the essential rites in the magic of an art that has as its object the creation of fervor. It is tragic animation itself, the way of the possession that tragedy maintains on the spectator, the instrument of the famous *catharsis*, which is not a moral purification of the passions but the movement by which the subject is rid of itself. (162)

The individual subject is rid of itself, of course, by being drawn into and possessed by the collective subject of delirium. The highest, "most civilized" form of poetry is also the most violent, destructive, and deadly form.

Racinian tragedy, the embodiment of the highest values of civilization, is thus necessarily bloody: "The poetry of Racine is never where fatality, blood, and suffering are not; it is not pure of cruelty" (165). "Racine knows only one way, it is the way of the knife. . . . He knows only the place of the truly fatal vein. . . . He leads his heroes to the temple, not to be absolved but to be slaughtered" (167–68). Poetic or tragic man, man at his *most civilized*, then, is not a "man-for-life but a man-for-death" (167). At the source of the poetic is the violence of the loss of self, of death, the ultimate fatality from which no one escapes. And it is not just tragic poetry, the highest form of poetry, that is rooted in such violence and in the radical dispossession of self in the name of poetic possession, and thus a higher, poeticized form of self-knowledge. In principle, all authentic poetry is violent, for a poetry devoid of cruelty and violence is an abstract, formalist, aestheticist poetry, a nonpoetic poetry. A people and a culture without violence are thus also a people and a culture without poetry. All authentic, "tragic" politics must also possess the supreme poetic virtue of violence and be the expression of being at its ultimate limits, of being-for-death.

But if violence is essential to the poetic, it alone cannot determine it. The character who is subjected to violence must remain conscious of his ordeal, for "lucidity is also one of the sovereign characteristics of Racinian humanity. There is not one character of Racine in whom violence and suffering abolish even for a single instant the acuity of his intellectual awareness" (177). What attracts Maulnier to Racine is precisely the fusion of violence and lucidity, the ultimate expression of force and poetic form, neither existing without the other: "The heroes of Racine are lucid only in violence; and they are poetic only in violence" (182). Racine's "exceptionally hard and brutal art, unique in the period for its savagery" (182), consists in fact of a perfect fusion of extremes: of the original, barbaric violence of existence, on the one hand, and of the most "civilized," lucid experience of such violence, on the other.

The goal of tragic art is not to moderate the brutality or savagery of these violent forces but rather to give them form, and to allow them to give form to themselves. The "purity" of Racine's art is "not just of art and style and form, but of man given over to the greatest and most dan-

gerous sentiments, without anything changing their violence or compos-
ing an equilibrium. No artist ever established such an exact coincidence
of being and its fundamental forces" (216). Such a coincidence of being
and force, form and delirium, the civilized and the barbaric, thus constitutes the paradoxical purity of art—its highest, most uncompromising
form. The coincidence of extreme force and perfect form is thus the essence of the poetic work itself, but it is also the essence of a new type of
humanity, "the totally new and totally living humanity which comes out
of [Racine's] work" (270). Racinian man thus represents a poetic, tragic,
but not aestheticized humanity, a humanity that has been fashioned
through the lucid confrontation with its own origin and limits, with the
savage and destructive forces that are nevertheless *productive*. The question that underlies all of Maulnier's political essays is how society can be
reconstructed in terms of these same poetic-tragic principles and violent
forces.[5]

The Greek or Nietzschean Racine in this way constitutes a beginning,
a point of departure, for Maulnier's pursuit of a nationalism beyond nationalism and a theory and practice of literature that would embody and
serve as a model for such an ultranationalist, absolute, spiritualistic politics. In his *Introduction à la poésie française* (Paris: Gallimard, 1939), a
text which was first published as a series of articles in *Je suis partout* but
which seems on the surface to be far removed from the partisan and extremist politics of the late 1930s, Maulnier elaborated a vigorous defense
and illustration of French poetry, both of what makes it truly *French*
and what makes it truly poetic. The text is an extended polemic against
French romanticism and a defense of sixteenth- and seventeenth-century
poetry, but it also constitutes a defense of all poetic theories and practices
that attack and attempt to destroy the prevailing formalist aesthetics and
poetic practices of their time. In fact, it even undertakes in its treatment
of the modern period a vigorous defense of surrealism in the name of
the poetic-cultural ideal of the fusion of classical form and revolutionary
violence.

Even though Maulnier severely criticizes its formalist limitations, surrealism also serves as the model of an authentic revolutionary poetic
movement, a violent, combative movement against the "common rationality" that limits poetry to "the materials supplied by the ordinary transparent consciousness." In this way it points to "a procedure of the spirit
which belongs to poetic activity of all times," which means that "every
poetic work whatsoever can in a certain sense be called surrealist" (19).
But if every authentic poetic work can be called surrealist in its capacity
to go beyond the transparent and the known, surrealism as such limits
itself by misunderstanding the higher form of poetic rationality onto
which its own procedures open. "The weakness of surrealism was not

234   CHAPTER NINE

just to forget everything rational that subsists in the hidden universe in which it believes it is fleeing rationalism, but also to forget everything miraculous which subsists in the universe of clarity" (17). Just as the constraints imposed by classicism made possible the actualization of violent intensities and were their expression, so the rational is considered the most "miraculous" (perhaps even, the most surreal) element of the poetic universe, present only when rationalism as such has been left behind.

As was the case in his analysis of Racine, Maulnier first separates poetry from the exterior, material manifestations of the French people and nation, and from the physical and geographic characteristics of France. And in this, France and French poetry are unique:

> If the poetry of foreign peoples can appear as the very song of these people, . . . French poetry is completely separated from the biological work of France; it is the skillful utilization of the most elaborated material of our culture. English or German poetry encompasses England or Germany, while French poetry ignores France, shows itself incapable of successfully making use of French tradition, French legends, French concerns, the geniuses of French soil. (32)

When it comes to poetry and the spiritual in general, biology and geography, blood and soil are certainly not determining factors. The vocation of French poetry is more spiritual than that of other countries, for unlike other poetries, which are expressions of the people, its land and history, "French poetry is first of all poetry, . . . its nature is to be essentially literary" (33). And this militant nationalist cannot be any more explicit as to what being essentially literary means: "The homeland of French poetry is less France than literature" (33). Nation, homeland, and even tradition and culture in their narrow nationalist sense, are irrelevant terms for the study of *French* poetry. What is most French about it is that it is so little French and so completely literary, at least on the surface.

Maulnier argues that, unlike other countries, and especially (Nazi) Germany, France "has never established links between its historical, popular, legendary traditions and its poetic tradition." This results in the radical separation of political manifestations and poetic expression: "Nothing is more prosaic than a French political ceremony. Nothing is more foreign to French life than a French poem" (35). This radical separation is the sign of the pure spirituality of the poetic in France, and thus of its superiority over other poetic traditions. But it also distinguishes French poetics and politics from the poetic-political manifestations of Nazi Germany (and fascist Italy), an aestheticizing or poeticizing of the political that Maulnier considers inferior to the prosaic French version of politics, just as he considers German poetry to be inferior to French poetry. In other words, a poetry too closely linked to historical events, specific national institutions and customs, and popular myths not only is a degraded form of poetry, but it also produces a degraded form of tradition, history, popular expression, and politics. Politics and poetry both suffer from their direct linkage, or from the determination of one by the other, from the explicit poeticizing of the political and the dogmatic politicizing of the poetic.

Maulnier sees the history of French poetry as the movement toward an ever-increasing immateriality, a continual purging of all exterior, non-poetic elements, and this process culminates in the manifestation of the true French national-poetic identity: "French poetry, literary and stark from the moment it began to merit the name French poetry, throughout the centuries has never stopped aiming at becoming more and more literary and stark" (44). For "the most literary people in the world" (43), to be poetic without compromise and to be French without compromise are parallel activities; each consists of a process of stripping away the inessential trappings of poetry and politics and purifying the essential spiritual core of the people. The poetic in its purest form transforms everything within its reach: "The effort of French poetry toward a pure poetry is not the effort to deprive the poem of all content other than poetry, which would have no sense, *but to give the poem the power to act poetically on the totality of its content*" (49). What ultimately defines a poem as authentically *poetic* is its ability to act poetically without exterior restraints, to transform the totality of its parts, no matter how apoetic or antipoetic, into integral components of the poem. What defines a people is exactly the same capacity for a people to act as itself and transform the totality of its history, experiences, and even the foreign elements within it into what could be called a cultural or political poem. The poetic and the national, the making of a poem and the making of a people, are homologous *acts*, and in this way national identity, tradition, and culture are reintroduced into the question of the poetic at its very foundation. Maulnier, the champion of a pure poetry is at the same time Maulnier the ultranationalist, advocate of a nationalism beyond nationalism, of a nationalism that takes the form of a poetic-political act consisting of the total transformation and rebirth of a profoundly literary people.

The Spiritual Revolution and the Ideal of Culture

Maulnier's complicated relation to fascism can be best understood in terms of the aesthetic principles that are at the heart of his radical concept of nationalism and that are derived from his notion of the total poetic act. For example, his collection of political essays entitled *Mythes socialistes* (Paris: Gallimard, 1936) consists of an extended critique of both socialism and totalitarian nationalist ideologies for being "barbarian"—that is, non-Greek, nonpoetic—and for demanding that intellectual and artistic productions be determined and controlled by material and political concerns. No matter whether it is done in the name of an ideology of the left or of the right, Maulnier denounced the restrictions imposed on the freedom of the mind as the source of all enslavement: "From the enslavement of thought to the enslavement of man, the distance is quickly breached" (6). His attacks were especially aimed at the Soviet Union and at all socialist myths that brought about the "fall of the spirit" (10) by assigning thought the task primarily of "serving primitive masses, crowds, political parties, myths, nations" (12). But Maulnier also severely criticized fascism and National Socialism for their populist characteristics and use of myth, thus linking them directly to communism and the destruction of the spirit.

Maulnier considered populism to be the most degraded form of humanism, the form institutionalized in modernity *by democracy*. And insofar as they were populist, he attacked Italian fascism and German National Socialism for representing the continuation rather than the reversal or destruction of democracy:

> The Italian fascist and German racist movements, which have been too often represented as anti-democratic reactions, are not exempt from certain dangerous affinities with democracy. I mean by that the call they make to the masses, by the respect in which they hold the values revered by the masses, by the concern the leaders have to mix with the masses and let themselves be carried off by them. Hitler is less a leader than a collective myth, the symbol of a community of the spirit and of dreams, a representative man in whom the German crowds recognize their incarnation—fascism and racism representing the most natural, extreme consequences of democracy, the passage from individualist parliamentary and liberal democracy to an authoritarian, religious, total, and devouring collectivism. (56)

Maulnier never deviated from this criticism of Italian fascism and German National Socialism, which is based on his fundamental distrust of the collective will, whether it manifested itself spontaneously or was imposed through the political manipulation of the symbolic manifestations of community and of "representative man." He felt that any political figure or principle originating in or closely associated with *the masses* represented in fact an extension of democracy and had collectivist, totalitarian, antispiritual (antipoetic) implications identical to those of Marxist forms of socialism.

The renewal of the nation and its people, the national revolution, "has to have its principle and its center located beyond [nationalist collectivism]" (57) in the hierarchies formed by the intellect. It should be led by an aristocracy of independent thinkers, like Maulnier himself, rather than follow or be associated with the passions of the crowd. The problem with all forms of political collectivism, he felt, with collectivisms of the right as well as the left, was that "in order to achieve the complete communion dreamed of by collectivism, . . . because one cannot obtain [it] by raising up the masses, it is necessary, whether one wants to or not, to bring art down in order to accomplish it" (92). To bring art (the spiritual) down to the level of the collectivity, however, was the greatest aesthetic *and political* sin. Maulnier always condemned any collectivism that moved in the direction of this leveling process for being too materialist—that is, too "democratic"—whether the collective was fascist or socialist in form and whether the collectivity was based on class, race, or even the cultural integrity of a people or nation. The "common" fascist aestheticizing of politics was thus too much of a politicization of art for Maulnier, a utilization of art for political purposes that seriously diminished the scope and effects of both art and politics.

According to Maulnier, once the poetic, the ultimate form of the spiritual, has been established in itself and on its own terms apart from historical-political determinations, it does not "ignore the world but dominate[s] it" from above or "beyond" (153). This means that writers and artists should resist what Maulnier considered the "easier" choice of direct political commitments and actions (154) in order to develop the resources of the spirit by artistic creation, and in this way act "politically" in a much more complicated and fundamental, poetic way. "It is good from time to time to remind those who forget, that is by their aesthetic and literary productions, not by their juridical and social natures, that civilizations survive and fight against time" (149). There is a fundamental element of political resistance built into Maulnier's position on literature and culture: it is the resistance of art to its own political determination or to its being used to serve specific political ends, whether they be ends determined by democracy, socialism, or fascism. In the name of nothing less than the "survival of civilization," the intellectual and the artist are required to serve art and ideas before politics and in this way bring about a true, profound spiritual revolution, not just an economic or sociopolitical revolution that would touch only the "surface" levels of society.

This does not mean that Maulnier had nothing to say about economics, politics, and social issues. On the contrary, what the priority and privilege he assigned to the spiritual allowed him to do was to interpret, judge, and criticize contending economic and political theories from an allegedly higher perspective, and especially to point out where they failed in the ultimate task of defending and advancing authentic values. In *Au-delà du nationalisme* (1938), Maulnier insisted on the necessity of going beyond not only traditional forms of nationalism or the "cult of the nation," which most often served as nothing more than a "refuge, a mystificatory outburst, or, still worse, a veritable diversion" from real social and political problems and the threat of war (7), but also going beyond nationalism in its "revolutionary," that is, fascist and National-Socialist, forms. Maulnier had particularly harsh things to say about the political expressions of nationalism in Italy and Germany, which he basically considered to be too emotive and unreflective to be supported, signs of the weakness of thought and of the spirit, rather than of its strength and development:

> The impotency of thought before the real and actual destiny of men has had the result that men, turning away from thought, looked to empirical pragmatism and mysticism for the way to resolve the problems before which their intelligence left them without weapons. The recourse to Action, Race, Blood, to the predestined Leader, to the superior mission of a people, the entire suspect paraphernalia of modern nationalism is nothing but a substitute for failing intelligence, the cry of man in darkness to regain mastery in a world where reason is powerless to guide him. (19)

All the signs of the unity of a people or nation, all the emotive devices used in the process of national identification of a people with its leader and through him with itself, were treated by Maulnier as symptoms of deficiencies within fascism and National Socialism, as emotional, irrational substitutes for true, rational, organic cultural unity.

Maulnier claimed that his spiritualistic view of nationalism was rooted in the deepest levels of history, in what remains historical after surface events have run their course. In this sense, only what negates and transcends history and politics in the usual sense of the terms could be considered truly historical and political: "The genuine historical event is the one that renders obsolete the entire state of things that preceded it. From this point of view, the political transformation of a people achieves its full historical value only to the extent that it goes beyond politics itself" (21). And what goes beyond politics itself, *what lasts*, is what is inscribed in the mind, what changes the way men think about what occurs in history:

> The only forms of society truly lasting are those which, beyond the powerful and passing waves of anger, of fear, . . . place their foundations in the substance itself of minds. The nationalist movements of our time, are they only spasms of national sensibility and the epics of adventurous dictators? Are they the beginnings of a new social era? (21–22)

The question Maulnier asks at the start of *Au-delà du nationalisme* is thus whether fascism and National Socialism have this capacity to do more than affect the surface of history, whether they have the *intellectual* (not emotional or political) force to go beyond the strictly historical and political realms and change the way men think about themselves and their society, and, as a result, radically change the way they live.

Italian fascism and German National Socialism were destined to fail, Maulnier decided, not in spite of but precisely because of their "astonishing affective power," which brought about the "sentimental reconciliation of classes and as a result the sentimental unity of the nation." No matter how powerful the immediate emotive effects produced by fascist celebrations of unity, they were of short duration, given that sentiment alone could not ever have a profound, transformative effect on the social structure (37). His criticism of this aspect of all totalitarian neonationalisms (and implicitly of the literary fascism of many of his friends and associates) was thus severe and relentless.[6]

At the same time, the nationalist doctrine or consciousness that he felt had been lacking in all nationalisms up to that point, and that he had attempted to provide in all his texts from this period, cannot be considered, strictly speaking, antifascist either. In their details, he considered the "reforms of National Socialism and fascism often to be perfectly valuable in themselves, . . . applied to the most critical points of contemporary society" (33). They were simply not sufficient, for they lacked a "general theory of labor in economic life and of the relations of economic life with the totality of collective life" (34), a cultural totality that encompassed and determined both the economic and the political levels of society. In his opinion, National Socialism and fascism were not rigorous enough and did not go far enough in pursuing their political ends, for they stopped short of a total vision and limited themselves to attempting to resolve the more practical problems of social existence and specific social, economic, and political conflicts. Maulnier thus considered their totalitarianism, no matter how extreme and ruthless, to be limited, not intellectually coherent, and in this specific sense, not sufficiently, not spiritually, fascist.

Whatever class allegiances individuals might have, however much they might have been formed by their economic situation and the values inherent in it, Maulnier claimed they always had a more basic, more complete, more immediate and natural allegiance to their national community: "Man adheres to the community, he participates in its historical duration not by 'the product of the material givens of the life of this community' alone, but by a adherence that one could call biological, by a total commitment of his personality, by a vital influence as natural as the penetration of its roots in the soil is for the plant" (60). Even for the most literary and spiritualistic of nationalists, then, as for culturalist anti-Semites such as Maurras, Barrès, Brasillach, and even for absolute "poeticist" racists such as Céline and Rebatet, the original national community was a natural, "biological" unity that preexisted the individual and all social divisions. It was the principle to which Maulnier felt society had to return in order to overcome the divisiveness of liberalism, capitalism, and parliamentary democracy.

In the essays from this collection, Maulnier constantly repeated that human society was not in its essence economic and political but "biological," by which he meant a society "constituted in the course of centuries by the intimate and inextricable collaboration of all of the forces of life" (68). No matter how divided, any society retained its original and "almost invincible force," that of "a common land, blood, and language" (62). Against Marxism, Maulnier will thus constantly evoke this "natural principle," which is the key principle he shared with the neonationalisms he criticized elsewhere, even if, as in the case of the other literary fascists studied, his notion of the true nature of a people was more culturally than racially determined. In a choice among democracy, Marxism, and fascism in terms of the nature of society, he was clearly more on the side of fascism, and his purpose was to provide a more rational and philosophically defensible basis for fascism, for a profoundly culturalist form of fascism beyond traditional nationalisms and existing fascisms and National Socialisms.

The meaning and function of the "biological" needs to be investigated further in order to understand better both what links Maulnier to political forms of fascism and what separates him form them. He clearly felt that the only way to achieve a nationalism beyond nationalism was through a "national revolution," a term in fact that he considered redundant, for all true nationalisms were by definition revolutionary—that is, antidemocratic, anticapitalist—and all true revolutions were nationalist. This was what Maulnier once again called "a fundamental biological fact":

> Every revolution that brings along with it progress and the surpassing of the existing mode of life is national by the same necessity that every organized life is stronger than its own metamorphoses. . . . Every valuable revolution will thus be "national" because the national community is the organized social mode of life in the West and as a result the real producer of the dialectical transformations of history. No life progresses by disassociation. (226)

Thus, even if he was most often critical of the fundamental role given to the myths of soil, blood, and race in fascism and National Socialism, it is clear that the national revolution he proposed was at the same time also an extension or radical spiritualization of basic fascist and National Socialist principles, rooted in the myths of blood and soil, not their negation. What fascist countries had accomplished was a totalitarian politicizing of aesthetics and culture; what he advocated was a totally autonomous aestheticizing of politics, with the self-determination of culture as the origin and end of politics.[7]

In "Il faut refaire un nationalisme en dépit de la nation," Maulnier anticipated the problem that a proponent of the National Revolution would have in the case of war: he could neither be completely for nor against his nation. In view of the alleged corrupt, decadent nature of the Popular Front government and of parliamentary democracy in general, the true nationalist could not hope for victory because "a war in which the victory of France would also be a victory of its repugnant allies would in a short time efface from the earth the most precious values of human civilization, would inevitably efface, in a return shock, France itself. . . . A victory of France risks being a defeat for the human species" (*Combat*, no. 14 [April 1937]). At the same time, a nationalist could never hope for the victory of the enemies of the nation, no matter how miserable the present state of the nation. The only solution was to act to prevent the outbreak of war and, as the title of the essay indicates, be a "nationalist in spite of the nation, and, so to speak, against it," having a "revolutionary attitude, in the most complete, the most demanding, and the most brutal sense of the word," attempting at all times to do nothing less than "remake France."

In 1938, Maulnier wrote two articles for *Combat* that are crucial for understanding his position after the defeat and during the Occupation: "Notes sur l'antisémitisme" (no. 26 [June 1938]) and "Notes sur le fascisme" (no. 30 [December, 1938]). Both can be seen as responses to Brasillach and the dominant tendencies of *Je suis partout* of this period, especially the first article, which is practically a point-by-point response to Brasillach's contribution to the special issue on the Jews published in April 1938. Not wanting to break totally with Brasillach and *Je suis partout*, Maulnier began his article on anti-Semitism by making a distinction between "philosophical" and "political" anti-Semitism, claiming that to condemn the first was not necessarily to condemn the second, for even if the philosophical premises of anti-Semitism were invalid, even if the Jews were not "*really* a power of corruption and enslavement," its political effects were for the most part positive, and thus it could still be defended on nationalist grounds. Anti-Semitism was, Maulnier argued, "a good method for crystallizing revolutionary tendencies."

In justifying anti-Semitism because it had always existed, the anti-Semite was relying on myth to support his beliefs and actions, claimed Maulnier, and he argued that it was necessary to separate the reality behind the myth from the myth itself: "The absurdity of anti-Semitism begins at the point where the anti-Semite begins to *attribute* to a particular people, a particular race, or a particular spirit the innumerable products of real evolution and history, whether fortunate or unfortunate, and the reason for the evils of humanity." The other side of the myth was the assumption or fear that the non-Jew—it should be noted that Maulnier did not use the term "Aryan"—is always inferior to the Jew and therefore always duped by him: "The non-Jew would thus everywhere and always be destined in the presence of the Jew, to irremediable defeat and faced with Jews he would have only one resource: to profit from their small numbers and eliminate them." Maulnier attacked both the myth of the Jewish people as "a demonic people . . . marching toward the conquest of the world," and the corresponding myth of the "inferiority of the non-Jew," on the general principle that all myths had to be destroyed, *especially* if they had a long history. Maulnier thus presented himself once again in this article as a ferocious opponent of nationalist myths in general, and therefore of the *myth* of anti-Semitism, of anti-Semitism as a myth, in particular. True culture had to be based on rational, truly spiritual principles and have nothing to do with such myths.

Like Brasillach and others, however, Maulnier did acknowledge the possibility of an "anti-Semitism of reason" that would not depend on myth, that would not assume that any people was demonic or inferior *by nature*. It would find, however, he claimed, that in Western societies Jewish minorities possessed a power and influence out of proportion to their numbers, and that they had not been assimilated into the societies they dominated from the outside. "Separated from myths, anti-Semitism finds its valid foundations in two particular traits which distinguish the Jewish element: its ever-increasing power, its irreducible heterogeneity."

Because most anti-Semitism was rooted in myth and intent only on eliminating Jews from positions of power, given that they were projected to be the source of *all* evil, it "[left] in place the political organization and social structure while partially changing the masters. It [was] therefore the mask of a reformism that [was] as violent as it [was] ineffective." Anti-Semitism was nonrevolutionary or even antirevolutionary and thus in no way was a proper basis for the National Revolution, whose unique goal should be "the suppression of the democratic state and the suppression of mercantile society," which were the bases of the power of Jewish and other financiers. Maulnier thus took what he considered to be a "moderate," "enlightened" position on anti-Semitism in the name of a more radical, revolutionary form of nationalism, and he tried to keep a distance from the anti-Semitic fanatics at *Je suis partout*, such as Rebatet—who also, it should be recalled, claimed to be rational and restrained in their anti-Semitism. He sought to locate the "Jewish question" within, rather than as, the basis for his general political position and therefore criticized any form of fascism—any proposed National Revolution that was rooted directly in the myth of race and a biologically determined people—for being reformist rather than truly revolutionary.

In "Notes sur le 'Fascisme,'" Maulnier attacked the Nazi leaders for giving anti-Semitism and fascism a bad name and for furnishing arguments to antifascists because of their violent persecution of the Jews. After separating Maulnier once again from Nazi racist policies, the article constituted a checklist of what Maulnier supported and could not support in Nazi Germany and fascist Italy. It thus was a condensed statement of the kind of fascism Maulnier advocated. He acknowledged in it that he agreed with and admired the following reforms undertaken by "fascist" authorities:

> Totalitarian regimes have given the state, as a political instrument, the servant of national destiny, an extraordinary efficacy. They have given . . . to the proletariat an organic participation in community life. They have invented an economic technique which, in spite of its imperfections, . . . has beaten capitalism . . . in the domain of productivity. They have invented a social morality in many respects very superior to the "morality" of democratic states.

These great successes of fascist regimes in the economic, political, and "moral" realms were, Maulnier argued, signs of the "historical value" of fascism, and they made the pillaging of Jewish stores and other injustices, what he called "certain gratuitous absurdities and truly excessive tyrannies," only the "minuscule foam of the waves of history" to which not too much attention had to be paid.

The problem, however, was that not only the enemies of fascism but most of the fascist countries as well were directing a great deal of attention to such "foam" and neglecting the principles that Maulnier argued would make fascism a lasting phenomenon. The fascist countries had failed "to construct values equal to their historical task." In burning books that they considered were opposed to their ideology, Maulnier claimed, the authoritarian regimes "condemn to death that very ideology" that in order to develop had to pass by way of "confrontation, doubt, *contradiction*"; that is, by conflict with adversaries and their ideas. A fascism that had "declared itself the enemy of intelligence" and proclaimed that "the forces of instinct and violence make history" advocated a false and dangerous path. Fascist countries, each of which claimed to be the premier country in the world, each of which put military values first and tended to organize society according to military structures rather than cultural values, manifested what he called "an infantile barbarism." He thus accused the fascist countries, just as he had accused the later Nietzsche, of falling back into barbarism. Maulnier prefered what could be called a "civilized" form of authoritarianism or fascism—a civilized barbarism?—a reasonable anti-Semitism, an authoritarian state in which the individual was not enslaved by the community, and which had an organized, centralized government that was the expression of the nation as the product of civilization, as an organic, *cultural*, rather than a strictly political, totality. As Germany and Italy tended toward becoming (assuming they had not already become) "barbaric societies," Maulnier demanded that France not imitate them but become again what it had been in the past and was always destined to be: a true (Greek) civilization.

Maulnier boasted in the preface to *La France, la guerre et la paix* (Lyon: Lardanchet, 1942), a collection of essays originally written from 1939 to 1942, that these essays revealed that his fundamental principles were the same before and after the defeat, that historical events had not made him change his political position in any important way. His principal argument in the essays was that France had to develop its own path and rebuild itself once again *outside* and *beyond* both "democratic and totalitarian myths" (9). Without claiming that the defeat was a good thing for France, Maulnier did accept the general Vichy political line that it was necessary to take advantage of the defeat, because it did have the merit of "displaying the evil [democracy] in full light and chasing from power those who thought only of supporting it or masking it. . . . On this condition alone, the *revolution* being undertaken can be brought to term" (94–95). Like Maurras, he pretended that even while occupied France would be able "to create its own future, and not receive it from the hands of foreigners," the only way for France to save itself was "to continue to be" (99). The continued existence of the nation (under Pétain) was the fundamental principle he supported and in terms of which he continued to argue for a national revolution. "Neither fascist nor democratic, neither authoritarian nor liberal, neither racist nor anti-racist" (158), France was to be left to itself, to be, in the terms of Maurras, "la seule France."

Violence et conscience (Paris: Gallimard, 1945), a collection of essays written in 1942 and 1943, consists of an extended diatribe against capitalism, which Maulnier considered to be the principal enemy and destroyer of the arts and therefore of the national community. Not only did "capitalism cut all the channels that had . . . carried on the flourishing of arts and letters, . . . the life [literally, *la sève*, sap] of the community," but while it was accomplishing this cultural devastation, it also claimed to be the unique support of civilization and accused its antidemocratic opponents of being "the adversaries of civilization" (18). This resulted in "'spiritual values' being embodied in the most materialist regime that ever existed" (19), and in their being cut off from their authentic spiritualist base. It also meant that the spiritual victims of capitalism—thinkers, artists, and writers—mistakenly rallied to support it, as the capitalist system continued to claim for itself the very values it was in reality destroying (21). To wage a spiritual revolution was to wage the only truly nationalist-socialist revolution, and the only true victory that could come

out of the war, therefore, would be "the victory of human consciousness over the powers that were unleashed by a non-dominated social
universe." Anything else would constitute only "the victory of one destructive element over the others in the midst of a unique process of destruction," which would be "a victory without historical value" (45).

Neither pro-German, nor pro-Russian, nor pro-American, nor pro-
English, but "pro-human," Maulnier presented himself during the war
and Occupation as occupying a transcendent *humanist* position: "There
is only one way to make history. It is to make human consciousness and
will present and sovereign where Destiny rules. It is to humanize history,
to make it human" (48). Specifically, it is to call for the "liquidation of
capitalism, . . . the abolishment of the capitalist structure society imposes
on us as a historical necessity" (59). It was also to work toward "saving
the values of civilization . . . by separating them from a rotting economic
structure, . . . saving authority and property by cutting them off from
capitalism" (60). The human, manifested in what Maulnier called a "superior historical consciousness" (59), clearly was not on the side of either
capitalism or liberal democracy. At the same time, it did have something,
though not everything, in common with fascism; namely, its "opposition
to proletarian Marxism . . . and the will to national power" (94). Maulnier was still trying to save something fundamental in fascism, something
that none of the various forms of fascism had ever realized but that he
continued to insist on: fascism with a human face, fascism as a privileged,
total form of humanism, the complete, modern realization of true classical civilization.

The complicated strategy of distancing himself from an ideology that
he, on a deeper level and in its ultimate, spiritualistic form, supported,
must have effectively succeeded in disguising the nature of his political
convictions, for Maulnier felt confident enough in 1946 to publish one
final collection of essays from the period of the Occupation. In his introduction to the collection, he characterized his writing from that period as
"an act of opposition"(*Arrière-Pensées* [Paris: La Table Ronde, 1946],
5). But it seems fair to ask, Opposition to what? At the very least, Maulnier's "opposition" constituted a defense of Pétain's decision to sign an
armistice in 1940 and collaborate actively with Hitler, as well as an implicit attack on all those who wanted to continue the war in order to
defeat Nazi Germany and liberate France by force. But as other essays
clearly show, his opposition was also toward those hard-line fascist collaborators whose criticism of and hatred for democracy—which were at
least for a time close to his own criticisms—led them eventually to what
he characterized as an antinationalist position. "It is in this way that a
number of French slipped, almost without knowing it, from the criticism
of democracy to anti-democratic passion, and from anti-democratic pas-

sion to anti-nationalist passion" ("Contribution à la psychanalyse de ce temps" [November 1943], 63).

Maulnier attacked without naming them militant French fascists, such as Rebatet, who made of the unhappy state of France after its defeat the sign of the great victory of *their* fascist ideas: "The defeat of France was first of all the defeat of the regime they detested, and without knowing it, their hatred was already directed at France itself, guilty of having been governed by such a regime. France was perishing; they were *triumphant* (61–62). He still advocated total opposition to democracy, but warned that it should never become too passionate or too triumphant, for if it did, it would pass quickly into opposition to the nation itself, even if it was under the banner of a *national* socialism. If Drieu la Rochelle constantly criticized fascism for not being European enough, Maulnier criticized it in this way for not being nationalist enough. The differences between them on this precise issue had to do with how each defined the spiritual and what each meant by a cultural, literary-aesthetic community "beyond nationalism." But in no way did their often pointed critiques of the limitations of various fascisms make either less of a fascist. Rather, their views made them demand more from fascism than fascism could ever possibly give.

The "clandestine opposition" Maulnier expressed in his essays during the Occupation was aimed primarily at anything that threatened to limit or destroy French culture, what he—like Barrès, Maurras, and all of the literary fascists treated in this book—considered the essence and ultimate truth of France itself.

> Other nations can have, as the principle of their unity, their territory, the form of their work, and, at very least, the relative homogeneity of their blood. Open to numerous invasions, dedicated to very diverse activities, born of ethnically disparate elements, France molded itself into a unique substance only by the slow work of history. It is a nation forged by the hands of man. French civilization has been one of the principal means by which the French nation was made; and the latter is obliged to the first by a debt that cannot be canceled. ("France, fille des arts . . ." [January 1942], 166)

As much as such a position showed Maulnier's opposition to the control of the arts by the fascist state and to censorship based on ideology or racist principles, as much as it might make him appear "liberal" when compared with more politically militant fascists and anti-Semites such as Rebatet, his notion that France was born of the arts and that it was the guardian of civilization and spiritual values in their most developed form did not in any way separate him from the antidemocratic intellectuals and writers of the extreme, fascist right. This was the camp of the literary fascists with whom he had openly collaborated before the defeat and with whom he then collaborated clandestinely and indirectly during the Occupation, even if was by attempting to "correct" and "purify" their nationalism, their anti-Semitism, and their fascism, and to make them even more aesthetic and spiritual.[8]

Maulnier's ideology of culture, or what could be called his national culturalism, should be considered, as he himself repeatedly affirmed, the basis for an extreme, ultranationalist position, for what Sternhell rightly calls a *spiritualistic* form of fascism. It was not the fascism of direct collaborators but of someone who attempted both to stand above the politics of the left and the right and to direct the nation and nationalist politics toward the extremist, antidemocratic culturalist position he derived from a radical, Nietzschean form of classical humanism. Maulnier's aesthetics, which were the foundation for an ultranationalist politics, thus represented one of the most uncompromising, rigorous, intellectual forms of literary fascism, a *literary* fascism beyond fascism. If this made it the "purest form" of fascism, as Sternhell argues, it was because its "purity" was a function of classical aesthetic principles and poetic autonomy. For authentic poetry is already in itself the ideal the political ought to and yet cannot ever achieve: a total, poetic transformation of the material into the spiritual. In this way, Maulnier, of all the literary fascists, most completely elaborated the ideal of an uncompromising, totalitarian form of poetic spirituality that was characteristic of the work of French literary fascists in general and that was the ultimate foundation and model for their politics.

Afterword

Literary Fascism and the Case of Paul de Man

DEMONIZING fascist writers and demeaning their intelligence and literary-critical skills are certainly not effective ways of understanding fascism and its attraction for a vast number of writers and intellectuals. But those who have taken the opposite tack and emphasized predominantly (or exclusively) the literary or critical talents of exemplary fascist writers, or the complexity of their work, have most often ended up excusing or mitigating the political responsibilities of literary fascists and obfuscating the particular nature of their fascism. As I have demonstrated in various ways in the course of this book, when it comes to literary fascism, it is never possible to separate the literary from the political, for even formalist or aestheticist concepts of literature that stress the autonomy and organic integrity of literature and art were used to support totalitarian forms of politics. To take the literary fascists' essays on literature and art seriously and to analyze them critically is not in this case to evoke the literary interests of fascist writers as a way of protecting them from their political responsibilities, but rather it is to confront the particular nature of their fascist politics. To say that a certain form of fascism is literary, therefore, means that it cannot be effectively analyzed and criticized on political grounds alone, given that it has profound roots in art and literature.

Recent controversies surrounding the extent of Martin Heidegger's commitment to Nazism, and the nature and implications of the young Paul de Man's collaborationist journalistic activities during the early years of World War II, have brought many of the issues at the very center of literary fascism into the forefront of intellectual debates and given them an interest and urgency that they have not had for quite some time. In both instances, the debates have often been partisan and polemical, with the demonizing of Heidegger and de Man and the condemnation of all of their work clearly the goal of many of the most polemical and distorted attacks on their prewar and wartime writings and activities. Crucial issues have been obscured by the desire of some to indict all of those interested in Heidegger's work and to attack and dismiss all of de Man's later critical work and especially that which is associated with deconstruction. But responses to such attacks, with rare exceptions, have also been unnecessarily polemical and defensive. The result has been to perpetuate the battles over these two figures and to escalate a general cultural war being waged over how best to understand the nature of the relation of art, literature, and intellectual and cultural activities in general with totalitarian and racist politics. Also at stake in the debates is the determination of the relation that art, literature, criticism, and theory have today with both past and new forms of extremist politics.[1]

Polemical battles obviously obscure more than illuminate the issues dividing the various factions and are soon forgotten as intellectual fashion moves on and becomes concerned with other issues, figures, and controversies. It would certainly be better, however, if the polemical battles surrounding the cases of Heidegger and de Man did not end up being simply forgotten but were instead transformed into more productive critical discussions. For underneath the violence and hyperbole of polemics, and distorted by them, in this case as in others, important issues are always at stake. In these particular cases, one such issue is the role of literature and aesthetics in the elaboration of fascist politics. My hope is that *French Literary Fascism* can play a role in the development of critical approaches to the general problem of the literary or aesthetic roots and dimensions not just of fascism but of politics in general, and in this way help to clarify important aspects of both Heidegger's and de Man's temptations with extremist nationalist and fascist politics.

Given de Man's own obvious national-aestheticist literary orientation at the time he wrote for the collaborationist Belgian newspaper *Le Soir*, the fact that he had positive things to say about almost all of the literary fascists treated in this book, and most important, because he focused on the same literary and political issues that concerned them, the case of de Man is especially relevant to the problems I have treated here. In his articles written from December 1940 through November 1942, like many of the French literary fascists *before* the war, he defended not Nazism per se but a particular form of literary fascism that was oriented first and foremost toward affirming and defending the autonomy of literature from history and politics. The principle of national political autonomy that he also supported was itself dependent on such literary autonomy. His literary goal was clearly to defend the integrity of French and Belgian literature and to keep each literature from being destroyed by or simply assumed into Nazi cultural politics; his political goal was to defend the relative autonomy and integrity of Belgium and to prevent it from being divided and to prevent Flanders and Flemish culture from being swallowed up into a greater German Reich. But his overall goal was at the same time to ensure that French and Belgian literature and the Belgian nation had a place within the "New Europe" being created by the victories of the German army and Nazi cultural and political policies. This meant that both the relative autonomy of Belgium within a Europe dominated by Nazi Germany and that of the Flemish and Flemish culture within Belgium itself were the political stakes of his defense of the autonomy of (a nationalist form of) literature.[2]

De Man's interest in and support of fascism were especially evident in those articles in which he praised the indigenous national characteristics of Mussolini's "national revolution" and treated Italy's realization of its "new grandeur" as a model for Belgium's own national regeneration.[3] His views were even more explicit in those articles in which he described the positive changes accomplished by Nazi Germany, defended the "revolution" brought about by Germany's victories in the war and the positive future for Europe that it promised, analyzed the causes and effects of the defeat in France, urged collaboration with the Germans as the only realistic political strategy, argued for a certain form of Belgian nationalism within a Europe dominated by Germany, or pursued the questions of national identity, nationalism, and national literature or art in general. This is not to say that de Man was a member of any fascist party, or a Nazi, but it is to locate his journalism in the context of the literary and political movements of the extreme nationalist and fascist right, which defended fascism as being in the national interests of their country.

Compared with the writers I have treated in this book, however, the young Paul de Man must certainly be considered a minor, almost insignificant figure. At the time of the war, he was too young to have been as widely published or as well known as the French literary fascists I have considered or as a Belgian fascist such as Robert Poulet, and he was much less directly concerned with the practical politics of fascism than even they were. His "case"—which is of interest only because of the stature he gained in the United States long after the war—reveals rather how widespread the influence of such literary and political ideas were, how great a temptation they constituted, and how acceptable they also were outside a militant fascist or pro-Nazi context. I return to de Man's wartime journalism to conclude this book because it dramatically reveals, in the case of a critic who after the war was associated with forms of criticism diametrically opposed to the major premises of literary fascism, the seductive power of particular *literary* ideals and the dangers of their political application.

Over the course of the two years during which they were written, the wartime articles maintained a fairly consistent ideological position. In its broad lines, the position was that of a right-wing nationalist who was sympathetic to fascism and at the very least tolerant of important aspects of (a certain mystified version of) National Socialism. It seems hard to deny—although some have tried—that the writer of these articles, like Drieu la Rochelle, Brasillach, and others, had placed his confidence in the "future of Europe" promised by the "fascist revolution," which meant that he had confidence in and supported the general Nazi cultural and political project for Europe, even if at the same time he also distanced himself from other aspects of Nazism. What interests me especially is the literary dimensions of his political involvement.[4]

De Man's approach to art and literature in all of the essays, even when he was arguing for a certain form of literary-aesthetic autonomy, cannot be separated from the questions of nationalism, national identity, and the future of Europe under Nazi domination; that is, from all of the most important political issues of the period. It is true that de Man often stressed that literature and art have their own history and are thus autonomous, and unconnected to the "surface" upheavals of social and political history. In a manner similar to that of Maulnier, de Man attempted in many of his more directly political articles to define what was lasting and thus beneath the surface of current events, and he constantly criticized those who confused surface and depth. In terms of the historical-political surface, art and literature were not treated as being political, and thus de Man's defense of their autonomy could in principle be considered a way of distancing himself from and even countering some of the political excesses of National Socialism and fascism: that is, book burnings, literary and artistic censorship, and direct party involvement in or control of literary-aesthetic production and distribution. And yet de Man also argued in these articles that literature and art, *because of* their autonomous histories, were the deepest expressions of the true identity or interiority, first, of an author, and then, by extension, of a people or nation. In this way they were linked to a more profound cultural history, one rooted in the land and tradition, and thus of long duration. In this way, art and literature on a profound level supported a nationalist politics that was closely related to if not identical with the politics of literary fascism in general.

In an article entitled "Après les journées culturelles germano-flamandes. Le destin de la Flandre" (September 1, 1941), de Man argued that Flanders should not be incorporated into an "artificial" German community but should be allowed to remain independent, "between the French and German blocks." He began his article by claiming that the ultimate test of whether a people could really be considered worthy of being considered a nation was if it had an art or a culture that was entirely its own:

> Among the criteria thanks to which one can determine whether a certain geographic area merits the name of nation, one of the most important is the existence of a specific culture, or, more precisely, of an art which belongs to the inhabitants of the country. This is a primordial factor—itself resulting from a great quantity of historical, racic [*raciques*], etc., components—among all those that permit one to determine whether yes or no a people has a nationality worthy of being respected. (*Wartime Journalism*, 139)

De Man's point, of course, was to defend Flemish autonomy by showing that Flanders did have an art rooted in the land and belonging to its people and thus had a nationality "worthy of being respected." The autonomy of a nation's art and literature was the ultimate sign of the autonomy and grandeur of its people, and it was also the best argument a cultural or literary nationalist could make that a people should be allowed to maintain itself in the "New Europe" as a semiindependent nation. What he called "racic" factors were not totally determining in the making of a people, but they certainly constituted an important component of its general historical-cultural constitution.

Of all of the articles that addressed the issue of the autonomy of art and literature, there is ample evidence that, for de Man, literary autonomy and the question of national and "racic" identity were intimately tied together and supportive of each other. This means, among other things, that de Man considered literature to be historical and political in the strongest sense of the terms, not in terms of the "surface" of history and politics, but in terms of the alleged origin and truth of each in the profound cultural identity of a people. It is the same argument that both Brasillach and Maulnier constantly made in their respective defenses of French nationalism, and in at least Brasillach's case, in his militant support for a French form of fascism.

The reservations that de Man expressed in various articles about the total German domination of Europe his hopes that Nazi Germany would not attempt to destroy the national identities of other countries and peoples certainly did not amount to an opposition to Nazism. The relative autonomy he proposed for Belgium and Belgian culture—which he presented as a fusion of Germanic and French cultural and "racic" traits— was officially acceptable to the Nazis during the period he wrote and was even for a time encouraged as a way of ensuring peace in the occupied countries. Collaboration did not necessarily mean—at least not during the period de Man wrote for *Le Soir*—having to give up one's nationalist principles and actually become a militant Germanophile or a Nazi. It meant supporting the political and "cultural revolution" undertaken by the Nazis, and this could be done in the name of the nation, race, national order, or traditional authority, or even literature and art. The grounds for de Man's support clearly situated him within a diversified group of Belgian and French nationalists and fascists who were willing to collaborate with the Germans. Some of them would *later* find themselves in disfavor with the Nazi occupiers, but at the start of the war they were supported by the Nazis and encouraged to publish. The question of German nationalism in all of de Man's articles, as well as the related questions of Belgian and Flemish specificity and autonomy, and the question of national identity in general, as concerns literature and politics, or literature as the most profound expression of politics, cannot be separated from the fascist context of the times and from de Man's specific literary and political associations and models.[5]

Even if he criticized aspects of the work of the various fascist and collaborationist writers about whom he wrote, de Man never questioned or distanced himself from the essential elements of their fascism. For example, in his numerous references to Brasillach, he never distanced himself from his anti-Semitism (or from the anti-Semitism of any of the other French fascist writers he discussed). De Man reviewed Brasillach's *Notre avant-guerre* on August 12, 1941, and he stated that he admired the fact that Brasillach showed no traces of "bad conscience" for the defeat, since he thought France never should have fought Germany in the first place: "Brasillach knows perfectly that he lived happy and luminous days [during the period 1920–1940] . . . and that he has nothing to regret in this period which ends however in a catastrophe for his country." De Man did consider Brasillach's "political sense" to be questionable in certain instances, because his true vocation was art and literature, not politics, but he also claimed that Brasillach's "enumeration of anecdotes," even if they often were "partial and superficial . . . and miss the heart of things," nonetheless are "always amusing" (*Wartime Journalism*, 130–31).

Eventually, de Man did distance himself from Brasillach, but he did so not because he was against collaboration or critical of Brasillach's overtly fascist political orientation or his anti-Semitism; rather, he criticized Brasillach's lack of political sophistication concerning what he had experienced when he had visited Germany in 1937. De Man chastised Brasillach for "a lack of political sense" in a very specific instance; namely, when he manifested "a certain terror before the 'strange' nature of this demonstration [that of the Nazi Party Congress in Nuremberg]." He went on to criticize Brasillach for not understanding the "sudden importance of the political in the life of a people" (613). De Man's criticism of Brasillach, who was certainly one of the most visible French collaborators and outspoken literary fascists, might indicate his own "independence as a thinker," as some have claimed, but it was an independence that moved him in this instance at least even closer than Brasillach to an explicit defense of Nazi Germany. A sympathy for important aspects of Nazism (and its aesthetics of politics) was thus "declared" here and elsewhere; and even though this did not make de Man a Nazi, it did show that he had been more sympathetic to important elements of National Socialism than his defenders have generally been willing to admit.

In fact, in this article de Man even misrepresents Brasillach's position in order to claim that Brasillach did not understand the true political sense of what he had witnessed at the Nuremberg Party Congress of 1937. For Brasillach was not as negative as de Man implied, and in fact he had given a very lyrical description of the demonstrations at Nuremberg and had admitted that he "had never seen a more prodigious spectacle in [his] entire life" (*Notre avant-guerre*, 278) and had been profoundly moved by it. In his description of the Congress, however, originally published in 1937 and republished in slightly revised form in *Notre avant-guerre* in 1941, Brasillach did resist *the form* of this "new politics"—or what he called this "poetry, all of which is certainly not for us [Frenchmen]" (285)—on nationalist grounds; that is, chiefly because it was German and thus foreign or "strange" to the French. Brasillach felt that France needed an indigenous, French form of fascism, a new *French* aesthetics of the political that would produce its own form of poetry and politics. His main point was that the French should not be forced to accept in a servile fashion a poetry and a politics originating elsewhere.

Brasillach was thus defending French political and aesthetic autonomy on nationalist grounds, and this would in no way interfere with or counter his commitment to fascism or collaboration. In fact, his defense of national literary autonomy supported his commitment to collaboration. Here and elsewhere, Brasillach's position was practically indistinguishable from that taken by de Man in his newspaper articles, where an acceptance and admiration for particular aspects of Nazi Germany go hand and hand with the desire for a relative autonomy for his own nation in the realms of art, literature, and politics. In numerous other articles, de Man himself emphasized the cultural and literary-aesthetic differences between the French and the Germans, as well as between the Belgians and the Germans, in order to argue for the specificity of the French and Belgian situations. De Man's criticism of Brasillach revealed that his own defense of a separation of literature and politics even more profound than that proposed by Brasillach was compatible with a greater understanding of and sympathy for "the sudden importance of the political in the life of a people" under Nazism—or at least with a greater acceptance of Nazi Germany in which Nazi politics and "poetics" were not considered foreign or "strange" but familiar.

In many of his articles, de Man showed himself to be sympathetic and supportive of basic nationalist-fascist principles, pro-German (which at the time meant pro-Nazi, no matter how nuanced, complicated, and even "nonconformist" one tried to make the "pro"), and, in at least *two* articles, overtly anti-Semitic. The two articles were the much discussed "Jews in Contemporary Literature" (*Le Soir* [March 4, 1941], in *Wartime Journalism*, 45) and the one entitled "People and Books: A View on Contemporary German Fiction," published in an even more militantly profascist Flemish journal, *Hat Vlaamsche Land* (August 20, 1942, in *Wartime Journalism*, 325–26). The author of these articles was certainly not a militant anti-Semite in the style of Céline or Rebatet, but at the very best he was insensitive to, or at the worst supportive of, the incredible injustices already suffered by the Jews at the hands of the Nazis in Germany (as well as at the hands of occupying and indigenous forces in France and Belgium)—insomuch as that was the price one had to pay to become part of the "New Europe" and to save literature and art from non-European influences. He was indifferent to or simply against all real political opposition to Nazism, fascism, and anti-Semitism and accepted with only minor reservations the future for Europe that Germany proposed in the name of the superiority of a racially determined notion of culture.

In "People and Books: A View on Contemporary German Fiction," de Man distinguished between two groups within postwar German literary production: foreign authors who produced non-German, nonaesthetic art, and true German authors who produced authentic art:

> The first of these groups celebrates an art with a strongly cerebral disposition, founded upon some abstract principles and very remote from all naturalness. The theses of expressionism, though very remarkable in themselves, were used here as tricks, as skillful artifices aimed at easy effects. The very legitimate basic rule of artistic transformation, inspired by the personal vision of the creator, served here as a pretext for a forced, caricatured representation of reality. Thus, [the artists of this group] came into open conflict with the proper traditions of German art which had always and before everything else clung to a deep spiritual sincerity. Small wonder, then that it was mainly non-Germans, and specifically Jews, who went in this direction. (*Wartime Journalism*, 325)

De Man contrasted this first group of Jews and other "foreigners" with the properly German group "which did not give in to this aberrant fashion." And he went on to say that "by not giving in to this temptation these writers have not only succeeded in producing an art of abiding value but also in securing the artistic future of their country" (325–26). The authentic artist was also, *as an artist*, the authentic patriot, the true nationalist.

It should be noted that, contrary to what Samuel Weber argues in "The Monument Disfigured," de Man not only separated the Jews from the truly German, the sincere, and the natural—as Weber acknowledges (*Responses*, 416–17)—but also from what he declared was true art, which was artifice but of a genuine aesthetic kind. This was why de Man's defense of the autonomy of art and literature in his articles in terms of nationalist principles cannot be separated from his two explicit expressions of anti-Semitism, because for de Man, as for almost literary fascists, the Jews represented the foreign, the unnatural, and the unaesthetic or anti-aesthetic in literature and art. At best he believed they were capable of "tricks," "skillful artifices," and "caricatures" of art and its "proper tradition." In other words, de Man thought that true art began where such "Jewish" tricks ended. A defense of art and literature on aesthetic grounds thus entailed an exclusion and denunciation of Jewish mimicry and subterfuge in art, and of all "foreign" theories and techniques that turned art away from itself and its authentic national destiny.

The second explicitly anti-Semitic article written by de Man, "Les Juifs dans la littérature actuelle," has been much more frequently cited in the polemics surrounding the discovery of his wartime journalism. As many of his defenders have rightly claimed, in it de Man did explicitly condemn *certain effects* of "vulgar anti-Semitism." It was the starting point for his discussion of the nature of literature in general and the role of the Jews in the creation of modern literature in particular. But it cannot be considered even an implicit criticism or demystification of anti-Semitism, because de Man replaced "vulgar anti-Semitism" with a more sophisticated version of anti-Semitism, which, despite its sophistication, was rooted in exactly the same myths as the vulgar version. The lethal mythology of the Jew that supported all forms of anti-Semitism remained intact in this article. What was demystified was a certain "vulgar notion" of modern literature and of the history of literature, both of which in their genuine forms, de Man argued, had nothing to do with this mythology or with the Jews in any way.

De Man claimed that the "vulgar anti-Semitism" that equated modern art and literature with the "degeneracy and decadence" equivalent to being "enjuivé" was in large part the responsibility of the Jews themselves, who "contributed to spreading this myth" and "glorified themselves as the leaders of literary movements that characterize our age." Even though de Man immediately claimed that this myth had a "deeper cause," he in no way discredited it, for the explanation of the "deeper cause" was no less anti-Semitic than assigning to the Jews themselves the responsibility for "vulgar anti-Semitism." The deeper cause that explained the "error" of vulgar anti-Semitism was the assumption that literature was simply a product of its time and that therefore the modern novel and poetry were a "monstrous outgrowth[s] of the world war." De Man certainly rejected this "monstrosity," but nowhere did he distance himself from the even more vulgar, monstrous, and unjust idea that, as he put it, "Jews have, in fact, played an important role in the phony and disordered existence of Europe since 1920." He simply did not agree that modern literature had its origin in this disorder, and for that reason he argued that it could not be considered "enjuivé." His rhetorical ploy thus consisted in his attempt to save literature from Jewish influence and the "disorder" for which Jews had allegedly been responsible throughout Europe. De Man did not, however, make the slightest effort to distance himself from the worst aspects of literary fascism and anti-Semitism. Saving modern literature and culture meant quite simply "losing" the Jews, ensuring that their negative influence was kept at a distance from true literature.

At bottom, De Man's text takes literally and uses some of the most blatant anti-Semitic clichés, for de Man consistently characterized Jews as "a foreign force," so foreign that if they were to live "in a Jewish colony isolated from Europe," European literature would not lose anything essential, for the simple reason that Jews had never contributed anything to literature that had to do with its "true" (that is, European) identity. There is no way this article can be considered a "demystification" of any important aspect of anti-Semitism, for it is totally determined by the "myth of the Jew," which the worst anti-Semitic literature perpetrated. The denunciation of "vulgar anti-Semitism," as we have repeatedly seen, was the favorite strategy of literary fascists, even of militant anti-Semites such as Rebatet. Its purpose was always to situate the form of cultural anti-Semitism being defended on a "higher" spiritual and rational level.

In fact, de Man's article suspiciously resembles an article published only *eleven days* before his own in which Drieu la Rochelle had made an almost identical argument with reference to the same authors. The title of Drieu la Rochelle's article is "De Ludovic Halévy à André Maurois ou l'impuissance du Juif en littérature" (*Je suis partout*, no. 500 [February 21, 1941]), and as the title of the article indicates, Drieu la Rochelle also asserted that the influence of Jews on French literature had been minimal because modern literature had been able to defend itself against their negative influence: "With a little distance we can see that the Jews have not contributed very much to France in the area of letters and arts." The list of names Drieu la Rochelle cited as proof of the inferiority of Jewish writers was almost the same as de Man's: André Maurois, Henri Bernstein, Tristan Bernard, and Julien Benda, but he added Porto-Riche and J. Richard Bloch as further proof.

Unlike de Man, Drieu la Rochelle did discuss the case of Proust, but he attributed Proust's greatness to the "French peasant blood" that he claimed flowed within him. By dropping the reference to Proust, de Man eliminated from his own text the most "vulgar" aspects of Drieu la Rochelle's anti-Semitism, evident in comments such as the following: "Crossbreeding [*métissage*] produces some rare but precious results: Proust, Bergson [who had a quarter of Aryan blood]. The slightest drop of our peasant, artisan blood permits them sometimes to achieve true form. But to obtain a Bergson or a Proust—whom I would be curious to reread before ranking them among the greatest French writers—how many fanatical Bendas, or boring J. Richard Blochs, or mediocre Maurois one has to be subjected to!" De Man's article, as much as Drieu la Rochelle's, however, clearly defended the authentic works of modern literature by opposing them to the works of "inferior" Jewish writers. In each case, the defense of modern literature consisted in separating authentic literature from the negative, antiaesthetic influence of Jews.[6]

The chain linking de Man's overtly anti-Semitic articles to his many articles on literature and nationalism is quite explicit. For it is not possible to ascribe to the Jews the primary responsibility for the sociopolitical "disorder" in Europe before the war and not have this affect one's approach to literature, even if literature in all instances is not *directly* determined by sociopolitical forces. It is impossible to see the Jews as a foreign, non-European presence within the various nations and not conclude that their absence would be beneficial to the development of national unity and autonomy and thus to the development of an autonomous and truly nationalist literature. If art and literature were designated to play an important role in the rediscovery of the various national identities and in the development of a new "European Order," then certainly it could not be argued that de Man was interested only in defending the cause of literature and had little if any concern for politics as such. As was the case for the literary fascists treated in this book, his defense of literature constituted in itself the basis for his politics.

De Man's inclusion of the name of Kafka on the list of great modern writers whose work was fully rooted in the "authentic" history of literature, and not the expression of artificial, foreign (Jewish) interests, does seem to counter or at least to complicate his general assertion concerning the inferiority and foreignness of Jewish writers in general.[7] References to Proust in other articles, which were uniformly positive—although it should be noted that by omitting Proust from this article, de Man excepted him not only from the category of Jewish writers of the second rank but *also* from the category of authentic European writers—also seemed to indicate that, for de Man, there were clearly exceptions to the general rule that authentic literature and foreign, "Jewish influences" did not mix. If a limited number of exceptional writers had in the past been excluded from Europe for being Jewish, it would seem that he felt that modern literature would have suffered, even if he argued that literature would not suffer from such an absence in the future, given the "mediocrity" of the writers he cited.[8] But as we have repeatedly seen, most literary fascists (even militant anti-Semites like Rebatet), who like de Man were attracted to modern literature and extremist forms of nationalism and even fascism, were in general willing to acknowledge the contributions of a limited number of exceptional Jewish writers and artists at the same time that they were denouncing the negative influence of "Jewish aesthetics" on art and literature. The exceptional Jewish writer or artist was obviously one who did not write (or paint or compose or play music) like a Jew, but rather like an "authentic" Frenchman, Belgian, or German.

It was quite common for literary fascists to love Proust and demean or even hate the Jews. Literary interests and tastes that did not conform to strict Nazi racist politics, or in the case of the French, Vichy cultural poli-

tics, supported their radical nationalist, fascist politics rather than countered them. The important point in the case of de Man is, as his two
anti-Semitic articles show, that there was clearly no place for Jews in the
future he and other Belgian and French nationalists envisioned for literature, no place for a people without a "national identity" (except a negative one), whose writings were a "foreign influence" that continually
threatened the identity of the various European peoples and nations and
their literature as well, even if the various national literatures had been
strong enough in the past to resist this threat.

Hope for literature was thus on the side of the continual resistance to
the foreign, and even if de Man did not make anti-Semitism the explicit
cornerstone of his own approach to literature and politics, he constantly
praised those who did. For example, in one of his entries for the *Bibli-
ographie Dechenne*—for which he continued to write until March 1943,
and after he stopped writing for *Le Soir*—de Man characterized Lucien
Rebatet's anti-Semitic best-seller, *Les Décombres*, as "an immense pamphlet of brilliant vigor and verve," a work that rightly attacked the evils
of democracy and presented hope for the future in its view of the total
destruction of the past:

> Lucien Rebatet, like Robert Brasillach, is one of the young French intellectuals
> who, during the period between the two wars, strove to combat with all their
> forces a politics [the politics of parliamentary democracy] whose catastrophic
> character and nefarious orientation they understood. . . . Each in his turn, all
> those guilty of having caused the current French decay, regardless of the milieu
> or party to which they belong, is passed in review and executed in a few lapi-
> dary and definitive sentences. But this great work of destruction also contains
> constructive elements: in trudging through the ruins of a dilapidated period,
> Lucien Rebatet also dreams of reconstructing: and that is undoubtedly why his
> ferocious book ends with words of hope. (*Wartime Journalism* [September
> 1942], 366)

Rebatet's hope was for a fascist Europe dominated by Nazi Germany in
which France, having itself become fascist, would play a major role. The
primary group that he held responsible for the "nefarious character" and
"decay" of modern France was of course the Jews; and in praising the
hope of fascism that Rebatet held out for the future, de Man was defending the links Rebatet himself had made between literature and art, on the
one hand, and fascism and anti-Semitism, on the other.

If aspects of de Man's approach to literature can in fact be shown to
constitute a defense of its autonomy from immediate historical-political
forces and interests, as many have argued, if his defense of the political
and cultural integrity of Belgium can be shown to manifest an openness
to a certain form of heterogeneity (but only as concerns the alternative,

either France or Germany, not in terms of what is considered "non-European"—that is, neither French, nor German, nor Belgian), then it is also important to analyze carefully what ends both this defense of literary autonomy and this form of nationalism serve. A limited heterogeneity can and in these articles does serve extreme right-wing nationalist interests. A defense of the autonomy of literature can and here does serve a political position that is much more supportive of fascism than it is opposed to it, and that even makes important concessions to the anti-Semitism at its base, all in the name of an interest in and a commitment to the future of modern literature.

The defense of modern literature undertaken by de Man in many of his articles in *Le Soir* should not be confused with the counterpropositions, counterstrategies, and countermovements that would have actually constituted an opposition to fascism and anti-Semitism. De Man's critique of the "vulgar" concept of literature should not be confused with the demystification and rejection of anti-Semitism in all its forms. His defense of the dual cultural heritage of Belgium should not be confused with the resistance to the "New European Order" dominated by Nazi Germany. And finally, his argument for the relative autonomy of literature should not be confused with a critical concept of literature whose autonomy would not be dependent on any notion of national, cultural, or "racic" identity. Rather, they all should be seen as supporting elements of his defense of a particular form of literary fascism, of a politics that was fascist *because* of the way it defended literature and gave the literary priority over the political.

The literary fascists treated in this book, whether they collaborated actively with the Germans during the Occupation or not, were all engaged in a cultural war long before the outbreak of the Second World War. This cultural war had been going on long before they entered it, from at least the time of the Dreyfus affair, and it is a war that clearly is not over yet, given that the questions of nationalism, the militant defense of a national culture or language, and the singularity of national literatures and works of art are still being polemically debated today. The war to which literary fascists were most deeply committed was not initially (or completely) a war fought with Germany or on the side of German National Socialism, but a war fought against all the enemies of French language, literature, and culture, whomever they were determined to be—a war primarily fought against the Jews.

It was always in the name of a "certain idea of France" (or in the case of Drieu la Rochelle, of Europe; and in the case of Céline, of an original "Aryan," natural man) that all of the literary fascists wrote and acted. It was also in the name of literature, art, and culture that they formulated their notions of fascist politics. Their fascism, however, cannot be attributed to one particular concept of literature or art, one literary strategy or tendency alone, for in all cases it constituted an amalgam of not just the aesthetic and the political, but of the traditional and the modern, of a classical aesthetics of form and a post-Nietzschean aesthetics of force, of humanist premises and totalitarian ends, of the defense of the most elevated, abstract, metaphysical, aesthetic ideals and the most mundane, petty, violent, xenophobic, anti-Semitic practices. It was in each case *the way* in which literature and art were linked to and used as models for politics, rather than any single facet of literature or art itself, that gave form to their fascism. Thus, neither classicism nor Nietzscheanism, neither aestheticism nor culturalism, neither humanism nor antihumanism, neither modernism nor antimodernism, and neither masculinism nor antimasculinism should be singled out as the determining factor in the creation of literary fascism—or, on the other hand, as the unique or best means for criticizing or condemning fascism and anti-Semitism and distancing ourselves from extremist ideologies and racisms in general.

What this also means is that no critical approach to the fascist aestheticizing of politics can legitimately situate itself entirely outside the history and tradition that produced fascism, for that history was so contradictory and multifaceted that it included both the forces crucial for the resistance to and undermining of fascism and those that most actively contributed to the creation and defense of fascism. The amalgam constituted by literary fascism indicates not that all of literature (or all of French, German, Italian or European culture) was somehow primary or exclusively responsible for fascism, but rather that specific approaches to culture and literature had important roles to play in its formation. In any case, a commitment to the organic integrity or the autonomy of literature never *in itself* isolated anyone from or served as a counter to totalitarian ideologies. In the case of French literary fascism, an extremist form of literary organicism and the arguments made in the name of the autonomy of literature and art were constitutive of totalitarianism and anti-Semitism rather than opposed to them. The ideal of an original, autonomous literature and the related ideal of an integral national culture were in a fascist context nothing less than the founding principles of a dogmatic and ruthless political ideology. It is in this sense that literary fascism represented an extreme aestheticization of politics and a politicization of literature and culture, nothing less than the totalization of the literary as the political.

Notes to the Chapters

Introduction

1. In their preface to their detailed and dispassionate study of French policy toward the Jews during the Occupation, Marrus and Paxton describe their book as one that "explores the indigeneous French roots for the antisemitic measures adopted by Vichy after 1940" (xiii), and they convincingly show how "Vichy measures against Jews came from within, as part of the National Revolution," and why they should be considered "autonomous acts taken in pursuit of indigenous goals" (13), rather than acts the French were forced to perform by a ruthless occupier. The chief goal served by Vichy France's actions against the Jews was cultural homogeneity: "Vichy's antisemitism . . . was part of a larger national effort to replace with homogeneity the enfeebling disunities of the 1930's. French political cultures from the Left to Right—from Jacobism to integral nationalism—have traditionally perceived cultural pluralism as dangerous. . . . Vichy leaders set about to restore the homogeneity that they imagined to have been the traditional state of France. . . . It was not a happy time to be different in France" (366). See also Robert O. Paxton, *Vichy France: Old Guard and New Order 1940–1944* (New York: Columbia University Press, 1972); and for Vichy's legacy, see Henry Rousso, *The Vichy Syndrome: History and Memory in France since 1944*, trans. Arthur Goldhammer (Cambridge: Harvard University Press, 1991).

2. For one of the most exaggerated presentations of this position, see Bernard-Henri Lévy, *L'Idéologie française* (Paris: Grasset, 1981).

3. Benjamin writes in "The Work of Art in the Age of Mechanical Reproduction" (in *Illuminations*, trans. Harry Zohn [New York: Schocken Books, 1969]): "Fascism attempts to organize the newly created proletarian masses without affecting the property structure which the masses strive to eliminate. Fascism sees its salvation in giving these masses not their right, but instead a chance to express themselves. . . . The logical result of Fascism is the introduction of aesthetics into political life. . . . Mankind, which in Homer's time was an object of contemplation of the Olympian gods, now is one for itself. Its self-alienation has reached such a degree that it can experience its own destruction as an aesthetic pleasure of the first order. This is the situation of politics which Fascism is rendering aesthetic. Communism responds by politicizing art" (241–42).

4. In "The Nazi Myth," trans. Brian Holmes, *Critical Inquiry*, v. 16 (Winter 1990), Jean-Luc Nancy and Philippe Lacoue-Labarthe analyze Plato's condemnation and exclusion of myth in terms that will be especially pertinent for an understanding of the literary-aesthetic dimension of fascism: "Myth is a fiction in the strong, active sense of 'fashioning' or, as Plato says, of 'plastic art': it is, therefore, a *fictioning*, whose role is to propose, if not to impose, models or types . . . by means of which an individual, or a city, or an entire people, can take possession of itself and identify with itself" (297, translation modified). In *Heidegger, Art*

and Politics: The Fiction of the Political, trans. Chris Turner (Cambridge: Basil Blackwell, 1990), Lacoue-Labarthe claims, in a similar vein, that "the political (the City) belongs to a form of *plastic art*, formation and information, *fiction* in the strict sense. This is a deep theme which derives from Plato's politico-pedagogic writings . . . and reappears in the guise of such concepts as *Gestaltung* (configuration, fashioning) or *Bildung*, a term with a revealingly polysemic character (formation, constitution, organization, education, culture, etc.)" (66).

5. See for example, Zeev Sternhell, *La Droite révolutionaire, 1885–1914: Les Origines françaises du fascisme* (Paris: Seuil, 1978), and *Maurice Barrès et le nationalisme français* (Paris: Colin, 1972); Robert Soucy, *Fascism in France: The Case of Maurice Barrès* (Berkeley: University of California Press, 1972), and *French Fascism: The First Wave, 1924–1933* (New Haven: Yale University Press, 1986); Michael Curtis, *Three Against the Republic: Sorel, Barrrès, and Maurras* (Princeton: Princeton University Press, 1979); Eugen Weber, *Action Française: Royalism and Reaction in Twentieth-Century France* (Stanford: Stanford University Press, 1962); Pierre-Marie Dioudonnat, *Je suis partout 1930–1934: Les Maurrassiens devant la tentation fasciste* (Paris: La Table Ronde, 1973); and in spite of his recent revisionist publications, Ernst Nolte, *Three Faces of Fascism: Action Française, Italian Fascism, and National Socialism*, trans. Leila Vennewitz (New York: Holt, Rinehart, and Winston, 1966).

6. See William R. Tucker, *The Fascist Ego: A Political Biography of Robert Brasillach* (Berkeley: University of California Press, 1975), for a meticulous presentation of Brasillach's life and politcal ideas.

7. See Pierre Hebey, *La Nouvelle Revue Française des années sombres (Juin 1940–Juin 1941): Des Intellectuels à la dérive* (Paris: Gallimard, 1992).

Chapter One
The Use and Abuse of Culture: Maurice Barrès and the
Ideology of the Collective Subject

1. Valois, a dissident member of the Action Française, was the founder of Le Faisceau, the first overtly fascist party in France.

2. The shift in emphasis is evident in the titles of Barrès's two trilogies: *Le Culte du Moi* and *Le Roman de l'énergie nationale*. The first trilogy consists of *Sous l'Oeil des Barbares* (Paris: Alphonse Lemerre, 1888), *Un Homme Libre* (Paris: Perrin, 1889), and *Le Jardin de Bérénice* (Paris: Perrin, 1891); the second, of *Les Déracinés* (Paris: E. Fasquelle, 1897), *L'Appel au Soldat* (Paris: E. Fasquelle, 1900), and *Leurs Figures* (Paris: Plon, 1902). In this chapter, I shall be quoting from a recent paperback edition of *Les Déracinés* (Paris: Gallimard ["Folio"], 1988). Unless an English translation is indicated, all translations from the French throughout this book are my own.

3. See *Heidegger, Art and Politics: The Fiction of the Political*, trans. Chris Turner (Cambridge: Basil Blackwell, 1990), where Lacoue-Labarthe discusses the power and function of myth in Nazi ideology: "It is a 'power' [*puissance*], the power that is in the gathering together of the fundamental forces and orientations of an individual or a people, that is, to say the power of a deep, concrete, embodied identity. . . . [The power] is that of the dream, as the projection of an image

with which one identifies through a total and immediate commitment. Such an image is in no way a product of 'fabulation,' to which myth is ordinarily reduced; it is the figuration of a *type* conceived both as a model of identity and as that identity formed and realized" (93–94).

4. Trans. Brian Holmes, *Critical Inquiry*, v. 16 (Winter 1990), 294; trans. modified.

5. In *The Origins of Totalitarianism* (New York: Harcourt Brace Jovanovich, 1973), Hannah Arendt argues: "An ideology is quite literally what its name indicates: it is the logic of an idea. Its subject matter is history, to which the 'idea' is applied. . . . The ideology treats the course of events as though it followed the same 'law' as the logical exposition of its 'idea.' . . . The movement of history and the logical process of this notion are suposed to correspond to each other, so that whatever happens, happens according to the logic of one 'idea' " (469). Arendt calls the application of this logic "the tyranny of logicality" (473).

6. Zeev Sternhell, in *Maurice Barrès et le nationalisme français* (Paris: Editions Complexe, 1985), gives an invaluable, detailed presentation and analysis of Barrès's political evolution, insisting on the significance of his particular contributions to an extreme form of French nationalism that Sternhell also argues served as a foundation for various forms of French fascism decades later. Sternhell describes Barrès's nationalism as "a complete vision of man and the collectivity; . . . its goal is to give the French back their authenticity and, in making them hear the voice of blood, to reestablish the compromised unity of the nation. . . . [It is] a new religion possessing its own mysticism and rejecting in its totality the world as it is" (24).

7. The "Examen" was republished in a later edition of *Sous l'Oeil des Barbares* (Paris: Plon, 1922), and I shall quote exclusively from this edition.

8. Even Sternhell, who goes to great pains to explain the logic of Barrès's views and the coherence of his system, considers him ultimately to be an irrationalist: "Reality for Barrès is fundamentally irrational; escaping totally from reason, it can only be felt" (*Maurice Barrès et le nationalisme français*, 314).

9. Robert Soucy, in his study of Barrès, *Fascism in France: The Case of Maurice Barrès* (Berkeley: University of California Press, 1972), takes the opposite position from the one I am taking here and claims that Barrès's extreme collectivist or nationalist position in the second trilogy constitutes an antihumanism and represents, in spite of what Barrès himself claims, a radical break with the first trilogy and *Le Culte du Moi*. In discussing the movement already evident in the first trilogy toward what I have called the collective or Nation-Self, Soucy claims that it represents "a reversal not a continuation of his former position" (71). And yet Soucy has to admit the "reversal" is evident almost from the start, at least by the time of *Un homme libre*, the second novel of *Le Culte du Moi*.

10. In much the same vein, Zeev Sternhell argues that it is possible to "discern already in Barrès's very first period the germs of his future nationalism" (*Maurice Barrès et le nationalisme français*, 36).

11. Lacoue-Labarthe and Nancy argue in "The Nazi Myth" that in Nazi racist ideology, "the Jew is not simply a bad race, a defective type: he is the antitype, the bastard par excellence. He has no culture of his own. . . . His form is formless. . . . The Jew is not an opposite *type*, but the very absence of type" (307).

12. The grandfather of one of the principal characters, Maurice Roemer-spacher, for example, is presented as the source, model, and guarantee of his grandson's eventual rerooting in the land. The grandfather is described as a "type, a storehouse of generations," and an excellent storyteller, for "in his stories, one follows the movements of a soul living on the border" of France (103–4), and thus one that has lived through the greatest national agony and knows the costs of the invasion of the foreign and the necessity of resisting it.

13. See, of course, on the problem of the positing of "the Orient" as the other of "the West," Edward W. Said's *Orientalism* (New York: Vintage, 1979). I am indebted to Elizabeth Constable, who, in a paper she wrote for one of my graduate seminars, first drew my attention to the importance of narrative in the formation of national identity in Barrès, as well as to the significance of "foreign stories" as the most basic threat to the mythical national community, a danger best represented by the seductive character and stories of Astiné Aravian, the full mythical embodiment for Barrès of the "Oriental woman."

14. The narrator also interjects that Astiné understood that it was her destiny as an "Oriental woman" to die tragically and that she undoubtedly preferred this "noble destiny" to old age and obesity: "Would she have wanted to get old? Oriental women [*les Orientales*] get so heavy!" (427).

15. Barrès in his journal in fact denounced the political effects of Hugo's writing and saw *Les Déracinés* as a counter to *Les Misérables*, serving the same function for nationalism as it had served for republicanism: "It was *Les Misérables*, *Les Châtiments*, that brought down the Empire. As *Les Misérables* provided the manure in which radical, republican thought was born, I would like *Les Déracinés*. . . ." (*Mes Cahiers*, v. 2, 163)—unfinished in the text.

Chapter Two
The Beautiful Community: The Fascist Legacy of Charles Péguy

1. Bernard-Henri Lévy's sensationalist work, *L'Idéologie française* (Paris: Grasset, 1981), which was one of the first and remains the most extreme example of an ever-increasing number of studies whose principal goal seems to be the denunciation of canonical literary and philosophical figures, accepts the "fascist version" of Péguy without question. Lévy attacks Péguy and everyone else, whether on the left or the right, that he can fit into a long French nationalist and socialist tradition, which he claims is from its origins predominantly anti-Semitic and which leads for him directly and unproblematically to fascism and collaboration. As "the French ideology" goes, so, for Lévy, goes Péguy and almost all of the rest of French literature, thought, and culture.

2. Jacques Derrida, in "Otobiographies: The Teaching of Nietzsche and the Politics of the Proper Name," trans. Avital Ronell, in *The Ear of the Other*, ed. Christie V. McDonald (New York: Schocken, 1985), formulates the problem in the following way: "We shall ask even why it is not enough to say: 'Nietzsche did not think that,' 'he did not want that,' or that he he would have surely vomited it, that there is falsification of the legacy and interpretative mystification going on here. We shall ask why and how what is so naively called a falsification

was possible (it was not with just anything)" (23–24; trans. modified). Later, Derrida adds: "The future of the Nietzsche text is not closed. But if, within the still-open countours of an era, the only politics calling itself—proclaiming itself—Nietzschean will have been a Nazi one, then this is necessarily signficant and must be questioned in all of its consequences" (30–31).

3. For example, Pierre Drieu La Rochelle claimed that "it makes little difference who invented fascism. France has played an important role in it: the France of Sorel, of Péguy, of Barrès, of Maurras, the France of Proudhon" (*Chronique Politique* [Paris: Gallimard, 1943], 192).

4. Even though Rey does not mention it, one of those "mutilating" Péguy's work to make it fit into a collaborationist context was Péguy's own son Marcel. In *Le Destin de Charles Péguy* (Paris: Perrin, 1946; originally published in 1941), Marcel Péguy presented his father as both the inventor of national socialism and a racist: "He moved close to certain old French socialists; I mean socialists who had died before socialism was definitively corrupted by Marxism and Jewry. . . . My father clearly aimed with *the socialist city* for the institution in France of a *national socialism.*" He then added in a note that the term "national socialism" belonged primarily to the French: "I use this term because until further notice it seems to me the property of the French in general, and mine in particular" (89–90). The following description made of another of his father's texts is even more direct: "*Jeanne d'Arc* is a racist manifesto. At no moment does France appear to Jeanne as a political combination but rather as the land of a certain race. . . . What is rather particular in the racism of Jeanne (which is, of course, the racism of my father) is that it is an *essentially Christian racism*" (102–3). Of course, a father cannot control what a son will do in his name any more than an author can control what his readers will do. But it is still not insignificant, no matter how exaggerated and misleading certain of Marcel Péguy's claims could be shown to be, that Péguy's fascist legacy passes in part by way of his own son.

5. In *Le Mécontemporain: Péguy, lecteur d'un monde moderne* (Paris: Gallimard, 1991), Alain Finkielkraut also attempts to rescue Péguy from attacks such as Lévy's, by defending not his practice of writing but his view of culture. Like Rey, Finkielkraut praises Péguy's distrust of modernity and attacks what he calls the injustice of all attempts to "condemn Péguy and banish his work from culture" (19) by associating it with extremist forms of nationalism and with anti-Semitism. Finkielkraut's principal claim is that Péguy was never a xenophobic nationalist but a humanist, that he always spoke in the name of a plural and nonexclusive, humanistic culture, a "we" consisting of a plurality of voices, rather than a rationalist, politically defined, singular "humanity" (150–51). Péguy, in Finkielkraut's interpretation, "never gives up the cause of humanity for that of the nation" (159)—even in his most nationalistic texts. To make such an argument, Finkielkraut, like Rey, has to ignore or pass over very quickly all of the texts that extremist nationalists and fascists quoted in order to make Péguy an important precursor of French fascism. Finkielkraut's claims for Péguy are in fact just as inflated as Lévy's; they are just their extreme opposite.

6. All references to Péguy's writings are to the recently published three-volume edition of his *Oeuvres en Prose Complètes*, edited by Robert Burac (Paris: Bibli-

othèque de la Pléiade, 1987, 1988, 1992), which replaced the earlier Pléiade edition, edited by Marcel Péguy.

7. Péguy's project here explicitly echoes that of the nineteenth-century historian he most admired, Jules Michelet. "No occasion should be lost . . . to proclaim again that Michelet is the very genius of history, first of all, because it is true, and, second, because it bothers so many people and because it's such a huge ordeal for our great friends, the moderns" ("Clio: Dialogue de l'Histoire et de l'âme païenne," v. 3, 1028). In his preface to *Le Peuple* (Paris: Garnier Flammarion, 1974; originally published in 1846), Michelet criticizes all previous portraits of the French people for lacking "a sense of the grand harmony," for not seeing that "the family, work, the most humble life of the people all have in themselves a sacred poetry" (63). He claims that the true goal of history in not narration or analysis but *resurrection* (73), specifically the resurrection of the unity of the people and the nation: "One people! One homeland! One France! We shall never become two nations. . . . Without unity, we die" (75).

8. This is why Péguy attacked Jean Jaurès the most severely of all political figures, because, for Péguy, he represented the worst aspects of this double game: "This is what makes the responsibility of Jaurès in this crime, in this double crime, in this crime to the second degree, the greatest. He among all others, he at the head of the operation, was a politician like the others, worse than the others, a sneak among sneaks, a deceiver among deceivers; but he pretended not to be a politician. This made his noxiousness the greatest. This made his responsibility the greatest" (91). In "L'Argent" (February 1913), he excuses himself for even referring to Jaurès at all, for his is "a name that has become so basely filthy [*ordurier*] that when I write it to send it to the printers I have the impression of fearing that I shall fall under the jurisdiction of some penal code or other. Jaurès, the man who contaminated radicalism, socialism, and Dreyfusism" (v. 3, 798).

9. In "Our History," Jean-Luc Nancy, referring to the wartime writings of Paul de Man, asserts that if a political position can be defined as a "national-populism of the *spirit*, it is not a racism" (in *Diacritics*, v. 20, no. 3 [Fall 1990], 99). At the extreme limits of each position, this may of course be true, but I would argue that there is much more overlapping of the two positions, much more intermixing of spirit and blood in both spiritually and strictly racially defined "national-populisms" or national-socialisms than Nancy's comments imply. The line between them is most often very difficult to draw; each position borrows substantially from the other, even if each also opposes itself to the other in terms of particular issues. The difficulty in separating the spiritual from the racial becomes even more difficult if we follow Lacoue-Labarthe's analysis of fascism and his argument that "racism—and anti-semitism in particular—is primarily, fundamentally, an aestheticism" (*Heidegger, Art and Politics*, 69).

10. Alain Finkielkraut attempts to free Péguy from his own militaristic nationalist arguments by claiming that the material roots of spirituality in his work are accidental rather than essential. He claims that "the idea [of freedom] takes on the countours of place, and place appears as the receptacle or the pinnacle of support of the idea. The spirit impregnates, without losing any of its sprituality, the vines and hillsides of the countryside of France. Far from choosing the solidity of the

earth rather than the ether of freedom, Péguy sees freedom *land* [literally, come to earth (*atterir*)], and this discovery leads him to place himself in the service of his country" (*Le Mécontemporain*, 89).

11. The only exception to the general rule that a spiritual people can exist only because the temporal had been measured off and secured, argued Péguy, appeared to be the Jews: "The Jews from the time of their dispersion appear to represent an example, and the only one, of a spiritual race being carried on, prolonged, growing without the support of a temporal and, in particular, a military armature, without the support of a state, and, in particular, an army. It is perhaps true" (905). He went on to add, however, again stressing the uniqueness of the case of the Jews, that "Israel, all things considered, for its dispersion took and had to take the world that Rome had made, the world that everyone else took. And it is in no way rash to say that Israel continued a spiritual city of temporal dispersion in the same form of world, in the same mold of world, in the same cradle of the world in which Christianity founded a spiritual city of temporal unification" (906).

Chapter Three
The Nation as Artwork: Charles Maurras and the
Classical Origins of French Literary Fascism

1. For a detailed history of the Action Française, see Eugen Weber, *Action Française: Royalism and Reaction in Twentieth-Century France* (Stanford: Stanford University Press, 1962); for a study of the influence of Maurras on various nationalist and fascist thinkers who were at one time or another linked to the royalist movement, see Paul Sérant, *Les Dissidents de L'Action Française* (Paris: Editions Copernic, 1978); and for studies of the Action Française as an important precursor of fascism, see Ernst Nolte, *Three Faces of Fascism*, trans. Leila Vennewitz (New York: Holt, Rinehart, and Winston, 1966), 29–141, and Zeev Sternhell, *La Droite Révolutionaire 1855–1914: Les Origines françaises du fascisme* (Paris: Editions du Seuil, 1978), 348–400.

2. Quoted in Pierre-Marie Dioudonnat, *Je suis partout 1930–1934: Les Maurrassiens devant la tentation fasciste* (Paris: La Table Ronde, 1973), 344. This is undoubtedly the most detailed study of the influence of Maurras's ideas on the most important and influential of the journals that were at their inception sponsored by the Action Française but which eventually moved away from Maurras and became militantly pro-German, fascist, and collaborationist.

3. This is the title Maurras gave to a collection of essays he published in 1941, in which he defended Pétain and his politics of collaboration because he argued they were in the best interest of France: "We have only one slogan: France. We are neither German nor English. We are French. *FRANCE ALONE [LA FRANCE SEULE]* or, if you prefer, *ONLY FRANCE [LA SEULE FRANCE]*" (*La Seule France: Chronique des jours d'épreuve* [Lyon: Lardanchet, 1941], 118). During his trial for collusion with the enemy, which ran from January 24 to 27, 1945, Maurras repeatedly argued that he had never collaborated because he had always been a Germanophobe. His support of Vichy and the politics he proposed during the Occupation had as their unique goal, he claimed, to protect France from fur-

ther German interventions: "I have explained to you in great detail that I asked the legitimate [i.e., Vichy] French authorities to act energetically to keep the Gestapo from intervening. I wanted to avoid the intervention of the foreigner" (*Le Procès de Charles Maurras* [Paris: Albin Michel, 1946], 26). He also claimed that he had repeatedly urged a rapid and severe repression of all dissidents only "to reestablish order, so that counter-terrorism would not be born" (26).

4. Even Pierre Drieu la Rochelle, in spite of his serious reservations concerning important elements of Maurras's approach to literature and politics, nevertheless wrote the following "Religious and Political Testament" (dated September 15, 1939) in his journal: "I die a Maurrasian, with the regret of not having served Maurras and the Action Française better. If I only had made myself worthy of being the successor of Maurras" (*Journal: 1939–1945* [Paris: Gallimard, 1992], 84). An entry of October 26, 1939, further emphasizes Drieu la Rochelle's paradoxical, but far from completely negative relation to Maurras: "But also while distrusting certain Maurrassian right-wing fixations—even if on the whole I adhere to the philosophy of Maurras, to his lively reasoning . . . which accounts at the same time for nature and society, the divine and the human—I am very much up in the air, very isolated" (109). Repeatedly during the period of the war and the Occupation he wished in his journal that Maurras would die, so that the image of the Maurras of the 1920s would not be destroyed by the writings of the Maurras of the 1940s. For example: "What a shame that Maurras and Daudet did not die around 1925" ([May 18, 1940], 203); and "Will Maurras finally have the tact to die?" ([June 21, 1940], 246).

5. The title of an article written in 1901 on the socialist leader Jean Jaurès, "Mademoiselle Jean Jaurès," indicates what Maurras thinks of Jaurès and socialism in general: "By Mademoiselle Jean Jaurès you will have understood, as I have intended, the orator Jaurès in person, the 'Mademoiselle' placed there to indicate the sex of his mind [*esprit*]. . . . His mind combines the weaknesses and the seductions of the feminine mind" (in *Enquête sur la Monarchie* [Paris: Nouvelle Librairie Nationale, 1924], 499). Maurras goes on to argue that socialism, as a manifestation of the disorderly feminine mind, in spite of the long French socialist tradition, is quite simply not French: it is "rejected by the nature of the French soil, of the French people" (517).

6. During his trial after the war for collusion, to show his utter contempt for the authorities trying him, he repeatedly referred to the Republic as "la femme sans tête [the headless, in the sense of brainless, incompetent, woman]" and to the prosecuting attorney as "Monsieur l'avocat de la femme sans tête." The term, he claimed, surprisingly enough, was taken from a friend of his old enemy Jaurès: "Do you know how the socialist Marcel Sembat, a friend of Jaurès, called the Republic? You don't know? I'm going to tell you: he called it 'the brainless woman.' Well, the brainless woman certainly conceived the organization of this trial. It's incoherence and madness" (*Le Procès de Charles Maurras*, 50).

7. In a note at the end of *Romantisme et Révolution*, Maurras quotes an article he wrote on the death of Mallarmé and sketches the following movement of the supposed decline of syntax and style in the history of French literature: "Before [Chateaubriand], syntax and style, that is, the genius of the French language and the thought of the author, were in first place. Thanks to him, they have fallen to

second place, having given up their place to vocabulary. The consequences of this revolution were continued not just in Hugo and his contemporaries but even in the work of this belated Romantic whom we have just lost, M. Stéphane Mallarmé (*Revue Enclyopédique du 15 octobre 1898*)" (272).

8. This is not to suggest that all organicism leads or is equivalent to political totalitarianism, for Maurras's organicism is of a very particular neoclassical type. It is his *application* of certain organicist principles to politics that makes his aesthetics a model for literary fascism, not the organicist principles in themselves. For an eloquent "defense" of the critical, nontotalitarian, even postmodern implications of a version of literary organicism that would have to be considered diametrically opposed to Maurras's version, see Murray Krieger, *A Reopening of Closure: Organicism Against Itself* (New York: Columbia University Press, 1989).

9. In his study of Heidegger's politics, *Heidegger, Art and Politics: The Fiction of the Political*, trans. Chris Turner (Cambridge: Basil Blackwell, 1990), Philippe Lacoue-Labarthe analyzes the stakes of the organic determination of the political in terms that apply as well to Maurras as to National Socialism: "In its essence the political is *organic*. We must allow the terms to resonate doubly here and hear the *ergon* that lies beneath the *organon*. This is where the truth of what is called 'totalitarianism' is concealed. To say that the political is organic does not simply mean that the State is conceived simultaneously as 'living totality' and as artwork. The State is still too abstract a notion, which is to say that it is too separate a reality. . . . The essential organicity of the political is in reality infra-political, if not indeed infra-social (in the sense of *Gesellschaft*). It is the organicity of the community, *Gemeinschaft*, . . . a natural or 'physical' determination of the community which can only be accomplished and revealed to that community by a technè—if not by technè itself, by art" (68–69).

10. Maurras had nothing but scorn for the word "individual" and considered it to be, strictly speaking, inhuman: "If we speak of French workers and laborers, we do not say individuals. This dog is an individual. This elm is an individual. . . . For a Man, for a Worker, for a Frenchman, I use the only appropriate term, I say that he is a person" (*Mes idées politiques*, 268).

11. That is why when the Pretender, the Duc de Guise, in November of 1937, affirmed that no identity existed between the Action Française and the royal house, it had little if any effect on Maurras's political position. As Eugen Weber shows, "the Action Française replied with protestations of complete devotion and the suggestion that it was largely the influence of bad advisers on the Pretender's staff that explained the blow" (*Action Française*, 404); but when the break was reaffirmed, Maurras persisted in his royalism without the support of the Pretender. Weber also argues that "the royal excommunication of 1937 hurt the Pretender far more than it did the Action Française. . . . Most old royalists were indignant that the Comte de Paris should dare to treat Maurras this way. . . . The royal condemnation was approved by those who condemned Maurras already, not all of them friends of royalism" (408).

12. Maurras wrote an article in the *Petit Marseillais* of February 9, 1941, with "La Divine Surprise" as its title: "A poet . . . said that when Poetry has just realized all the points of its consummate perfection, when it has reached even the

sublime, something still is missing from it if it has not produced what could be called The Divine Surprise. . . . It's in the same sense that he spoke of the "divine part" of the art of war. Well, the divine part of political art has been reached by the extraordinary surprises that the Maréchal has given us. We expected so much from him, we could and we ought to expect everything. To this natural expectation he was able to add something. Afterwards, nothing more was missing" (quoted in Eugen Weber, *Action Française*, 447). Weber is certainly right to claim that for Maurras, "without its ever being actually said, Pétain took the place of a king, and to Pétain the royalists transferred the loyalty they had heretofore reserved for the Pretender" (*Action Française*, 446).

13. In a letter written on September 8, 1944, just before he was arrested, Maurras even claimed that Pétain could be considered to have "resisted": "There is no more firm *résistant* than he in France, nor certainly outside of France" (in *Lettres de Prison* [Paris: Flammarion, 1958], 8). In the project for a letter to be written to *France Soir* while he was in prison, Maurras claimed that he too was a heroic member of the true Resistance: "I did everything bad I could [to the Germans], and I never hid it. Not content to '*resist*' them, using the word in fashion, I made war on them with my pen for four years, an *offensive* war in all its forms and in all respects. . . . On the rare occasions when a member of the Action Française had the misfortune to turn to collaborationism and philokrautism, he was automatically kicked out, and he was told this to his face" (55–56). The first part of the statement was of course self-serving and absurd, equivalent to Pétain's defense of his own "resistance" to Hitler; the second part was basically true.

14. See chapter 25 of Eugen Weber's *Action Française*, "The Divine Surprise" (442–56), for a description of the importance of the Action Française for Vichy France, and especially pages 136–233 of Robert Paxton's *Vichy France: Old Guard and New Order 1940–1944* (New York: Columbia University Press, 1972) for an analysis of the nature and effects of Vichy France's "National Revolution," of exactly what it owed to Maurras and where it differed from his views.

15. Marrus and Paxton in *Vichy France and the Jews* describe the Statute in the following terms: "The law was virtually constitutional in scope. It assigned, on the basis of race, an inferior position in French civil law and society to a whole segment of French citizens and to noncitizens and foreigners living on French soil. The *Statut des juifs* began by defining who was Jewish in the eyes of the French state, and then excluded those Jews from top positions in the public service, from the officer corps and from the ranks of noncommissioned officers, and from the professions that influence public opinion: teaching, the press, radio, film, and theater. . . . The law, finally, promised that a quota system would be devised to limit Jews in the liberal professions" (3). "[It] went farther than the German ordinance [for the Occupied Zone] of the previous week. Where the German ordinance defined Jewishness reticently by religious practice, the Vichy statute spoke bluntly of race. The Vichy Statute was also more inclusive. . . . [It] included in its definition those with only two grandparents 'of the Jewish race' in cases where the spouse was also Jewish" (12). Marrus and Paxton also argue that "any simple notion of German *Diktat* can be dismissed summarily. . . . Years of scrutiny of the records left by German services in Paris and Berlin have turned up no trace of German orders to Vichy in 1940 . . . to adopt antisemitic legislation" (5).

Chapter Four
Fascism as Aesthetic Experience: Robert Brasillach and the
Politics of Literature

1. For example, Robert Brasillach's close friend and brother-in-law, Maurice Bardèche, was the most persistent of the many revisionists defending Brasillach: "How could this peaceful man, this 'scholar,' this writer whose entire work expresses the goodness, the love of beings, which was in fact his chief aptitude, how could he have been involved in this tempest, carried along at the center of this night in which the winds blew? . . . Nothing prepared Robert Brasillach for politics, and I don't believe I am falsifying the truth by saying that at the beginning of his literary life, it didn't interest him" ("Introduction," *Ecrit à Fresnes* [Paris: Plon, 1967], 12). For Bardèche, Brasillach was never a "political leader, but rather a carefree young man who took great pleasure in throwing snowballs" (18). Bardèche's testimony is, of course, more than suspect, not only because of his close relationship to Brasillach but because he continued to defend fascism after the war and himself remained an unrepentant revisionist and anti-Semite. In the same "Introduction," Bardèche claims that Brasillach's trial was the way "the Jews and the Popular Front settled their quarrel with *Je suis partout*." In explaining why Brasillach was executed, he points out that "the director of General de Gaulle's cabinet was Georges Boris, a Freemason and Jew" (40–41).

2. The unsigned material that appears on the back cover of the recent Plon editions of Brasillach's work describes him in exactly these terms: "The tragic destiny of Robert Brasillach, victim at the age of thirty-five of one of the dramas of the Purge Trials, brought an end to a career that was one of the most promising. . . . His work expresses the love of life, a sensibility for tenderness, friendship, courage facing life, the poetry of beings and feelings. . . . If he is still remembered, it is not only because of this death that is today regretted, it is because young people are pleased to discover in his books an image of themselves and of what they want to be" (*Notre avant-guerre* [Plon: Paris, 1981]).

3. Brasillach's literary talents and his critical skills were in fact very much in question during his trial for collusion with the Germans. The prosecutor, Marcel Reboul, evoked his "misuse" of these skills as one of the principal proofs of Brasillach's treason, as if his real crime were to have betrayed French culture: "Brasillach possessed to the highest point the sense of penetration of texts that a vast erudition and the perfect knowledge of classical rules gives. . . . In an affair of this kind, confronted with an accused of this intellectual quality, . . . it cannot be a question of attenuating circumstances" (in Jacques Isorni, *Le Procès de Robert Brasillach [19 janvier 1945]* [Paris: Flammarion, 1946], 126). Reboul added later that "Brasillach's treason is above all an *intellectual treason*. It is the treason of pride" (146). But Jacques Isorni, Brasillach's lawyer, evoked these same skills and talents in order to defend him: "How, Mister Commissioner, can you claim that he betrayed France, he who so profoundly penetrated the soul itself of France? Brasillach . . . is a part of the literary glory of France, a part of the glory of France" (173). Isorni then asked rhetorically: "Do civilized peoples execute their poets?" (177). And later in his defense, he asserted that "one does not betray his country by ensuring its intellectual or literary primacy" (187). Isorni con-

cluded his plea by saying: "You are going to judge a young man, a pure man, a great writer, a poet. . . . Justice does not have the right to execute souls. It is not possible that this great mind [*esprit*] of which the most illustrious writers have spoken will be extinguished forever" (208–9).

4. Brasillach himself contributed to the creation of his own "mythical" status as a victim of the Purge Trials by comparing himself to another "poet-martyr," André Chénier, the poet on whom Brasillach himself worked while in prison and with whom he clearly identified in the months before his execution: Chénier, victim of the Terror of the Revolution; Brasillach, "martyr" of the terror of the Liberation and especially of the communist elements of the Resistance. In two texts written while he was in prison and published in *Ecrit à Fresnes*, Brasillach makes an explicit connection between his own situation and that of Chénier. In his "Journal d'un homme occupé," he writes: "Decidedly, the First Republic had on its hands for eternity the blood of André Chénier and the blood of Lavoisier. The Fourth Republic wanted to exceed it" (60). And in his lyrical text entitled "Chénier," Brasillach describes how he read this poet: "It is in fact in a cell on death row in the prison at Fresnes, with my ankles linked together by a lead chain, that I assiduously read Chénier. The coldest of Januarys easily brought back to life for me the ancient Thermidor of revolutionary carts, and in a world in flames, the eternal return had brought back many similarities" (471).

5. At his trial, Brasillach's lawyer tried to show that Brasillach had always remained a patriotic French nationalist by insisting on the fact that he broke with *Je suis partout* when he felt that its support for Nazi Germany was harming France. Brasillach, himself, gave this version of the break between what he calls the "two parties at *Je suis partout*": "The first, consisting of myself and two or three friends, supported a politics of Franco-German collaboration but demanded that this politics be above all a French politics. The others were . . . 'ultras.' They wanted to go way beyond the politics of Vichy, they wanted an extremely active politics with Germany" (*Le Procès de Robert Brasillach*, 60–61). Pierre-Marie Dioudonnat argues that the origins of the crisis at *Je suis partout* dated at least from the previous year, but he supports for the most part Brasillach's version of the split: "Two groups at the heart of the *Je suis partout* team were opposed. The first, favoring the 'ultras' of collaboration, the P.P.F. of Jacques Doriot and then the Milice of Joseph Darnand, decided to remain faithful right to the end to fascist ideology and to Germany in its collapse. They accused the other group of being tepid. The latter, with Brasillach, remained closer to traditional nationalism, more supportive of Maréchal Pétain. It refused the politics of disaster and was skeptical of the extremists" (*Je suis partout, 1930–1944*, 366). See also Michel Laval, *Brasillach ou la trahison du clerc* (Paris: Hachette, 1993), for a dramatic account of Brasillach's trial and the political controversies that have surrounded it ever since. Laval points out that Brasillach's claim that it was out of principle that he broke with *Je suis partout* was refuted at the trial by showing that Brasillach continued to write for other collaborationist journals and never retracted his active support not just for collaboration but for fascism and National Socialism as well. For a good biography of Brasillach, see William R. Tucker, *The Fascist Ego: A Political Biography of Robert Brasillach* (Berkeley: University of California Press, 1975).

6. Brasillach naively hoped that Maurras would approve of his decision to continue publishing *Je suis partout* in Paris under the German occupation, but even after Maurras violently condemned the newspaper, Brasillach refrained from replying in any direct, polemical way. His criticisms of Maurras were fairly gentle and indirect and invariably preceded by an admission of what he and others owed to Maurras. For example, in "De l'Epopée aux Décombres" (*JSP*, no. 579 [September 4, 1942]), Brasillach argues that "to have been 'cleansed' in your youth of all democratic ideas is a gift that prepares you especially well for understanding the new world, even if [the Action Française] tried to instill in you at the same time several prejudices against this world." But having acknowledged this great "gift," he then proceeds to lament the positions taken by the Action Française during the Occupation: "Even its doctrine became feebler: what was the anti-Semitism of 1942 compared to that of 1912?"

7. Just before the outbreak of war in France, Thierry Maulnier, in "Sur la Prochaine 'Après-Guerre'" (*Je suis partout*, no. 485 [March 8, 1940]), gave a more developed justification for such a view of literary history as a continuity more fundamental than any surface disruption caused by war or social unrest. He argued that "great collective upheavals, great disasters, do not always play the role in the evolution of minds that one would be tempted to give them. The activity of the man who writes books, paints, or composes escapes in large part from the imprint of events. . . . Contrary to a widely accepted but crude idea, it is not great destructions that bring in great creative novelties." This meant for Maulnier that what was called the "postwar" period was on its most profound level really an extension of the "prewar" period: "As for the totality of its products, the postwar period is not the product of the war, but of the prewar period, whose continuation, after an interuption, it becomes."

8. This article has an interesting history. It appeared twice in *Je suis partout*, the first time as "A Propos de Mallarmé," no. 498 (June 7, 1940), and the second, in a slightly revised form (with the explicit references to Maulnier eliminated, even if the title he gave to Mallarmé is now the title of Brasillach's essay), in the next issue of the paper, no. 498 bis (February 7, 1941), as "Mallarmé, alchimiste du langage." Because of the defeat, *Je suis partout* was not published in the interim period, and when it did reappear in occupied Paris, Brasillach and the rest of the editorial board denounced Maulnier and the others who had published issue no. 498 as traitors, because they made no mention of the fact that the director and editor had been arrested. This marks Brasillach's break with his friend Maulnier as well as with Maurras and the Action Française in general. It is not without interest that the break is indicated by the double publication of an article on Mallarmé, which attempts to separate his poetry from his prose, what enriches the national language from what risks destroying it.

9. To my knowledge, Brasillach mentions the deportation of Jews from France only once in his columns from *Je suis partout*, and then it is to agree that the separation of children from their parents who are being deported is unwise—not because it is cruel and unjust but rather because it is not rational for the State to keep any Jews at all, young or old. "The Archbishop of Toulouse protests against the measures taken against the stateless Jews in the unoccupied territory. . . . He speaks of the brutalities and separations of which we are all ready to disapprove,

because it is necessary to free oneself of the Jews in block and not keep the little ones. Here humanity is in agreement with wisdom" ("Les Sept Internationales Contre la Patrie," *Je suis partout*, no. 582 [September 25, 1942]). Brasillach also criticizes the archbishop for not naming those he considers the real culprits responsible for the brutalities: "But he forgets to say that these brutalities are the work of police *AGITATORS* who want to make the poor Aryan idiots feel sorry." This practice was in fact soon stopped because of general public sentiment against such separations. Vichy had to ask for and finally received permission from Germany to send the children with the adults, which meant of course that the children also accompanied their parents to the gas chambers. See Marrus and Paxton's *Vichy France and the Jews*, especially 263–69, for an analysis of this change of policy.

10. Gerhard Heller, in *Un Allemand à Paris 1940–1944* (Paris: Seuil, 1981), a memoir clearly written to give as positive a picture of his own role at the Propaganda-Staffel as possible, claims that he heard Brasillach take a very different position on what should be done with the Jews. He quotes Brasillach as having said: "They should all be killed, even the little children" (90).

11. In *Heidegger, Art and Politics*, Lacoue-Labarthe argues in much the same way that Germany itself looked to Greece for such a model of *self-formation*: "What the German *imitatio* was looking for in Greece was the model—and therefore the possibility—of a pure emergence, a pure originality: the model of self-formation" (79). In relation to the German *imitatio*, Brasillach is proposing that France, in order to be itself, imitate a model of self-formation that is itself an imitation of a model of self-formation which is projected as being that of the Greeks.

12. In *Reproductions of Banality: Fascism, Literature, and French Intellectual Life* (Minneapolis: University of Minnesota Press, 1986), Alice Yaeger Kaplan considers Brasillach primarily from the perspective provided by the *Histoire du Cinéma* (Paris: Denoël, 1935), which he coauthored with Maurice Bardèche. Kaplan shows how, for Brasillach, "moviegoing constitutes a rite of friendship, an aesthetic experience against which political experience is later measured. . . . It is as film that fascism calls for unmediated experience and only with film that men can follow *en masse*, as though creators; and yet the debt of fascism to film must be denied, because ideological activity must be understood by the fascists not as created but as the most natural, the most spontaneous, of experiences" (151). See also Mary Jean Green, "Fascists on Film: The Brasillach and Bardèche *Histoire du cinéma*," in Richard J. Golsan, ed., *Fascism, Aesthetics, and Culture* (Hanover, N.H.: University Press of New England, 1992). The importance of film as a model for political experience is undeniable. But the French literary fascists in general not only acknowledged but praised the aesthetic, "creative" side of fascism, for it was this "creativity" that was considered the most natural side of man and the highest form of politics In any case, the debt of fascism to film, art, and literature is often overtly proclaimed by them all.

13. The prosecutor at his trial gave great importance to statements such as this, as have almost all commentators of Brasillach's work and life, from Sartre on. See Chapter 6 for an analysis of Jean-Paul Sartre's claim that such statements

represent the proof that collaboration was a profoundly unmanly, un-French, homosexual act—in "Qu'est-ce qu'un collaborateur?" in *Situations* III (Paris: Gallimard, 1976; originally published in 1945).

Chapter Five
The Fascist Imagined Community: The Myths of Europe and Totalitarian Man in Drieu la Rochelle

1. See also Ernest Gellner, *Nations and Nationalism* (New York: Oxford University Press, 1983), and E. J. Hobsbawm, *Nations and Nationalism Since 1780: Programme, Myth, Reality* (New York: Cambridge University Press, 1990). Gellner argues that the idea that the nation is a fact of nature or a historically inevitable destiny is mythical: "Nations as a natural, God-given way of classifying men, as an inherent . . . political destiny, are a myth; nationalism, which sometimes takes pre-exisiting cultures and turns them into nations, sometimes invents them, and often obliterates pre-exisiting cultures: *that* is a reality" (48–49). Hobsbawm also stresses what he calls "the element of artefact, invention and social engineering which enters into the making of nations" (10), in his study of the problem, but he tends to see Anderson's notion of the nation as an "imagined community" as something that fills "the emotional void left by the retreat or disintegration, or the unavailability of *real* human communities and networks" (46), which is to limit seriously the impact of imagination and myth by rooting them in the space once occupied by the genuine and the real. For a more nuanced approach to the problem, see Etienne Balibar, "Racism and Nationalism" and "The Nation Form," in Etienne Balibar and Immanuel Wallerstein, *Race, Nation, Class: Ambiguous Identities* (New York: Verso, 1991).

2. See Paul Valéry, "L'Idée de dictature"—originally published in 1934—in *Regards sur le monde actuel* (Paris: Gallimard, 1945). Valéry relates this dictatorial aspect of the spirit to the aesthetic faculty, one which in pursuing an "ideal" of order or justice reduces men to the status of figures appropriate for being combined together and "makes of human society a sort of work in which it recognizes itself. There is something of the artist in the dictator and something aesthetic in his conceptions. He must fashion and work his human material and make it appropriate for his designs. . . . In this way, the (political) spirit . . . achieves under a dictatorial regime the plenitude of its development" (99–100).

3. The collection of essays that Drieu la Rochelle published in 1934 to announce his conversion to fascism is entitled precisely *Socialisme fasciste* (Paris: Gallimard, 1934). Robert Soucy, in *Fascist Intellectual: Drieu la Rochelle* (Berkeley: University of California Press, 1979), argues that Drieu la Rochelle's " 'socialism' was more rhetorical than real, an antiestablishmentarianism which masked a basic economic traditionalism" (117). "It was a strange kind of socialism, . . . if it was a socialism at all, denouncing Marxism as decadent and related only tangentially to past French utopian socialisms. . . . Drieu's socialism stemmed from his revolt against bourgeois materialism and hedonism, not from compassion for the hardships of the working classes or a desire to improve their economic well-being: he was essentially interested in 'spiritual' regeneration" (115).

4. In *Mesure de la France*, Drieu la Rochelle argues that war became modern and thus inhuman with the invention of gunpowder: "Modern war was already at the time of Napoleon and even before, really since the use of gunpowder, which was the first serious attack carried out by industrial practices on the fundamental institutions of humanity, a simple machine to destroy the most robust bodies, . . . the systematic carnage of generations of males" (128). World War I simply realized the full potential of modern war for carnage; it did not invent it.

5. For Drieu la Rochelle, the literary compromise of the Surrealists, in their attempt to "discredit fixed literary form," consisted in their faith in and commitment to words as ends in themselves, and he considered what he called their attempts at "automatic writing" and other experiments to "drown words in words, . . . to wash them of all their tired and dried up significations" (78), a failure. "In abandoning yourselves to the race of your pen, you give yourselves over to the worst literature, that which is made of, which rots of memory. . . . If there is a bourgeois decadence, you are the most decadent of bourgeois writers" (78–79).

6. Drieu la Rochelle polemically linked Marxists and nationalists together by claiming they grew out of the same source: "Nationalists are certainly of their century, that is, the last century. Their sect in the nineteenth century grew out of the same source as that of Marxists. There is a definite kinship, within limits, between men such as Marx and Taine, who both descend from Hegel, whose teaching they corrupted. And the grandsons are cousins in spite of the dissimilarity of the transplants: Maurras and Mussolini, on one side, Lenin, on the other" (*Genève ou Moscou*, 163).

7. Drieu la Rochelle claims that no book more than Barrès's *Un homme libre* represents not just the narrowness but also the attractiveness of nationalism for a previous era: "It's a manual of exclusiveness which is locked up in its own logic; it's a secret poem, with an incredible attractiveness. This book was superb for twenty years; it's a book we should burn today" (*Genève ou Moscou*, 172). He also calls Barrès's writing "pure poison," and his political actions to restore France to itself, "the gestures of an embalmer of death more than of a doctor who wants to help revive life" (173–74).

8. The student claims in fact that nationalist myths are nothing more than "G-strings" covering over both the absence of natural or historical determining factors and the violence and power of the state: "The principle of France and the principle of Germany are the same: the reason of State. Except vital principles are always covered by a G-string that is an image. Here, natural limits or mutual consent (with kicks in the ass), there blood and language (with kicks in the ass)" (193).

9. Drieu la Rochelle also argues that compared to the violence and the number of people killed as part of France's own history and struggle to determine its national borders, Nazi Germany had done very little, and the way to ensure that Hitler would not imitate his French predecessors was simply not to oppose his actions: "The French could also recall that to establish these limits [their national boundaries], they turned Europe upside down under Louis XIV, the Convention, and Napoleon, who together killed millions of men. Hitler is still far from having

assassinated as many as any of these monsters. We could perhaps save him the trouble of a deplorable imitation of them" (198).

10. Drieu la Rochelle wrote in his journal during the battle for France that he was a prophet of history and that he could therefore clearly see that history was on the side of the Germans: "I am not a Germanophile, I am a prophet and philosopher of history. I see the present role that fatality and fortune and the laws of human nature have given to the Germans" (*Journal 1939–1945* [Paris: Gallimard, 1992], [May 29, 1940], 225). After the defeat, he immediately became disillusioned with the Vichy government and saw it as too conservative and not forceful enough. Vichy was "a rough compromise between democracy and fascism. They grossly imitate fascism without taking from it its virtues and assuming almost all of its inconveniences. An authoritarianism without authority, an autocratism without autocrats, without manly impetus" (*Journal* [July 13, 1940], 266).

11. Drieu la Rochelle admits in *Récit secret* (Paris: Gallimard, 1951) that he held Hitler responsible for the destruction of fascist Europe: "I restrained myself from indicating too overtly in my own writings all the scorn that I felt for Hitler who was losing Europe just as much as his enemies" (29). In his journal, he frequently blames the Germans and Hitler himself for not living up to fascist ideals: "The Germans are not at all revolutionary and have been completely left behind by events. Hitler no longer does anything but make war; he no longer has any political plans for Europe. I have known this for a year and a half" (*Journal* [March 5, 1943], 335). As early as April 22, 1942, he asserts that he "no longer believes in collaboration" (*Journal*, 294).

12. Much of the latter part of Drieu la Rochelle's novel, *Les Chiens de Paille* (Paris: Gallimard, 1964; first published in 1944), consists of a justification for the actions of the principal character of the novel, Constant, who is described as a heroic traitor. The model evoked in the novel for his apocalyptic vision and of the *literary-religous* traitor is, as in Drieu la Rochelle's political essays, Isaiah. But the figure of Judas also haunts and tempts Constant as the biblical model for the *political* traitor. Judas is presented as a necessary force in the dialectic of history and spirituality, and if he brings death, destruction, and eternal condemnation on himself, it is with the possibility of salvation for humanity: "Now, betrayal is a job of the greatest utility in the human comedy. It is the gear system that allows all of the wheels to contribute to the same movement. Traitor, traditor, translator, transmitter. . . . Judas is an indispensable, necessary character. Without Judas, the universe does not stir, without Judas, God neither leaves nor returns to himself. Without Judas, no opening, no window. . . . One can acknowledge that Judas did more than any other man for the salvation of humanity because he accepted not only transitory torture but also eternal torture" (115–17).

13. Drieu la Rochelle describes a meeting with his friend Malraux in Paris before Malraux had joined the Resistance: "Saw Malraux in Paris. He no longer believes in anything, denies the Russian force, and thinks that the world has no meaning and is heading toward the most sordid solution, the American solution. But that's because he himself has renounced being anything but a literary hack [*littérateur*]. Will he be great enough in this order to justify himself? But literature

can no longer justify anyone. Advises me to do as he does. Sure" (*Journal* [May 8, 1943], 345).

14. For a presentation and analysis of Drieu la Rochelle's suicidal tendencies, see once again Robert Soucy's *Fascist Intellectual* and perhaps the most serious and complete biography of Drieu la Rochelle, Pierre Andreu and Frédéric Glover's *Drieu la Rochelle* (Paris: Hachette, 1979).

15. For example, see Etiemble, "L'Ecrivain et la collaboration," in *Hygiène des lettres, II: Littérature dégagée* (Paris: Gallimard, 1967), who argues that "Drieu, however, was not vile: his death saves him and allows us if not to absolve him completely (for there are his quasi-denunciations of Emmanuel and Aragon), at least to judge him less severely" (192).

Chapter Six
Literary Fascism and the Problem of Gender: The Aesthetics
of the Body in Drieu la Rochelle

1. Republished in Jean-Paul Sartre, *Situations, III* (Paris: Gallimard, 1976). See Denis Hollier, *Politique de la prose* (Paris: Gallimard, 1982), for an analysis of Sartre's version of literary-nationalism and his criticism of writers who are "outsiders."

2. Sartre is just one of many examples of the characterization of French fascists as being predominantly homosexual. In his long interview with Patrick Modiano, Emmanuel Berl, for example, explains the attraction of fascism in the 1930s to a number of French intellectuals in the following way: "It didn't represent anything serious in public opinion, it was limited to small circles, to little cells. . . . They had an idea of the 'leader,' of a guy who could represent France without everyone laughing at him. . . . In this fascination with the leader and with force, there was also much latent femininity, a certain form of homosexuality. At bottom, in most of these fascist intellectuals—I'm thinking of Brasillach, Abel Bonnard, Laubreaux, and Bucard—there was the unconscious desire to get buggered by the S.S. They were not at all models of Aryan beauty, you know, these fascist intellectuals. . . . I always thought that these fascist intellectuals did not have the physique of their ideas. They wouldn't have lasted one minute in a ring with the Jewish boxer Max Baer" (*Interrogatoire* [Paris: Gallimard, 1976], 73–74).

3. Volume 1, *Women, Floods, Bodies, History*, trans. by Stephen Conway (Minneapolis: University of Minnesota Press, 1987); Volume 2, *Male Bodies: Psychoanalyzing the White Terror*, trans. Erica Carter and Chris Turner (Minneapolis: University of Minnesota Press, 1989).

4. Theweleit acknowledges a great debt to Gilles Deleuze and Félix Guattari's *L'Anti-Oedipe: Capitalisme et Schizophrénie* (Paris: Editions de Minuit, 1972), and the debt is certainly evident in his frequent use of terms such as "desiring-machines" and "deterritorialization." But because of the very particular and limited application of their critical apparatus to fascism, I would claim that Theweleit owes much more to Reich and even to Marcuse than to them.

5. Theweleit's post-Reichian, post-Marcusian utopia of desire is one in which through a certain type of orgasm—here, too, there is a norm—all traces of fascism are destroyed and even gender differences are undone through a "pleasurable

commingling" determined by what in the entire work is related to the unbounded, flowing traits of feminine desire and sexuality: "If human beings were to begin to achieve release through orgasms in which they experienced the other, the diverse and the different as equal, they might well become non-fascists. (Anti-fascism is no more than a political position that can be taken up at will; it has little signification for the defascizing of our lives.)" (v. 2, 104).

6. Kaplan's view of Theweleit is, however, more positive than my own. See her essay, "Theweleit and Spiegelman: Of Men and Mice," in *Remaking History*, ed. Barbara Kruger and Phil Mariani (Seattle: Bay Press, 1989). For a feminist analysis of the implications of the instability of the notion of "female" (and thus also of "male"), see Judith Butler, *Gender Trouble: Feminism and the Subversion of Identity* (New York: Routledge, 1990).

7. For example, in "PPF, Parti du corps vivant" (August 1937), he claims that Doriot's party was intent on restoring the health of the nation: It is "the political movement that goes the most openly, the most radically in the direction of the great revolution of behavior, in the restoration of the body—health, dignity, plenitude, heroism" (*Chronique politique 1934–1942* [Paris: Gallimard, 1943], 50). He also argues that "Doriot will create a France in which the thousands of young couples who each season rush off to the primordial pleasures of skiing, kayaking, camping, and swimming will be at ease. With him, the France of camping will defeat the France of cocktails and congresses" (55). In fact, he presents Doriot as nothing less than "our champion against death" (58).

8. Like the narrator of *La Comédie de Charleroi*, Drieu la Rochelle went off to fight in World War I with a copy of *Thus Spoke Zarathustra* in his pocket, and even though he admits that he never had a "philosophical mind" and that his readings of Nietzsche, therefore, were anything but analytical or philosophically rigorous, Drieu la Rochelle acknowledges that "it was toward this life [Nietzsche's], toward this work, toward this name that [his] intellectual sensibility had always gravitated" ("Encore et toujours Nietzsche," *Je suis partout* [March 3, 1939]; reprinted in *Sur les Ecrivains*, 92). And the Nietzsche that especially interested him was the one who revealed a mysticism at the heart of Greek genius that was equal to its rationalism, the Dionysus who was always beside Apollo (93).

9. See Alice Kaplan's discussion of what she calls "abortion anxiety" in Drieu la Rochelle (*Reproductions of Banality*, 101–7).

10. This novel was originally published in a censored version in 1939 and then republished during the Occupation in 1942, with the censored parts restored and with a new preface by the author. All quotations from the novel and the preface are from the reedition of the 1942 edition in Gallimard's Folio Collection (Paris: Gallimard, 1988). In his preface to the 1942 edition of the novel, Drieu la Rochelle presents the novel predominantly in terms of its decadence: "[Decadence] alone explains the terrible insufficiency which is the foundation of this work. This novel appears insufficient because it treats the terrible French insufficiency and treats it honestly, without looking for equivocations or alibis. In order to show insufficiency, the artist must limit himself to being insufficient" (16).

11. See Susan R. Suleiman, "Ideological Dissent from Works of Fiction: Toward a Rhetoric of the *roman à thèse*"(*Neophilogus*, no. 60 [1976], 170–73), and Alice Kaplan, *Reproductions of Banality* (99–100) for an analysis of the ideo-

NOTES TO CHAPTER SEVEN

logical function of the most negative of the female characters presented in the novel.

12. In the novel, only one of Gilles's lovers, Pauline, becomes pregnant, and he awaits the birth with great pride and high expectations. But to save the life of Pauline, when a cancer is discovered, the baby is sacrificed: "The operation was a success. The doctors took out along with the child, this full promise of life, an enormous embryo of death. But death had not been uprooted. Cases of cancer in thirty-year-olds are rare and thus mortal" (567). And Pauline's death is tied explicitly to the unproductive future of France: "France was dying while Pauline was dying" (603).

13. These essays were collected near the end of the war in *Le Français d'Europe* (Paris: Editions Balzac, 1944), and the page numbers given here refer to this edition.

Chapter Seven
Literary Anti-Semitism: The Poetics of Race in Drumont and Céline

1. *The History of Anti-Semitism*, v. 4, "Suicidal Europe: 1870–1933," trans. George Klim (New York: Vanguard Press, 1985), 31.

2. Even the most formally "innovative" of anti-Semites, Céline, has been rightly accused of plagiarism. One of the early negative reviews of Céline's first "pamphlet," *Bagatelles pour un massacre*, was that of Emmanuel Mounier, founder and director of the spiritualist Catholic journal, *Esprit*, who claimed that the intention of the book was to "incite people to murder" (*Esprit*, no. 66 [March 1938]; republished in *Cahier de l'Herne: Céline* [Paris: Livre de Poche, 1988], 291). Mounier then went on to dismiss Céline's supposed erudition and to accuse him of plagiarizing other anti-Semitic books and brochures. Mounier proved his point by placing in facing columns passages from *Bagatelles* and almost identical passages from the two brochures in question. Alice Yaeger Kaplan, in *Relevé des sources et citations dans Bagatelles pour un massacre* (Tusson: Du Lérot, 1987), does an outstanding job tracking down the various sources for both the acknowledged and the unacknowledged quotations in Céline's first anti-Semitic pamphlet.

3. See Bernanos's homage to Drumont in *La Grande peur des bien-pensants* (1931); in *Essais et écrits de combat I* [Paris: Bibliothèque de la Pléiade, 1971]). In his introduction, Bernanos raises the question that he feels readers might ask of his essay: "'What does he want to do with this Drumont?' you ask. Well, I want to honor him, that's all" (45). "I will have completed my task, served in accordance with my forces my old, dead master, if I am able to transmit to some young people of my race the lesson in heroism I received long ago [from Drumont] when I was only a young boy" (56). After the war, in a letter (dated September 2, 1947) sent from Denmark to an American professor of literature, Milton Hindus, and in which Céline is trying to downplay the importance of the anti-Semitism of his previous works, Céline denies having read Drumont, but his characterization of Gobineau is enough to put into doubt his comments on Drumont as well: "I never read Drumont either—only Gobineau in this area, and he is a philo-Semite" (in *Cahier de l'Herne: Céline*, 414). In *L'Ecole des Cadavres*, Céline in fact claims

that "all Aryans ought to have read Drumont" (35), implying, of course, that he himself had done so.

4. Michel Winock describes *La France juive* in the following way: "[Drumont's] work constitutes, we wouldn't dare say the first synthesis in the French language—pasting together would be more exact—of modern anti-Semitism, bringing together the anti-Judaic heritage of the Christian tradition, the Judeophobic anticapitalism of popular and socialist levels of society, and finally the racist theses of the new anthropological science. Because Drumont picked up on—regardless of the contradictions!—everything that could stimulate his obsession" (*Nationalisme, antisémitisme et fascisme en France*, 80–81). Later in the book, Winock argues that Drumont makes of the different forms of anti-Semitism "a *totality* which has an answer for *everything* [un *tout* qui a réponse à *tout*]" (132).

5. According to Léon Poliakov, this text was "the best-seller of the latter half of the nineteenth century: 114 editions in one year, not counting a short popular version and several 'sequels'" (*The History of Anti-Semitism*, v. 4, 40). Michel Winock reports that in 1887, just over a year after it had been published, *La France juive* was in its 145th edition. He estimates conservatively that this means that around 150,000 copies had been sold in a year. A condensed, one-volume edition was published in 1890, and this went through ten editions. In 1914, the complete work reached its 200th edition, with the last edition coming out in 1941 (*Nationalisme, antisémitisme et fascisme en France*, 118–19).

6. Because one of the most visible traits of Céline's style is his use of ellipses, in order not to confuse matters I have put between brackets—[. . . .]—the ellipses that I have added to the quotations to indicate where I have omitted something from the text. All other ellipses are Céline's own.

7. See for example, André Gide's review article of *Bagatelles pour un massacre*, "Les Juifs, Céline et Maritain," originally published in the *Nouvelle Revue Française* (April 1, 1938), in which he criticized all of those who responded negatively to the ravings of the text for having themselves "raved" and missed the point: that it was all just a "joke," that "[Céline] does everything he can to make us not take him seriously. . . . Céline excels in invective. He latches on to whatever he finds. Jewry is here only a pretext that he chose, the dullest imaginable, the most trivial, the most accepted, the one which cares the least about nuances, which allows the most summary judgments, the most enormous exaggerations, and has the least concern about fairness, allowing the most intemperate carelessness of the pen. And Céline is never better than when he is the least measured. He's a creator. He speaks of the Jews in *Bagatelles* in the same way that in *Mort à crédit* he spoke of the maggots his evocative force had just created" (*Cahier de l'Herne: Céline*, 296). Gide thus defends and explains away Céline's anti-Semitism in the name of his creativeness, what he calls his creation of "pitiful jokes without importance, as we hope he will continue to do in the books that will follow. . . . And Ferdinand continues to get angry to the point of the most stunning lyricism; his complaints and his harangue spill out for the greatest amusement of his readers" (298).

8. See "D'une identité à l'autre" in *Polylogue* (Paris: Seuil, 1977) and the last hundred pages of *Pouvoirs de l'horreur* (Paris: Seuil, 1980), which are devoted to

Céline. All references will be to the English translations of these texts: "From One Identity to An Other," which is found in *Desire in Language: A Semiotic Approach to Literature and Art*, ed. Leon S. Roudiez (New York: Columbia University Press, 1980); and *Powers of Horror: An Essay on Abjection*, trans. Leon S. Roudiez (New York: Columbia University Press, 1982).

9. Philippe Muray, in his *Céline* (Paris: Seuil, 1981), argues along similar lines that the scandal of the pamphlets is profoundly literary in nature, first of all because the "revolutionary writing" of the pamphlets and that of the novels is basically the same: "If [Céline's] racist books created a scandal, it is not so much because they were racist—others held the same opinions and got away with it—but more because they placed a writing considered 'revolutionary' in the service of racist hatred without their being the slightest noteworthy modification of that writing. . . . The pamphlets perfectly exploited the surplus value of the writing of the novels without any break being discernable on the level of this writing" (105). Muray is especially critical of approaches that focus exclusively on either the poetic or the political level of Céline's texts at the expense of the other level, thus denying the way one level intesects with and is dependent on the other: "The Célinian scandal is above all of a literary kind. . . . Everything in him is mixed together. Anyone who would approach his work to analyze or celebrate exclusively his writing, would see the anti-Semitic beast who lies dormant there spring up. Anyone, on the contrary, who would impose on his work a strictly political treatment, would never finish struggling against a technique of language which never stops disintegrating or recomposing the meanings with which it continuously intersects" (12–13).

10. Kristeva describes the abject near the beginning of her study as "a massive and sudden emergence of a foreignness which, as familiar as it might have been to me in an opaque and forgotten life, now harries me as something separate, loathsome. Not me. Not that. But not nothing, either. A 'something' that I do not recognize as a thing. A mass of non-sense that is anything but insignificant and that crushes me. At the border of nonexistence and hallucination, of a reality that, if I acknowledge it, annihilates me. There, the abject and abjection are my safeguards. The beginnings of my culture" (*Powers of Horror*, 2; trans. modified).

11. Henri Godard's *Poétique de Céline* (Paris: Gallimard, 1985), on the contrary, defends the pleasure he claims Céline's texts produce in the reader who is able to read Céline's "liberating writing" *as writing*, not ideology. "If one of the functions of literature is certainly to make us take pleasure in our language [*jouir de notre langue*], it is first of all on this account that Céline deserves the place that has henceforth been given him" (30). Godard also claims that all of Céline's most racist and essentialist propositions, even "in their most aggressive form, if they do not become the only subject of discourse, . . . are in a sense defused by the writing that conveys them" (207). What he calls the liberating characteristics of Céline's writing constitute such a fundamental poetic "truth" that even when Céline's formulates his most "negative convictions concerning freedom," he does it in such a way that "everything invites us to define it as a writing of freedom" (207). Here poetics clearly has "defused" and neutralized everything else and made of the most extreme, dogmatic expression of unfreedom the most accomplished poetic practice of freedom.

12. In a similar mode, Philipe Muray, in spite of what he initially claims is the fundamental interconnection of writing and politics in all of Céline's work, ends up trying to save literature and writing on their deepest level from ideological contamination. He claims, for example, that "the pamphlets are written *only in appearance*, that they are books only in appearance" (*Céline*, 128), even if the distinction between novels and pamphlets, he also argues, is not absolute or systematically sustainable. It is, however, still "the bad literature of Céline [that] is anti-Semitic," not the good (148). Ultimately, even if he admits that "if there were not two Célines, it was because the Céline of the pamphlets was located inside the other, like the malady of the body inside the soul," Muray still sees Céline's novels as constituting his self-cure from the malady of anti-Semitism: "Slowly, book after book, Céline cures himself by means of his books of his own malady which consisted in wanting to cure otherwise than by disappearing into his books. It's a totally literary tragedy" (229).

13. Philippe Lacoue-Labarthe summarizes the portrait of the Jews given by the Nazi racist ideologue, Alfred Rosenberg, which Céline in his own style repeats and dramatizes: "[The Jews] are a formless, unaesthetic 'people,' which by definition cannot enter into the process of self-fictioning and constitute a subject, or, in other words, a being-propre (*être-propre*). It is this unassignable (and formidable) im-properness of the Jews which makes them, says Rosenberg once again, not the direct opposite (a counter-type) of the Teuton, but his contradiction—the very absence of type. Hence their power . . . to insert themselves into every culture and State and then to live a life that is parasitic upon these, constantly threatening them with bastardization. All in all, the Jews are infinitely mimetic beings, or, in other words, the site of an *endless mimesis*, which is both interminable and inorganic, producing no art and achieving no appropriation. They are destabilization itself" (*Heidegger, Art and Politics*, 96).

14. In Céline's racist mythology, the Jew was a Negro or a mixture of races: "The Jew is a Negro, the Semite race doesn't exist, it's an invention of Freemasons, the Jew is the product of the crosssing of Negroes and Asiatic barbarians" (*Bagatelles*, 191–92). The fact that the "Semite race" did not exist never kept him from referring to the Jews as a race, or from representing them in various forms as *the enemy race*.

15. In a letter to Milton Hindus (June 14, 1947), Céline claimed that "anti-Semitism is no longer possible, conceivable— Anti-Semitism died in a very simple, dare I say, physical way" (*Cahier de l'Herne: Céline*, 395). But he went on to add that racism, on the contrary, was not dead, but just for the moment dormant, and he claimed it would undoubtedly be revived—to show how little dead his own anti-Semitism was—this time by Jews: "It is time to put an end to anti-Semitism on principle and for reasons of fundamental idiocy, anti-Semitism doesn't mean anything—we shall undoubtedly return to racism, but later and with the Jews— and undoubtedly under the leadership of the Jews" (396).

16. Even as knowledgeable a reader as Alice Kaplan, who certainly has no interest in mitigating the seriousness of Céline's anti-Semitism and the ideological implications of his work, claims that "the biggest problem in writing about any of the critically recognized Céline's is figuring out what technical languages to call upon and which passages to call up in support. If you quote an anti-Semitic pas-

sage, chances are you can find another sentence in the same paragraph or chapter, or certainly in the next book, that will contradict it" (*Reproductions of Banality*, 107). Kaplan's examples of contradiction all have to do with the extension of the accusation of "Jewification" to almost everyone and everything, a radical, total generalization of the figure of the Jew and thus of mimeticism into every realm. As she argues, in the realm of literature, for example, everyone from the most cerebral writers to the surrealists are accused of being "Jewified": "Céline asserts that Jews pervert direct emotion. This seems near enough to the standard racist attack on Jews as hard-hearted, rootless intellectuals. But as one reads on, Jews become indistinguishable from the surrealists, and even from the Soviets. In the course of the text's long lists, everyone becomes 'jewified' until the identification of Jews is impossible" (107).

17. In an interesting recent essay on Céline, "Style, Subversion, Modernity: Louis-Ferdinand Céline's Anti-Semitic Pamphlets," Rosemarie Scullion, like Kaplan, argues that the generalization of the signifier "Jew" represents a contradiction in Céline's strategy and weakens the force of his argument: "[Céline's] pronouncements in the pamphlets often overtly contradict themselves and are so ludicrously totalizing that they defy reason altogether, rendering it impossible to gauge precisely or definitively stabilize the author's political identity" (in *Fascism, Aesthetics, and Culture*, ed. Richard Golsan [Hanover, N.H.: University Press of New England, 1992], 181). In a note, Scullion also claims that, as the "dizzying inventory of the individuals, organizations, political and artistic movements Céline labels Jewish in *Bagatelles* clearly illustrates, the author scatters the identity to such an extent that the signifier *juif* is divested of much of its signifying potential" (269, n. 12). I am arguing that in fact the opposite is true: that the signifying potential of the Jew is maximized not scattered through such totalization; it is maximized by being scattered.

18. In *Entretiens avec le Professeur Y* (1955), the character who speaks for Céline responds to a question about foreign languages in a way that recalls Céline's diatribes against the "Jewification" of the French language in *Bagatelles*: "There is only one language, . . . one valid language! one acceptable language! the imperial language of this world: our own! . . . the others are gibberish, you understand? . . . dialects that came too late! . . . badly put together, badly polished, buffooneries, raucous or mewing cries for gaudy foreigners!" (107). In Céline's novel *Féerie pour une autre fois* (Paris: Folio, 1952), which relates the last days of the Occupation and his own detention in Denmark, the doctor who is the main character of the novel claims that "a torturer who would speak French to me, I would forgive him for almost everything . . . so much I hate foreign languages! it's not believable that such gibberish exists! what frauds!" (83).

Chapter Eight
The Art of Anti-Semitic Rage: Lucien Rebatet's Aesthetics of Violence

1. Lucien Rebatet, *Les Décombres* (Paris: Denoël, 1942). A revised version of this text was published in 1976 as *Les Mémoires d'un Fasciste I: Les Décombres, 1938–1940* (Paris: Payot, 1976). References to the original 1942 edition will be indicated in the text. The editor of the new edition, Jean-Jacques Pauvert, claims

that even with a shortage of paper, the original edition sold over 100,000 copies. As Pauvert admits in his preface to the reedition, Rebatet cut almost eight pages from the first 536 pages of the original edition and then the entire last section of the book (pages 537–664). The effect of the various changes was to clean up the original version and make it somewhat less violent and less anti-Semitic. For example, when in the 1942 version Rebatet wrote "a little wandering kike [un petit youtre errant]" (105), he changed it in the 1976 edition to "a little wandering Jew" (113). Alice Kaplan is right to criticize Pauvert for not republishing the original text and for letting Rebatet purge the text of its worst references, especially given that Pauvert defends his republication of it in the name of the memory of past injustices that would prevent the reappearance of fascism in the future. Kaplan correctly argues that "by editing—by refusing to publish what is most referentially damning—[Pauvert] is abetting forgetfulness" (*Reproductions of Banality: Fascism, Literature, and French Intellectual Life* [Minneapolis: University of Minnesota Press, 1986], 140, n. 1). Pauvert is is also abetting a form of revisionism that would argue that the anti-Semitism of French literary fascists has been greatly exaggerated.

2. It is now available again, because Gallimard reissued it in 1991. Its few admirers, however, do constitute a strange and heterogeneous group. For example, Maurice Bardèche, close friend and brother-in-law of Robert Brasillach, fascist and revisionist, in an interview conducted by Alice Kaplan in 1982, expressed the opinion that Rebatet rather than Céline was the greater writer: "I'm not at all fascinated by Céline. . . . Rebatet, he's more interesting than Céline. Except that Rebatet was killed as a writer by those politics. Rebatet first spent five years in prison during which time he wrote *Les Deux étendards*, a magnificent novel. Then he left prison but no one wanted anything to do with him. . . . He was an extraordinary man, by his culture, the accuracy of his judgment, his verve, his talent; admirably learned about both painting and music" (*Reproductions of Banality*, 179). Another admirer, Etiemble, had the opposite political convictions, and his highly favorable review of *Les Deux étendards*, "A Propos de Lucien Rebatet," in *La Nouvelle Revue Française* (March 1953), provoked Sartre to remove him from the editorial committee of *Les Temps Modernes*. In the review, after condemning the "stupidities" of Rebatet in *Les Décombres*, Etiemble asks: "This Nazi, this bastard, how not to admire the writer that he has become?" (reprinted in Etiemble, *Hygiène des lettres, II: Littérature dégagée* [Paris: Gallimard, 1967], 204). He ends his review by comparing Michel, the main character of the novel, to Stendhal's Lucien Leuwen: "Michel is you, he's me. Michel, he's our youth—he's also Rebatet! He's really Lucien Leuwen" (210). In the same collection of essays, see his attack on Sartre for denouncing his review and excluding him from *Les Temps Modernes*: "Lettre ouverte à Jean-Paul Sartre sur l'unité de mauvaise action" (142–57). Another surprising admirer of Rebatet is George Steiner, who ends "Cry Havoc," an essay largely devoted to Céline, by praising *Les Deux étendards* as a "greater work than any of Céline's, with the possible exception of *Journey*, and one of the masterpieces of modern literature. . . . Unlike Céline's fiction, Rebatet's novel has the impersonal authority, the sheer formal beauty of classical art" (in *Extra-Territorial: Papers on Literature and the Language of Revolution* [New York: Atheneum, 1971], 45). Steiner considers it

a "mystery" in the theological sense of the term that "a profoundly generous imagination, a grasp of the sanctity of individual life . . . [can] coexist with Fascist doctrines and aims of murderous action openly avowed" (46). It is to unraveling the logic of this "mystery," as well as the political role in literary fascism and anti-Semitism of the ideal of "the formal beauty of classical art," that the present chapter and this book as a whole are devoted.

3. He claimed, of course, that the Jews were responsibile for the fact that he and his colleagues had become more aggressive anti-Semites: "My best journalist friends and myself have been treated as mortal enemies by the Jews, who were right to do so. In our group, we once had a traditional mistrust concerning the Jews: nothing destined us to an aggressive anti-Semitism. The Jews, by their works and their proliferation, were the essential artisans of it" (*Les Décombres*, 25).

4. Alice Kaplan links the scenes of collective readings at *Je suis partout* to the fact that Rebatet worked briefly for the Vichy Journal de la Radio in 1940, and, with Rebatet as her pretext, she analyzes the relation of "radio talk" and radio technology to fascist discourse in general and suggests how radio "created a need for what it could satisfy—in this case, amplified, telephonic invective. . . . It fostered a notion of the nation as a group of like speakers. . . . Radio is an available interpretive instrument for xenophobic diatribe, for the protection of one imaginary tribe against another" (*Reproductions of Banality*, 133).

5. Rebatet's other experience with the radio occured in Sigmaringen, Germany, after having fled France with the retreating German army, when he was asked by Jean-Hérold Paquis to work for Radio Patrie, a tool of the Nazis that broadcast into France the news that the French were suffering under the "American occupation" and would soon be liberated again by the Germans. Radio, in this case, once again did not seem to him an appropriate technology for disseminating the true voice of fascism (or his voice), but rather because of what he called the political charade it was being used for, left him (and fascism) without a voice: "The military chronicle, the speciality of Paquis, alas, left me speechless [literally, without a voice]. It was to reedit the grotesque aspects of the old journalist-generals of 1940 who declared that the German armored divisions had made cavalry charges without any strategic importance and that Hitler, being eight days late on his calender, had lost the battle. . . . I preferred working in a factory to participating in this lamentable parody" (*Mémoires d'un fasciste, II: 1941–1947* [Paris: Pauvert, 1976], 214).

6. Nancy describes this scene, which he calls the scene of myth, in the following way: "We know the scene: there are men assembled together, and someone tells them a story. These assembled men, it isn't yet certain if they constitute an assembly, if they are a horde or a tribe. But we call them 'brothers,' because they are assembled together, and because they listen to the same story. . . . They were not assembled before the story, it's the recitation that assembles them" ("Le Mythe interrompu," in *La Communauté désoeuvrée* [Paris: Christian Bourgois, 1986], 109). Nancy goes on to argue that "there is a co-implication of the thought of myth, of the mythical scenography, and of the production and staging of a 'Volk' and a 'Reich' in the sense that Nazism gave to these terms. . . . In this sense, we have nothing more to do with myth" (117).

7. In *Les Décombres*, Rebatet described how he and others at *Je suis partout* made light of the accusation that they were all "Hitlerites": "Self-righteous people began to speak on the sly of our Hitlerism, which was for us a superb subject for farces. Wagnerian, Nietzschean, anti-Semitic, anti-clerical, knowing in detail the National-Socialist folklore, I was naturally chosen in our group to play the role of the crack S.A. man. I fulfilled my function with resounding *Horst Wessel Lied*'s and 'Heil's'" (64).

8. Rebatet published an anti-Semitic pamphlet during the Occupation, *Les Tribus du cinéma et du théâtre* (Paris: Nouvelles Editions Françaises, 1942), which elaborates at great length on this theme, using the cinema as the best example of how an art can supposedly be exploited and ruined if taken over by Jewish interests. Hollywood, of course, was the name that stood for all such "Jewish exploitation."

9. In *Les Mémoires d'un fasciste, II*, Rebatet admitted that as the situation of the German army deteriorated, the more vigorously *Je suis partout* supported the Nazi cause: "At *Je suis partout* we hid our powerlessness by means of a disoriented agitation" (174).

Chapter Nine
A Literary Fascism beyond Fascism: Thierry Maulnier and the Ideology of Culture

1. *Au-delà du nationalisme* (Paris: Gallimard, 1938).

2. The one important exception to the general picture I have just drawn, however, is Zeev Sternhell, who considers Maulnier to be not just one French fascist among many others but rather, along with Marcel Déat and the Belgian Henri De Man, to be one of the most representative and important fascist theorists of the period. In the last chapter of *Neither Right nor Left* (213–65), which is called "Spiritualistic Fascism" and largely devoted to Maulnier, Sternhell treats Maulnier's antimaterialist, antidemocratic and anti-Marxist political position as one of the purest, intellectual forms of fascism.

3. See Jacques Derrida, *De l'Esprit: Heidegger et la question* (Paris: Galilée, 1987), for an analysis of the contradictory sense of the concept of spirit (*Geist*) in the work of Heidegger, as well as in the humanist tradition that is so often evoked to criticize or condemn Heidegger's work. See especially Derrida's analysis of Heidegger's Rectoral Address (54–73), in which he shows how Heidegger's spiritualization of National Socialism is both the sign of his commitment to it in the form of an attempt to "save it" and at the same time an apparent break with Nazi ideology, for such a "discourse *seems* no longer simply to belong to the 'ideological' camp in which obscure forces are appealed to, forces that would not be spiritual but natural, biological, racial" (64–65). Derrida argues that the break with biologism and racism is limited and only apparent, however, because it takes the form of an *opposition* to them that is ultimately rooted in the same "metaphysics of the subject." For Derrida, the Rectoral Address "capitalizes the worst, that is, two evils at the same time: the approval given to Nazism and the procedure that is still metaphysical" (66). Maulnier's even more overtly spiritualistic approach to fascism is caught in the same contradictions.

4. This contrasts with Brasillach's study of the life and work of another neo-classical dramatist, *Pierre Corneille* (Paris: Librairie Arthème Fayard, 1938), in which Brasillach describes what he calls "the fascism of Pierre Corneille" in the following terms: "A nationalism pushed to the point of the most vibrant sense of identity, the incarnation of authority in a dominating and absolute figure, and preferably a royal dictatorship, the opposition to liberal ideas, parliamentary government, to the old generations that never understood anything, the hope in youth and in the future, the construction of that future through faith, sacrifice, through everything that lifts man above materialism. . .—these are the bases for what could be called the politics of Corneille. Aren't they strangely contemporary?" (298).

5. Until the war, Maurice Blanchot shared many of Maulnier's violently extremist, tragic-humanist, ultranationalist principles and was a frequent contributor in 1936 and 1937 to *Combat*, the militantly anti-Blumian, anti-Popular Front journal that Maulnier cofounded and ran. In "Terrorisme, méthode de salut public" (no. 7 [July 1936]), Blanchot argues that there should be no restrictions placed on the means used to bring down the Popular Front government, which he describes sarcastically as a "beautiful union, a holy alliance, this conglomerate of Soviet, Jewish, and capitalist interests. Everything that is anti-national, everything that is anti-social will be served [by it]." For these reasons, Blanchot feels justified in asserting that "it is good that people who believe they possess total power, . . . who seem truly to be the masters of beautiful French blood, experience suddenly their weaknesses and are recalled to reason through fear. . . . We have to be ready at the same time to do everything, through all means and especially violence. . . . It is necessary that there be a revolution, because you do not reform a political regime that controls everything, that has its roots everywhere; you don't suppress it, you cut it down. It is necessary that this revolution be violent, because you do not draw out of a people as feeble as ours the forces and passions necessary for a renewal by decent measures but by bloody jolts, by a storm that will shake it up in order to awaken it."

6. This is one of the places where I part company with Sternhell, who, I believe, seriously understates and even at times distorts the significance of Maulnier's criticisms of fascism and nazism. Sternhell claims, for example, that "not only did Maulnier accept the Nazi ideology, but he wished to use it as an example for the regeneration of France" (*Neither Right nor Left*, 234). He also claims that Maulnier's criticism of National Socialism for not developing a serious critique of capitalism "is the only adverse criticism that Maulnier has to make of nazism and fascism" (236). Maulnier's criticisms were in fact numerous and substantial, and the radical spiritualistic nature of his concept of fascism made it impossible for him to accept Nazi ideology as a model for a French ultranationalism "beyond nationalism." This, however, does not necessarily make him less of a fascist, just a different and more demanding kind of fascist.

7. Here, as in many other places, Maulnier's position and strategy could be compared to Heidegger's, his desire to spiritualize fascism and nazism compared to Heidegger's project, during a limited period, to accomplish similar although not identical goals. For example, in his Rectoral Address, "The Self-Assertion of the German University," Heidegger has this to say about the spirit: "The *spiritual*

world of a people is not the superstructure of a culture, no more than it is an armory stuffed with useful facts and values; it is the power that most deeply preserves the people's strengths, which are tied to earth and blood; and as such it is the power that most deeply moves and most profoundly shakes its being [*Dasein*]. Only a spiritual world gives the people the assurance of greatness" (trans. Karsten Harries, *Review of Metaphysics*, no. 38 [March 1985], 474–75).

8. Paul Sérant, in *Les Dissidents de l'Action Française* (Paris: Editions Copernic, 1978), claims, on the contrary, that "it is easy to see that if [during the war] Thierry Maulnier condemns the different partisans of an alliance of France with one of the foreign coalitions, it is all the same toward the Allied forces that his preferences go. The Parisian press was not mistaken, and except for Brasillach who maintained his friendship with him, the journalists of the Action Française who rallied to collaboration didn't hesitate to accuse Thierry Maulnier of 'Gaullism'" (225). I put much less stake in such accusations coming from the most extreme fascists and collaborationists than Sérant does and find no evidence in Maulnier's wartime writings of his alleged "Gaullist" sympathies

Afterword
Literary Fascism and the Case of Paul de Man

1. For essays on various sides of the battle over the nature and implications of de Man's wartime journalism, see especially *Responses: On Paul de Man's Wartime Journalism*, ed. Werner Hamacher, Neil Hertz, and Thomas Keenan (Lincoln: University of Nebraska Press, 1989), and *Critical Inquiry*, v. 15, no. 4 (Summer 1989), which includes "Biodegradables: Seven Diary Fragments," Jacques Derrida's polemical response to various criticisms of his initial essay on de Man, "Like the Sound of the Sea Deep within a Shell: Paul de Man's War," trans. Peggy Kamuf and originally published in *Critical Inquiry*, v. 14, no. 3 (Spring 1988), and republished in a slightly expanded form in *Responses*. See also my own response to Derrida's essay, "The Temptation of Fascism and the Question of Literature: Justice, Sorrow, and Political Error (An Open Letter to Jacques Derrida)," in *Cultural Critique*, no. 15 (Spring 1990).

2. De Man's articles have been collected in *Wartime Journalism, 1939–1943*, ed. Werner Hamacher, Neil Hertz, and Thomas Keenan (Lincoln: University of Nebraska Press, 1988). In terms of de Man's support for the "New Europe," see, for example, "Dans nos murs" (August 26, 1941), where he praises a book published by Pierre Daye, previously a member of the Belgian parliament from Léon Degrelle's extremist Rexist Party and a frequent contributor to *Je suis partout*, for "showing that the present war, besides being an economic and national struggle, is the beginning of a revolution that aims at organizing European society in a more equitable manner" (138).

3. See his reviews of a series of conferences given in Brussels at the Institut de Culture Italienne in March 1941: "Les Systèmes impériaux de la Rome antique," "Le 'Risorgimento' italien," and "La Formation de la jeunesse en Italie" (*Wartime Journalism*, 48, 50, 54).

4. In *Responses*, texts by Els de Bens, "Paul de Man and the Collaborationist Press," and Ortwin de Graef, "Aspects of the Context of Paul de Man's Earliest

Publications," give a detailed description of the situation of the press in Belgium at this time and its control by the Nazi occupiers. De Man's relation to Raymond de Becker, editor-in-chief of *Le Soir* from the end of 1940 until he was removed in September 1943, his connection to militant collaborationists such as the Didiers and *Les Editions de la Toison d'Or*, and finally his involvment with the Dechenne agency (to whom the Germans granted the monopoly of the distribution of dailies and weeklies), where de Man continued to work after leaving *Le Soir*, all indicate an extended involvement with the collaborationist press and its leaders. In addition to Derrida's essay, see especially Alice Yaeger Kaplan, "Paul de Man, *Le Soir* and the Francophone Collaboration (1940–1942)," and William Flesch, "Ancestral Voices: De Man and His Defenders," for essays that deal with concerns close to my own. See also Werner Hamacher, "Journals, Politics: Notes on Paul de Man's Wartime Journalism," trans. Susan Bernstein, Peter Burgard, Jonathan Hess, Eva Geulen, and Timothy Walters, in *Responses*, for a detailed analysis of the complications and contradictions in what he calls the Belgicist position of de Man's wartime journalism and the "politics of realism" that de Man constantly called on to justify collaboration.

5. Werner Hamacher meticulously documents the changing situation of those maintaining a "Belgicist postion" throughout the war, as well as the different versions of this position (see once again "Journals, Politics," in *Responses*, 441–46). For example, Hamacher describes how Raymond de Becker, chosen editor-in-chief of *Le Soir* on December 5, 1940, and thus obviously acceptable to the Nazi occupiers, "collaborated with the Nazis in the hope of achieving 'free collaboration' until it became clear to him (very late) that the Nazis were conducting a systematic policy of denationalization. . . . Becker was relieved of his duties as editor-in-chief of *Le Soir* in September 1943 and was taken into German custody" (445). Even so, after the war, he was sentenced to death by a Belgian court because although he had "supported a politics of national independence and restitution of the state . . . he had betrayed the contents of that politics by linking it to the ideal of a 'new Europe' under German hegemony and by repeatedly taking a position in favor of recruiting Belgians for the German army and for 'labor service' in Germany" (446).

6. In his review of Drieu la Rochelle's *Notes pour comprendre le siècle*, de Man criticized Drieu la Rochelle's anti-rationalism, his subordination of thought to a broad and superficial historical schema, and his confusion of aesthetic and ethical determinants. He did, however, praise the "*élan* and conviction with which [Drieu la Rochelle] throws himself into the struggle to create a radically new human [that is, fascist] type. That is an undeniable sign of vitality, all the more promising in a country which has fallen as low as France" (*Wartime Journalism*, 171).

7. As numerous commentators in *Responses* have indicated, this list is not originally de Man's, but except for his elimination of the name of Proust from the list, it is a list he took from Aldous Huxley, and one de Man had already used before the war (but in quotation marks and with attribution) in a very different context: in an article on the contemporary English novel that he wrote for the liberal student journal he helped run, the *Cahiers du Libre Examen* (January 1940); in *Wartime Journalism*, 17). Much has been written about the importance

of the inclusion of Kafka's name in the list given by de Man in "Les Juifs," but the most eloquent and convincing analysis of this list is in my mind that of Werner Hamacher: "The name *Kafka, could* have and *should* have decided all of that. It could have and should have been cited—plainly, clearly, unambiguously—as the name of resistance against racist terror; instead it functions, at best, as an anti-anti-semitic allusion. In the ideological-political context of the time, the name *Kafka* could have and should have been a protest against the division of the world and of literature into the Jewish and the non-Jewish. Only when used decisively— as the name of a decision, clear and discernible to anyone—could the name have opposed that division. Accordingly, in the Belgium of 1941 the name should have been not *Kafka* but *Proust*. . . . They were, objectively, names against the politics of black-listing and denunciation of names, through names; but in de Man's article they are *not*. He participates in ths politics by leaving the significance of the name *Kafka* unclear and by going so far as to include in his text a second, clearly denunciatory list with names from Maurois to Benda" (*Responses*, 461).

8. Brasillach, in spite of his militant anti-Semitism, also took a position similar to de Man's in other articles, for he considered Proust to be "a great French writer, one of the greatest French writers. . . . It has been claimed that *La Recherche* is not a novel, when it is perhaps the only pure novel" (*Je suis partout* [February 12, 1943]). As for Hemmingway and D. H. Lawrence, other names on de Man's list, both were, for example, favorites of Drieu La Rochelle, who translated and wrote introductions for a novel of each of them. Drieu la Rochelle had also been a friend of Huxley's.

Index